Corporate Restructuring

Lessons from Experience

Corporate Restructuring

Lessons from Experience

Edited by

Michael Pomerleano

William Shaw

THE WORLD BANK

Library of Congress Cataloging-in-Publication Data has been applied for.

ISBN 0-8213-5928-2   978-8-213-59282-6

Cover Design: James E. Quigley, World Bank Institute.

Photo Credit: Malcolm Fife, Photodisc.

Contents

Chapter 5
Are More Restructuring Regimes Becoming Like the U.S.
Chapter 11 System? **127**

James H. Zukin, with the assistance of Alan Fragen and Dorian Lowell

Chapter 6
The Successful Asset Management Companies **141**

*Ruth L. Neyens, Dató Zukri Samat, Beom Choi, Yang Kaisheng,
and Shinjiro Takagi*

Chapter 7
Progress toward the Resolution of Nonperforming Loans **171**

Jack Rodman

Part II: War Stories from the Crises

Chapter 8
Restructuring in Weak Legal and Regulatory Jurisdictions:
The Case of Indonesian Restructurings **185**

Ray Davis

Chapter 9
Government Policy Responses in Korea **205**

Hogen Oh

Chapter 14

The Contingent Claims Approach to Corporate Vulnerability Analysis: Estimating Default Risk and Economywide Risk Transfer **261**

Michael T. Gapen, Dale F. Gray, Cheng Hoon Lim, and Yingbin Xiao

Chapter 15

Developing an Effective Framework for Insolvency and Credit Rights **301**

Gordon W. Johnson

Appendix 1
Financial Restructuring: Techniques and Negotiating Dynamics . . 331

Alan D. Fragen

Boxes

Figures

Tables

Preface

The severe financial crises that devastated emerging markets over the past decade underlined important gaps in our ability to deal with corporate distress. The Asian crisis, and ensuing crises in Turkey and Argentina, led to massive declines in output and corporate profitability and to widespread corporate insolvencies. Moreover, corporate difficulties are not limited to countries that have suffered a recent, spectacular crisis. In many countries, corporate weaknesses or "silent" distress may be setting the stage for future financial crises. There is no magic bullet for addressing systemic corporate distress. Coping with it requires a host of simultaneous measures, such as financial engineering techniques for restructuring, consideration of the impact of the tax system on incentives for restructuring, policy approaches to the disposal of bad debts, efforts to strengthen bankruptcy courts and the legal framework for insolvency, and the establishment of procedures for out-of-court workouts. It has become clear that governments, as well as the multilateral institutions, often lack the resources and expertise required to address corporate distress on a large scale and that policies, institutions, and legal frameworks may not be adequate to the task. A scarcity of skills (legal, financial) in the private sector and in the judiciary is also found to be an impediment in many countries.

The World Bank organized a conference in March 2004, entitled Corporate Restructuring—International Best Practices, to improve our understanding of how to cope with systemic corporate distress. This conference brought together policymakers, regulators, investment bankers, tax lawyers, and other restructuring specialists to share their experiences with corporate restructuring in crises. The emphasis was heavily toward practical solutions, with the goal of helping participants to learn what has worked and what has not. The high quality of presentations, significant interest in exchanging ideas during discussions, and substantial participation from some of the leading experts in corporate restructuring were gratifying for those of us involved in organizing the conference.

This book collects the papers presented at the conference. It provides an overview of the state of corporate distress and efforts at restructuring, discusses approaches to monitoring corporate distress, reviews the main policy lessons from systemic corporate crises, and evaluates the success of different financial techniques for restructuring troubled debtors. The opening chapter advocates an integrated approach to corporate restructuring, and an introductory chapter distills the key lessons from the papers gathered in this volume. We hope that the book will be of benefit to our clients that confront systemic corporate distress and will make some contribution to improving crisis prevention and reducing the costs of recovery.

CESARE CALARI
Vice President, Financial Sector
World Bank

Acknowledgments

This volume relies extensively on presentations at the Corporate Restructuring: International Best Practices conference hosted in Washington, D.C., by the World Bank Group in March 2004. We would like to acknowledge the efforts of the participants at the conference as well as those of the contributors to this book. We are also indebted to the referees (Sri-Ram Aiyer, Won-Dong Cho, and Bob Litan) and to the peer reviewers (Lily Chu, Stijn Claessens, Sophie Sirtaine, and V. Sundararajan), whose insights enriched the manuscript. In addition, we thank Colleen Mascenik for providing research assistance, Elizabeth Forsyth for editing the manuscript, James Quigley for designing the book, and Myrvet Alyeldin Cocoli and Sema Muslu for providing administrative support.

Contributors

Beom Choi is executive director of the International Business Group of Korea Asset Management Corporation (KAMCO). He manages international relations and is the main liaison officer with government restructuring agencies in China, Indonesia, Japan, Malaysia, and Thailand. He is also the coordinating officer of the Nonperforming Loan Forum, which involves more than 800 executives from over 15 countries, and has headed teams in the Corporate Disposition and Investment Management departments. Prior to joining KAMCO, he was head of Equity Sales at the Seoul Branch of Credit Suisse First Boston (1996–98) and head of Equity Business and Corporate Finance for the Seoul Branch of W. I. Carr (1994–96). He holds a BA in finance from the University of Wisconsin, a degree from Hankook University of Foreign Studies in Korea, and an MBA from Western Michigan University.

Stijn Claessens has rejoined the World Bank after teaching international finance at the University of Amsterdam. He has worked in the World Bank in various capacities, including as lead economist of the Financial Sector Strategy and Policy Group, Financial Sector Operations Vice Presidency. He has led World Bank missions to numerous countries, helping governments to develop strategies for external debt restructuring and asset-liability management and providing advice on financial sector restructuring and reform. He has lectured and published extensively on external finance and domestic financial sector issues. He holds an MA in business economics from Erasmus University, the Netherlands, and an MA and a PhD in business economics from the Wharton School of the University of Pennsylvania.

Richard H. Daniel retired in mid-1993 as vice chairman, director, and chief credit officer of Mellon Bank, where he managed the corporation's credit-related functions. He came to Mellon in 1986, with more than 35 years of credit experience, developed largely through a long career with Security Pacific National Bank, Los Angeles, and a year as executive vice present in charge of the Special Assets Department of Crocker National Bank. He is a founding member of Robert Morris Associates, served as director of the organization's domestic lending division, and founded the Senior Workout Officers' Roundtable. He holds a BS from the University of California, Berkley, and is a graduate of the Pacific Coast Banking School in Seattle.

Ray Davis leads RN Davis & Company, an advisory firm executing mergers and acquisitions and restructuring assignments with clients in North America and Asia. He is a former managing director of Credit Suisse First Boston, where he spent more than five years working on restructuring assignments in Asia, Europe, and the Middle East, and spent 16 years at Lehman Brothers, both in the Restructuring Group and the Oil and Gas Group. He worked extensively in Mexico after the peso crisis and has been involved in numerous in-court and out-of-court restructurings in Canada and the United States. Before joining Lehman Brothers, he worked for the U.S. Department of Energy and taught finance at Emory University and Temple University. He has a BS in mechanical engineering from the University of Pennsylvania, an MBA from Temple University, and a DBA from Indiana University.

Alan D. Fragen is managing director in the Financial Restructuring Group in the Los Angeles office of Houlihan Lokey Howard & Zukin. Over the past 12 years, he has managed numerous complex restructurings, including assignments that incorporate distressed merger and acquisition activity and outside capital-raising events. He is an expert in the communications industry and in the precious and base metals mining and processing industries. He holds a BA in economics and mathematics from Northwestern University and an MS in econometrics from the London School of Economics and Political Science.

Michael T. Gapen is an economist in the Capital Markets Financing Division of the International Monetary Fund (IMF). He has participated in IMF missions to Iceland, Panama, Suriname, and, most recently, Brazil, where he focused primarily on capital market issues. Prior to joining the IMF, he was a visiting assistant professor in the Mendoza College of Business at the University of Notre Dame.

Jack Glen is lead portfolio officer in the Portfolio Management Department of the International Finance Corporation (IFC). Before joining the IFC in 1991, he taught international corporate finance at the Wharton School. He has a PhD in international finance from Northwestern University.

Mario Gobbo is in charge of Life Sciences Investments for the International Finance Corporation, a World Bank Group institution dealing with private sector investments. He previously worked with Lazard Brothers in London, where he managed the company's Central and Eastern European practice. In 1982 he began his career as a banker in Milan with Continental Illinois National Bank and subsequently moved to London, where he worked with Swiss Bank Corporation International, among others. He has more than 20 years of banking experience, which spans pharmaceuticals and biotechnology as well as oil and gas, telecommunications, power, and financial institutions. He has a BA from Harvard College, an MSc from University of Colorado; an MBA, an MA in business economics, and a PhD from Wharton School, University of Pennsylvania.

Dale F. Gray is president of Macro Financial Risk Corporation, M*f*Risk. In a joint venture, Moody's Investors Services and M*f*Risk have developed web-based interactive models for more than 18 countries and provided macrofinancial research for banks, investors, and international institutions. From 1995 to 1998, he was an adviser at the International Monetary Fund for the Russia Team, working on capital market development and corporate and financial sectors, and for the Fiscal Affairs Department. From 1985 to 1995, he worked at the World Bank on Eastern Europe, Former Soviet Union, Middle East, and major Latin American countries. From 1982 to 1985, he was an adviser to the minister of finance and the central bank in Indonesia. He has an MA from Stanford University and a PhD from Massachusetts Institute of Technology; he is a certified financial risk manager.

Gordon Johnson is legal counsel for the World Bank on matters pertaining to corporate insolvency and creditor rights systems. He has experience in approximately 40 emerging-market countries on matters of legal, judicial, and regulatory reform and routinely provides legal support to emergency recovery teams in crisis situations, such as Argentina and Turkey. He spearheaded the Bank's Insolvency Initiative, in collaboration with international partners, to develop the Principles and Guidelines for Effective Insolvency and Creditor Rights Systems, a benchmark for assessing the effectiveness of country systems worldwide. Prior to joining the Bank, he practiced for more than a decade with the international law firm of Weil Gotshal & Manges in the areas of business finance and restructuring and electrical power transactions He holds a BS from Abiline Christian University, a JD from Pepperdine University School of Law, and an LLM in international banking and finance from the University of London.

Yang Kaisheng is president of China's Huarong Asset Management Corporation, an independent legal entity, a wholly state-owned financial institution, and the largest of four asset management companies. Founded by the government to tackle the problem of nonperforming loans and support the reform of China's state-owned enterprises, Huarong purchases, manages, and disposes of the nonperforming loans acquired and maximizes the recovery value, while minimizing any losses resulting from the disposition.

Ira Lieberman is former senior adviser to the World Bank and a senior adviser to the Open Society Institute of the Soros Foundation.

Cheng Hoon Lim is deputy division chief in the Capital Markets Financing Division of the International Monetary Fund. She joined the IMF in 1994 and has worked primarily on crises in emerging markets, including Korea during the Asian crisis and, more recently, Argentina and Turkey. She was banking supervisor at the U.K. Financial Services Authority and has worked at the Urban Development Division of the World Bank. She has a PhD in applied macroeconomics from Cambridge University.

Dorian Lowell is senior vice president of Houlihan Lokey Howard and Zukin, an international investment bank established in 1970 that provides a wide range of services in the areas of mergers and acquisitions, financing, financial restructuring, and merchant banking.

William P. Mako is lead private sector development specialist in the Beijing Office of the World Bank. He has worked in various regions and countries, advising authorities on measures to alleviate and resolve corporate distress, on procedures and institutional arrangements to facilitate corporate workouts, and on the development and implementation of enterprise privatization and capital markets programs. Prior to joining the World Bank, he worked at PriceWaterhouse from 1983 to 1997 and at Booz Allen & Hamilton in 1982. In the United States, he has experience in Chapter 11 and Chapter 7 insolvency cases. He holds a BS in foreign service from the Georgetown School of Foreign Service and an MA in public and private management from Yale University, School of Management.

Ruth Neyens is program manager of Banking and Financial Restructuring, Operations and Policy Development in the World Bank's Financial Sector Vice Presidency. She is responsible for developing and delivering a comprehensive program focused on strengthening banking supervision and regulation, improving the performance of banks through restructuring, and undertaking corporate restructuring, including asset management. She has served as program manager for financial sector reform in Indonesia and provided advice and technical assistance in these areas in Argentina, Bolivia, Korea, and Turkey. Before joining the Bank, she was senior vice president at Bank of America, responsible for asset resolution. In addition, she has held senior positions in credit risk management and credit training. She has taught finance and bank management courses at the University of Maryland.

Hogen Oh is chairman of Lazard Asia, which provides strategic and merger and acquisitions advisory services for multinational and major Asian corporations. From 1998 to 2000, he was executive chairman of Korea's Corporate Restructuring Committee, where he chaired a special committee to evaluate so-called Big Deals. He also served as chairman of the Corporate Restructuring Committee and the board of directors of Daewoo Companies, where he supervised and coordinated all restructuring efforts. He has served as representative for the Global Strategic Service (1994–98), as chairman of Younglim Cardinal, Publishers (1992–99), as chairman and chief executive officer of the Korea Merchant Banking Corporation (1984–90), and as a member of the Advisory Committee to the Minister of Finance (1982–90). He holds a BA in economics and an MA in economics from Pace University.

Michael Pomerleano is lead financial sector specialist in the Financial Sector Operations and Policy Department of the World Bank. He has extensive international financial consulting experience in Asia and in the transitional economies of Eastern Europe and Central Asia, advising governments, central banks, and commercial banks on financial sector reform. Before joining the World Bank in 1992, he worked for the National Banking Group of Citicorp, was managing partner of MBC Associates (an owner-operator of commercial real estate), and worked in the supervision and regulation division of the board of governors of the Federal Reserve System. He has an MA in business economics, a joint degree awarded by the Harvard Business School and Harvard Economics Department.

Dató Zainal Abidin Putih is chairman of the Pengurusan Danaharta Nasional Berhad. He is a fellow of the Institute of Chartered Accountants of England and Wales, a chartered accountant of the Malaysian Institute of Accountants, and a certified public accountant of the Malaysian Institute of Certified Public Accountants. He has extensive experience in the audits of banks, insurance, energy, transport, manufacturing, government agencies, plantations, properties, hotels, investment companies, unit trusts, distributors, timber, and wholesalers. He is joint chairman of Ernst & Young Malaysia and chairman of the Malaysian Accounting Standards Board.

Jack Rodman is managing director of Asia-Pacific Financial Solutions, a profit center he founded within Ernst & Young in 1995 to provide financial services related to the nonperforming loans of banks and government agencies in the Asia Pacific. He was credited by the *Wall Street Journal* with creating a market for the sale of nonperforming loans in China and Japan. Before founding Asia-Pacific Financial Solutions, he worked with Kenneth Leventhal & Company for more than 30 years, holding several senior management positions with the firm. He has a BA in accounting from San Jose State University and an MA in business administration from the University of California, Los Angeles.

Dató Zukri Samat is managing director of Pergurusan Danaharta Nasional Berhad, Malaysia. At Danaharta, he has held various positions, including general manager and director of the Operations Division. He has wide experience in the banking sector, having served both local and international financial institutions in various capacities. Prior to joining Danaharta, he was general manager of Credit Agricole Indosuez Labuan and worked in Commerce International Merchange Bankers Berhad. He holds an MBA from the University of Hull, United Kingdom.

William Shaw is former lead economist in the World Bank's Development Prospects Group. Since joining the research department in 1995, he worked on various editions of *Global Economic Prospects* and *Global Development Finance* (the Bank's annual publications on current development issues) and on debt sustainability analysis for the Heavily Indebted Poor Countries Initiative. From 1988 to 1995, he worked in the Bank's operational departments, serving as the country economist for Tanzania, private sector development specialist for the Caribbean, and country economist for Bolivia. Before joining the Bank, Mr. Shaw worked on the administration of a food assistance program for the U.S. Department of Agriculture. Since retiring from the Bank, Mr. Shaw has served as a consultant on various issues in development economics.

Shinjiro Takagi is chairman of the Industrial Revitalization Committee of the Industrialization Revitalization Corporation of Japan. The committee examines the restructuring plans of companies, identifies which companies to support, and determines the purchase price of loan claims from nonprimary lenders. Mr. Takagi formerly served as Justice of the Tokyo High Court and is an experienced lawyer.

Christopher Vale is founding director of Rexiter Capital Management, a London-based global emerging markets fund manager. He has managed two corporate restructuring funds in Korea: Arirang and Mukoonghwa. Before founding Rexiter Capital Management, he worked for Kleinwort Benson Investment Management (KBIM) as a U.K. fund manager. In 1989 he transferred to the Hong Kong Office of KBIM, where he spent eight years managing Asian funds primarily for U.S. and U.K. clients. He became head of KBIM's Asian Team and a director of KBIM in 1994. He has a BA in economics and agricultural economics from the University of Exeter, United Kingdom.

Yingbin Xiao is an economist in the Capital Markets Financing Division of the International Monetary Fund. She has performed financial analysis on the Argentine corporate sector, highlighting balance sheet risks facing the sector, and has conducted a comparative study of trade and investment liberalization. She holds an MS in financial engineering, an MA in economics, and a PhD in financial economics from the University of Michigan, Ann Arbor.

James H. Zukin is senior managing director and founding board member of Houlihan Lokey Howard & Zukin, an international investment bank established in 1970 that provides a wide range of services in the areas of mergers and acquisitions, financing, financial restructuring, and merchant banking. Prior to joining Houlihan Lokey in 1976, Mr. Zukin was founder and director of the ESOT Valuation Group at Marshall & Stevens and vice president for mergers and acquisitions at Niederhoffer, Cross & Zeckhauser. He has a BA in economics from the University of California, Berkeley, and an MBA from Harvard Business School.

Introduction: Toward Better Practices in Systemic Corporate Restructuring

Michael Pomerleano

Recent systemic crises have underlined how widespread, severe weaknesses in corporate finance and governance, combined with inappropriate macroeconomic policies or a sudden loss of confidence, can have unforeseen and extremely serious consequences for the economic and social fabric of a country. Paul Romer, the Stanford economist, remarked: "A crisis is a terrible thing to waste." Those are profound words and resonate true for at least three reasons. First and most obviously, a crisis is a terrible and costly event. The recent fiscal costs of recapitalizing banks during the Asia crisis are estimated at 28 percent of GDP in Malaysia and over 55 percent of GDP in Indonesia (Caprio 2003). The crisis-induced decline in GDP has been as great as 10 percent of GDP, and hard-to-quantify intangible costs may include slow growth and lower long-term productivity if bank and corporate restructuring is not successful. Second, the recent corporate crises underlined the gaps in our ability to deal with corporate distress. Crises can teach us what works and what doesn't, although we need to continue searching for additional practical solutions that were not tried during the crisis.[1] And, finally, crises may make it possible to force through necessary but politically difficult changes in law, policies, and institutions.

This chapter seeks to distill the lessons from recent crises and offers a range of suggestions, some of them controversial, on measures to help prevent crises and manage recovery. Recommendations are grouped into five sections, covering the role of government, the legal framework for corporate restructuring, the tax regime, skills required for restructuring, and financial engineering techniques. Clearly, one size does not fit all, and these recommendations will need to be adapted to the circumstances and conditions in a specific country. Measures that are acceptable in a disciplined setting where the culture is homogeneous might not be enforceable in a country where the rule of law is ineffective.

The Government's Role

Governments have been intensively involved in resolving systemic crises, including extensive interventions in the process of corporate restructuring, driven by the huge costs of crises, the government's responsibility (explicit or implicit) for the banking system, and the necessity of addressing widespread business failures and unemployment (see table 1). The role of government should be considered in terms of steps to monitor and intervene in the corporate sector prior to a crisis, ways to organize the immediate response to a crisis, the strategy for addressing corporate and financial sector insolvency, and creation of an appropriate regulatory framework for corporate restructuring.

Monitoring

Officials responsible for economic policy, as well as the public at-large, need adequate information on the financial soundness of the corporate sector. For example, while some of the weaknesses of East Asian businesses, such as poor governance and high leverage, were recognized prior to the 1997 crisis, the full impact of cross-guarantees and the extent of foreign exchange exposure in corporate finances were not fully understood until after the fact. In Indonesia, for instance, private corporations were borrowing directly offshore. Because the international bank debts were owed mainly by the corporate sector, public officials did not have adequate data on the extent of foreign debt incurred. Thus government could not properly evaluate the impact of foreign exchange depreciation on the solvency of the corporate sector and on the economy as a whole. Establishing a central monitoring

Table 1: Taxonomy of the Role of Government: Legal, Regulatory, Tax, and Financial Engineering Measures

Issue	Agency responsible	Prevailing practice	Measures	Extent of intervention or intrusion
Information on the financial soundness of the corporate sector	Ministry of finance or central bank	Limited: Colombia (Superintendency of Companies)	Collection and analysis of data	Low
Tax regime	Ministry of finance or tax agency		Carry of losses; deductibility of write-offs	Low
Effective insolvency regime in terms of legislation and capacity	Justice department	Some: for example, Colombia (Superintendency of Companies), Korea, Malaysia, the Philippines, and the United States (Securities and Exchange Commission)	Specialized courts	Medium
Out-of-court infrastructure	Banking supervision and regulation agency	Some: for example, Thailand		Medium
Financial engineering, such as asset management companies, corporate restructuring funds, corporate restructuring vehicles, secondary market in distressed debt	Ministry of finance, central bank, tax authority, justice department	Some: for example, Korea	Funding for asset management companies, corporate restructuring funds; legal setting for securitizations	High
Regulatory initiatives	Banking supervision and regulation agency	One: Korea	Corporate deleveraging and corporate action plans	Very high

unit within the government offers the advantage of developing and centralizing expertise for monitoring the corporate sector.

This government unit could take on the responsibilities for detailed data collection. The kinds of data that might be recorded include the composition of corporate debts, exchange rate denomination of debt, residence of debt owners, profit and loss accounts, and governance structures. The amount of resources devoted to these efforts would vary, depending on fiscal resources, the nature of corporate vulnerabilities, and the level of development. It would be important to minimize the burden of data collection on companies and to take into account legitimate needs for confidentiality. In some countries, government might be able to rely on private companies (for example, credit bureaus and rating agencies) to collect the data or might assign this responsibility to bank supervisors. This government unit also could take on coordinating responsibilities relative to ongoing corporate restructuring and act as an advocate within the government to push for the legal, regulatory, tax, and financial engineering reforms aimed at creating a sound corporate sector.

One of the few examples of a government agency devoted to corporate sector monitoring and intervention is Colombia's Superintendency of Companies. Centralizing this responsibility within a government department was seen as necessary because the judicial system did not have sufficient expertise or capacity in business matters and was often ineffective in resolving insolvency proceedings. For example, before 1995 some companies had been in the process of liquidation for more than 12 years without paying their debts, and this was having an adverse impact on financial institutions.

The Superintendency of Companies was established to monitor and, on occasion, intervene in businesses with the goal of preventing crises, ensuring confidence in the legal system, and generating reliable accounting and financial data to ensure transparency. The superintendency can review any company that is registered with the Chamber of Commerce, for the purpose of obtaining all information necessary to understand the company's legal, accounting, economic, and administrative status. It also oversees corporate restructuring and has the capacity to enforce compliance when companies are found to be in violation of laws.

Intervention

The extent to which an agency should intervene in corporate decisionmaking prior to a crisis is controversial. Government officials may lack sufficient information to make efficient decisions on corporate restructuring. Moreover, in some cases, government interventions may simply serve the interests of particular corporate groups with influence on government. The ability of government to intervene, and the effectiveness of interventions, will depend greatly on the country context and specific circumstances. For example, the Korean government made concerted efforts to force the five big chaebols to rationalize operations through mergers (the so-called Big Deals) in the midst of the crisis, with debatable results. In Republic of Korea, where close ties had long existed between government and corporate interests, it is possible that using government influence to help rationalize the chaebols prior to the crisis might have been more effective.

In most cases, however, government interventions in corporate restructuring have come in the aftermath of a crisis. And, typically, interventionist steps have been taken either through the banking system—for example, Korea's enforcement of benchmarks for corporate deleveraging by stipulating that banks could not lend to corporations that did not meet these targets—or by government agencies that have purchased nonperforming loans and thus become creditors of bankrupt companies and perforce involved in their restructuring. In this context, the government strategy for dealing with corporate restructuring is critical to the prospects for recovery from systemic crises.

The agency responsible for restructuring insolvent companies should divide corporations by size and by viable versus nonviable companies. This should enable the agency to focus on the largest debtors that warrant immediate attention. Government needs to demonstrate its determination to liquidate companies that have little prospect of survival and to force viable companies to take the necessary financial and operational steps to regain solvency. A firm stand is required to avoid moral hazard. Korea learned this lesson the hard way, as policymakers believed that the largest chaebols were "too big to fail." With the exception of Daewoo, the seven largest chaebols were allowed to undertake voluntary restructuring along the lines of the Big Deals, which went nowhere after months of talk.

Governments should forge stronger links between corporate and bank restructuring. It is impossible to address the problems of banks successfully without addressing the underlying problem of bad corporate loans. By contrast, rehabilitating banks with the intention of addressing corporate weaknesses at a later time is a recipe for failure: banks can be recapitalized, but they remain with a huge portfolio of bad loans. Turkey adopted this approach, in anticipation that a more robust financial system would be in a better position to restructure the corporate sector, with poor results. An integrated approach to bank and corporate restructuring often involves putting pressure on the banks to address corporate weaknesses, as was done in Korea.

Malaysia's experience is a valuable model for tackling corporate and bank restructuring in unison. The National Economic Action Council, created in January 1998 as a high-level consultative body (including the prime minister and governor of the central bank), formulated an agenda for comprehensive restructuring of the banking and corporate sectors. Three agencies—Danaharta, Danamodal, and the Corporate Debt Restructuring Committee (CDRC)—were established for this purpose: Danaharta was an asset management company with functions similar to those of the U.S. Resolution Trust Corporation; Danamodal Nasional Berhad was established to recapitalize the banking sector, especially to assist banks whose capital base had been eroded by losses; and CDRC was established to reduce stress on the banking system and to repair the financial and operational positions of corporate borrowers. These three agencies linked their efforts effectively. A bank in trouble because of the huge amount of bad loans on its books could see Danaharta to sell its nonperforming loans. Thereafter, if the bank was still in financial trouble and the shareholders could not recapitalize, the bank could seek financial assistance from Danamodal, at a cost. Effectively, new money would be injected into the bank, diluting the original shareholders. This meant that Danamodal could facilitate consolidation of the sector by selling its stake to a stronger bank and thereby fostering mergers. Meanwhile, CDRC acted as an informal mediator, facilitating dialogue between borrowers and their creditors to achieve voluntary restructuring schemes. If CDRC could achieve this, then nonperforming loans would be resolved voluntarily. If not, Danaharta would take over the bad loans.

While the government needs to be actively involved in the resolution process, this role should rely, to the extent possible, on market forces rather than government fiat to establish the right incentives for sound financial behavior. For example, an appropriate mix of carrots and sticks can induce financial institutions to take steps to resolve nonperforming loans, such as by conveying excess nonperforming loans to an asset management company for resolution. Time-bound capital adequacy forbearance might be appropriate where the deteriorating capital position is attributable to the disposition of nonperforming loans.

The application of sticks and carrots in Taiwan (China) offers a model for reducing substantially banks' nonperforming loans. Taiwan (China) initially had difficulty finalizing the sale of nonperforming loans. However, President Chen Shui-Bian imposed stringent rules (the 2-5-8 Plan), which specified that, in two years, all banks were to reduce their bad loans to below 5 percent and to achieve an 8 percent risk-adjusted capital ratio. Banks that failed to achieve these goals were subject to a series of restrictions, including no new branches, lower salaries for directors and supervisors, and limited hiring, long-term investment, and loans to related parties. Banks that continued to miss the plan's targets could be subjected to fines, replacement of management, and revocation of their banking license. At the same time, tax holidays were implemented, while other regulations were eased or removed. This approach and its decisive execution by the government was a huge success: in the 18 months after initiation of the program, 25 market sale transactions to third-party investors were completed.

In other countries, banking laws and regulations may impede restructuring, and time-bound relief might be appropriate during a crisis. Banking laws or regulations may restrict the amount of converted corporate equity that a financial institution can hold or else require its prompt sale. Moreover, preemptive rights of shareholders may delay or obstruct debt-equity swaps, and therefore minority shareholders may hold out for preferential terms.

Legal Framework for Corporate Restructuring

Many countries need to strengthen the legal framework governing corporate bankruptcy, including improving laws, training court personnel, and making administrative systems more efficient. In several countries hit by crises, the legal system provides insufficient protection for creditor rights, greatly impeding progress in the resolution of bankrupt companies.

An effective insolvency framework is the prerequisite for efficient corporate restructuring and, indeed, is an important support for financial intermediation. Weak creditor rights and slow enforcement limit recoveries and raise the risk of lending, thereby reducing access to credit. Effective insolvency systems serve as a disciplinary force in establishing a deterrent against which voluntary corporate restructuring takes place, both in and out of court.

The goals of an insolvency framework should be to reduce legal and financial uncertainty, promote efficiency, and provide fair and equitable treatment of stakeholders in the insolvent firm. There are clear advantages to a Chapter 11–style bankruptcy reorganization framework, which helps to facilitate asset resolution in a way that minimizes the deterioration of asset values, supports the continuity of operation for viable firms, and allows the transfer of the assets of nonviable firms to better uses. However, Chapter 11–style bankruptcy processes can also provide scope for delays and require a highly specialized judiciary.

The huge number of bankruptcies in the aftermath of crises, in conjunction with existing weaknesses in the court system, requires the establishment of officially sanctioned out-of-court workout processes. It is essential for such processes to include time-bound measures that enforce the resolution of disagreements between debtors and creditors. Corporate restructuring agencies that oversee out-of-court workouts should have the authority to terminate the mediation and refer the case for initiation of bankruptcy proceedings. Korea's adoption of the London approach illustrates the value of binding deadlines and mechanisms for resolving inter-creditor differences. The typical medium-size Korean corporation, with a financial exposure of $1.5 billion, usually has anywhere between 40 and 60 institutions lending to it in one form or another. With so many creditors, it could be difficult to achieve the 75 percent threshold for agreement provided for in the accord. Therefore, the accord provided for a corporate restructuring committee, with an executive chairman, which would review proposals for corporate restructuring. If 75 percent of the creditors could not reach agreement, the restructuring proposal would be submitted to the committee, which then would issue a binding judgment on it.

Out-of-court workout processes, while essential for many of the crisis countries, can also exacerbate delays and uncertainty, especially when the majority shareholders are ill intended. In Thailand in the case of Thai Petrochemicals, for instance, the procedures were slow and gave the intransigent majority owner enormous scope for delay. Thus out-of-court restructuring should be governed by clear principles and processes, including:

- A corporate restructuring accord among domestic and international creditors that binds all the creditors and contains binding deadlines

- Reliable mechanisms to resolve differences among creditors—that is, a reasonable threshold for binding agreements and cram-down (for example, 75 percent)
- A coordination committee that arbitrates inter-creditor differences and binds the creditors.

Tax Issues

In virtually all of the developing countries, tax impediments to corporate restructuring exist and can bring the corporate restructuring process to a grinding halt. There are several recurring types of tax impediments. The tax treatment of debt may forbid creditors from claiming a tax deduction for discharged debt and may treat forgiven debt as taxable income for the debtor. In other countries, mergers and acquisition transactions can generate a taxable event. For instance, in some cases, tax losses cannot be assumed by the acquiring corporation. The transfer of distressed debt to a pool such as a trust may be considered a sale and therefore generate sales or transfer taxes.

Restructuring should be viewed as an ongoing process and be permitted to take place for reasons of economic efficiency rather than tax considerations. Therefore, it is desirable to enact tax policies that are neutral to corporate restructuring. However, in periods of severe corporate distress, governments have introduced time-bound tax incentives designed to accelerate corporate restructuring. For example, in Thailand, the government recognized the impediments and specified temporary and permanent measures to facilitate corporate restructuring. The temporary measures were intended to enable debtors and creditors to speed up the restructuring process and were set to expire by December 31, 1999. They included (a) deduction of written-off debt from the taxable income of the creditor, (b) elimination or deferral of corporate income tax on written-off debt for the debtor, (c) elimination of all taxes on asset transfers from debtor to creditor, and (d) elimination of taxes on accrued but unpaid interest and limitation of taxes on restructurings that involve interest rate reductions by creditors. Permanent measures designed to support corporate restructuring included (a) provision for tax-free mergers and non-cash acquisition of assets in the case of full mergers and (b) elimination of the value added tax and specific business tax on the transfer of assets to special-purpose vehicles.

Skills and Capacity

The buildup, duration, and severity of corporate crises, as well as the restructuring that occurs in the aftermath of crises, are related to the availability of skills in financial sector services (see table 2). Countries that have capable professionals such as appraisers and insolvency experts recognize and respond more swiftly to crises than countries with a limited base of expertise. The same is true of countries with a wide range of investment and risk management mechanisms, including a secondary market for debt, corporate financial restructuring funds, corporate restructuring vehicles, real estate investment trusts, and securitization. However, the development and implementation of such instruments require a solid base of human capital, including insolvency experts, appraisers, financial analysts, and actuaries.

The Asian financial crisis has led to calls for the development of international standards with the intent of strengthening public financial institutions, particularly in areas such as securities and bank regulation. There is an equal need to strengthen the capacity of the private financial sector through international standards in the essential professions and improvements in the institutional setting. Critical professions that are lacking and whose absence impedes the process of restructuring include insolvency experts, lawyers, accountants, appraisers, financial analysts, and actuaries (see table 3). Effective regulations can increase the efficient supply of such professionals by establishing standards for quality (see table 4), introducing safeguards against fraud, and establishing requirements that encourage private sector demand (for example, requiring proper audits increases the demand for auditors, thus raising their salaries and encouraging more entrants to the field). Governments should also abolish restrictions on foreign competition to encourage greater access to professionals. There is ample evidence that the

Table 2: Employment in Finance, Insurance, Real Estate, and Business Services as a Percentage of Total Employment in Select Countries, 1997

Country	Share of total employment
Indonesia	0.754
Philippines	2.442
Malaysia	5.219
Japan	8.769
United States	11.399

Source: United Nations (1997).

presence of foreign banking, insurance, and securities benefits the sectors in which they invest (Litan, Masson, and Pomerleano 2001). Liberalization of entry in the financial services professions offers policymakers a venue through which to import financial sector expertise.

Table 3: Appraisal, Actuarial, and Insolvency Professionals in Select Countries

	Appraisers		Insolvency experts		Actuaries	
Economy	Number per million population	Number	Number per million population	Number	Number per million population	Number
Argentina	—	—	0.92	34	4.54	168
Australia	—	—	31.57	606	—	—
Austria	—	—	2.84	23	—	—
Belgium	—	—	0.68	7	—	—
Brazil	29.39	5,000	—	—	2.40	408
Canada	—	—	34.89	1,071	—	—
Czech Rep.	535.37	5,500	1.56	16	—	—
China	10.64	13,420	0.01	8	0.01	8
Finland	28.96	150	—	—	18.73	97
France	29.74	1,750	2.53	149	21.78	1,282
Germany	97.38	8,000	0.99	81	20.22	1,661
Hong Kong (China)	159.46	1,084	—	—	29.27	199
Hungary	—	—	2.20	22	12.87	129
India	0.34	350	0.03	33	0.11	111
Indonesia	6,665	1,400	0.02	4	0.03	7
Israel	—	—	0.16	1	—	—
Italy	—	—	0.80	46	—	—
Japan	44.96	5,700	0.04	5	6.73	853
Korea, Rep. of	36.47	1,724	0.02	1	0.23	11
Lithuania	126.01	466	—	—	—	—
Malaysia	21.50	500	1.12	26	—	—
Mexico	30.62	3,000	0.02	2	1.95	191
New Zealand	—	—	49.86	191	—	—
Nigeria	—	—	0.03	4	—	—
Norway	—	—	2.00	9	—	—
Pakistan	—	—	—	—	0.10	14
Philippines	—	—	0.01	1	0.90	68
Poland	77.62	3,000	0.28	11	0.10	4
Romania	—	—	0.62	14	—	—
Russia	27.48	4,000	—	—	—	—
Singapore	129.17	519	2.74	11	20.41	82
South Africa	—	—	7.13	305	—	—
Spain	—	—	0.30	12	—	—
Sweden	56.38	500	1.58	14	27.74	246

Table 3: Appraisal, Actuarial, and Insolvency Professionals in Select Countries (cont'd)

Economy	Appraisers		Insolvency experts		Actuaries	
	Number per million population	Number	Number per million population	Number	Number per million population	Number
Switzerland	—	—	0.84	6	48.05	345
Thailand	—	—	0.13	8	0.21	13
United Kingdom	334.79	20,000	27.02	1,614	79.75	4,764
United States	284.14	80,000	6.54	1,841	53.16	14,968

— Not available.

Source: For insolvency, membership database of the International Federation of Insolvency Professionals; for appraisers, the International Valuation Standards Committee; for actuaries, the International Actuarial Association.

Table 4: Qualification Requirements of Insolvency Experts in Select Countries

Country and field	Qualification requirements
Insolvency experts	
Canada	Membership requirements in the Canadian Insolvency Practitioners Association (CIPA) include the association's standards of admission, prescribed course of study, and passage of required examinations. In 1997 the National Insolvency Qualification Program was created to harmonize qualification requirements.
New Zealand	Government is opposed to occupational registration, so there is no registration of insolvency practitioners. The following cannot qualify for appointment: persons under 18 years of age and creditors, shareholders, directors, auditors, or receivers of the company.
Switzerland	Insolvency is not a specialized profession. Activities are performed mostly by other specialized professions (lawyers, accountants).
United Kingdom	Insolvency experts are licensed and regulated by one of eight recognized professional bodies (for example, the Institute of Chartered Accountants in England and Wales plus the Secretary of State for Industry).
Actuaries	
Argentina	Examinations, university courses
Brazil	University degree program
Finland	Examinations of other bodies, government examinations
Germany	Examinations, university courses
Hungary	University degree plus 18 months of practice
India	Own examinations
Japan	Own examinations of other bodies
Mexico	University degree program
Singapore	Examinations of other bodies, university degree program
Sweden	University degree program
Switzerland	University degree plus at least three years of qualified professional experience, in line with international guidelines of ASTIN (International Actuarial Association)
United Kingdom	Examinations, university courses
United States	Own examinations of other bodies

Source: International Actuarial Association.

Financial Engineering:
Financial and Operational Restructuring

Countries should avoid easy solutions, such as interest and principal forbearance and stretching the maturity of debt, while ignoring corporate operational and financial restructuring. Such measures create moral hazard with far-reaching implications. Financial stabilization and financial restructuring should only buy time for more fundamental financial restructuring (the dilution of equity and sale of new equity) and operational restructuring (for example, changes in management and major assets sales). The crisis countries have used various techniques to address corporate restructuring.

Asset Management Companies

President Yang of China's Huarong Asset Management Company has said, "Nonperforming loans are like an ice cream cone. If you don't get rid of them, they melt all over your hands, and you don't have anything left to sell. The key issue for the seller is the price it is willing to accept today to avoid the wait and the commitment of resources required for potential collection." Asset management companies should focus on rapid disposition. Their success is contingent on good governance and policies, transparency, purchase of loans at market prices, and the realization of losses prior to purchase.

The history of government-established and -managed asset management companies does not inspire confidence. Mexico's Bank Savings Protection Fund (FOBAPROA), for example, has witnessed massive disappearance of assets as well as failure to identify assets due to inadequate documentation. The resolution process has been extremely slow. Turkey's asset management company is still unable to quantify the stock of assets that it holds. The Indonesian Bank Restructuring Agency (IBRA) has only disposed of a small percentage of its holdings. By contrast, there have only been isolated success stories: Danaharta in Malaysia is the leading success, and the Korea Asset Management Corporation (KAMCO) has been successful to a lesser extent.

Danaharta's success can be attributed to three key elements. It was given substantial up-front government funding, which provided leeway for operations and recognition of losses. It was established with a finite lifespan. And perhaps most important, it was founded not with a pool of permanent government staff but rather with staff taken on secondment from the private sector, including reputable banks, investment banks, and big accounting firms.

Why are government-established and -managed asset management companies prone to failure? First, they are invariably staffed by government bureaucrats, who tend to lack the expertise found in the private sector, who are timid and reluctant to be blamed for realizing losses, and who therefore prefer to sit on assets. Second, government asset management companies typically transfer assets at book value rather than market value. Due to political realities, they are not given sufficient working capital to acquire assets or fiscal headroom to incur losses and move on. As KAMCO discovered after the first round of asset sales, the public outcry against recognition of losses is very strong, and working capital is limited by political pressure. Third, centralized government asset management companies are too big and too unwieldy to get a complex job done. At its peak, IBRA owned 70 percent of the financial and industrial sector in Indonesia. At this size, the agency becomes too inflexible and unwieldy to take risks or try new financial techniques. Finally, as has been well argued by economist and Nobel laureate James Buchanan, bureaucracies are in the business of self-preservation (see Buchanan 1960; Buchanan and Tullock 1962; Buchanan and Wagner 1977). Asset management companies that are not explicitly limited in their lifespan or that lack the incentive to wrap up the job and dissolve will find ways to prolong their business.

What are the lessons of experience from successful asset management companies? First, and foremost, transparency, good governance, and clear policies and procedures are essential to success. Second, asset management companies should engage the private financial sector in asset disposition. Finally, they should employ a broad menu of financial instruments rather than tie the restructuring process to a single financial technique such as outright auctions.

Alternatives to Asset Management Companies

A better alternative is to adopt smaller-scale solutions that involve the private sector in resolving nonperforming loans, as in the good bank–bad bank approach. Although these models may not be feasible in all instances, they offer better incentives, as well as more efficient and speedy resolutions, than asset management companies. A good example is the establishment by Mellon Bank of a subsidiary bank—Grant Street Bank—with the transfer of

Mellon's nonperforming loans (about $1 billion at net asset value). Prior to transfer, the loans were written down to their liquidation value, including the projected cost of administering the loans until they would be collected, or about 60 percent of face value. Grant Street took approximately five years to liquidate all its assets, and Grant Street shareholders made a reasonable profit. The model proved successful: by the fourth quarter of 1988, the confidence level among Wall Street, regulators, clients, and staff had rebounded, and Mellon Bank witnessed a surge in new business.

An important lesson to take from the Mellon Bank approach is the value of a permanent joint venture of a bank with an investment bank. In Mellon's case, the relationship with E. M. Warburg Pincus was critical to providing the infusion of capital and expertise that would get the good and bad banks through the difficult disposition process. This method could be replicated for other banks with large stocks of nonperforming loans, through joint ventures with other reputable investment banks (a number of investment banks, such as Cerebus, Deutsche Bank, Goldman Sachs, Lone Star, and others, were involved in the restructuring process in the aftermath of the Asia crisis).

Another promising experiment is taking place in China. Rather than establish a centralized asset management corporation as a government agency, China established five major asset management companies, one for each of the five big banks. Instead of a behemoth run directly by the government, these asset management companies have been operating relatively more flexibly. We have not yet seen the results of this approach, but the potential benefits of this structure are promising.

Use of Financial Techniques

Greater use should be made of market-based financial instruments in restructuring, including a secondary market for debt, corporate financial restructuring funds, corporate restructuring vehicles, debt rescheduling, and conversion of debt-for-equity swaps or convertible bonds.

Secondary Market for Distressed Debt

In the typical insolvency process, a distressed company is restructured by the creditors and owners. In situations of extreme distress, the creditors liquidate the company. With a secondary market for distressed debt, investors accumulate the debt from the banks and attempt to restructure the company.

In this context, development of a secondary market in distressed corporate debt would support the corporate restructuring process in several ways. It would help troubled banks to dispose of poorly performing loans and therefore enable more efficient management of loan portfolios. It would create a market-signaling process for the valuation of troubled loans. And, finally, it would allow prospective acquirers to accumulate a strategic equity interest in corporations or real estate projects and to exert influence over the restructuring.

In emerging markets, the secondary market in distressed corporate debt is nascent. Markets in Asia, Australia, and Latin America are at early stages of development, while markets in Africa and the Middle East are relatively undeveloped. Efforts to sell distressed debt are subject to lengthy due diligence and lack of standard documentation, leading to variable—sometimes protracted—settlement periods and creating the potential for failed trades and substantial legal costs. The situation discourages transactions in the secondary market.

Three ingredients foster the development of the distressed debt market. The first is transparency of information. In order to evaluate the investment, potential investors have to be able to understand the accounting principles and the financial statements. The second ingredient is reasonable certainty in the application and interpretation of the laws in troubled situations. The third is uniformity in the standards for trading distressed debt to facilitate the sale of loans.

In conclusion, while secondary markets for distressed debt harbor potential, it is important to acknowledge that their development might not live up to their potential, due to uniform reluctance of banks to recognize losses on the disposition of loans. Regulators have to complement the development of markets with powerful incentives for the disposition of distressed debt.

Corporate Restructuring Funds

The Korean government contracted with foreign investment firms to create and manage a portfolio of investments with both policy and performance objectives. The funds had to rely on funding from Korean financial institutions, as neither foreign markets nor Korean investors had significant appetite for funds with policy objectives. Although the funds had considerable design problems, this does not detract from a fundamentally sound idea that can be refined in the future.

Corporate Restructuring Vehicles

Corporate restructuring vehicles are special-purpose vehicles created in Korea to acquire nonperforming loans from KAMCO and the banks. The goal was to centralize expertise in collections, to unite the holdings of separate creditors to realize economies of scale and minimize intra-creditor conflicts, and to relieve banks of the burden of managing nonperforming assets (and allow them to dispose of equity acquired during debt-for-equity swaps).[2] These vehicles focused on viable medium and large companies and raised debt or equity financing from qualified institutional investors (but not the general public). As a limited-life company, corporate restructuring vehicles enjoyed tax and leverage advantages.

Despite their appeal, corporate restructuring vehicles were not widely adopted, and only three to four transactions took place. Underprovisioned bank creditors were reluctant to assign loans to corporate restructuring vehicles and thus realize losses as well as undermine their relationship with clients. Further, senior creditors were reluctant to give up their seniority and be treated pari passu with other rights holders, and loan guarantors were reluctant to fulfill their liabilities earlier than under the usual process of loan restructuring. Also, it was difficult to designate a paid asset manager among multiple leading creditors. As a result of the objections, holdout creditors requested cash to exit and undermined the structure of corporate restructuring vehicles. In the absence of the threat of court-imposed liquidation, corporate debtors also were reluctant to agree to the draconian measures, such as asset sales, equity dilution, and diminution of management control, necessary to transfer a corporation to a corporate restructuring vehicle. Finally, the vehicles were hampered by serious technical issues: the legal structure was new and challenging, and it was difficult to employ "transfer pricing" in valuing different classes of debt.

Other countries can learn from Korea's experience. The positive aspects of special-purpose vehicles—going-concern value higher than liquidation value, removal of financial and management burden from the banking sector, more efficient allocation of resources, improved prospects to realize values, supportive tax treatment of debt-equity swaps, and non-cash forms of consideration (paper debt) that provide accounting flexibility—led to acceptance and commitment on the part of financial authorities, investment advisers, and investors.

Securitization

There is a growing range of securitization mechanisms for assets such as distressed loans and commercial real estate. Securitization can help to transfer liquidity, market, and credit risks from the balance sheets of banks to whoever is better equipped to value and manage these risks, and in the process such mechanisms can help to rehabilitate banks. For instance, the benefits of securitization of distressed debt for banks include improved balance sheet structure and better risk management.

Securitization holds great promise for banks in emerging markets to dispose of distressed assets, but the experience in the crisis countries has not been encouraging. In part, the failure is attributable to the prerequisites for securitization. First, trusts need to be recognized as a legal vehicle. In countries where there is a civil law tradition, the concept of trust, which separates management from beneficial ownership, is not recognized, and special legislation has to be passed. Second, the tax code should be neutral to securitized transactions, and there should be no sale, transfer, duty, or value added taxes on the transfer of impaired assets. Finally, many developing countries lack the financial expertise to package securitization transactions. Therefore, securitized assets impose significant compliance or administrative costs on the originator and do not provide adequate protection to investors. As a result, in at least one crisis country, the securitization transactions that took place provided full recourse to the buyer from the seller, thereby defeating the intended objective of transferring risks.

References

Buchanan, James. 1960. *Fiscal Theory and Political Economy*. Chapel Hill: University of North Carolina Press.

Buchanan, James, and Gordon Tullock. 1962. *The Calculus of Consent: Logical Foundations of Constitutional Democracy*. Ann Arbor: University of Michigan Press.

Buchanan, James, and Richard E. Wagner. 1977. *Democracy in Deficit: The Political Legacy of Lord Keynes*. New York: Academic Press.

Caprio, Gerard. 2003. "Episodes of Systemic and Borderline Financial Crises, Year(s) 1970s–2002." World Bank, Washington, D.C., January 22. Available at http://econ.worldbank.org/.

Litan, Robert E., Paul Masson, and Michael Pomerleano, eds. 2001. *Open Doors: Foreign Participation in Financial Systems in Developing Countries.* Washington, D.C.: Brookings Institution Press.

United Nations. 1997. *Statistical Yearbook 1997.* New York.

Notes

1. Distressed debt qualifies in this category.
2. The volume of these equities held on the books of banks has been growing since the workout initiatives were introduced.

Synopsis of Conference Papers

William Shaw

The financial crises of the late 1990s devastated the most affected emerging-market economies. Unemployment jumped, interest rates shot up, output plummeted, and massive exchange rate depreciation further reduced living standards. The crisis engendered huge shifts in the profitability of business activities and left an enormous overhang of bankrupt corporations and bad loans on the balance sheets of banks. Despite the key role that corporate sector weaknesses played in many of the crises, information on government actions to remedy corporate distress remains limited.

This volume addresses corporate restructuring during systemic crises, relying on the experience of senior public officials, private businessmen, and staff of the World Bank and International Monetary Fund. The papers that follow were commissioned as part of a World Bank seminar held in Washington, D.C. in March 2004. This initial chapter summarizes the main contributions, grouped into three parts: overviews of the crisis experience and general principles, war stories of particular experiences by practitioners, and technical issues.

Overviews of the Crisis and General Principles

In chapter 2, Stijn Claessens emphasizes the importance of establishing the appropriate incentives for both corporates and banks. Out-of-court workouts were more successful in countries with strong bankruptcy regimes—for example, in Korea and Malaysia (and, to some extent, Turkey)—than in countries with weaker legal systems—for example, in Indonesia, Mexico, and Thailand. Governments are often driven to intervene to support the banking system during systemic crises, but they should nevertheless maintain appropriate incentives for resolving nonperforming loans—for example, by linking government assistance for bank recapitalization directly to the pace of corporate restructuring. While regulatory forbearance is often necessary during systemic crises, it should not condone excessive risk taking and "cosmetic" corporate restructuring.[1]

Incentives for appropriate banking and corporate behavior can be improved by limiting ownership links between banks and corporations, by strengthening corporate governance, by requiring disclosure of nonperforming loans and (perhaps phased-in) adequate loan-loss provisioning, and by amending tax, accounting, and other legal rules to avoid discriminating against corporate restructuring.

Political pressures, the massive number of insolvent corporations, and a lack of expertise in managing corporate activities limited the success of banks and asset management companies in achieving corporate turnarounds and underlined the need to dispose of assets rapidly with limited consideration for price. However, large-scale disposal of assets can be difficult because of depressed asset prices and political pressures. One alternative is for ownership to remain with the state for some period, but to outsource the restructuring to private sector professionals. Greater differentiation by the type of assets is also useful—for example, between ongoing businesses and real estate, which is relatively homogeneous and has less potential for loss of value (and can therefore be held by asset management companies).

In chapter 3, Ira Lieberman and his co-authors review the experience with out-of-court workouts. Restructuring strategies should be differentiated by the type of firm: (a) small business failures may be addressed through blanket rollovers and injection of liquidity; (b) mid-size firms require rollovers and extensions of bank credits to help them ride out the crisis; and (c) the largest firms must be dealt with on a case-by-case basis, with deep corporate restructuring and avoidance of simple bailouts. It is important to impose losses on all stakeholders, including managers, creditors, and owners.

Improvements in policy and institutions are required to prevent and cope with future crises: stronger transparency rules could limit insider lending, institutions need greater capacity to manage corporate restructuring, and a menu of tools should be available to deal with crisis-induced insolvencies (including restructuring funds, formal bankruptcy systems, prepackaged bankruptcies, asset management companies, market solutions to divest asset management company assets, and voluntary workout schemes). As coping with systemic crisis can take years, procedures for out-of-court workouts should provide for a second round of modifications once economic conditions have stabilized.

In chapter 4, William Mako emphasizes the government's role in forcing debtors to cooperate in corporate restructuring. Workout procedures can be based on best practice examples, such as the model memorandum of understanding for Korean workouts. Legal and regulatory impediments to restructuring can be eliminated quickly, assuming sufficient political consensus. Governments can and should invest in capacity to deal with future workouts and should use existing capacity efficiently by segmenting firms by size (as in Malaysia). More difficult obstacles to successful restructuring involve the ability of creditors to impose losses on a debtor (given weak legal frameworks and political pressures), the government's readiness to force creditors to recognize losses from corporate restructuring, and the resolution of inter-creditor differences regarding the allocation of losses and risk.

The appropriate structure of bankruptcy law in industrial economies is evolving with the level of economic development. As James Zukin writes in chapter 5, earlier bankruptcy regimes emphasized tangible property rights, the rights of secured creditors, and the realization of assets to discharge debts. However, in modern economies, the value of the firm as a going concern often exceeds the value of tangible assets, due to advantages such as human resources, organization, and brand-name recognition. Thus modern bankruptcy regimes, as exemplified by the U.S. Chapter 11 system, emphasize maintaining firms as going concerns. Restructuring regimes in industrial countries are moving toward the Chapter 11 system. Some limited progress has been made in emerging markets, although care must be taken to ensure time-bound resolution of disputes, as Chapter 11-style frameworks can engender delays.

1

After an introduction by Ruth Neyens of the World Bank, chapter 6 gives presentations by managers of the more successful asset management companies, including Dató Zukri Samat from Danaharta, Beom Choi of the Korea Asset Management Company, Yang Kaisheng, president of China's Huarong, and Shinjiro Takagi, chairman of the Industrial Revitalization Corporation of Japan (IRCJ). Asset management companies took nonperforming loans off of the books of banks, thus allowing them to focus on the core activities of financial intermediation; minimized the incentive for banks with dwindling (or negative) capital to take large risks; severed the ties between banks and corporates that impeded asset resolution; and enabled banks to clean up their balance sheets, a prerequisite for raising further capital. Setting up new agencies with special powers also allowed governments to eliminate some of the legal obstacles to restructuring, while maintaining control over the process. And centralizing extremely scarce restructuring expertise in one or a few agencies helped to achieve economies of scale in restructuring.

But the landscape is full of failed asset management companies, such as in Mexico and Indonesia. The relatively successful agencies presented here are the exceptions. First and foremost, each agency emphasized transparency as a key principle of operations and employed governance structures that ensured efficient administration, open transactions, and checks and balances on management. Engaging private sector cooperation and ensuring competitive markets were critical, and successful asset management companies adopted a menu of asset disposition strategies.

In chapter 7, Jack Rodman provides an overview of progress in reducing the nonperforming loans of banks. Asian economies have cut the volume of nonperforming loans in half over the past two years, mostly through write-offs and transfers to government agencies rather than through disposition of assets. Rodman emphasizes the importance of strong government leadership, including the willingness to devote money to loan resolution. Governments can substantially reduce the costs of resolving nonperforming loans by clarifying the legal structure for transactions, strengthening creditor rights and the role of the court system, opening the market to foreign competition, and encouraging a wide range of instruments for selling nonperforming loans (for example, asset-backed securitizations and joint ventures). Asset holders, including governments, need to adopt a more realistic understanding of asset values and be willing to absorb losses.

War Stories from the Crises

In chapter 8, Ray Davis criticizes the lack of predictability in insolvency procedures in many emerging markets. Ineffective legal frameworks for bankrupt companies make restructuring negotiations more dependent on intervention by government or the organization and skill of the negotiating parties.

Davis cites several ingredients for successful restructuring. Strong creditor leadership is essential to impose discipline on the company and on dissident creditors. Lengthy negotiations should be avoided due to the potential for destruction of value, particularly in countries where law enforcement is weak. Cash controls are needed to prevent owners and managers from siphoning funds from the business during negotiations. The presence of at least some local creditors can be helpful in gaining favorable treatment by regulators and the courts and in facilitating acceptance of draconian measures. In Davis's experience, government intervention has been useful in achieving successful restructurings in Malaysia and Mexico, but less so in Indonesia, where the Jakarta Initiative has been relatively ineffective in larger, more complex cases.

In chapter 9, Hogen Oh, former executive chairman of Korea's Corporate Restructuring Coordination Committee, reviews government measures to unify supervision of the financial system, provide fiscal resources to support restructuring, and require banks (and by extension corporations) to adopt international accounting standards. The recognition of losses, the elimination of cross-guarantees within corporate groups, and guidance to banks aimed at reducing corporate leverage forced chaebols to restructure. Workouts for some 102 corporations, including Daewoo companies, were managed, with almost all reaching a successful conclusion. The demise of Daewoo was a watershed event that dispelled the notion of implicit government guarantees for "too-big-to-fail" chaebols in Korea.

In chapter 10, Dató Zainal A. Putih, chairman of Danaharta (the Malaysian asset management company), reviews government efforts to restructure the banking and corporate sectors. Danaharta enjoyed special powers that sped up the transfer of assets and bypassed court processes for foreclosure on collateral. Danamodal required banks receiving capital injections to write down shareholders' capital, submit recapitalization plans, and meet monthly reporting of performance against a list of identified targets. And the Corporate Debt Restructuring Committee (CDRC) mediated voluntary out-of-court restructuring of large debt cases involving viable borrowers with multiple major creditors. All three agencies were created as finite-life agencies in order to minimize moral hazard.

In chapter 11, Richard Daniel discusses the resolution of nonperforming loans, based on his experience heading the Grant Street National Bank (set up to liquidate low-quality assets from Mellon Bank). The first step is to take the portfolio of bad loans away from the original lenders, who may be unwilling to acknowledge their own mistakes and may lack appropriate skills. Recovery also requires an effective credit quality control and asset classification, access to a well-functioning legal system to help force collection, sufficient reserves, and the will to stop making, or renewing, bad loans. This latter quality can be a major problem in countries trying to move from a state-managed to a free-market economy.

Christopher Vale provides a manager's perspective on the Korean corporate restructuring funds in chapter 12. Corporate restructuring funds provided critical equity financing to small and medium enterprises, motivated merchant banks to get involved in restructuring, and generated interest by other investors in targeted companies. But the dual objectives of improving performance and achieving policy goals (for example, encouragement of new investments and technological development) led to difficult tradeoffs. For example, there was little international appetite for funds with policy objectives, so funding had to be mobilized from domestic banks. The funds could only invest in newly issued debt or equity, which hindered transactions such as buying old debt at a distressed price. Also, requirements for a small size and large number of transactions were difficult to achieve with any reasonable administrative cost.

Technical Issues

In chapter 13, Jack Glen uses the interest coverage ratio (ICR—the ratio of earnings before interest, taxes, and depreciation expense to interest expense) as a measure of firm viability: firms with a ratio below 1 do not generate adequate cash flow to service their debt. He analyzes the relationship between the ICR and factors specific to the firm, as well as macroeconomic events, for a large number of firms in a broad cross section of countries during the period 1994–2001. In Thailand, for example, for every 10 percentage point decline in GDP growth, the ICR drops about 1 percentage point. Thus the 16 percent drop in Thailand's GDP from 1996 to 1998 would, by these estimations, have doubled to about 25 percent the share of Thai firms with an ICR of less than 1.

In chapter 14, Michael Gapen and his co-authors estimate corporate sector credit risk using the contingent claims approach, a concept widely applied to measure the default probability of a firm. The contingent claims approach uses options theory to measure the value of the firm in terms of the market price of securities in the capital structure (because equity can be thought of as a residual claim with limited liability, there is a correspondence between equity and a call option). The authors compute the *distance to distress*, which is the difference between the implied market value of firm assets and an indicator of the level of debt, scaled by a one standard deviation move in firm assets. This model would have provided an accurate view of the pending financial difficulties facing the Brazilian corporate sector in the buildup to the crisis and would have signaled serious problems for many Thai firms nearly 18 months before the floating of the baht. The authors also show that a complete analysis of the risks involved in corporate sector vulnerabilities must take into account third-party guarantees, such as government guarantees of the financial system.

In chapter 15, Gordon Johnson reports on a joint initiative of the World Bank and the International Monetary Fund to set standards for each step in the credit process, including access to credit, companies in financial distress, and formal systems for resolution and recovery. For creditor rights, about half of the emerging markets assessed are operating more or less at a functional level, while the rest fail to meet standards in most areas. Most systems involved in the legal frameworks for insolvency are not working effectively, rehabilitation procedures for companies undergoing restructuring are not much better, and institutional and regulatory frameworks are worse. There is enormous need for greater capacity to oversee corporate restructuring in court systems and regulatory bodies. Johnson emphasizes the weak treatment of employee rights and social protection of labor, the lack of access to financing, and tax provisions that penalize restructuring as major obstacles to successful corporate workouts.

Note

1. For example, forbearance on the capital adequacy ratio is preferable to forbearance on provisioning for nonperforming and classified loans. Both

1

methods reduce the absolute amount of capital required during periods of distress, but the latter masks the extent of losses and creates adverse incentives to addressing classified loans.

Part I
Overviews of the Crisis Experience

2

Policy Approaches to Corporate Restructuring around the World: What Worked, What Failed?

Stijn Claessens

A number of countries experienced a financial crisis in the past decade. In several of these, the corporate sector was an important factor contributing to the crisis. And many of the crises involved large-scale corporate sector distress. In turn, in many cases corporate restructuring was recognized as key to the recovery. More generally, corporate sector restructuring and reform have recently been considered essential to economic recovery, the long-term viability of corporations, and a lower risk of (subsequent) financial crises. This paper surveys the policy approaches and legal and regulatory changes adopted in response to widespread corporate failure in eight countries over the past decade (Brazil, the Czech Republic, Indonesia, Republic of Korea, Malaysia, Mexico, Thailand, and Turkey). After surveying the various decisions made and measures taken, the paper offers an assessment of which policies were most effective given country circumstances, which were ineffective, and why.[1]

Overview of Approaches

Restructuring refers to a multidimensional process (see box 2.1). Corporate sector restructuring, as the term is used here, refers to the process of sepa-

2

rating financially distressed firms into viable firms and nonviable firms, followed by arranging the financial structure of the viable firms to create sustainable financial and operational situations and then liquidating or restructuring nonviable (parts of) corporations. In the immediate aftermath of a financial crisis, two main approaches to corporate restructuring can be distinguished: a centralized and a decentralized approach. Most countries studied here, and also more generally, employed elements of both approaches. In terms of the decentralized elements, banks and other creditors were expected to work out the problems of over-indebted corporations on a case-by-case basis, while governments provided support in various forms to the banking system—through recapitalization, tax relief, and other measures. Most countries, however, also recognized that a completely decentralized approach would not suffice given the large scale of corporate sector distress and the coordination problems among creditors. A large direct role for the government was deemed both necessary and unavoidable. The response was typically twofold: adopt a stricter set of rules for corporate restructuring and create a government-owned asset management company.[2]

For most countries, the mixed model became large-scale corporate restructuring under a government-sponsored out-of-court process—the so-called London approach—with specific rules for restructuring. Outside

---

Box 2.1: Definitions of Restructuring

Restructuring refers to several related processes: recognizing and allocating financial losses, restructuring the financial claims of financial institutions and corporations, and restructuring the operations of financial institutions and corporations. Recognition or resolution involves the allocation of existing losses and associated redistribution of wealth and control. Losses—that is, differences between financial institutions' and corporations' market value of assets and nominal values of liabilities—can be allocated to shareholders by dilution, to depositors and external creditors by reduction (of the present value) of their claims, to employees and suppliers by payment of lower wages and prices, and to the government—that is, the public at large—through higher taxes, expenditure cuts, or inflation. Financial restructuring for corporations can take many forms: rescheduling (extension of maturities), lower interest rates, debt-for-equity swaps, debt forgiveness, indexing of interest payments to earnings, and so on. The main aims of financial restructuring are separating and treating appropriately viable and nonviable firms and creating the right incentives for operational restructuring. Operational restructuring, an ongoing process, includes improvements in efficiency and management, reductions in staff and wages, sales of assets (for example, reduction in subsidiaries), enhanced marketing efforts, and so on, with the expectation of higher profitability and cash flow.

the London approach, and typically for smaller firms, purely market-based restructuring took place through in-court restructuring (bankruptcy proceedings) or voluntary actions, including mergers and acquisitions. In terms of centralized approaches, the first role of public asset management companies in separating nonperforming loans from the banking system was to restore financial stability. Because of their large holdings in many countries, asset management companies played important roles in corporate restructuring. Much operational and financial restructuring happened *outside* these forums, driven often by the lack of new financing, especially for small and medium enterprises. In some countries, special schemes were adopted for large corporations and sometimes also for smaller firms. The strengthening of the capital bases of weak banks, structural reforms in the financial system, and reforms in corporate governance complemented these approaches. Also changes to the accounting and tax regimes for the treatment of restructured debt were typically part of the reforms.

I review these approaches for eight countries, each of which had a financial crisis involving corporate sector distress in the 1990s: Brazil, the Czech Republic, Indonesia, Korea, Malaysia, Mexico, Thailand, and Turkey. The crises differed in timing: the Asian crises all started in late 1997, the crisis in the Czech Republic began in 1997, the crisis in Brazil began in early 1999, and the crisis in Turkey began in early 2001. The crisis in Mexico occurred earlier in the decade, starting in late 1994 and deepening in early 1995. I start the review with government-sponsored voluntary workouts, followed by court-supervised restructuring and then asset management companies, and finish with voluntary and special schemes.

The paper does not review the general causes of the crisis. But the degree to which the corporate sector contributed to the crisis did affect the responses. In turn, when reviewing the policy responses, it is important to take into account the condition of the corporate sector before the crisis and the presence of structural weaknesses in the corporate sector. As an illustration of the differences among the crisis-affected countries, figure 2.1 provides data on corporate sector financial conditions before the crisis. In countries like Korea and Thailand, corporate sector leverage was high, while in Malaysia and the Czech Republic corporate leverage was low and interest coverage was quite high. At the same time, the return on assets was low in many non-Asian countries, suggesting longer-term structural weaknesses in operational performance.

Figure 2.1: Financial Conditions and Performance of the Corporate Sector before the Crisis in Eight Countries

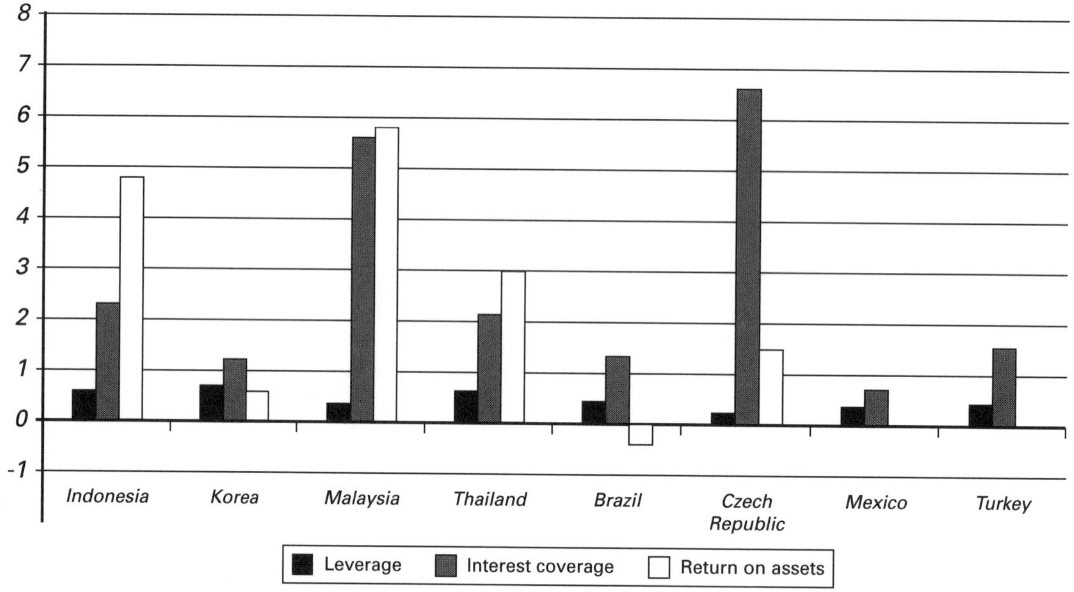

Legend: ■ Leverage ■ Interest coverage □ Return on assets

Note: The data are for the year prior to the crisis in each country: 1994 for Mexico, 1996 for Asian countries and Czech Republic, 1998 for Brazil, and 2000 for Turkey.

Source: Country sources (a complete list is available from the author).

Government-Sponsored Voluntary Workout Schemes

Recognizing the scale of the restructuring challenges and realizing that the markets did not function sufficiently, many countries set up, through agreements among creditors or through laws and regulations, out-of-court processes for screening and restructuring large, distressed corporations. The out-of-court frameworks themselves built on the London approach for corporate reorganization first enunciated in the United Kingdom in the early 1990s. The London approach encourages creditors in out-of-court agreements to follow certain principles: minimize losses to creditors, avoid unnecessary liquidation of viable debtors, and offer continued financial support to viable borrowers. Since the London rules were not designed for cases of system-wide corporate distress and the acts of the Bank of England were merely informal sanctions, most crisis-affected countries adopted more formal approaches. These involved accords under contract law through which creditors agree among themselves to follow certain processes and actions. Mexico used this model for a subset of corporate sector claims (Unidad Coordinadora del Acuerdo Bancario Empresarial, UCABE). The East Asian countries were the first to adopt these models on a larger scale, followed by Turkey. Brazil and the Czech Republic did not use this model.

Governments enhanced their out-of-court frameworks in several ways, with three important features easily distinguished. First, did all (or most) financial institutions sign on to the accord under regular contract or commercial law? If so, agreements reached among the majority could be enforced on other creditors without going through formal judicial procedures. In Korea, for example, with encouragement from the Financial Supervisory Commission, 210 local financial institutions signed the corporate restructuring agreement in July 1998. Second, was formal arbitration with specific deadlines part of the accord? Without such arbitration, an out-of-court system had to rely on the formal judicial process to resolve disputes, with the associated costs and delays. Third, could penalties for failure to meet deadlines be imposed under the accord?

Not all countries had these three features in place immediately after the crisis (table 2.1). In Indonesia, for example, no formal arbitration was in place by mid-1999. Malaysia's Corporate Debt Restructuring Committee was meant to provide a platform for workouts, but it did not initially have any legal powers. The severity of penalties and deadlines also varied by country, with several countries initially having no penalties at all for failing to comply with deadlines and other breaches. In many countries, however, the design and implementation of sanctions were weak. Mexico's regime had none of the three features; in addition, the only deadlines were those of the normal insolvency and liquidation regime, which was very weak. In addition, the effectiveness of sanctions varied across countries. There was no out-of court system in Brazil (although the central bank did begin to monitor banks with large nonperforming loans more actively) or in the Czech Republic.

As lessons were learned within countries, and also applied to later crises, enhancements were added over time. East Asian countries put in place more meaningful sanctions and deadlines between 1998 and 2001, and by mid-2003, all countries except Indonesia had at least two of the three key features in place (see table 2.2). Korea ended up with the best-defined setup, as

2

Table 2.1: Features of Out-of-Court Corporate Restructuring Processses in Eight Countries

Feature	Indonesia	Korea, Rep. of	Malaysia	Thailand	Czech Republic	Turkey	Mexico	Brazil
Name of initiative or coordinating body	Jakarta Initiative Task Force (JITF)	Corporate Restructuring Coordination Committee (CRCC)	Corporate Debt Restructuring Committee (CDRC)	Corporate Debt Restructuring Advisory Committee (CDRAC)	None	Istanbul approach	Unidad Coordinadora del Acuerdo Bancario Empresarial (UCABE)	None
Basic approach	Forum for negotiations, followed by adoption of time-bound mediation procedures	Forum for negotiations	Forum for negotiations	Forum for facilitation, superseded by contractual approach (debtor-creditor agreements)	None	Forum for negotiations, superseded in the fall of 2001 by a legal approach (Law on Corporate Restructuring)	Promotion of a voluntary debt workout program for the largest 40 corporations (only about 10 percent of all bank lending)	None
Onset of the crisis	Late 1997	Late 1997	Late 1997	Late 1997	1997	February 2001	Late 1994	January 1999
Resolution of inter-creditor disputes	No special procedure	Possibility to have loan of opposing creditor purchased; also arbitration committee consisting of private experts	Nothing special, apart from persuasion by central bank	Three-person panel to attribute differences, but any concerned creditor can opt out	No established framework for creditor coordination; efforts to reach settlements frequently undermined by minority and dissenting creditors	None	Possibility to form a *convenio*; all creditors are treated equally and decisions bind all creditors	No possibility of consensual resolution among parties or establishment of creditor committees
Current default structure for failure to reach agreement	JITF may refer uncooperative debtor to government for possible bankruptcy petition[a]	Foreclosure, liquidation through court receivership	Foreclosure, liquidation or referral to asset management company with super-administrative powers	If less than 50 percent support the proposed workout, debt-or-credit agreement obliges creditors to petition court for collection of debts	Regular bankruptcy	Regular bankruptcy	Criminal bankruptcy procedures or "suspension of payments" to banks permitted by courts	Financial institutions not allowed to invoke insolvency relief pledge for secured debt; unsecured debt can be deferred or reduced (*concordata*)

a. This option has not been used since mid-2001 (Mako 2003).

Source: Country sources (a complete list is available from the author).

Table 2.2: Status of Out-of-Court Corporate Restructuring Processes in Eight Countries, 1999 and 2003

Indicator	Indonesia	Korea, Rep. of	Malaysia	Thailand	Czech Republic	Turkey[a]	Mexico[b]	Brazil
All or most financial institutions signed on to accord								
Mid-1999	No	Yes	Yes	Yes	n.a.	No	No	n.a.
Mid-2003	No	Yes	Yes	Yes	n.a.	Yes	No	n.a.
Accord provides for formal arbitration with deadlines								
Mid-1999	No	No	Yes	Yes	n.a.	No	No	n.a.
Mid-2003	Yes	Yes	Yes	Yes	n.a.	Yes	No	n.a.
Accord imposes penalties for non-compliances								
Mid-1999	No	Yes	No	Yes	n.a.	No	No	n.a.
Mid-2003	No	Yes	No	Yes	n.a.	Yes	No	n.a.

n.a. Not applicable.

a. The first date is end of 2001, and the second is end of 2003.

b. The first date is end of 1994, and the second is end of 2003.

Source: Country sources (a complete list is available from the author).

it codified the framework in the fall of 2001—with all three features as well as others—in a law on corporate restructuring (which, however, is in force only for a limited time). Malaysia strengthened its framework in August 2001, and Thailand also established a relatively strong framework. The framework in Indonesia remained weak, since not all financial institutions were obliged to sign on to the accord and there were few effective sanctions for failing to meet deadlines. Turkey, which established its regime (the so-called Istanbul approach) later, quickly incorporated all three features in its out-of-court regime. In Mexico, the approach remained largely consensual.

Reflecting, in part, improvements in design and general experience with restructuring, the number of corporations and amount of debt being restructured under out-of-court programs increased steadily (table 2.3). The greatest progress was achieved in Korea, where restructuring agreements were reached by mid-2003 for about 80 percent of registered cases representing 95 percent of total debt, with the remaining typically converted into court-supervised bankruptcies. In Malaysia, 77 percent of the debt referred to the Corporate Debt Restructuring Committee was resolved by mid-2003. The

Table 2.3: Scope of Out-of-Court Corporate Restructuring in Four East Asian Countries, as of Mid-1999 and Mid-2003

Indicator	Indonesia	Korea, Rep. of	Malaysia	Thailand
Number of registered cases				
Mid-1999	157	83	27	430
Mid-2003	—	83	54	14,917
Number of restructured cases				
Mid-1999	22	46	10	167
Mid-2003	—	68	46	6,345
Ratio of restructured debt to total debt (percent)				
Mid-1999	13	40	32	22
Mid-2003	56	95	77	48

— Not applicable.

Source: Country sources (a complete list is available from the author).

least progress was recorded in Thailand, where only 48 percent of debt was restructured as of mid-2003.

In Mexico, little information has been made available. In 1997, three years after the crisis, some 30–40 companies reportedly had been restructured through UCABE, but no results or proceedings of its operations have been published. This is also true for the London approach, in which confidentiality has been maintained. In the Czech Republic, although there was no formal out-of-court system, large not-in-court corporate restructurings were still being registered. Of these registered cases, less than half were started as of 1999. In Turkey, the process started only in July 2002 and so far has resulted in the restructuring of $3.8 billion in debts owed by 109 companies from 28 groups.[3] Most of the restructuring has entailed rescheduling debt, with only 3 percent of debt being restructured, mostly because little time has passed since the crisis. As of 2003, 1,561 cases were registered. In Brazil, there was no formal out-of-court restructuring process.

While the out-of-court processes helped to accelerate restructuring, in practice, and regardless of the tightness of the framework, implementation experienced problems in many countries. In several countries, much of the restructuring in the initial years following the crisis was in the form of temporary financial relief. As restructurings were based on unrealistic assumptions or as operational restructuring and profitability lagged, some of the restructured debt reverted back to nonperforming status, sometimes even within a few months after restructuring. In Thailand, for example, about 30 percent of the debt restructured in 2002 reverted to nonperforming status in just a few months. In Mexico, some workout cases, such as Mexicana de Aviación and Aeroméxico, which were problematic state-owned firms that were privatized in the early 1990s, emerged again as problem cases in recent years. In general, especially initially, debt restructuring agreements were favorable to the debtors. For debt restructuring agreements mediated by the Jakarta Initiative Task Force even as late as 2000, for example, terms were extended to seven years on average, and 87 percent of the rescheduled principal was subject to a two- to three-year grace period. About a third of the debt was converted into equity, and just 5 percent of the restructured debt was repaid promptly (for example, from existing cash balances, sale of assets, or debt-for-assets swaps).

Regardless of the quality of the out-of-court procedures, an important requirement for success was a credible threat of liquidation under a normal insolvency or bankruptcy regime. Since those countries that had reasonably functioning bankruptcy regimes also adopted stronger out-of-court systems, the importance of the features of out-of-court regimes is hard to pinpoint separately. Furthermore, many other factors played a role. Nevertheless, for those countries in which the crisis occurred longer ago, there appears to be a link between the strength of the out-of-court rules and the intensity of the restructuring process, as shown by Korea and Malaysia. Furthermore, the fact that restructuring accelerated as the out-of-court procedures were tightened supports the view that the strength of the out-of-court regime was an important aspect in the speed of restructuring. In Turkey, as of August 2003, $5 billion of loans of 220 firms were restructured. The restructuring is still relatively recent, however, and it is too early to judge the success of what is a relatively strict approach.

Court-Supervised Restructuring and Bankruptcy

Initial weaknesses in bankruptcy regimes made court-supervised restructuring an unattractive option for creditors in most countries, and it was little used. The exceptions in East Asia were Korea and to some extent Malaysia. Of the other countries, the bankruptcy system in Turkey was relatively strong in terms of formal rules. For the rest, bankruptcy systems were weak

2

and played only a small role in restructuring.[4] These weaknesses in the bankruptcy systems related to poor creditor rights, poor rules for conducting insolvency procedures, and the general nature of the legal system, with many countries having a long history of pro-debtor bias. In many countries, this pro-debtor bias was aggravated by the limited efficacy of the judicial system. The lack of a credible threat of restructuring or liquidation through bankruptcy procedures impeded the in-court restructuring but also the out-of-court restructuring, as creditors lacked the means to force borrowers to come to the negotiating table in good faith.

Some of the legal deficiencies were corrected following the crisis. All countries undertook to improve their insolvency regimes (table 2.4). Thailand introduced a reorganization procedure in its bankruptcy law in 1998 and made further amendments in 1999, including the important step of revoking the exemption of individual guarantors of debt from bankruptcy suits. It also established a Central Bankruptcy Court by June 1999, which has been reasonably effective, and is making further changes.[5] Indonesia revised its bankruptcy law in 1998 and set up special commercial courts to facilitate corporate restructuring. In Korea, bankruptcy and restructuring procedures were working relatively well before the crisis. Nevertheless, amendments were made to the Corporate Reorganization Act, the Composition Act, and the Bankruptcy Law to improve the speed and efficiency of the system (Korea is now considering revamping all of these laws to make them more efficient).[6] The Malaysian bankruptcy system was also working relatively well before the crisis, and few changes were made in the years immediately following the crisis. Later, some improvements were made. In 2003, for example, to create conditions for more market-driven corporate restructuring, the 1965 Malaysian Companies Act was amended to ensure that an ailing company could not make an ex parte application to a court for a restraining order against probable action by creditors.

In Brazil and Mexico, bankruptcy systems were especially weak before the crisis and did not improve much afterward. In Mexico, the reform of the bankruptcy system did not take place until 2000, and in Brazil, the bankruptcy regime did not change over this period (some reforms are in Parliament now, though). In the Czech Republic, some amendments to the bankruptcy law were passed only in 2000, and completing the new bankruptcy law was still a priority in 2003, in addition to more timely court decisions. In Turkey, on July 17, 2003, Parliament passed amendments to the Execution and Bankruptcy Act, which enhanced effective creditor rights.

Table 2.4: Creditor Rights in Bankruptcy Regimes in Eight Countries, 1999 (or the Crisis Period) and 2003

Indicator and period	Indonesia	Korea, Rep. of	Malaysia	Thailand	Czech Republic	Turkey	Mexico	Brazil
Restrictions on reorganizations								
1999 (or crisis period)[a]	1	1	1	1	1	1	0	1
2003	1	1	1	1	1	1	0	1
No automatic stay on assets								
1999 (or crisis period)[a]	0	0	0	1	1	0	0	0
2003	0	0	1	1	1	0	0	0
Secured creditors paid first								
1999 (or crisis period)[a]	0	1	0	0	0	1	0	0
2003	0	1	0	0	0	1	0	0
Management does not stay on in reorganizations								
1999 (or crisis period)[a]	1	1	0	1	0	0	0	0
2003	1	1	0	1	1	0	0	0
Creditor rights score								
1999 (or crisis period)[a]	2	3	1	3	2	2	0	0
2003	2	3	2	3	3	2	0	1
Rule of law indicator								
1999 (or crisis period)[a]	3.98	5.35	6.78	6.25	—	5.18	5.35	6.32
2003	3.98	5.35	6.78	6.25	—	5.18	5.35	6.32
Effective creditor rights								
1999 (or crisis period)[a]	7.96	16.05	6.78	6.25	—	10.36	0	6.32
2003	7.96	16.05	13.56	6.25	—	10.36	0	6.32

— Not available.

a. The crisis period is 1994 for Mexico, 1999 for Brazil and the Czech Republic, and 2001 for Turkey.

Source: Country sources (a complete list is available from the author).

In addition, prepackaged bankruptcy provisions were included to further improve the insolvency regime.

Most important, the improvements in some of the formal regimes did not do away with many of the institutional problems weakening the judicial system and functioning of the courts in several countries. A rating of the effectiveness of the insolvency systems shows that most of the crisis-affected countries lagged far behind OECD countries in terms of the time and cost it takes to resolve estates (table 2.5). This is attributable, in part, to the insol-

Table 2.5: Effectiveness of Insolvency Systems in Select Regions and Countries

Economy	Actual time (years)	Actual cost (percent of estate)	Goals of insolvency index	Court powers index
High-income countries (OECD)	1.8	7	77	36
Middle-income countries	3.4	16	48	60
Indonesia	6.0	18	35	100
Korea, Rep. of	1.5	4	91	67
Malaysia	2.2	18	52	33
Thailand	2.6	38	62	33
Czech Republic	9.2	38	22	0
Brazil	10.0	8	24	67
Mexico	2.0	18	61	67
Turkey	1.8	8	51	67

Source: World Bank (2003).

vency goals as defined in the law, where most crisis-affected countries fall short of OECD average, although not much so from other middle-income countries (higher scores of the index mean a higher likelihood of success in reaching the goals of insolvency). Courts in several crisis countries had more power than typical courts in OECD countries (higher scores mean more involvement of the court). More power is a poor combination with weak capacity and high corruption, however, and thereby accounts for much of the delays and costs in restructuring.

As far as available, table 2.6 provides figures on bankruptcies in the crisis-affected countries. The figures are difficult to compare across countries, however, because they refer to different types of bankruptcy (corporate, personal). Bankruptcy rates were still low in 1999 in East Asian countries, and only a small percentage of debt was being restructured using formal bankruptcy procedures. Improvements in bankruptcy regimes and the establishment of specialized bankruptcy courts in some countries nevertheless did have some payoffs, and over time bankruptcy was used more often to resolve financial distress.

In East Asia, from very low bases, the number of cases filed under bankruptcy procedures increased sharply between mid-1999 and mid-2003 by about 30 times in Indonesia and about 60 times in Thailand.[7] In Korea, bankruptcy rates were already high, as the regime was well able to deal with financial distress, at least for small firms. In East Asia, corporations tended to defer the government-sponsored, out-of-court programs in favor of court-supervised restructuring. In Thailand, for example, about half of the court-supervised restructuring in 1999–2001 came from the government-sponsored, out-of-court process. In Indonesia, bankruptcy judges remained in short supply, and creditors had little ability to clamp down on recalcitrant borrowers. As a consequence, the number of cases actually completed remained very low; as of mid-2000, only 65 large cases were completed in Indonesia, and this number rose to only 230 as of 2003.

For the other countries, no good data are available on the degree of in-court restructuring. In the two Latin American countries, the rise in bankruptcy was much lower after the financial crisis. This is partly explained by the differences in corporate sector leverage before the crisis: many Latin

Table 2.6: In-Court Restructuring in Four East Asian Countries, of Mid-1999 and Mid-2003

Indicator or period	Indonesia[a]	Korea, Rep. of	Malaysia	Thailand
Number of registered cases				
Mid-1999	88	48	52	30
Mid-2003	2,656	—	1,200	1,830
Number of cases started				
Mid-1999	78	27	34	22
Mid-2003	2,348	—	—	135
Number of restructured cases				
Mid-1999	8	19	12	8
Mid-2003	230	—	—	50
Ratio of restructured debt to total				
Mid-1999	4	8	—	7
Mid-2003	—	—	—	—

— Not applicable.

a. Refers to Indonesia Bank Restructuring Agency cases only.

Source: Country sources (a complete list is available from the author).

2

American corporations had relatively low leverage. This limited debt financing reflected, in part, a weak legal infrastructure and macro instability, making the supply of savings, including from abroad, less abundant and banks more conservative in their lending decisions. The low leverage and limited external financial dependence meant that firms were able to absorb the various shocks better. As such, the poor insolvency systems were not a particularly severe constraint in the short run, although they hampered businesses very much in the long run, as external financing was difficult to obtain. The same applied (to a lesser degree) in Turkey, where long periods of high inflation limited the willingness of investors to provide debt financing to firms and leverage was low. In terms of interest burden relative to cash flows or income, however, Mexican and Turkish firms were similar to or worse than firms in East Asia, given the high real interest rates in these countries.

As institutional reform took time and institutional capacity, including human capital, was spare, restructuring was limited initially. The shortage of capital was a particularly severe bottleneck that could not be resolved quickly. As a consequence, in many countries private sector interventions did not make much progress in reducing the open financial distress, at least in the short run. Other forms of government intervention were consequently necessary to address the most severe consequences of debt overhang in the corporate sector. This happened through the assumption of nonperforming assets in many of the crisis countries. Governments themselves became large claimants on the corporate sector and, as such, a major direct party to the restructuring.

Restructuring by Public Asset Management Companies and State-Owned Banks

All four crisis countries in East Asia established a publicly owned asset management company, although the timing varied, with Thailand only establishing its asset management company in 2001.[8] The Czech Republic and Turkey also established asset management companies, although the one in the Czech Republic took on its role in 2000, after the start of the corporate sector crisis, whereas the one in Turkey was created quickly after the crisis in 2002. A deposit insurance agency managed assets from defunct financial institutions in Mexico, but no special agency was created in Brazil.

The purposes of the asset management companies differed somewhat among the countries. Some were set up largely to support the banking system. Mexico's FOBAPROA (Bank Savings Protection Fund), established in 1995 and funded fully by the Mexican central bank, was created to buy the subordinated debt of undercapitalized banks and to restore their capital adequacy. In exchange, it acquired a claim on the possible recovery of non-performing loans, but the responsibility for recovering the loans remained with the bank. As a consequence of the diffused responsibility, FOBAPROA undertook very little restructuring. In December 1998, a new banking law was approved and a new deposit insurance agency was created: the Institute for the Protection of Bank Savings (IPAB). This time, the law provided for a more solid legal framework and set a time table for the sale of bad assets. In the Czech Republic, Konsolidacna Banka took on debts from banks earlier in the transition, but that was for reasons of maturity mismatch; these loans were to large corporations and often became nonperforming. Only in 2000 did the Czech Republic establish a formal asset management company: Cezka Konsolidacna Agentura (CKA).

The mandates of most asset management companies were mixtures of bank recapitalization, asset disposal, and restructuring tasks. In principle, they allowed the disposition of assets to the private sector through various means. This was intended to minimize the direct role of government in the restructuring of individual corporations, which would improve the likelihood of sustainable financial restructuring and proper operational restructuring. In practice, however, asset disposition was slow, in most cases due to difficulty in valuing assets, thin markets for selling assets, fears of selling too cheaply, and social and political pressures. Most asset management companies therefore ended up restructuring corporations. Claims on large corporations, in particular, then remained with the asset management company, often for long periods of time, as these were the most difficult to sell or restructure (as, for example, the Hyundai Engineering and Construction and Hynix Semiconductor chip factory in Korea). At the end of 2003, for example, 70 percent of the remaining loans held by Korea Asset Management Corporation (KAMCO) related to the large, bankrupt chaebol Daewoo.

Disposition and restructuring often were delayed not only because of concerns about the social impact of deeper restructuring but also because of political connections or fear of revealing "skeletons" hidden among the nonperforming loans. In Mexico, FOBAPROA sold virtually no assets. Although (foreign) investors showed interest as Mexico recovered from its crisis, the agency was reluctant to reveal information on the defaulted borrowers out of fear of exposing the causes of the nonperforming loans and was constrained from engaging in asset sales by political pressures. Only when the agency was reconstituted in the form of IPAB were assets sold, but this was some five years after the crisis.

Thus in most countries holdings by asset management companies remained large for several years after the crisis started (see table 2.7). The four Asian asset management companies together still held some $150 billion in assets as of mid-2002, four years after most of them were constituted. Disposition accelerated, however, over time. In Korea, KAMCO had a 59 percent disposition rate in 2002, and even its restructuring of Daewoo assets eventually involved significant financial and operational restructuring. In Malaysia, the rate of disposition also accelerated, with Danaharta disposing of nearly all nonperforming loans by end-2002. For political economy and institutional reasons, the asset management companies in Indonesia and Thailand were slower to dispose of assets. The Indonesian Bank Restructuring Agency had disposed of only about 20 percent of its large holdings of nonperforming loans as of May 2003. However, disposition accelerated in 2003: as sales mechanisms and market conditions improved, IBRA was able to resolve 70 percent of the nonperforming loans acquired by September 2003 and to complete its asset resolution by February 2004, when its mandate expired.[9] Similarly, although Thai Asset Management Company (TAMC) only started its operations in June 2002, its rate of asset resolution as of end-2003 (70 percent) compared favorably with that of other countries in the region (although there were concerns about sustainability, as half of the asset resolution involved debt restructuring).

To a lesser extent, this happened in the Czech Republic and Turkey as well. CKA in the Czech Republic and State Deposit and Insurance Fund (SDIF) in Turkey held, respectively, $8 billion and $9 billion in assets. CKA had disposed of only 23 percent of nonperforming loans as of 2002, but, since then, sales of assets have accelerated and are proceeding expeditiously. In Turkey, the crisis is more recent, but as of 2003 SDIF already had disposed of some 23 percent of nonperforming loans (SDIF collected $2.1 billion, with $1.8 billion via direct collection and the sale of subsidiaries, tangible and intangible assets, and banks and $0.3 billion via deferred sales). In Mexico, FOBAPROA had only disposed of 0.5 percent of assets by the end of 1999, five years after the crisis. As of today, Mexico's IBAP has disposed some 10 percent of nonperforming loans.

As banks reduced their holdings of nonperforming loans and as asset management companies bought up the remaining, often more difficult,

Table 2.7: Holdings of Nonperforming Loans and Powers of Asset Management Companies in Eight Countries, 2003

Feature	Indonesia	Korea, Rep. of	Malaysia	Thailand	Czech Republic	Turkey	Mexico	Brazil
Nonperforming loans								
Holdings (US$ bill.)	39.41	91.75	12.6	18.23	8.09	9.27	1.06	n.a.
Purchased (as a percentage of total nonperforming loans)	91.72	79.31	41.5	57.9	n.a.	81.3	10	n.a.
Disposed (as a percentage of nonperforming loans acquired)	70	59	100	73	23	22.7	10	n.a.
Special powers	To seize debt- or assets	None	To appoint a special administrator for business restructuring; foreclose on collateral	To bypass court processes (for TAMC-administered business restructuring); foreclose on collateral	To seize debt- or assets	To participate in any bankruptcy estate in its capacity as a privileged creditor for the amount it paid to depositors	For IPAB, to receive priority in the recovery of assets for the amounts it paid as deposit insurance agency	n.a.
Asset disposition and management	Debt and business restructuring; outsourcing of medium-sized loans; auctions of smaller loans	Auction; public sale; equity partnership; securitization	Private auction; tenders; securitization; special administration (business restructuring)	Debt and business restructuring; outsourcing; foreclosure	State workout units with limited capacity; investment bank Lazard manages a large share of disposition	Can take assets from the intervened banks and assign assets to third parties; a strategy for the sale of core banking assets announced by SDIF on September 20, 2002	Under FOBAPROA, management and administration of assets until their sale is left with the banks; FOBAPROA only has an interest in the cash flows	n.a.

n.a. Not applicable.

Note: For Indonesia, IBRA; for Korea, KAMCO; for Malaysia, Danharta; for Thailand, TAMC; for Czech Republic, CKA; for Turkey, SDIF; and for Mexico, FOBAPROA before 1999 and IPAB since 1999.

Source: Country sources (a complete list is available from the author).

loans, asset management companies became the holder of most nonperforming loans. At the end of 2002, about 75 percent of all nonperforming loans in the crisis-affected East Asian countries were held by asset management companies. By the end of 2002, in Indonesia IBRA held more than 90 percent of all remaining nonperforming loans, and in Korea KAMCO held some 80 percent. In Turkey SIDF held 80 percent of nonperforming loans.

With their large holdings, most asset management companies played a large role in the restructuring of corporate loans and often led other investors. Most of this happened under out-of-court mechanisms, if established. Furthermore, some asset management companies had special powers. In Malaysia, for example, Danaharta was allowed to foreclose more easily on collateral; and in 2003 the government introduced special powers under the Danaharta Act, which allows for the appointment of special administrators to manage distressed companies. In Indonesia, IBRA could seize debtor assets, and in Thailand, the TAMC-administered restructuring largely bypassed the court process. As lessons were learned from earlier crises, these special powers were often added to the charter of asset management companies established later. In Mexico, IPAB handles and settles all claims arising from a bank resolution. Although IPAB does not hold title to many of the assets, it is the beneficiary of recovery flows and can liquidate assets or alienate these assets to a specialized liquidation firm, which administers and liquidates assets on its behalf. In the Czech Republic, CKA can confiscate debtors' assets, and in Turkey, SDIF can seize assets, assign them to a third party, and exercise other "superpowers."

Their large stake and special powers gave asset management companies the ability to set the pace and intensity of restructuring, introducing additional financial as well as social and political dimensions to it. In several cases, asset management companies played the lead role in complex restructuring cases. In East Asia, this included some of the large distressed debtors, such as Renong and UME in Malaysia, ATP in Thailand, and the chaebols Daewoo and Huyndai in Korea. In these cases, asset management companies, together with other (government) agencies, such as the Korean Development Bank and the Malaysian Employee Provident Fund, took the lead in providing financial relief and initiating debt restructuring, although not always efficiently. In the Czech Republic, much of the management was outsourced to an investment bank, Lazard, thus shielding it from political pressures. CKA and its fully owned subsidiary (managed by Lazard) dealt with even the large workout cases mainly by selling quickly to (foreign) strategic investors. Examples of enterprises sold are Aliachem, CKD

PrahaHolding, SkodaHolding, Tatra, Vitkovice, and Zetor. In the other two countries with asset management companies, this was much less the case. In Mexico, FOBAPROA only delayed restructuring because political factors were introduced, but IPAB was more successful. Turkey's experiences are recent and not yet focused enough, in part due to the large number of loans (as of June 2003, more than 125,000 loans were transferred to the Collection Department of SDIF: around 1,000 were majority shareholder loans, more than 10,000 were other corporate loans, and approximately 114,000 were individual loans).

Although asset management companies assisted in financial restructuring, there remained many concerns about whether they were facilitating corporate restructuring, including in the large cases. The Renong case in Malaysia, for example, involved very few concessions by the firm and its owners (no changes in management, no assets sales) and very generous debt restructuring (including conversion of short-term debt into seven-year zero-coupon debt). Experiences in other countries also suggest that asset management companies often delay, rather than accelerate, operational restructuring (see box 2.2). These experiences show that ingredients for successful restructuring using asset management companies are numerous and more likely met in advanced and developed countries than in emerging

---

Box 2.2: Cross-Country Experiences with Asset Management Companies

A review of seven centralized approaches using asset management companies shows that most did not achieve their stated objectives when it came to corporate restructuring (see Klingebiel 2000). The review distinguishes corporate restructuring asset management companies from bank rehabilitation asset management companies. In two out of three cases, corporate restructuring asset management companies did not achieve their narrow goals of expediting restructuring. Only the Swedish asset management company successfully managed its portfolio, acting in some instances as lead agent in the restructuring process. Rapid asset disposition vehicles fared somewhat better, with two out of four agencies—namely, the agen-

cies in Spain and the United States—achieving their objectives. The successful experiences suggest that asset management companies can be used effectively, but only for the narrowly defined purposes of resolving insolvent and nonviable financial institutions and selling off their assets. But even achieving these objectives requires many ingredients: a type of asset that is easily liquefiable (real estate), professionally trained management, political independence, a base of skilled human resources, appropriate funding, adequate bankruptcy and foreclosure laws, good information and management systems, and transparency in operations and processes.

markets. The nature of the claims (mostly corporate sector claims) and the conditions in some crisis-affected countries (limited skills, weak institutional frameworks, and political constraints) suggest that asset management companies should focus on fast disposition of assets and only attempt a limited role in corporate restructuring. This model was largely followed by KAMCO, which, after an initially slow start, disposed of its assets quickly (except for the Daewoo and some Hyundai assets).

Other Forms of Government-Directed Corporate Restructuring

In addition to the asset management companies, some countries also engaged in other forms of government-directed corporate restructuring. In Korea, the government set a number of targets for the mid-tier chaebols (known as the 6–64 chaebols). This so-called Five Plus Three Program, launched in January 1998 and later expanded, sought to impose more financial discipline on large chaebols not in immediate distress. It eliminated domestic cross-guarantees, established requirements in capital structure improvement, lowered the ratio of liabilities to equity to 200 percent by end-1999, imposed tighter exposure limits on financial institutions, streamlined business lines, and increased transparency. It included Fair Trade Commission actions against anticompetitive intra-chaebol transactions. A 1998 February amendment to the Fair Trade Act prohibited further cross-guarantee in the 30 largest chaebols and ordered chaebols to abolish existing cross-guarantees by the end of March 2000. In 2002 the ban on cross-guarantees was extended to groups with assets of more than 2 trillion won, which covered 43 corporate groups. The lifting of cross-guarantees among affiliated firms allowed individual firms to be declared insolvent and improved governance in chaebol firms.

Furthermore, in 1998 Korea adopted a special, government-led form of restructuring for the five largest chaebols, some of which had serious financial problems. The restructuring program focused on voluntary restructuring efforts submitted by the chaebols, so-called capital structural improvement plans (CSIPs), to be agreed and monitored by their lead banks. The CSIPs furthermore encouraged asset swaps and mergers among the largest chaebols as a way of rationalizing some industries, such as car manufacturing and chips production.

The Korea program for the 6–64 chaebols provided useful benchmarks and some quantitative restrictions but still required the banks, as lead creditors, to take further initiative in the restructuring of individual chaebols and businesses. It was quickly enhanced with the out-of-court procedures described above. Progress with restructuring the five largest chaebols was initially slow, and in addition banks accepted CSIPs that included accounting measures such as asset revaluation to reduce leverage. Supervisory actions revised these, although in the case of the largest two chaebols, banks put themselves at continued risk by not trying to reduce their exposure to the conglomerates. Still, for three chaebols there was much progress, and in 1998 the debt-to-equity ratio of the top five chaebols dropped to 386 percent, from 470 percent in 1997 (yet the initial target of 320 percent was not met).

Greater progress was made in 1999, with considerable differentiation, though. The two largest chaebols relied much on funds raised by affiliated investment trust companies to finance their cash flow needs. Attracted by rates of return above deposit rates (which mainly reflected past capital gains), retail investors and commercial banks channeled a large amount of resources through investment trust companies to the largest chaebols, in particular Daewoo, much of it in the form of bond financing. This led to a financial crisis in the investment trust company sector, which then required liquidity support from the banking system, thus increasing the fragility of the banking system and triggering a new round of bank restructuring. Eventually, the problems were absorbed by KAMCO and KDIC and to some extent by Korean Development Bank.

In the end, the CSIPs had limited value, as those chaebols already undertaking restructuring and in relatively good financial condition needed few additional incentives, whereas those that did need them were not specifically put under greater pressure. Furthermore, by having a direct role in the restructuring, the government introduced more political economy factors, particularly for asset swaps. After 1999, the CSIPs faded away as a tool for restructuring. This shows that it is difficult for the government to initiate restructuring by setting specific targets without addressing the fundamental issues; often these efforts backfire, as firms either try to meet them in appearance, but not in practice, or see them as a way to increase their political influence.

State-Owned Banks

Besides restructuring through the asset management companies and other actions aimed at specific classes of large firms, governments in all countries had a large role in corporate reform through their ownership—direct and indirect—of the banking systems. In all countries, due to nationalization and other restructuring, state ownership of financial institutions rose sharply. Combining the holdings of asset management companies and state-owned financial institutions, the state owned, on average, more than 50 percent of financial assets in crisis-affected East Asian countries in 2000, which equaled more than 75 percent of GDP. In Indonesia, as of January 2000, state-owned banks and IBRA together held about $42 billion out of the $60 billion in domestic corporate sector claims, with the share of nonperforming loans held by the state even larger. In Thailand, the three state-owned banks controlled 27 percent of assets, with TAMC further adding to the state's share. Altogether the Thai state banks now have a 45 percent market share, with privately owned Thai banks showing little or no growth. In Korea, state-owned and state-controlled banks represented more than half of total banking system assets in 2001 and an even large share of nonperforming assets.

In Mexico, assets held by FOBAPROA represented some 8 percent of all bank assets in 1996. In Brazil, very little new direct or indirect ownership occurred, as the government did not establish an asset management company and the privatization of many regional banks meant that the share of state-owned banks declined (in 2002 federal and state banks accounted for more than 33 percent of financial assets, compared with 51 percent in 1993). In the Czech Republic, bank privatization meant that the share of state-owned bank assets declined to 4.6 percent in 2002, down from 18.6 percent in 1998. In Turkey, the share of the state-owned banks grew from 34.9 percent in 1998 to 40 percent in 2002.

This large state ownership and transfer of distressed assets was, in most cases, effective in isolating problems in the financial sector and in providing financial relief to corporations. While perhaps inevitable, it further delayed corporate restructuring. Besides direct ownership, in many countries the government fully guaranteed the liabilities of banks, thus mitigating banks' incentives to restructure.

Voluntary Workouts outside Government-Sponsored and In-Court Frameworks

Much of the restructuring took place outside the government-sponsored programs, formal in-court processes, or asset management companies. In Korea, for example, the less distressed, smaller chaebols were not included in the out-of-court program but experienced significant restructuring. Furthermore, the restructuring of almost all small and medium enterprises was voluntary in all countries. This was, in part, because such firms experienced larger shocks and had little access to new financing, thus leaving them no choice but to restructure. In most countries, smaller listed companies were more adversely affected than large and mid-size companies. In Turkey, losses amounted to some 20 percent of sales for small and medium enterprises versus 5 percent for large and mid-size companies, the burden of financial expenses was 30 percent of sales for small and medium enterprises versus 20 percent for large companies, and on average their interest coverage fell to 0.50, meaning that most could not service their debts. Not only was the impact of shocks often larger for small and medium enterprises, but they also had less access to financing with which to smooth the shocks. Korean banks' lending to small and medium enterprises during 1998, for example, fell almost 10 percent, while their lending to larger corporations rose 9 percent. In part, this was due to spillover from the distress of larger corporations. In many countries, suppliers, for example, were less able to use their most important assets—that is, inventories and accounts receivables—as collateral to obtain bank loans. The distress in the banking system often created a credit crunch in which the supply of financing to small and medium enterprises was reduced even further, while loans to larger corporations were rolled over.

The large shocks and the lack of new financing for most small and medium enterprises (and many smaller publicly listed firms as well) and the pressure on them to repay loans meant that they were forced to restructure on their own, through asset dispositions and operational adjustments, including labor shedding, or face a quick demise. These hard-budget constraints thus led to speedy, although not necessarily efficient, corporate restructuring, as they were applied unevenly and did not always consider financial viability. As firms sometimes were not even able to receive financing for working capital or trade, their activity came to a halt, which slowed the overall economic recovery. Some governments tried to counter the tendency of banks to reduce their loans to small and medium enterprises by developing special programs or restructuring approaches (see box 2.3). But in spite of these measures, many small and medium enterprises were still heavily affected due to their links to larger firms, which cut them off from suppliers' credit or even forced them to extend financing. In Korea, for example, the crisis may have had the biggest impact on small and medium enterprises, many of which were suppliers to large chaebols, and the number of small and medium enterprise failures climbed to 8,200 in 1997 and to 10,500 in 1998.

Another voluntary channel for restructuring was mergers and acquisitions (M&As). M&As, particularly cross-border ones, increased sharply following the crisis. In East Asia, total cross-border M&As—defined as acquisitions of more than 50 percent equity by foreign investors—increased from $3 billion in 1996 to $22 billion in 1999. The rise was the strongest in Korea, accounting for $13 billion of M&As in 1999, and in Thailand, accounting for $4 billion. Malaysia, which had a history of significant foreign direct investment, however, saw a decline in mergers and acquisitions following the crisis. For the four Asian countries as a group, the rise in M&As did offset a decline in foreign direct investment in greenfield projects (those designed to build new means of production), keeping foreign direct investment resilient overall. These trends continued in 2000 and thereafter, as investors reevaluated countries. M&A activity in Malaysia, for example,

---

Box 2.3: Special Programs and Restructuring Approaches for Small and Medium Enterprises

Governments have responded to the distress of small and medium enterprises with streamlined approaches both for resolving their debt and for facilitating financing.

In Korea, as the recession deepened in 1998, the authorities strengthened banks' incentives to lend to small and medium enterprises and improved their access to credit. Important policies were the required rollover of loans and the expansion of credit guarantees, which reduced the default risk on banks' books and implied a lower risk weight in the calculation of Bank for International Settlement ratios than did collateralized loans.

In Malaysia, company borrowers with total outstanding credits of less than RM 50 million could seek financing support from the Loan Monitoring Unit of the central bank while the company pursued restructuring.

In Thailand, where about 600,000 small and medium enterprises accounted for about 40 percent of nonperforming loans, the Corporate Debt Restructuring

Advisory Committee introduced a simplified process to reach agreement in a small or medium enterprise within 45 days and identified more than 12,000 cases for monitoring and follow-up. By the end of July 2001, 73 percent of these cases were completed or in process, while the remaining 27 percent were subject to legal action. In addition, the Bank of Thailand set targets for financial institutions to resolve 15,000 small and medium enterprise cases each month: in practice, each month about 12,000 small and medium enterprise cases were resolved. The Bank of Thailand also led a consortium to purchase promissory notes issued by creditworthy small and medium enterprises at a discount. Bank of Thailand priced the facility at below the average cost of funds to the banks in order to encourage its use.

In Indonesia, no special measures were taken for small and medium enterprises. Neither were there special programs for small and medium enterprises in Brazil, the Czech Republic, Mexico, or Turkey.

increased in value to $9.5 billion, with Malaysia's financial sector accounting for a large share.

In Asia, the wave of mergers and acquisitions was triggered, in part, by some important policy changes following the crisis. These included the liberalization of investment in nontraded sectors, changes in competition policy, and other reforms. In Korea, for example, hostile takeovers were difficult to execute, but M&A funds were introduced that aimed to take over the control rights of target firms or to provide capital solely to raiders or target firms.[10] Much of the M&A activity was directed to wholesale and retail trade as well as real estate services and had an important impact by increasing competition and introducing new, modern operational practices. Cross-border M&As were typically less of a direct force in corporate restructuring, however, in part as their size was small relative to the total debt to be restructured. Also, the benefits of M&As were of longer term, making them less important as a stimulus for short-term corporate sector recovery. Yet mergers and acquisitions were useful in bringing capital and expertise to some deeply affected sectors.

M&As helped particularly with the reprivatization of nationalized financial institutions, which indirectly supported corporate sector restructuring. In Mexico, for example, foreign banks acquired many of the weak local banks, thus providing skills and capital for restructuring (today the banking system is largely foreign owned). In the Czech Republic, M&A activities in the financial services sector represent the largest segment, with investments of more than $800 million in 2002, including an increase in foreign ownership in Erste Bank. In Turkey, tax incentives were introduced to facilitate M&As of banks, including their subsidiaries, which led to an increase in M&As; the total asset size of banks subject to mergers and acquisitions was about $26.5 billion in 2001.

Supporting Policy Changes

Apart from weaknesses in the insolvency-foreclosure framework (which provided few incentives for debtors to cooperate with creditors or to accept dilution or loss of control), various tax, legal, and regulatory impediments discouraged mergers, acquisitions, and other corporate reorganizations. Besides changes in bankruptcy regimes, government undertook many supportive measures by changing the overall framework. These included

2

loan classification criteria, loan-loss provisioning rules, changes in tax and accounting rules, and changes in corporate governance.

Loan Classification Criteria and Loan-Loss Provisioning Rules

Rules for loan classification and criteria for loan-loss provisioning need to force financial institutions to acknowledge problem loans and to undertake restructuring rather than continue rolling loans forward. Many countries did not have these rules, however, or were slow to adopt them. An analysis shows that loan classification criteria in some crisis-affected countries were not always forward-looking enough to force financial institutions to come

Table 2.8: Framework of Regulatory and Loan Restructuring in Eight Countries, as of Early 1997 (Outside of East Asia), 1999 (in East Asia), and 2003

Indicator and period	Indonesia	Korea, Rep. of	Malaysia	Thailand	Czech Republic	Turkey	Mexico	Brazil
Loan classification								
Early 1997 (Asian countries) or 1999 (non-Asian countries)	2	2	2	1	2	0	1	3
2003	2	2	2	2	2	—	2	3
Loan-loss provision								
Early 1997 (Asian countries) or 1999 (non-Asian countries)	1	3	3	1	2	—	2	2
2003	3	3	2	2	2	—	1	2
Interest accrual								
Early 1997 (Asian countries) or 1999 (non-Asian countries)	1	3	3	1	—	—	—	—
2003	2	4	3	4	—	—	—	—
Overall index								
Early 1997 (Asian countries) or 1999 (non-Asian countries)	1.3	2.7	2.0	1.0	—	—	1	—
2003	2.3	3.0	2.3	2.7	—	—	—	—

— Not available.

Note: Countries are scored on a scale from 1 to 4 for each variable, with 4 indicating best practice and 1 indicating farthest from best practice.

Source: Country sources (a complete list is available from the author).

to grips with problem debtors quickly (table 2.8). In Malaysia, for example, banking institutions were initially given an option of reporting nonperforming loans using the standard of either three or six months past due, but they were not required to use forward-looking criteria. Later, loan classification criteria and capital adequacy requirements were tightened, and banks with a ratio of nonperforming loans above 10 percent were required to resolve the excess promptly or else sell the excess to Danaharta. In Korea, the government tightened loan classification requirements for firms that had undergone restructuring, bringing them under the new forward-looking criteria, but only in late 2000. As a consequence, many of the banks continued to roll over nonperforming loans.

Many other countries did not require the corporation to have a sustained record of repayments or viable financials before allowing the upgrading of restructured loans. Indonesia did not have tight criteria for loan provisioning and interest accruals as of mid-2001. Mexico did not adopt forward-looking loan classification criteria until long after the crisis. Brazil had been reforming its regulations for some time and did not especially accelerate loan classification and loan-loss provisioning criteria. In the Czech Republic and Turkey, changes were limited.

Tax, Legal, and Accounting Rules

Issues such as the tax treatment of mergers and debt-for-equity swaps, personal liability of state-owned banks' management in extending relief, protection for public shareholders, transfer taxes, accounting rules, and other policies can hinder the restructuring process. At the same time, they may serve useful public policy purposes. Although it is very difficult to generalize across countries as to which policy is best and what measures need to be changed, it is clear that, regardless of whether there is a financial crisis, the rules should not discriminate against corporate restructuring, as that is a normal part of any economic process. In many of the countries, these rules did so, however, especially during the early phases (Mako 2003).

In Indonesia, gains from debt rescheduling were potentially taxable for the debtor, while losses to creditors were not tax-deductible. Restructuring agreements that would be too slow to reduce corporate debts below single-borrower exposure limits could constitute a violation of legal lending limits. Other issues included time limits for financial institutions to dispose of

2

converted corporate equity, high transfer taxes, and potential delisting of restructured companies from local stock exchanges.

In Thailand, impediments included the treatment of some non-cash corporate reorganizations (for example, mergers) as a taxable event, the inability to transfer net operating losses to reduce the tax liability of a corporate acquirer or a new merged entity, waiting periods of up to six months for creditor review of proposed mergers, and personal liability of any employee of a state-owned financial institution (for example, a nationalized bank) responsible for a loss to the institution, including a loss from corporate debt restructuring.

In Turkey, as well as in other countries, tax losses for write-offs were allowed only when legal proceedings had commenced to recover the debt, although commencement was of itself sufficient. This created a perverse incentive for banks to pursue legal action to get the benefit of the tax loss, even where such proceedings were futile. It also contributed to congestion in the courts. Also debt-to-equity conversions were only allowed for shareholder loans. This, combined with unfavorable legislation regarding collateral for movable assets and inefficient enforcement and insolvency procedures, hindered meaningful workouts and restructurings. As a consequence, debt rescheduling was the primary, if not the exclusive, method for restructuring debt in Turkey.

Corporate Governance

Changes in corporate governance were important for two reasons. Since corporate sector investment and financing behavior was often one of the major sources of vulnerabilities that led to the financial crisis, changes were necessary to prevent a recurrence. And the restructuring process itself put greater emphasis on owners being able to discipline management, oversee financial transactions of the firm, and assure equal treatment of all shareholders.

Important among the corporate governance reforms were the rights of shareholders. Table 2.9 summarizes the specific progress that was made in enhancing the rules for equity investors in four key areas: one-share, one-vote; proxy by mail; inability to block shares; and possibility for cumulative voting. The table shows that countries came somewhat closer to international standards in the rules governing corporations. Following the crisis, Korea made the most progress, as it satisfied three of these four key criteria for effective corporate governance in 2003 compared to only one in 1996.

Table 2.9: Equity Rights in Eight Countries, as of 1996 and Mid-2003

Indicator and period	Indonesia	Korea, Rep. of	Malaysia	Thailand	Czech Republic	Turkey	Mexico	Brazil
One-share, one-vote								
1996	1	1	1	0	1	0	0	0
Mid-2003	1	1	1	1	1	1	1	1
Proxy by mail								
1996	1	0	0	0	0	0	0	0
Mid-2003	1	1	1	1	0	1	0	0
Shares not blocked								
1996	1	0	1	1	0	0	0	0
Mid-2003	1	0	1	1	0	0	1	0
Cumulative voting								
1996	1	0	0	1	1	0	0	0
Mid-2003	1	1	0	1	1	1	0	0
Equity rights score (sum)								
1996	4	1	2	2	2	0	0	0
Mid-2003	4	3	3	4	2	3	2	1

Note: 1 denotes that equity rights are in the law.

Source: Country sources (a complete list is available from the author).

Significant deficiencies remained, however. Legislation on class-action suits, which promote the rights of minority shareholders and transparency in the management of companies, for example, is still pending in Korea. The corporate governance frameworks of Malaysia and Thailand were also not complete as of 2002. Indonesia had well-established equity rights in 1996, but enforcement was weak. Significant corporate governance reforms were undertaken in Turkey following the crisis, but much less so in Mexico and even less so in Brazil. The most important changes in Brazil were limits on the presence of nonvoting shares, but only for new issues. In the Czech Republic, few changes were adopted between 1996 and 2001.

In addition to these changes, countries implemented other measures enhancing the rights of equity holders. Many countries, including Brazil, Korea, Malaysia, and Thailand, adopted a code on corporate governance. Although these were most often nonbinding, by requiring corporations to comply or explain why they could not, they put pressure on corporations. In

Korea, the threshold to file a derivative action against a company was lowered, and all listed companies were required to appoint independent directors. Several countries strengthened their accounting and auditing standards and boards. As disclosure was a key weakness, Thailand, for example, focused on reinforcing accounting and auditing standards and practices. Many new or improved accounting and auditing standards were issued, an accounting standards board was established, and disciplinary measures for noncompliance were enhanced. Thailand also clarified the roles and duties of company directors. However, progress on other critical aspects of corporate governance was slow and mostly limited to clarifying the duties of company directors.

The implementation and enforcement of many of these changes were still limited, especially in countries where enforcement of minority rights was weak. In Korea, for example, although a cumulative voting system enhancing minority rights was introduced in the commercial code, about 80 percent of listed companies were able to exclude it from their articles of incorporation. In addition, as of end-2000, not a single company had implemented a cumulative voting system for electing board members. Furthermore, more than half of the chaebols continued to spend more on donations than on dividends, indicating that they did not focus on shareholder value. Intragroup transfers, for example, continued to occur among Korean chaebols at the expense of minority shareholders. In Indonesia, many laws were poorly enforced, including the laws on minority rights. In Mexico, shareholder abuses continued in the 1990s, even when Mexican firms started to list on international stock exchanges (Siegel forthcoming).

Other Changes

Restructuring requires a broad set of options, not only debt rescheduling and principal and interest reductions but also debt-for-equity swaps, asset sales, securitization, and spin-offs. The relative importance of these restructuring techniques varies over time, as creditors await proposals by debtors and information on the true viability of firms is revealed. The choice of the particular restructuring instrument also varies with the demand of investors, with domestic institutional investors more likely seeking securitized obligations, "vulture" funds seeking distressed assets that can be turned around quickly, and direct investors seeking a longer-term investment through a merger and acquisition. The use of any of the instruments depends primarily on the willingness of the controlling owner of the corporation to dilute its ownership stake and on the ability and willingness of the holder of the distressed claim to absorb the losses. Yet the use of various tools also depends on whether regulations and laws allow for these instruments.

Tax, accounting, legal, and other institutional barriers initially limited the scope for productive use of these tools by the private sector. In particular, the legal structures for off-loading nonperforming assets and managing debt were often lacking, including corporate restructuring vehicles, venture funds, equity partnerships, and other tools. A corporate restructuring vehicle, for example, can temporarily manage debt-swapped equities obtained by commercial banks, receiving funding initially from an investment group and later from the capital markets. Corporate restructuring vehicles facilitate the disposal of assets by creditor banks, facilitate effective management, and improve governance of companies in the workout process. Although Korea assigned corporate restructuring vehicles a formal role in the out-of-court restructuring process in 2000, including in the new corporate restructuring law, no corporate restructuring vehicles were established until 2002.

Outcomes in Corporate Restructuring

In this section, I review a number of measures to assess the progress and success with corporate restructuring, including financial and operational restructuring measures. The successes are hard to assess and even more difficult to compare across countries. Each country developed over time its own set of indicators against which progress could be measured, but difficulties in developing objective indicators on the quality and intensity of restructuring remained. For a comparison across countries, a further problem is that the crises occurred at different times and that global developments played a role in the success or failure of corporate restructuring. I provide first some financial restructuring measures and then some operational restructuring measures.

Nonperforming Loans and Financial Indicators

The most commonly used indicator of the degree of restructuring done is the amount of nonperforming loans. These typically increase sharply and continue at that level during the first years after the crisis, with only a slow decline after that. The rise reflects the increased distress but also the introduction of better loan classification standards for banks and other financial

Table 2.10: Share of Nonperforming Loans, Including Shares of Debt Transferred to Asset Management Companies, in Eight Countries, 1998–2003

Year	Indonesia	Korea, Rep. of	Malaysia	Thailand	Czech Republic	Turkey	Mexico	Brazil
1998	48.6	—	15.0	—	20.7	6.7	11.3	5.3
1999	32.9	19.7	15.0	40.5	21.9	9.7	8.9	8.7
2000	56.3	13.9	10.6	26.8	19.9	11.0	5.8	8.4
2001	49.8	9.9	10.7	22.3	13.7	29.0	5.1	5.7
2002	42.0	—	9.6	—	9.6	17.0	4.8	6.1
2003[a]	—	—	—	15.7	7.6	15.0	—	—

— Not available.

a. March 2003 for countries outside of East Asia.

Source: Country sources (a complete list is available from the author).

2

institutions. The subsequent slow decline reflects the difficulties in restructuring loans. Although in many countries asset management companies took a lot of debt off the books of the banks, the overall volume of nonperforming loans did not decline quickly. Using officially reported figures, the gross share of nonperforming loans in total debt fell in East Asia only after 1999 (see table 2.10). Only after 2000 did the decline in the ratio of nonperforming loans accelerate, dropping some 14 percentage points in Thailand between end-1999 and 2001 and declining further to reach 16 percent in 2002. In Indonesia, the ratio of nonperforming loans declined steadily but was still about 50 percent in 2001 and above 40 percent in 2002. Only in 2001 did Korea and Malaysia have a ratio of nonperforming loans in (close to) single digits.

In the other crisis countries, the patterns were similar: nonperforming loans rose initially, sometimes sharply. In Brazil, the ratio of nonperforming loans was high as early as 1995. In Mexico, as interest rates rose and economic activity sharply decelerated, banks faced increasing nonperforming loans. The government had to intervene in banks, and a series of mergers and acquisitions took place. This strengthened the banking system, and banks were better prepared to deal with the 1998 crisis. Still, loan classification standards were relatively tight to begin with, and nonperforming loans rose further in 1998, followed by a slow decline. Standards remained weak for long periods of time, and the figures on nonperforming loans did not show the true problems. From 1999 on, nonperforming loans started to fall, reaching about 5 percent in 2002.

In the Czech Republic, the ratio of nonperforming loans was very high before the crisis, due to the restructuring involved with the transition from the planned economy. The crisis did, however, lead to a further rise in nonperforming loans, with a peak in 1999, followed by a sharp decline, reaching single digits in 2002. In Turkey, most nonperforming loans of state-owned banks were transferred to SIDF, yet their balance sheets remained weak; although banks showed small positive earnings in 2001, their overall capacity to generate income remained poor. As in many other countries, nonperforming loans in Turkey were masked by inter-enterprise arrears. Signs of this were the increase in the average maturity of payables as corporations unable to generate cash flow delayed payments to suppliers and others. The average maturity of payables in the metals sector, for example, increased from 38 days at the end of December 2000 to 58 days at the end of March 2001, and other sectors, except paper and printing, also had longer maturities as well. At the same time, the level of reported nonperforming loans in the banking sector was low at the end of March 2001, suggesting underreporting. Corporate sector, bottom-up analysis, in contrast, suggested that system-wide distressed assets accounted for about 36 percent of loans compared with the public figure given for nonperforming loans of 11 percent at end-2000. But banking figures caught on in 2001, when the end-of-year ratio of nonperforming loans rose to 29 percent.

While there was progress with reducing nonperforming loans in most countries, many corporations did not achieve viable financial structures in terms of leverage, share of short-term debt, and interest coverage. Comparability across countries in terms of leverage and the degree to which it has been reduced is an issue, and the trend is often more important as differences across countries can make for long-standing variability. In the short run, leverage typically increased, frequently reflecting currency devaluations that raised the foreign currency components of debt. The short-run increase also reflected the fact that debts were being rescheduled and not being converted into equity. In some countries, large amounts of debt financing, both bank financing and bonds, went to weak corporations, and only limited amounts of debt were converted into equity. The limited progress reflected the large share of claims held by weakly capitalized commercial banks. Banks had little ability and few incentives to engage in debt-for-equity conversions, as they often were unable to write off debts and could continue

2

to carry loans at low provisioning requirements. As they lacked the skills to manage equity, both commercial banks and asset management companies often preferred, especially in the first years, to roll over claims rather than reduce principal or convert to equity.

The lack of improvement in leverage also reflected an unwillingness of current owners to dilute their claims and invite more outsider owners. This was typically aggravated by the shortage of equity. Domestic stock markets were typically depressed, and foreign direct investors showed limited interest, at least initially, to commit fresh resources, except at very low, "fire-sale" prices. The low stock prices raised the opportunity costs of new equity even higher, thus deterring controlling shareholders from converting debt into equity or from issuing new stock.

Over a longer period, more progress was made (table 2.11). In East Asia, most progress was made in Korea, where the ratio of debt to assets fell by about half between 1997 and 1999 before stabilizing at 40 percent in 2002–03. This was partly a direct result of government policies that explic-

Table 2.11: Corporate Leverage in Eight Countries, 1994–2003 (ratio of debt to assets)

Year	Indonesia	Korea, Rep. of	Malaysia	Thailand	Czech Republic	Turkey	Mexico	Brazil
1994	0.32	0.60	0.25	0.42	—	0.25	0.37	0.23
1995	0.38	0.60	0.28	0.47	0.26	0.23	0.38	0.28
1996	0.41	0.64	0.31	0.48	0.24	0.23	0.35	0.36
1997	0.60	0.71	0.37	0.61	0.27	0.29	0.36	0.38
1998	0.74	0.70	0.67	0.56	0.27	0.32	0.34	0.43
1999	0.61	0.67	0.52	0.88	0.40	0.39	0.36	0.56
2000	0.94	0.55	0.45	0.74	0.22	0.45	0.30	0.50
2001	0.67	0.46	0.70	0.68	0.19	0.64	0.30	0.48
2002	0.57	0.40	0.67	0.66	0.14	0.48	0.30	0.59
2003	—	0.38	0.41	—	—	—	0.31	—
Average number of firms	158	438	390	235	40	90	90	184

— Not available.

Source: Computed using Worldscope database.

itly required corporations to bring their debt-to-equity ratio down to 200 percent.[11] Malaysia was generally also successful; although the approach was unconventional in many ways, including capital controls, the end results were favorable. After a peak in 1998, the debt-to-asset ratio declined to about 40 percent at the end of the period. In Thailand, the debt-to-asset ratio of publicly listed corporations at the end of 2000 was still above that in 1995–96 and even close to the peak levels of 1997. The debt-to-asset ratio in Indonesia had a more erratic pattern, in part due to large currency swings, but it was down to about 57 percent by the end of 2002.

In the other crisis-affected countries, leverage at the start of the crisis was not as high as in East Asia. In Turkey, leverage was generally low but had begun to rise even before the crisis, in large part because there had been other shocks (the 1998 Russian crisis and the 1999 earthquakes). It peaked in 2001 and then declined, but experiences are still too recent to judge. In Brazil, the Czech Republic, and Mexico, leverage was strongly influenced by currency devaluations. In Brazil, for example, more than half of the debts of listed firms in 2000 were in foreign exchange or indexed to the dollar, even for firms in nontradable sectors. The devaluation of Brazil's currency therefore had a major short-run adverse impact on leverage.[12] Otherwise, data show little progress being achieved in lowering debt ratios in these countries, at least over this period. In Mexico, no substantial progress was made on adjusting debt structures until late in the 1990s, after which the ratio stabilized. In the Czech Republic, the distressed state of the banking system, until its recapitalization and privatization, allowed very little scope for reducing debts until long after the crisis, with a drop not occurring until 2000.

In most crisis countries, the structure of debt financing improved somewhat. Typically, the share of long-term debt in total debt increased or at least stabilized, as investors came to realize the risks associated with holding too much short-term debt. But the adjustments were also due to restructuring, initially involving the extension of maturities, the lowering of interest payments, and other financial relief measures. In some countries, such as Korea and Malaysia, large corporations (Daewoo and Hyundai being the most notable, but not the only, examples) increased their reliance on corporate bonds, while decreasing their bank debt. Yet many of these bonds resulted from forced conversion or were not sold on market terms: some bonds were issued by very weak corporations that were considered too big

2

Table 2.12: Interest Coverage Ratio of the Corporate Sector in Eight Countries, 1994–2003

(median of listed firms' ratio of fixed charge coverage)

Year	Indonesia	Korea, Rep. of	Malaysia	Thailand	Czech Republic	Turkey	Mexico	Brazil
1994	4.33	1.38	7.47	4.04	—	2.56	0.71	2.89
1995	3.49	1.33	7.79	3.13	—	4.42	1.90	1.66
1996	2.91	1.22	5.58	2.13	6.61	3.25	3.11	1.35
1997	0.89	1.11	3.96	1.30	6.92	4.21	3.11	1.88
1998	0.33	1.11	1.58	2.24	7.23	2.16	1.75	1.33
1999	2.17	1.81	1.92	1.14	5.24	1.53	2.94	0.85
2000	0.33	1.74	3.51	1.70	6.38	2.18	2.91	1.22
2001	1.74	1.80	3.21	2.97	7.91	1.12	2.69	1.22
2002	3.45	1.80	3.65	4.10	8.48	2.12	2.57	0.96
2003	—	—	4.78	—	—	—	—	—
Average number of firms	158	438	390	235	40	120	93	185

— Not available.

Source: Computed using Worldscope database.

to fail. In a second round, many bonds had to be restructured, with banks absorbing some of the losses.

The financial restructuring schemes adopted in the workouts, especially initially, typically involved one or a combination of debt restructuring and capital reduction. Although these restructurings provided corporations with some temporary relief, they rarely led to sustainable financing scenarios in the first round. The ratio of EBITDA (earnings before interest, taxes, and depreciation allowance) to interest payments for publicly listed corporations reached a low in 1998 (or 1999) in the East Asian crisis-affected countries, where interest rates were high and earnings were depressed (table 2.12). The coverage ratio recovered afterward, largely due to a decline in interest rates, and in 2000 it was still below that in 1995–96 in all East Asian countries, except Korea.[13] Since then, the interest coverage ratio has improved in all East Asian countries.

In the other crisis-affected countries, real interest rates typically rose sharply and remained high for longer periods of time. The interest coverage ratio dropped further and did not stabilize. Brazil stands out, as its interest coverage ratio declined sharply, although the interest coverage ratio of corporations was high before the crisis due to a conservative financing structure. And in Turkey, corporations saw a sharp decline in interest coverage following the crisis.

In the years immediately following the crises, many firms struggled to cover interest expenses from operating income, and on an international basis the interest coverage ratios remained typically low in crisis-affected countries. For comparison, the average interest coverage in the United States in the late 1990s was around 5; in order to earn an A rating based on Standard & Poor's rating requirements, a U.S. company typically must have a ratio of operating cash flow to interest of more than 8. The share of East Asian corporations with nonviable financial structures, as measured by interest coverage of less than 1, was about 23 percent in 2000, three years after the crisis (table 2.13); although this was below the peak of 1998, it was still high. Similar patterns prevailed in the other crisis-affected countries. In Turkey, for example, in the first quarter of 2001, 69 percent of companies listed on the Istanbul

Table 2.13: Percentage of Corporations in East Asia with Interest Coverage Less Than 1, 1995–2000

Indicator	Indonesia	Korea, Rep. of	Malaysia	Thailand	Average
1995	4.90	4.46	6.08	13.77	7.30
1996	7.34	9.20	9.58	15.55	10.42
1997	16.30	12.97	14.55	25.78	17.40
1998	37.13	24.19	33.75	41.90	34.24
1999	33.48	10.50	29.13	32.39	26.38
2000	29.05	9.97	27.47	24.19	22.66
Average number of firms	259	200	456	317	n.a.

n.a. Not applicable.

Source: Calculations using Bloomberg data; composed of corporations whose stocks are included in the composite indexes of the respective markets. For Korea, only the companies comprising the KOSPI 200 (Korean Stock Price Index) are included. The interest coverage ratio is computed as EBITDA (earnings before interest taxes and depreciation allowance) divided by interest expense. Companies with negative reported equity values are excluded.

2

Stock Exchange had either interest coverage below 1 or insufficient liquid assets to cover their bank debt, a further increase from 63 percent in the first quarter of 1999. Firms still had very risky financial structures.

Operational Restructuring Measures

Financial restructuring is only a means to achieving improved operational performance. A proper financial structure can create incentives for more and deeper operational restructuring. In Korea, for example, through court-supervised receiverships and out-of-court workouts, the controlling shareholders and management of many chaebols—including some of the biggest pre-crisis names—completely lost out or saw their shareholdings severely diluted and their managerial discretion circumscribed in the years immediately after the crisis. These types of financial restructurings, and their signaling value toward other controlling shareholders and managers, helped to accelerate operational restructuring. Much of the financial restructuring was a response

Table 2.14: Profitability of Corporations in Eight Countries, 1994–2003

(percent)

Year	Indonesia	Korea, Rep. of	Malaysia	Thailand	Czech Republic	Turkey	Mexico	Brazil
1994	6.6	1.8	6.5	5.1	—	14.0	0.0	3.6
1995	6.0	1.6	6.7	4.3	5.0	14.4	3.1	−0.8
1996	4.8	0.6	5.8	3.0	1.5	14.8	6.5	0.0
1997	−3.7	−1.9	1.3	−11.21	1.8	13.6	4.6	1.8
1998	−10.4	−8.3	−8.3	1.7	−1.0	9.9	1.7	−0.4
1999	4.9	0.2	−2.2	−2.2	−5.0	3.4	2.5	−5.0
2000	−5.9	−1.9	−2.7	−3.7	5.0	0.0	4.3	−7.3
2001	0.5	0.0	−3.6	2.1	4.0	−6.8	−0.6	−13.6
2002	9.7	5.9	−7.1	6.6	3.0	2.9	1.0	−7.6
2003	—	—	−1.5	—	—	—	—	—
Average number of firms	158	438	390	235	40	120	93	185

— Not available

Note: Profitability is measured as dollar return on assets, which is net income in U.S. dollars divided by total assets in U.S.dollars.

Source: Computed using Worldscope database.

to a systemic crisis, however; although it achieved some temporary financial stabilization, it was not always sustainable and did not always promote real operational restructuring. In particular, much of financial restructuring did not alter the incentive structures in a way that encouraged owners, creditors, and managers to pursue sustainable operational restructuring. A final measure of the degree of success of financial restructuring efforts is therefore the operational performance of firms. I now consider the return on assets as well as some other evidence.

In the first phases, operational restructuring involved the rapid disposition of non-core assets, simple forms of labor reductions, and fast price and wage adjustments. These were the relatively easy parts and typically occurred early in the crisis. As such, there was typically a short-run improvement in operational performance, which was not necessarily sustainable. Data on profitability and other performance indicators suggest that this restructuring typically resulted in quick gains. In East Asia in 1999, following the sharp decline in 1998, publicly listed firms saw some recovery in return on assets (table 2.14). With the exception of Korea and Indonesia in 1999, however, the return on assets was still negative in 1999 and 2000. The average return on assets in 2001 was still low, and only in 2002 was there a return to pre-crisis levels in all countries, except Malaysia.

In the other countries, the patterns were less clear. In the Czech Republic, the return on assets was low even before the crisis of 1997, stayed negative for two years after the crisis, and has now returned to levels between 3 and 4 percent. In Mexico, the return on assets was still 3.1 percent in the year of the crisis (1995) and stayed between 1.7 and 6.5 percent, with a drop in 2001. In the case of Brazil, the return on assets did not drop in the years after the crisis, and this continued until 2002, but the return on assets is very volatile in Brazil, making a comparison difficult. Although the negative return on assets in Turkey in 2001 was clearly caused by the crisis and a recovery in 2002, the case is too recent to assess. Furthermore, Turkey's return on assets has experienced a long decline.

This pattern in profitability shows that the restructuring efforts during the first few years following a crisis could lead to some quick operational gains (through increased efficiency, divestiture of unprofitable businesses, and adjustment in prices). Profitability has a large cyclical component, however, and it is consequently hard to separate the effects of restructuring from the effects of the overall environment. Nevertheless, it is clear from anecdotal evidence that operational restructuring typically takes several years and that much of the more difficult restructuring in crisis-affected countries was often postponed, at least for the large corporations. The need to undertake deeper operational restructuring was all the more necessary as the profitability and cash flow income of corporations in many of the crisis-affected countries was already low.

Other data also suggest that relatively little operational restructuring initially occurred, at least for the large corporations, and that the large corporate restructuring deals continued to emphasize financial over operational restructuring. For example, an examination of the deals concluded under the Jakarta Initiative Task Force during 2000 showed a large reliance on term extensions and conversions into equity or convertible bonds. Other, more fundamental, restructuring averaged only 5 percent of deals over all of 2000, after falling steadily to only 2 percent of deals in the last quarter of 2000 (Mako 2003). In Korea, workouts under the corporate restructuring accord implemented through June 2002 involved 32.7 trillion won of financial restructuring (for example, rate reductions, payment deferments, debt-to-equity conversions, and surety obligations by affiliates) and only 6.4 trillion won of operational restructuring and other "self-help" (for example, asset sales, divestitures, new equity, cost savings). In other words, only 20 percent involved operational restructuring. In many cases, with perhaps Korea as a main exception, management did not change, and existing owners remained in control, with TPI in Thailand being the most extreme case. Banks typically did not force much operational restructuring on large corporations. They were reluctant not only to take measures such as selling off nonperforming loans or converting debt into equity but also to force corporations to close nonviable business, sell overvalued assets, and undertake other forms of operational restructuring.

Policy Lessons

Corporate restructuring depends on many factors and policy measures, including financial sector reform, development of restructuring mechanisms, choice of lead agent undertaking restructuring, and willingness to change the corporate governance and competition frameworks. Since countries adopt many policies and otherwise differ in numerous ways, the link between policies and outcomes is difficult to establish. Furthermore, it is the overall consistency between the various reforms that determines the likelihood of success, making it difficult to point to specific policy instruments. Nevertheless, specific policy lessons emerge from this and other cross-country comparisons.

An Efficient Insolvency System

An efficient court-supervised process is a necessity, and without it an out-of-court corporate restructuring framework can only help to a limited degree.

The effectiveness of the out-of-court system depends on the formal court system. The fact that the frameworks for out-of-court corporate workouts were more effective in countries like Korea and Malaysia, and to some extent Turkey, than in Mexico, Thailand, and Indonesia reflects clear differences in the ability of each country's insolvency and creditor rights system to impose losses on debtors. In Korea, because of a bankruptcy regime that was credible at the beginning of the financial crisis, many controlling shareholders saw their shareholdings severely diluted and managerial discretion controlled. However, even in Korea, bankruptcy affected small and medium enterprises much more than large corporations, and some heavily indebted corporations were able to avoid bankruptcy for long periods of time. In Malaysia, bankruptcy was an effective threat, but again not for large or politically connected firms. In other countries, like Brazil and Mexico, the inability to force out existing shareholders was more widespread, and bankruptcy was not a viable threat for any firm.

Although the formal bankruptcy regimes can be improved relatively quickly, and they have been in many countries, legal enforcement often remains limited. This is both for technical and political reasons, as courts are overworked, understaffed, and often subject to political pressures. Anecdotal evidence of the uncertainties introduced by the courts is plentiful, and the comparative data presented on costs and time delays back up the large discrepancy between developing and developed countries. Although it takes considerable time, reforms to enhance the efficiency and integrity of the bankruptcy process, including the introduction of specialized bankruptcy courts, are often necessary. In the meantime, introducing London-type approaches even when not in a crisis can be useful. However, the regime needs to be tighter than some of the crisis-affected countries allowed and backed up by those aspects of in-court regimes that operate relatively strongly. Furthermore, market-based alternatives to debt resolution mechanisms should be explored, with the powers and involvement of the courts to remain limited.

Adequate Loss-Absorption Capacity

Loss-absorption capacity is necessary, but preferably with as many private sector incentives as possible and without perverse links.

To restore bank capital adequacy, recapitalization by the private sector is preferred but is rarely sufficient in times of a systemic financial crisis. If the government steps in, as is typical in a systemic crisis, it should try to preserve as many private sector incentives as possible, which is a tricky tradeoff. Incentives can be strengthened by linking government financial resources directly to the financial corporate restructuring undertaken by banks, as was done in some countries. For example, the capital support scheme in Mexico linked fiscal resources to actual corporate restructuring through loss-sharing arrangements. This was expected to induce banks to conduct deeper restructuring but was not effective in the end because the responsibility for restructuring was unclear. A similar scheme in Thailand, which also required some dilution of equity stakes by controlling bank owners, did not see much interest because the largest banks preferred not to grant control rights to the government and the threat of closure of the bank was missing. Still, such schemes can work, as has been shown in more developed countries.

A proper incentive structure also means limited ownership links between banks and corporations. This is necessary in order to reduce the chances of the same party being both debtor and creditor. In many countries, extensive links between banks and corporations limited the restructuring. In Indonesia, the Widaja family was the controlling owner of a financially distressed corporation that had large debts to the defunct bank that was also controlled by the same family. Such links cannot be removed overnight, but restructuring approaches have to take them into account. More broadly, links between the financial and corporate sectors, through the political system and otherwise, have to be considered.

A Proper Framework of Incentives

To facilitate the restructuring of workout firms, it is necessary to have a proper incentive framework at the level of individual loans.

The incentive framework needs to include proper accounting, classification, and provisioning rules. In many crisis countries, loan classification criteria were not always forward-looking enough to force financial institutions to come to grips with problem debtors quickly. If not under pressure to realistically mark their assets to market, financial institutions tend to postpone restructuring in the hope of a recovery of the debtor or some other form of relief. While loan-loss provisioning can be phased in to deal with a shortage of capital, disclosure of nonperforming loans should not be phased in.

Other barriers to corporate restructuring, such as tax and accounting rules and certain legal rules, need to be addressed. Issues such as the tax treatment of mergers and debt-equity swaps, personal liability of state-owned banks' management in extending relief, protection for public shareholders, transfer taxes, and a host of other policies can hinder the restructuring process, as they did in many countries during the early phases. Since these rules can also serve a useful public policy purpose, countries should continuously evaluate which policy is best and what measures need to be changed. Regardless of whether there is a financial crisis, the guiding principle should be that rules should not discriminate against corporate restructuring, as that is a normal part of any economy.

This includes a proper incentive framework under which financial institutions operate.

The prudential and legal systems need to limit forbearance and ensure that undercapitalized financial institutions are properly disciplined, while giving an incentive for banks to come to grips with their problem loans. Apart from providing the right incentives at the level of individual loans, incentives need to be proper at the level of the institution. Marginally capitalized banks tend to engage in cosmetic corporate restructuring, such as the extension of maturity or the reduction of interest rates on loans to nonviable corporations, rather than debt write-offs. Ad hoc forbearance condones this behavior. If forbearance is applied, it has to be done uniformly across all financial institutions, maintain disclosure, and have time limits.

A Limited Role for Banks and the State

The role of banks and the state in restructuring, while inevitable in the first phases of the crisis, eventually needs to be limited, and this issue should be considered up-front.

Banks—often owned by the state or operating under an extensive government safety net—and public asset management companies played a large role but were slow to divest assets. The formal policy statements and directions were typically clear: banks needed to divest, encouraged by a proper prudential framework; asset management companies needed to dispose of their assets faster with less consideration for price; and state-owned banks needed to be privatized to strategic shareholders. However, while a larger role for private investors was often formally supported, there were many delays, sometimes for good reasons, but often for not so good reasons. Banks and asset management companies were thus left to undertake the restructuring.

Experiences from these and other countries made clear, however, that commercial banks and asset management companies are best used for financial restructuring, not for operational reorganization. Some of this arose from the lack of expertise and skills related to operational restructuring at commercial banks and asset management companies. As elsewhere, banks also had limited experience in managing corporate shareholdings or exercising corporate governance. Nevertheless, political economy factors also limited the ability of publicly owned agencies to force through the difficult restructuring. Too often insiders—those with a part in causing the crisis or other political interests—ran the asset management companies. In addition, governments had to balance the interests of various constituencies, such as demands for higher wages from workers, with the viability of the corporate sector. More generally, governments practiced various forms of regulatory forbearance vis-à-vis banks and other financial institutions to soften the impacts of operational restructuring. This not only was directed toward mitigating the social impacts but also involved propping up large distressed companies, often controlled by the politically well connected.

More and earlier involvement of outside investors is necessary to achieve deep operational restructuring. Because of better skills and freedom from political pressures, operational restructuring is best left to the private sector. Encouraging quick divestiture of assets by asset management companies, state-owned banks, as well as private banks is thus the most effective approach to further operational restructuring. Banks should not be allowed to continue carrying nonperforming or poorly restructured loans at low provisioning levels and should be encouraged to divest assets. State-owned banks and asset management companies should be directed to divest with set time limits.

A Menu of Approaches

To dispose of assets, a menu of approaches should be available to banks and asset management companies. When large-scale disposal of assets is difficult, because of depressed asset prices or political sensitivities, solutions may have to be mixed public-private arrangements and assets may have to be reprivatized in other ways. Under these arrangements, ownership remains for some period with the state, but private sector incentives are used to manage the assets. To the extent that banks and asset management companies retain assets, outside professionals—on the basis of some incentive compensation, whenever possible—should conduct due diligence, structure and negotiate corporate workouts, and manage asset sales. Thus the management of converted equity should be outsourced more to asset management or corporate professionals, including through equity partnerships.

There also needs to be more differentiation by type of assets. Some assets, such as real estate, can be more easily held by asset management companies, as there is less loss of value and, because they are relatively homogeneous, can be easily sold off (for example, through real estate–backed securities). In some countries, quick divestiture (would have) placed assets in the hands of the same or similar owners who had contributed to the crisis. In other countries, foreign ownership was a politically sensitive issue. Solutions that could have dealt with these concerns, such as the temporary allocation of assets to privately managed, but publicly owned, funds or the privatization of assets to employees or the general public, combined with share-purchase schemes (as have been used in Chile and some transition economies, such as Poland), were not used in any crisis but should be considered up-front.

Corporate Governance and Other Reforms

Corporate governance reforms must accompany the crisis resolution. Changes in the corporate governance framework ought to be part of the structural reform process and not just focused on publicly listed corporations. Spurred by a global emphasis on corporate governance, many countries in recent years have been improving the rules on how corporations are monitored and governed. Changes in corporate governance cover a broad spectrum of issues: trying to ensure better discipline by the domestic financial system, requiring enhanced disclosure of financial transactions, adopting better rules for internal management of corporations, and implementing better capital market regulation and supervision. The need to focus on corporate governance relates to corporate restructuring because the investment and financing behavior of the corporate sector was often one of the major vulnerabilities that led to the financial crises. Yet changes in the rules alone are not sufficient. In many crisis countries, great difficulties remain in implementing and enforcing the changes in corporate governance. Ratings of the quality of corporate governance of individual corporations and of countries' frameworks are still below international benchmarks.

References

The word "processed" describes informally produced works that may not be commonly available through libraries.

Asia Development Bank, Morgan Stanley, and PriceWaterhouseCoopers. 2003. *The Asia-Pacific Restructuring and Insolvency Guide, 2003/2004*. London.

Dado, Marinela E., and Daniela Klingebiel. 2002. "Decentralized Creditor-Led Corporate Restructuring Cross-Country Experience." Research Working Paper 2901. World Bank, Financial Sector Learning Program, Washington, D.C. Processed.

Johnson, Gordon W. 2001. "Principles and Guidelines for Effective Insolvency and Creditor Rights Systems." World Bank, Finance, Private Sector, and Infrastructure, Washington, D.C. Processed.

Kim, Hyoung-Tae. 2003. "Corporate Restructuring in Korea and Its Application to Japan: Corporate Restructuring Vehicles." Korea Securities Research Institute, September. Processed.

Klingebiel, Daniela. 2000. "The Use of Asset Management Companies in the Resolution of Banking Crises, Cross-Country Experience." Working Paper 2284. World Bank, Washington, D.C. Processed.

Mako, William P. 2003. "Facilitating Out-of-Court Workouts in a Crisis: Lessons from East Asia, 1998–2001." Forum on Asian Insolvency Reform (FAIR), Seoul, Korea. Processed.

Siegel, Jordan. Forthcoming. "Can Foreign Firms Bond Themselves Effectively by Renting U.S. Secrities Laws?" *Journal of Financial Economics*.

Stone, Mark. 2000a. *The Corporate Sector Dynamics of Systemic Financial Crises*. Policy Discussion Paper 00/114. Washington, D.C.: International Monetary Fund.

———. 2000b. *Large-Scale Post-Crisis Corporate Sector Restructuring*. Policy Discussion Paper 00/7. Washington, D.C.: International Monetary Fund.

World Bank. 2003. "Doing Business in 2003: Understanding Regulation." International Finance Corporation and the World Bank, Washington, D.C. Processed.

2

Notes

1. I do not review the origins of corporate sector financial distress, although the causes clearly condition the most appropriate response. A situation of large-scale corporate sector distress caused by a macroeconomic shock—for example, a sharp change in commodity prices for a commodity-dependent economy—will require a different response than a crisis caused by a weak institutional environment—say, a lack of an effective bankruptcy regime. For reviews of corporate restructuring experiences, see Dado and Klingebiel (2002), Stone (2000a, 2000b).

2. I use the term asset management company both for agencies especially set up to take over large nonperforming loans and for (existing or new) deposit insurance agencies that take over distressed assets in the context of the resolution of defunct financial institutions whose deposits are insured.

3. A billion is 1,000 million.

4. For more details on Asia, see Asia Development Bank, Morgan Stanley, and PriceWaterhouseCoopers (2003). For the other countries, see Johnson (2001).

5. After more than two and a half years of review, the Legal Reform Committee for Development of Thailand finally submitted a three-point revision of the Bankruptcy Act on September 15, 2003, including the reform of liquidation for individual debtors. Currently, the act is in parliamentary process.

6. The new insolvency bill is currently under review by the related committees of the National Assembly. The new bill aims to consolidate and strengthen three separate bankruptcy codes on corporate failure, composition, and liquidation.

7. The numbers should be considered as rough indicators, given the poor reporting in some countries. Furthermore, and to varying degrees, some of the increase in the number of cases is accounted for by personal bankruptcies and small enterprises, which represent a very small fraction of overall nonperforming loans.

8. Thailand did have the Financial Restructuring Agency, which was involved in auctioning off the assets of defunct finance companies. The Financial Restructuring Agency has been criticized heavily for selling half of its $15 billion in assets to foreigners, which were quickly "flipped" back to original creditors, providing huge profits. It is estimated that one

foreign investment bank bought $2.5 billion in bad assets at 19 cents at an auction in December 1998 and flipped them back at 60 cents to the original creditors within six months, earning profits of more than $1 billion. Some "profit sharing" with the Financial Restructuring Agency was subsequently challenged in the courts. Since much of its assets concerned real estate, however, the Financial Restructuring Agency is less germane to the issue of corporate restructuring.

9. According to its own announcements, IBRA has completed its targeted programs. Holding companies, however, have been established to manage IBRA's remaining assets, thus keeping nonperforming assets in state hands (Mako 2003).

10. Amendments to the Securities Investment Company Act and the Securities Trust Business Act are necessary to make these funds effective (Kim 2003).

11. The progress in lowering debt-to-equity ratios among Korean chaebols was partly achieved using various accounting measures, including overvaluation of affiliated party transactions and revaluations of securities and foreign exchange holdings. Furthermore, reflecting the limited desire of corporations to adjust their financial structures, much of the new equity raised in 1999, when the Korean stock market was experiencing a sharp recovery, was used to acquire new assets rather than to retire debt.

12. A major reason that the large currency devaluation in Brazil did not trigger much corporate sector distress is that many corporations anticipated the devaluation and repaid their loans or otherwise created hedges. This large currency outflow led to a large loss of foreign exchange reserves and indirectly created large fiscal costs.

13. In many countries, these ratios themselves were inflated as firms obtained financial relief through rescheduling or lower interest rates, lowering their actual interest payments and increasing the coverage ratio. Furthermore, in East Asia at least, interest rates following the crisis were below historic averages, thus alleviating debt service burdens, but rates rose as economies recovered further. In the other countries, real interest rates remained high following the crisis or even increased, thus worsening debt sustainability.

Chapter 3

Recent International Experiences in the Use of Voluntary Workouts under Distressed Conditions

Ira Lieberman, Mario Gobbo, William P. Mako, and Ruth L. Neyens

Bank failures and systemic distress in the financial sector are facts of life in the industrial world as well as developing and transition economies. Since the late 1970s, 112 episodes of systemic banking crisis have occurred in 93 countries, with an additional 51 borderline crises recorded in 46 countries (Caprio and Klingebiel 1999). These crises have cost, on average, 12.8 percent of GDP, with the percentage still higher in developing countries (14.3 percent). But in many countries the costs have been much higher. Argentina and Chile spent as much as 40–55 percent of GDP to resolve their crises in the early 1980s, and the recent East Asian crisis is expected to cost in the vicinity of 20–55 percent of GDP (Honohan and Klingebiel 2000).

These numbers do not include the indirect—human—costs incurred, such as the loss of or delay in accessing deposits, lack of credit, payment of higher interest rates charged to cover the losses on nonperforming loans, loss of wages as a result of layoffs, and the opportunity costs associated with forgone investments. Moreover, the effects (and costs) may not be limited solely to the country experiencing the crisis. In a global economy, financial instability can be easily transmitted to neighboring countries or more distant trading partners.

Nonperforming loans are a growing and global challenge. By one account, troubled loans in the transition economies alone amounted to

$26 billion (or 16 percent of total loans) at the end of 2000 (Sherif 2002).[1] These stocks of nonperforming loans exact a heavy price. They weaken the repayment ethic, as borrowers see others default without penalty. They lock up scarce financial capital in nonproductive projects and impede the resumption of efficient intermediation, which is vital for sustainable economic growth. The burden of this misallocation of capital—stagnant growth, lack of capital formation, and lost opportunities—falls hardest on the poor, as large amounts of government resources are redirected from badly needed social programs to recapitalization of the banking sector.

In the wake of the financial crises of the late 1990s, the international financial institutions and many experts have recognized the inextricable link between corporate and bank restructuring through a process known as workouts, in which one sector's debt is the other's asset.[2] The condition of the portfolio of the banking sector is the mirror image of the health of the corporate sector, and successful bank restructuring is contingent on effective corporate restructuring. Indeed, the ability to contain the fiscal cost of financial crisis appears to be linked directly to the success of implementing a program that recognizes this linkage.

During financial crises or periods of liquidity tightening, it may be necessary for banks and large corporations to come together and resolve the inability of debtors to meet their obligations. This is often difficult when multiple creditors are involved in each case and when a large number of such cases must be resolved. Weak bankruptcy systems cannot handle a large number of cases at one time.

Informal workout proceedings or out-of-court settlements between banks and corporates are a widely applied method of asset resolution. They have been used to resolve nonperforming loans in many countries since the London approach was first conceived by the Bank of England in the mid-1970s.[3] As other countries, particularly those with weak legal and institutional environments, have experienced financial-economic crises, they have adopted variations of the London approach to aid in the resolution process.

This paper reviews the recent experience with voluntary corporate workouts during periods of financial distress or crises. We begin with the United Kingdom and the London approach, where the Bank of England used its powers of persuasion to bring debtors and creditors to the negotiating table. During the East Asian crisis, Indonesia, Republic of Korea, and Thailand each adopted variants of the London approach. We focus on the most effective example—Korea—where the Financial Supervisory Commission undertook both bank and corporate restructuring. During the tequila crisis, Mexican authorities reacted to the need for corporate workouts by establishing a presidential commission to handle a select number of workouts. During the recent Turkish crisis, the government, the banks, and representatives of industry came together, assisted by the World Bank, to design a voluntary workout program that soon became known as the Istanbul approach. We also explore the Polish case, where the government developed a decentralized, bank-led approach to workouts with a view to restructuring the banks before their eventual privatization.[4] We conclude with an overview of lessons learned.

In each of these cases the institutional structure for informal workouts may vary, but the rules have common features:

- A standstill period while negotiation takes place
- The role of a lead creditor institution and a creditors committee to oversee each case
- A higher authority that can push cases to resolution and arbitrate disputes
- Professional due diligence, usually an audit firm and, in large cases, insolvency experts
- A majority agreement, normally a super majority of creditors, binding all creditors
- Rescheduling of financial obligations complemented by operational restructuring
- Willingness of both creditors and debtors to absorb losses
- Availability of new working capital that will allow the company to operate once an agreement is reached.

The London Approach

The United Kingdom entered a period of industrial recession during the mid-1970s, and commercial banks experienced a rapid buildup in nonperforming loans. The banks had little experience in organizing internal workout units and little expertise in dealing effectively with both the debtor and the other creditors short of formal action under insolvency legislation, which was out of date and unsuited to the constructive survival of banks and firms alike. Insolvency legislation did not provide the tools necessary for voluntary restructuring, including the protection of new money and a process to limit the ability of a small group of creditors to block a workout settlement between the majority of creditors and the company.

Against this backdrop, the Bank of England chose to play an interventionist role, largely through suasion, by bringing together both the debtor and its banks and brokering a restructuring of the lending arrangement. The Bank of England's main objectives were the following:[5]

- To minimize losses to banks and other parties from unavoidable company failures through the use of well-prepared workouts
- To avoid unnecessary liquidation of viable companies, through the use of reorganization and the preservation of employment and productive capacity
- To provide support in cases where creditors could not agree to the terms under which a workout could be concluded.

The involvement of the Bank of England in company workouts was possible because its statutes did not limit its activity to a narrowly defined role. In fact, the Bank of England's policy was entirely unconnected with banking regulation. As far as companies were concerned, the Bank of England was trusted because it was considered impartial, independent, and confidential. In many cases, the Bank of England would call the participating banks together and, if there was no lead banker, arrange for one of the major lenders to assume that position. The Bank of England, together with the lead bank and a merchant bank hired as a financial adviser, would work to facilitate solutions to problems that arose during the course of workouts, such as payment of wages, or to avoid premature liquidation by banks calling in their loans (renegade banks). The Bank of England was quite ready to use its moral suasion to ensure the success of the workouts and to resolve difficult issues that arose during the workout process. However, intervention did not result in corporate bailouts or lead to the commitment of funds by the Bank of England or the government.

Following the election of more market-oriented governments in the United States and the United Kingdom, long and sustained economic growth occurred during the mid-1980s, while the financial industry underwent significant changes.[6] As a result, the Bank of England reviewed its policy on corporate workouts. It decided to reduce its direct contact with companies in difficulty, leaving the task of developing restructuring strategies to the private sector. This smaller role as diplomat and catalyst[7] was intended to motivate the parties involved to work toward generally agreeable workout solutions.

After consultations with the banking community, the Bank of England decided during the early 1990s not to formalize its restructuring framework, now called the "London rules" by some, although the Bank of England preferred to retain the more informal term "London approach."[8] It was feared that foreign banks might challenge strictly formalized rules in court. In addition, the framework had to remain flexible and adaptable. The bank, therefore, chose to define and communicate the framework for corporate workouts through the British Bankers Association (which included foreign banks), speeches, and published articles rather than through formal policy documents.[9]

The London approach provides general guidance to banks and other creditors on how to react to a company facing serious financial difficulties. This guidance, however, is not statutory, and the Bank of England does not have any powers of enforcement. It remains separate from the Bank of England's role as regulator. By ensuring certain rules for restructuring, the London approach aims to avoid unnecessary damage and foster solutions that benefit all banks or creditors involved. The key features of the London approach are as follows:

- *Voluntary resolution.* The main creditors have to be willing to consider a voluntary resolution to a company's financial difficulties rather than resort to a formal insolvency procedure (liquidation, administration, or a company voluntary agreement), without recourse to other enforcement procedures such as receivership and administrative receivership.
- *Due diligence.* As part of this consideration, the creditors generally commission an independent review of the company's long-term viability, drawing on information made available by, and shared between, all the likely parties to any workout.
- *Standstill.* During the period of the review, the company's bankers agree to maintain their facilities (effectively operating at an informal standstill) to allow the company to operate normally, subject to the preparation, approval, and monitoring of cash budgets.
- *Lead bank and creditors committee.* To facilitate these discussions, a coordinating or lead bank may be designated and a steering commit-

tee of creditors formed.[10] Drawing on the independent review, the company's main creditors work to reach a joint view on whether, and on what terms, a company is worth supporting in the longer term.

- *New money.* In addition to the maintenance of existing facilities, it may be necessary to provide new money, in the event of an immediate liquidity shortfall. New money may be provided on a pro rata basis by all existing lenders, by specific lenders with priority arrangements, or through the release of asset disposal proceeds subject to priority considerations.

- *Seniority of claims and sharing of losses.* Other principles underlying this critical period of financial support include the recognition of seniority of claims and the sharing of losses equally between creditors in a single category.

- *Financial restructuring.* If, on the basis of the review, there is agreement among creditors that the company is viable in the long term, the creditors consider financial restructuring, such as an interest holiday, extension of loan maturities, further lending of new money, and conversion of debt into equity.

- *Operational restructuring.* Longer-term financial changes need to be conditional on the implementation of an agreed business plan, which may well involve changes in management, the sale or division of assets, or even the takeover of the company.

Three key elements of the London approach are notable. First, it does not guarantee the survival of a company in difficulty. In many cases, the due diligence reveals that the company cannot be restructured, at which point formal insolvency or liquidation proceedings are initiated. Second, not all creditors participate in the London approach. Instead, the framework is reserved for the major creditors, usually commercial banks, which have no ability to bind nonparticipating creditors. For this reason restructurings done under this approach usually provide continued funding of working capital needs. And, third, regulatory authorities do not intervene at any point in the process. Instead, the decisions are made directly by the parties at risk: the debtor and its primary creditors. Because of its voluntary nature, the London approach can only be effective as long as both the banking and business communities are supportive and believe that the outcome is no worse than the treatment they would have received in an insolvency proceeding.

During the recession of the early 1990s, the London approach served to ensure the survival of many companies whose banks, bondholders, and other creditors reached a voluntary solution for the financial restructuring of viable businesses. The Bank of England has been actively involved in more than 160 restructuring cases since 1989, and numerous workouts have been achieved without the direct intervention of the Bank of England. As important, in most developed countries, banks routinely form creditors committees and negotiate voluntary out-of-court workout schemes with their borrowers in accordance with these principles. Thus the London approach provides a mechanism to preserve value for creditors and shareholders and save jobs as well as productive capacity.

Many countries naturally turned toward the London approach, or a similar mechanism, when it became obvious that a general scheme was needed for corporate debt restructuring. However, many of the approaches, though based on the London approach, were developed in response to conditions particular to the country's situation at the time. The type of relationship between business and government, the nature of corporate debt, the amount of debt denominated in foreign currency, and the percentages held by domestic or foreign banks were all factors that influenced the frameworks adopted in each country.

Corporate Restructuring in Korea

When contagion from the East Asian crisis spread to Korea in 1997, it found an economy with a crisis waiting to happen.[11] The financial system was weak and subordinate to the strong industrial conglomerates—chaebols—that dominated the economy. Loans were often politically directed, and major banks served as the "house" banks to the major chaebols. Loans were based on collateral and depended on a spider's web of cross-guarantees from chaebol affiliate to chaebol affiliate within the same group, in the absence of a legal holding company structure.[12] Historically the ties between government and industry were very close, and the chaebols built their diverse lines of business often with encouragement from and licensing by the government. By 1997 there was significant over-capacity in the economy in several industries, such as oil refining and petrochemicals, chip production, auto assembly, and heavy industry (machine building), as the large chaebols competed fiercely with one another in most of these basic

3

sectors. As a result, profit margins, return on equity, and return on assets were all low by Western standards. The families that controlled the chaebols often did so with minority shareholdings, so expansion was fueled by heavy over-borrowing to avoid dilution of their existing shareholdings. Debt-to-equity ratios for the largest five chaebols averaged 470 percent in 1997 and, for many mid-tier chaebols, were in excess of 500 percent (Financial Supervisory Commission 1999b). There was significant variation among the top five, with Daewoo and Hyundai retaining very high debt-to-equity ratios throughout 1998, while Samsung LG and SK began to move into compliance with a government-mandated restructuring program (Financial Supervisory Commission 1999b).

When the government sought to contain a run on the won in 1997, interest rates spiked to 30 percent, and most of the chaebols were technically bankrupt, with inadequate cash flow to cover their debt service payments. Debt coverage ratios for many of the mid-tier chaebols were well below 1, and their debt-to-equity ratios continued to rise sharply, especially if asset revaluations were excluded from the equity base.[13] During 1997–98, some 13 major groups, including Hanbo Steel and Kia, went into bankruptcy. The cross-guarantees within groups proved to be a major problem. For example, in the KIA Group the car company was profitable, but affiliates such as Kia Steel were large loss makers. The cross-guarantees made it impossible to separate good assets from bad assets, and as a result entire groups fell into bankruptcy.

Initial Government Response

By late 1997, the government had begun a series of ad hoc rescue or bailout programs for several mid-tier chaebols, which largely consisted of calling the banks to the table and asking them to lend money to these companies. The government was forced to deal with a parallel crisis in the financial sector, starting with the liquidation of some 18 merchant banks and the intervention of several of the largest commercial banks. It soon became clear to the government and the Financial Supervisory Commission, which was charged with resolving both the banking and the corporate crisis, that a systemic approach was needed to resolve both sets of issues. On the financial sector side, the government created the Korea Asset Management Corporation (KAMCO) in 1997 to lift highly distressed assets off the books of the banks.

On the corporate side, the government utilized a variety of approaches or mechanisms and institutions to address what was a very large and very complex problem: how to resolve the excessive indebtedness of Korean industry without resorting to bailouts.

The corporate restructuring program had four objectives:

- Reduce systemic risk and the potential for a secondary crisis
- Liquidate nonviable corporations and restructure potentially viable ones
- Restore viable chaebols to creditworthiness
- Foster a competitive real and financial sector.

Policy Measures

The government first adopted a series of policy measures to facilitate corporate restructuring. These included the following:

- Tax exemptions and reductions to encourage merger and acquisition (M&A) transactions
- A series of incentives to encourage foreign direct investment, in the end almost completely liberalizing entry for foreign direct investment
- Modified labor standards to allow layoffs in corporate restructuring and M&A
- Higher ceilings for bank holdings, increasing from 10 to 15 percent of a company's capital
- Progressive limitations on interest deductibility for corporate taxes
- International accounting standards to be fully adopted by 2000
- Improved disclosure and reporting requirements for public companies
- Creation of dedicated bankruptcy courts
- A series of corporate governance measures to protect minority shareholder rights and to require that at least 25 percent of directors be independent.

The government started by segmenting the problem as follows.

First, a number of highly indebted companies or chaebols were allowed to enter the court-supervised insolvency process. In total, some 13 chaebols with 46 trillion won in assets and 28 trillion won in debt entered into the formal insolvency process during 1997 (Mako 1999). For an overview of Koreas corporate restructuring program, excluding KAMCO's asset purchases, see table 3.1.

Second, the largest or top five chaebols—Hyundai, Samsung, Daewoo, SK, and LG—were required to submit capital structure improvement plans (CSIPs) to the government. These restructuring plans were to be monitored by their house banks, the Financial Supervisory Commission, and eventually the president's office. The restructuring programs focused on lowering debt and increasing the equity base by reducing the ratio of debt to equity to 2:1 over a period of three years, injecting new equity by the owners, raising capital in both the domestic market and abroad, and selling assets. The top five were required to begin focusing on core businesses and were expected to shed many of their affiliates. In addition they were expected to cease giving cross-guarantees in support of loans to affiliates. As part of the workout program, all cross-guarantees were eventually cut, so viable companies in a group could be separated from insolvent companies and restructured. The top five were required to report on their programs quarterly. When it became clear that Daewoo and Hyundai were not progressing, they were required to report in monthly meetings attended initially by the president or his economic advisers as well as the Financial Supervisory Commission and the lead banks.[14]

Table 3.1: Size of Korea's Corporate Restructuring Program

Indicator	Amount (trillions of won)
Bankruptcies by the end of 1997	28
Top five asset sales and recapitalization	47
Corporate workouts	44
Daewoo restructuring-workout	63
Small business liquidity support	24
Total	206[a]

Note: Excludes KAMCO's asset purchases. KAMCO purchases had a nominal value of 101 trillion won and an actual value of 38.7 trillion won, as of end-2001.

a. Approximately $171.6 billion at 1,200 won to the U.S. dollar.

Source: Analysis of data provided by the Korean Financial Supervisory Agency.

Third, the next tier of chaebols—titled 6–64, ranked by the size of their assets—were evaluated by their banks and the Financial Supervisory Commission and categorized on a scale of A (satisfactory) to E (extremely unsatisfactory). Of these 59 chaebols, 41 went into a voluntary restructuring program similar to the CSIPs of the top five, 15 were assigned to a workout program, and three went into court receivership.

Fourth, in addition to the CSIPs, the government sought to reduce over-capacity in industry by forcing the major chaebols and some of the state-owned companies into a series of asset swaps, the so-called Big Deals, in industries such as petrochemicals, chip making, heavy industry, aerospace engineering, and construction. The plan was to require their banks to agree to long-term loan rescheduling, debt-for-equity swaps, and the provision of fresh loans, when these mergers took place. The Big Deals proved very elusive, primarily failing on the issue of valuation. But some swaps did take place, for example, in chip making and heavy industry.

Finally, the government dealt with small and medium companies, many of which were satellites or captive suppliers of the chaebols, by requiring the banks to roll over their loans, provide grace periods for repayment, and inject liquidity into the sector. Early in 1998, some 4,000–5,000 small and medium enterprises were failing each month; by mid-1998, with the program in place, that figure was reduced to 1,000–2,000 per month.

Workout Program

In July 1998, 210 local financial institutions signed a corporate restructuring agreement, a contractual approach to out-of-court workouts. The Korean government, under the auspices of the Financial Supervisory Commission, encouraged lead banks to focus first on voluntary (that is, out-of-court) workout of the 6–64 chaebols. These chaebols tended to be in the deepest distress, lacking the financial resources and clout to restructure on their own. A large number of insolvencies among this group could have created an upsurge in unemployment and provoked a secondary financial crisis. The 6–64 chaebols tended to be less complex and, therefore, potentially easier to restructure than the top five chaebols. In the view of the Financial Supervisory Commission, experience gained in restructuring chaebols from among the 6–64 group would prepare lead banks (and their professional advisers) to take on the top five chaebols, whose size and complexity placed them in a league of their own.

Figure 3.1: Korea's Approach to Debt Restructuring—Following the London Approach

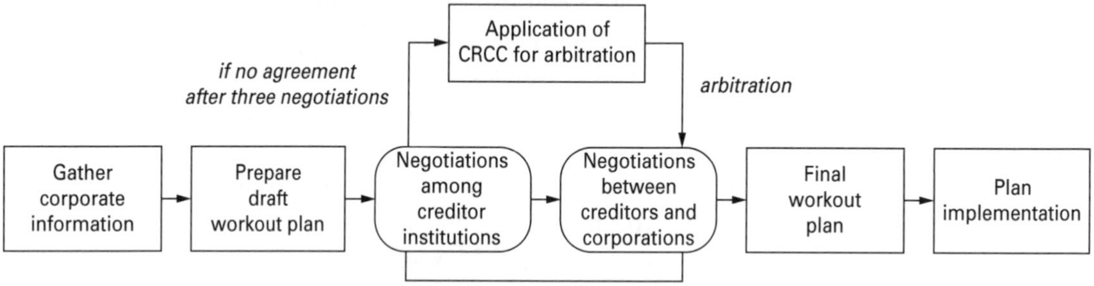

Approach: London Principles focus on out-of-court restructuring of debt

The workout process followed the London approach for out-of-court resolution of financial restructuring cases (see figure 3.1). Key provisions of the corporate restructuring agreement included the following:

- A steering committee was formed, consisting of 10 representatives from participating financial institutions responsible for implementing, amending, and terminating the corporate restructuring agreement.
- The Corporate Restructuring Coordination Committee (CRCC) was created to act as an arbitration committee. CRCC was responsible for assessing the viability of corporate candidates for restructuring, arbitrating differences among creditors, enforcing its decisions, and, when necessary, modifying workout plans proposed by participating creditors.
- Six lead banks were nominated to take charge of corporate restructuring for the first- and second-tier corporate groups. Workout units focusing on corporate restructuring were created within all commercial banks.
- The Council of Creditor Financial Institutions, organized by either the nominated lead bank or the bank holding the largest amount of debt for a company, was formed to allow creditor financial institutions to participate in the restructuring process. Each council was convened within 10 days of a request from any financial institution

holding more than 25 percent of a debtor's financial institution debt (that is, signatories to the corporate restructuring agreement).

- Financial institution creditors holding a majority of credits in a chaebol affiliate could decide to pursue joint workouts with one or more other chaebol affiliates of the same group, if a majority of their financial institution creditors agreed.
- From the date of notice that convened the council, signatories to the corporate restructuring agreement deferred their rights for the discharge of debts, including repayment of debt, and their claims for the discharge of guaranteed obligations. In essence, a standstill agreement went into effect.
- A workout could involve some combination of debt-to-equity conversions, term extensions, deferred payment of principal or interest, reduction of interest rates, waiver of indebtedness, provision of new credits, cancellation of existing guarantee obligations, sale of non-core business and assets, and issue of new equity.
- Council decisions required approval by financial institution creditors holding at least 75 percent of the financial institution credits. A presiding bank could apply to CRCC for arbitration at any point in the process to clarify an issue or after failing three times to get voluntary agreement among creditors on a proposed workout.
- Within one month of an application for arbitration from a presiding bank, CRCC provided a written opinion to all the debtor's financial institution creditors as well as the relevant regulatory agencies.
- If a signatory to the agreement failed to comply with an approved workout agreement or an arbitration decision, CRCC could fine this signatory up to 30 percent of the credit amount in question or up to 50 percent of the cost of non-compliance. The council would decide the criteria for distributing the fine among the other financial institutions.

The corporate restructuring agreement provided expedited procedures and tight deadlines. The time frame, while aggressive, encouraged an initial emphasis on balance sheet restructuring prior to asset sales and new equity investment, which tended to be more time-consuming. It took some three to six months, on average, to reach an agreement on workout plans. Under the pressure of tough deadlines, the initial due diligence prior to a workout agreement tended to focus on financial viability and projections, with little

3

Table 3.2: Application of Debt Restructuring Methods in Korea

Method	Amount (billions of won)	Percent	Typical application
Rate reduction and deferral of interest	23,302	67	Secured debt
Deferral of interest	4,857	14	Secured debt
Debt-for-equity swaps and convertible bonds	4,329	12	Excess debt
Other	2,412	7	Cross-guarantees
Total	34,900	100	

Source: Financial Supervisory Commission and Corporate Restructuring Coordination Committee. In Kawai, Lieberman, and Mako (2000, p. 109).

emphasis on sensitivity analysis and alternative restructuring scenarios. Moreover, inadequate emphasis was placed on deeper restructuring, replacement of management, and analysis of fundamental viability of the business in the longer term.

The initial round of workouts was largely agreed to by the middle of 1999. By September workout plans had been completed for 41 affiliates of 16 chaebols and 38 large to medium-size, stand-alone corporations (not conglomerates or chaebols)—some 79 companies in total (excluding Daewoo affiliates). These workouts represented some 44 trillion won in restructurings: some 21 percent from corporate restructuring (asset sales and injection of new equity) and 79 percent from debt restructuring. Debt restructuring involved a mix of rescheduling (the primary focus of the workout), debt-for-equity swaps, convertible bond issue, limited debt forgiveness, and some new money (see table 3.2).

Initially, reported results suggested that the workout process was successful. However, there was concern that the initial workouts deferred debt for some three to seven years, with virtually no debt reductions or write-offs. This created the potential for a balloon effect in a few years, when the restructured debt matured. Most of the debt workouts were completed by the end of 1999. However, new financing took place in a series of operations (tranches) and took a few years to complete. Moreover, the chaebols needed to demonstrate that they could operate profitably in order to attract substantial new capital.

A review of the workout terms agreed to by debtors and creditors supports the following conclusions (see table 3.3):

- Significant operational restructuring (for example, asset sales) and new equity issues were under way or being contemplated in many cases. However, over-saturation of asset and equity markets made it impracticable to rely solely on asset sales, foreign investment, and new equity issues for initial restructuring of the 6–64 chaebols.
- Self-help contributions from major shareholders were modest at best.
- Initial implementation of these workout deals featured concessionary debt restructuring (interest rate reductions, convertible bonds, and unwinding of complex cross-guarantee arrangements among chaebol affiliates), which accounted for about two-thirds of the voluntary restructuring in 1998 among the 6–64 chaebols. Very little debt was written off.

Many of the workouts agreed on initially needed to be renegotiated over the next one to three years. A number of the highly indebted companies in workouts remained "zombie" companies because they were unable to attract fresh working capital from their creditors. Insufficient emphasis was placed

Table 3.3: Corporate Restructuring Measures Agreed as Part of Workouts in Korea, 1999

Category	Amount (billions of won)	Percentage complete
Real estate sales	3,956	23
Affiliate sales	1,047	7
Other asset sales	995	46
Foreign capital	1,650	58
Rights issue	433	53
Ratio of cost reductions to capital contributions	1,262	44
Total	9,343	34[a]

a. Average

Source: Financial Supervisory Commission and Corporate Restructuring Coordination Committee. In Kawai, Lieberman, and Mako (2000, p. 109).

on fundamental restructuring, following the initial debt rescheduling and other workout steps. Some of these companies were eventually liquidated. Within the context of a systemic crisis, however, the first round of restructuring deals yielded reasonable initial results and provided breathing space to both the banks and the companies.

Daewoo: "Too Big to Fail?"

Daewoo was sui generis among the workouts. Daewoo's chairman resisted all efforts by the government to compel restructuring. In a lunch meeting with the authors, late in 1997, he vehemently denied the need to restructure.[15] Based on Daewoo's prior history, he clearly expected a government bailout. The company was rolling over some 12 trillion won in commercial paper. Potentially it could take a number of non-bank financial institutions (investment trust companies) into bankruptcy and provoke a secondary crisis or, as some analysts noted, a third wave of corporate distress (for a discussion of the case, see Kawai, Lieberman, and Mako 2000, pp. 79–80, 90, 109). Daewoo had nominal debts of some 60 trillion won ($50 billion) and a debt-to-equity ratio of 527 percent prior to asset revaluations at the end of 1998 (Financial Supervisory Commission 1999a). At that time, Daewoo had a 12.2 trillion won ($10.2 billion) negative cash flow, so it was clear that the group was bleeding heavily. Daewoo companies represented 5 percent of GDP, 10 percent of exports, and 10 percent of asset holdings by the investment trust companies (Kawai, Lieberman, and Mako 2000, p. 80, note 3). Based on Korea's bankruptcy experience during 1997, it was clear that contingent liabilities and offshore liabilities not reported in the group's financial statements would drive up the nominal amount by 20 percent—to more than $60 billion.

In 1999 the government finally pulled the plug on Daewoo. The restructuring involved more than 100 group companies in 65 countries. Eight of 12 affiliates to be worked out in Korea were declared insolvent, and three affiliates had negative equity of 23 trillion won. CRCC oversaw the workout and, by December 1999, had formulated an agreed workout plan involving some 63 trillion won in debt, with 27 trillion won (42 percent of the total) in debt-for-equity swaps and essentially zero-yield convertible bonds. During the due diligence process, it became clear that Daewoo had moved some $7.5 billion offshore to support its international operations, leading foreign lenders to agitate for a consolidated settlement. On January 22, 2000, CRCC,

Daewoo representatives, and the steering committee of foreign creditors reached agreement on the purchase of $4.8 billion in loans made by foreign creditors to four Daewoo affiliates. In addition, the debtors were expected to receive out-of-the-money warrants as part of an overall settlement (Kawai, Lieberman, and Mako 2000, pp. 109–11; Mako 2001).

The Daewoo case signaled that times had changed in Korea: no group was too big to fail. It was a courageous policy decision on the part of the government. The alternative could have led to the subsequent bailout of many more companies. The Daewoo Group as such was broken apart and lost its status as one of the top five chaebols; individual group affiliates, such as its automobile operations, were auctioned off.

Special-Purpose Vehicles, Restructuring Funds, and M&A Transactions

In addition to the voluntary workout process, the government, realizing that the companies required credit and new equity, moved to establish a series of restructuring funds (three debt and one equity fund), managed by international, accredited fund managers. The Korean Development Bank was the primary investor. The government also established a real estate investment trust to allow companies to sell their land and buildings and to lease them as necessary. The companies were given an option to repurchase the real estate in the future. Having observed the collapse of the real estate market in Japan and Thailand, the government was keen to avoid this situation in Korea.

Korean analysts credit the creation of these restructuring funds and other special-purpose vehicles, but most of all policy measures to liberalize foreign direct investment and facilitate corporate restructuring, as the real driving force behind corporate restructuring in Korea. Korea had long been considered a closed economy in the West, but liberalization in the wake of the crisis brought in significant foreign investment and, above all, know-how in corporate restructuring. A significant percentage of these funds came into Korea as part of M&A transactions, initially to buy out joint venture operations from Korean partners in distress and subsequently to purchase corporate assets (see Kim 2003; Sohn 2002; Sohn, Yang, and Kim 2002).

Strengthening the Corporate Restructuring Process within the Banks

Finally, recognizing a need to strengthen efforts within the banks to deal with problematic holdings in their portfolio, the government took additional steps in 2001 to expedite corporate restructuring. The government introduced a continuous credit risk assessment system, which requires banks to assess high-risk companies every six months (World Bank 2003a). As a result of this process, the banks selected 1,246 companies for review. Of these, 66 were deemed nonviable and scheduled to be liquidated, 83 showed signs of distress and were restructured, and another 274 companies were seen as high risk and in need of change. Corporate reform in Korea evolved gradually to become a market-driven, rather than a government-driven, process. To the extent that it becomes a continuous part of bank operating procedures and not episodic during times of financial distress, this system reflects an important change in the operating procedures of banks and their relationships with borrowers.

Corporate Restructuring in Turkey: The Istanbul Approach

The Turkish crisis, which began in February 2001, proved to be the deepest of a series of recent economic crises that have adversely affected the Turkish economy.[16] The crisis led the government to intervene in some 19 private banks and to restructure the major state banks—Halk, Vakif, and Ziraat—at great cost to the economy. The intervened banks were acquired by the State Deposit and Insurance Fund (SDIF), which, in effect, became a public asset management agency. The Banking Regulation and Supervision Agency (BRSA) was strengthened and became truly independent, with the backing of the International Monetary Fund and the World Bank.[17] BRSA adopted a program to audit and flush out nonperforming loans in the non-intervened banks, including the five or so largest banks in the country. At the end of the process, the banks were due to be recapitalized to meet Basel standards (BDDK 2002).

Initially, the reform program ignored corporate distress. But during the course of 2001, it became clear that deep distress in the corporate sector had to be addressed. Unlike their Korean counterparts, Turkey's large corporations were not overly leveraged, although a number of the groups had borrowed in foreign exchange. When the Turkish lira was devalued during the crisis, debt service coverage ratios quickly dropped below 1. Also, mid-cap companies were faced with a severe credit crunch, and to the extent that they could borrow, real interest rates exceeded 30 percent (World Bank 2003b).

Legal Framework and Structure

The Turkish Bankers Association, working with government and industry representatives, took the lead in developing a voluntary, non-judicial work-out program based on the London approach. Building on the lessons learned from the East Asian experiences, the Istanbul approach also addressed the policy and regulatory implications and the tax incentives normally required to make such a program operational. These elements required the strong backing of the Treasury and the Ministry of Finance.

The Istanbul approach was enacted in Banking Law 4743 and in a circular issued by the Banking Regulation and Supervision Agency in February 2002. In addition, BRSA established clear rules for provisioning work-outs and for coordinating workouts with intervened banks (World Bank 2003b).[18]

At the heart of the Istanbul approach is a framework agreement (inter-creditor agreement) approved by BRSA and signed in June 2002 by 34 commercial banks, non-bank financial intermediaries, as well as intervened banks and state banks.

The workout program has the following elements (see figure 3.2). First, creditors must signal that they are willing to pursue a non-judicial resolution of a company's financial difficulties rather than resort to a formal process of seizing collateral or an insolvency procedure. Second, the out-of-court process is case-by-case—that is, each large company entering the process is addressed by a separate creditors committee. The committee is directed by a lead bank holding the largest share of the credits or is appointed by the other creditors holding 75 percent of the credits by value. While the inter-creditor agreement is signed by banks and non-bank financial institutions, other creditors such as trade creditors may join the workout process through the creditors committee. Third, the creditors committee has a maximum of 90 days plus three 30-day extension periods in which to reach a resolution and agree to a workout with the debtor. If there is no resolution and less than 55 percent of creditors agree to a proposed workout plan, then the case is dropped from consideration. Fourth, if between 55 and 75 percent

Figure 3.2: Istanbul Approach to Debt Restructuring

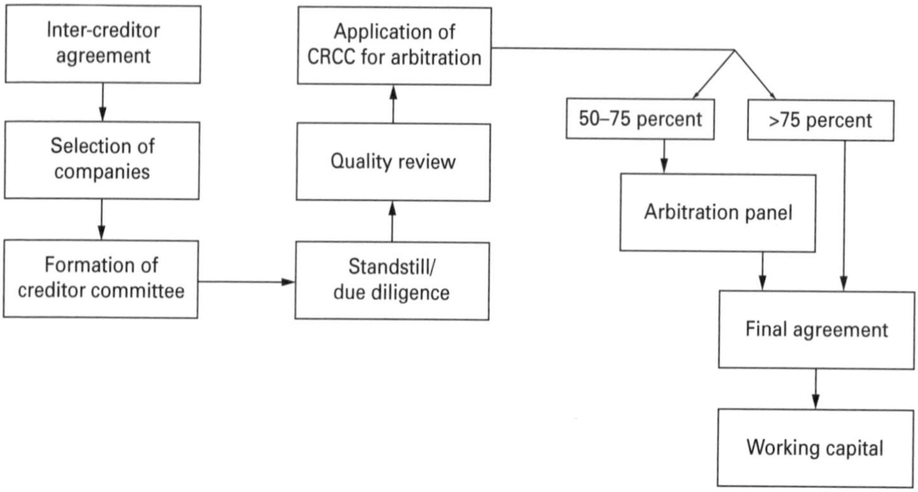

of creditors, by value, approve, the plan is brought to an arbitration panel, which has the authority to approve it. Minority creditors are then "crammed down" on. The arbitration panel can also opine on any individual matter that the creditors committee brings to its attention. Fifth, the creditors committee commissions an independent due diligence review of each distressed company's long-term viability, drawing on comprehensive information made available by and shared among all the likely parties to any workout.

The creditors agree to support a standstill during the period of the review and negotiation. That is, each of the creditors agrees to maintain its credit facilities and not to move against its collateral to the disadvantage of other creditors. This maintains the confidence of the workers, suppliers, and customers by allowing the company to continue operating. At the end of the due diligence period, the creditors have to form an opinion with respect to the company's viability and decide whether or not to proceed with the workout. Until the workout is agreed on, creditors preserve their legal rights to pursue the debtor through the courts in the event a workout agreement is not reached.

The Istanbul approach contains provisions allowing companies to supplement their borrowing in case of a liquidity shortfall or pressing maintenance needs. New money can be provided on a pro rata basis by all existing lenders, by specific lenders with priority arrangements, or by release of the proceeds of asset disposals subject to priority considerations. (Other principles underlying this critical period of financial support include recognizing the seniority of existing claims and sharing losses on an equal basis between creditors in the same category.)

If creditors agree that a company is viable over the long term, they consider a formal rescheduling—such as an interest holiday, recapitalization of interest in arrears, extension of loan maturities, lending of new money, or conversion of debt to equity. These longer-term financial changes are conditional on implementation of an agreed business plan that may well require restructuring of the company over the term of the workout. Restructuring may include changes in management, injections of fresh equity, sale or division of assets, and mergers or even company takeovers by new owners.

Once a workout is agreed to, the creditors and the debtor (the company) sign an agreement stipulating the terms and conditions of the workout, reporting requirements of the debtor, and events that would trigger a review of the agreement. The creditors also sign an inter-creditor agreement specific to the particular case.

Large and mid-cap manufacturing firms and small and medium enterprises (covered by a modified form of the process handled primarily by the lead bank) are eligible to apply for restructuring. However, for a large firm to qualify for the initial round, it had to meet at least two of the following criteria by the end of 2001: have two or more banks as creditors, debt of more than $10 million, more than 100 permanent employees, annual exports of $15 million, total annual turnover of at least TL 25 trillion, and assets on an audited balance sheet of at least TL 15 trillion. Excluded from the process were marketing and trading firms (that is, nonproducing firms) and firms with more than 50 percent state ownership.

Implementation of the Istanbul Approach

The government announced the start of the Istanbul approach as of June 1, 2002. However, implementation was delayed until the government's effort, through BRSA, to flush out nonperforming loans and recapitalize the banks was completed toward the end of September. At that point, newly capitalized banks had the proper incentive to have loans reclassified and to collect every penny of provisioned loans, as improvement in the classification of loans and the collection of provisioned loans would fall directly to the profit line and increase the capital of the banks. Banks also could benefit from the tax incentives for a period of three years, with the option of extending the program.

Companies that defaulted on loans could face seizure of their collateral if they abstained from the workout process. However, Turkey's weak bankruptcy framework served as an obstacle to the workout program. Debtors sought shelter from their creditors through the bankruptcy process, while banks sought to leverage their position and have the government and international institutions bail them out of their distressed debt. As in other crisis countries, getting the incentives right, so that creditors and debtors enter a workout process voluntarily, proved difficult.

In addition to the Istanbul approach, the government had discussed with the World Bank and other advisers market-oriented ways to dispose of the assets of 19 intervened banks held by the State Deposit and Insurance Fund.[19] SDIF, in effect, became a public asset management agency but showed little capacity to develop market-oriented solutions to dispose of its distressed assets.

At the end of 2003, a total of 34 cases had been considered for workouts under the Istanbul approach, involving some 161 separate companies. Loans equal to $4.6 billion were restructured, while some $5.4 billion in loans came under the framework of the Istanbul approach (see table 3.4).[20] Of the total,

Table 3.4: Summary of Workouts in Turkey, as of September 30, 2003

Status of workout	Number	Value (millions of U.S. dollars)
Agreements	20	4,561
Agreed but not signed	6	622
In progress	7	223
Rejected	1	17
Total	34	5,423

Source: Information provided by TSKB, Istanbul Approach Coordination Secretariat.

$2.3 billion of the total was accounted for by the Cukrova Group, a banking and corporate conglomerate that was subject to a separate workout.

The cases had the following characteristics:

- Dependence on long-term rescheduling of debts ranging from five to 10 years, with certain classes of secured creditors benefiting from shorter reschedulings
- Grace period from six months to two years for repayment of principal
- Consolidation of debt past due at interest rates ranging from 1.5 to 5 percent over Libor, with 3 percent over Libor the mode
- Debt-for-asset swaps in an amount of $273.6 million or 6 percent of restructured debt
- Debt-for-equity swaps in an amount of $313.9 million or 7 percent of restructured debt
- Fresh capital, with $79 million in cash and $132.9 million in non-cash (letters of credit, guarantees, construction bonds) for a total of $211.9 million or 4.6 percent of restructured debt, with interest rates on fresh capital ranging from 5 to 7 percent over Libor, presumably reflecting the perceived risk
- Write-off of only $3.6 million of debt
- Minimal company restructuring, with agreement to a change of management in only one of the 20 cases and some limited agreement regarding the swap or sale of assets.

Impediments

Several impediments have prevented the Istanbul approach from becoming a more robust restructuring process beyond this initial round. The first impediment pertains to category two loans: loans that are impaired, but overdue less than 90 days, and as such do not require provisioning.[21] The banks were unwilling to bring potentially viable borrowers that fell under category two into the workout process but did not want to be forced to automatically provision for these loans because the borrower entered a workout process. The banks sought agreement with BRSA on forbearance for a period of six months following the workout. If the loans were serviced during that period and continued to be serviced, no provisioning was required.

Anxious to flush out all nonperforming loans, BRSA was reluctant to sign off on a blanket forbearance agreement as part of the workout process.

The initial mistake was having a category two without some level of provisioning. This was the most important issue limiting the use of the Istanbul agreement and impeding the real restructuring of companies. Three problems were related to category two loans. First, the law governing the Istanbul approach is ambiguous concerning whether these loans automatically require provisioning, if they are restructured under the Istanbul approach. According to the Turkish Bankers Association, they do require provisioning. Second, a number of category two loans were denominated in foreign exchange, with 12–18 months maturity. If these loans were rescheduled in January 2003 or thereafter, they would lose eligibility for the Istanbul approach. Third, the Istanbul approach requires a 90 percent vote of creditors to approve workouts of performing loans. This is too restrictive. In the end, these loans were not brought into the Istanbul approach, and many workouts simply did not occur.

The second impediment concerned the differences between state and SDIF banks and commercial banks. Commercial banks claimed that three to four large commercial banks bore most of the burden of restructurings under the Istanbul approach. State and SDIF banks could not participate in debt-for-equity swaps, could not take real estate collateral, and were reluctant to extend new financing. This was a material issue, as the state banks represented $601 million (22.4 percent of workouts), SDIF banks represented $688 million (25.6 percent), and Vakifbank represented $534 million (20 percent). State banks claim that they would have adhered to the rules of the Istanbul approach if there had been independent due diligence of cases by TSKB or by external investment banks or accountants. Also, to provide new money, the state bank must be given first priority, and this new money needs to be backed by new or shared collateral. To the end, the state banks remained reluctant players, and the banks overall showed great reluctance to provide fresh cash during workouts. Some domestic banks and virtually all foreign banks opted out of the Istanbul approach. This proved to be difficult in some cases but overall was not the greatest impediment to the process.

The third impediment was that banks focused their efforts on rescheduling and not on fundamental restructuring of problem companies. Most of the companies that entered the Istanbul apprpoach process were in significant distress, and their loans were fully provisioned by the banks. A number of these companies had problems before the recent crisis. The banks opted for long-term rescheduling (six to 14 years) to lower the companies' debt amortization burdens and to increase free cash flow in the companies. A number of these cases were restructured through debt-for-equity swaps, debt-for-asset swaps, and even change of management. The lack of an adequate bankruptcy law limited the ability of the banks to bring more pressure on the companies. Most of the workouts required some fresh cash. But managers of the banks were reluctant to increase their exposure to these companies. This was also the experience initially in Korea, where the banks focused on rescheduling. In the end, 50 percent of the companies in Korea went through a second and third round of restructuring, with a number of companies needing to be liquidated. This is likely to happen in Turkey as well.

Looking ahead, experience from East Asia points to other issues that are likely to come up over the course of implementation of the Istanbul approach. One is the disposition of the assets as loans are restructured. SDIF is operating a public asset management company. However, public agencies have often found it hard to operate such companies because of the commercial nature of the work. One option is for SDIF to consider co-participation transactions that allow companies to participate in the disposal of assets. In Korea this was done through a profit participation arrangement with the Korea Asset Management Corporation. Companies that go through restructuring may well need funds to manage assets that are difficult to dispose of during a crisis. International debt and equity funds could manage these assets for banks and potentially bring in institutional capital. Such a role might be ideal for Turkey's private development bank, supported by commercial banks. Distressed companies and banks may also seek to divest land and other fixed assets from their portfolios. To smooth this process and possibly limit the decline in prices, Turkey could establish real estate investment trusts run by institutional investors.

The banks continue to point to the lack of a viable bankruptcy law. The system lacks a "stick" to require corporate restructuring. The Ministry of Justice has drafted a revised bankruptcy law, and, following review, elements of the law have now been adopted. In countries lacking an adequate bankruptcy system (for example, Indonesia, Mexico, and Thailand), voluntary workouts proved very difficult. In Korea, in contrast, the bankruptcy system complemented the voluntary workout program.

The banks would like to reschedule debts due to the tax authorities, as well as debts owed to state-owned utilities, pari passu with their own credits. Banks are of the view that the regulations from BRSA governing the reversal of provisions following a workout are too stringent and should be modified or a grace period should be given for the resumption of debt service for restructured loans.

In conclusion, the Istanbul approach could have been a far more robust process. The bank owners were reluctant to bring in fresh capital to recapitalize the banks, while the banks were unwilling to provide much in the way of fresh cash to the workout companies. The workout companies were highly distressed, and in a number of cases will prove nonviable. Had an agreement been reached with BRSA on forbearance for workout companies under category two loans, an estimated $5 billion in loans would have entered the workout process. According to the banks, they would have supported real restructuring in these cases. We perhaps will never know or will need to wait until the next period of financial-corporate distress to know for sure. It is clear that the banks remained fragile due to impaired loans that were not adequately provided for. By the end of 2003 the banks had stepped up their provisioning, and there was a sense that this was less of a problem. What totally failed to work was any restructuring of corporate assets under the public asset management company. SDIF canceled its only scheduled round of asset sales to date and seems unable to arrive at a market-based solution to dispose of its assets.

Corporate Restructuring in Mexico

Following reprivatization of the Mexican banks in 1992,[22] credit expanded very rapidly, reaching a peak of $117.8 billion in 1994 (World Bank 1998, p. iii). Faced with an acute shortage of foreign reserves, in December 1994 the Mexican central bank allowed the peso to float against the dollar. The resulting sharp rise in interest rates and the cost of foreign debt created a liquidity crisis that was exacerbated by a slump in domestic demand. The crisis, known generally as the "tequila crisis," forced a number of the groups, which had diversified and grown very rapidly in the early 1990s, to restructure their debts.

The Mexican Bankruptcy Law, perceived by virtually all analysts of Mexico's financial system as very weak even before the crisis, is clearly an ineffective instrument for orderly workout or liquidation of troubled companies.[23] It permits many debtors to stave off creditors' claims almost indefinitely; during the tequila crisis, debtors used bankruptcy as a threat or weapon more often than creditors did. The law does not provide for consolidated bankruptcy, so a company with many subsidiaries and affiliates would have many separate bankruptcy cases under separate judges. Any company that was insolvent (liabilities exceeded assets) was likely to be put into liquidation by a motion of its creditors and would not be reorganized (Davis 1998, p. 113). The Mexican government and the Association of Mexican Banks concluded that, "satisfactory progress in large corporate debt restructuring was not being made by the workout groups in the individual banks and that the relationships between debtors and creditors had deteriorated to such a degree that productive negotiations had become severely impeded" (Jones 1996, p. 113).

As a result of the lack of progress and the shortcomings of the Bankruptcy Law, in December 1995 the Mexican government created an institutional structure known as Unidad Coordinadora del Acuerdo Bancario Empresarial (UCABE) to orchestrate the voluntary restructuring of 30–40 of the largest debtors.[24] The Mexican Banking Commission and FOBAPROA (a bank support fund, in effect an asset management agency), responsible for purchasing distressed assets from Mexican banks, also helped to organize the banks so that they could deal with their large cases using a unified approach (Jones 1996, p. 115).

UCABE was a mediator in large cases of corporate restructuring, targeting companies with $150 million–$500 million of bank debt. Holding some $8 billion in debt, these companies represented approximately 8 percent of total outstanding loans in the Mexican banking system at the end of 1995. UCABE sought to preserve the viability of these firms, sustain employment, and promote economic recovery. It worked out potentially viable companies—defined as those having a positive cash flow, a significant base of employment, and a competitive cost structure as well as being a leader or an important player in their market niche.

Banks operating within the UCABE framework needed to compensate for the weaknesses in the legal framework—namely, the absence of a viable bankruptcy system and any formal framework for workouts. Thus they agreed to follow specific rules of conduct regarding selection of a lead negotiator bank and agreed to reach decisions by majority rule (Jones 1996, pp. 2–3, 12). In addition, standstill agreements were adopted, and seniority of secured creditors was recognized. Provisions were made for the preferential treatment of new voluntary loans together with the subordination of existing guarantees. And once a sustainable amount of debt had been identified, the banks were allowed to enter into debt swaps among themselves and to use debt capitalization and other financial engineering techniques to reduce the overall debt burden and facilitate exit from the credit.

Shareholders and debtor companies also followed rules regarding the provision of new capital, the dilution of ownership rights, and the strengthening or replacement of company management in order to facilitate reaching a final agreement.

The advantages of the scheme are clear: a flexible and agile voluntary process to meet the needs of the debtor and the creditors, top-level government commitment through the Office of the Presidency, and provision of new financial resources. The disadvantages are that the process was discretionary and ad hoc: it lacked published guidelines, did not address the fundamental weaknesses of the Mexican bankruptcy system, and was an extra-legal system that could be subject to court challenge.

In total, 30–40 companies were restructured through UCABE, although no results or proceedings of its operations have been published. Nevertheless, there is information on a number of major workouts, some of which were handled with UCABE's support. Some of the workout cases, such as Mexicana de Aviación and Aeroméxico, were problematic state-owned firms in the 1980s that were privatized in the early 1990s—apparently without adequate restructuring—and emerged again as problem cases during the tequila crisis.

Poland: Decentralized Workouts Pursuant to Privatization of State-Owned Banks

The discussion of the Polish experience with corporate restructuring usually centers on the use of a decentralized, bank-led approach. Although this framework was not modeled directly on the London approach, it contains some key elements of that approach. Moreover, the results provide an interesting basis of comparison with the more traditional approaches in Eastern and Central Europe, which relied on an asset management company or, as in the case of Hungary, the eventual use of the formal bankruptcy system.

During the transition reforms of 1990–91, the portfolios of most banks, and especially of Poland's nine state-owned institutions, deteriorated rapidly. Doubtful or lost loans made up 9 percent of the loans of the best state-owned bank but more than 60 percent of the loans of the worst state-owned bank.[25]

In March 1993, with the assistance of the World Bank, the Act on Financial Restructuring of Enterprises and Banks was adopted to supplement and accelerate court-based bankruptcy and liquidation options. The procedure adopted by this act remains unique in Central Europe, as it designated the newly created commercial banks, many still under government control, as the principal agents for designing and implementing enterprise restructuring.

The bank conciliation procedure, as the restructuring process became known, was formalized by the Law on Financial Restructuring of Enterprises and Banks, in effect from 1993 to 1996. This new law provided the banks with three new tools, or instruments, for use in the workout process: (a) bank-led conciliation agreements, (b) the public sale of nonperforming loans on the secondary market, and (c) debt-for-equity swaps. Bank-led conciliation agreements also provided for debt-for-equity swaps as well as for the rescheduling or write-off of debts and the extension of new credit. The bank conciliation procedure was designed as a temporary process to bypass the existing judicial debt workout procedure that dated from 1934. Although significantly amended in 1990, it remained extremely inflexible (Gray and Holle 1996, p. 6).

In addition to flexibility in restructuring instruments, the bank-led conciliation procedure provided several additional advantages. First, it was somewhat quicker and less cumbersome than judicial proceedings. Second, the voting majority required for approval of an agreement was lowered, thereby limiting the ability of small creditors to block agreements. And lastly, responsibility for monitoring the agreement was explicitly delegated to the lead bank. If the restructuring plan was violated and the lead bank did not terminate the plan, it could become liable for any additional losses incurred by other creditors.

The plan shared several key elements with a more traditional London approach framework:

- Placing the responsibility for negotiations and subsequent monitoring of the plan squarely on the banks rather than on a government entity
- Designing the approach to provide an efficient and effective process to preserve viable companies and jobs

3

- Introducing new priority rules by eliminating the Treasury's superiority
- Developing provisions preventing small creditors from blocking agreements.

The overall conciliation process took about two years, and by mid-1995 approximately 85 percent of the conciliation agreements had been finalized. The speed of the process was enhanced by deadlines imposed by the law. These were, by and large, complied with, although the original deadline of March 1994 was extended to April.

While only 23 percent of firms entered bank conciliation (see table 3.5), they accounted for 46 percent of debt owed to the main banks at the end of 1991. Firms entering bank conciliation were, on average, more profitable in 1991–92 and had more employees than firms on other paths. The overall decision for a firm to enter bank conciliation does not appear to have been heavily affected by the sector in which it operated. In only a few cases was the conciliation proceeding triggered by aggressive action by creditors to collect their money. In half of the cases, it appears that the enterprises sought the agreements to obtain additional working capital or debt relief to continue covering weak performance.

Two universal provisions in conciliation agreements were debt write-offs and extensions of the payment period, with small creditors usually receiving much more favorable treatment than larger creditors. In part, this is attributable to the fact that banks (the large creditors) had consistently been capi-

Table 3.5: Financial Resolution Paths of 787 Firms in Poland, by Type of Instrument Used

Type of instrument	Percent
Repayment	40
Bank conciliation	23
Court conciliation	2
Sale of debt	8
Liquidation	5
Bankruptcy	17
Other	5

Source: Gray and Holle (1996).

talizing interest not paid in the past (approximately 44 percent of total debt subject to conciliation agreements), while other creditors had not.

Other financial restructuring tools were less common. Immediate partial payback was required in only six cases, and the amounts were less than 1 percent of total claims. Additional collateral was sought in only two cases, perhaps explained by the weakness of the Polish collateral system. No evidence was seen of any reduction in interest rates.

Debt-for-equity swaps occurred in 25 of the 62 bank conciliation cases and covered, on average, 33 percent of the debt. The swaps almost exclusively involved large creditors, with the weakest banks most active in swapping debt for equity and more or less matching the stronger banks in the amount of loans they agreed to write off. This may reflect the fact that the weaker banks had the worst clients and thus fewer options. New loans were relatively uncommon. Restructuring plans were overly optimistic, vague, and unrealistic. They generally contained little detail on operational restructuring, with half or fewer committing to specific changes such as sales of assets or changes in staffing levels. No management changes were envisioned in any plan.

The main impact of the conciliation process was probably to provide firms with breathing room. The reform was clearly innovative, well designed, and forced the banks into taking action against bad debtors. In addition, agreement was reached rather quickly in most cases. Generally, better firms pursued the conciliation procedure, while financially weaker firms went into bankruptcy or liquidation. However, bigger firms, especially those with a large number of employees, often entered conciliation even if they were financially weak and poorly managed, as they were politically much more difficult to close. On average, profitable companies with more than 1,000 employees either repaid their debts or took part in successful bank reconciliation procedures, while smaller firms with negative profitability either sold off their debts or entered a process of liquidation or bankruptcy. One of the more successful aspects of the program was that loans were written down or swapped without creating an environment of general debt forgiveness. This, in turn, helped banks to extend new loans on market-oriented terms, which eventually resulted in a faster economic and banking recovery.

On the less positive side, debt-for-equity swaps were not used as widely as originally anticipated. Many of the banks were not privatized immediately as part of the restructuring process and did not rapidly divest their equity holdings, and therefore the process did not result in extensive change in

Figure 3.3: Profit Measures for 57 Firms in Bank Conciliation in Poland, 1991–95

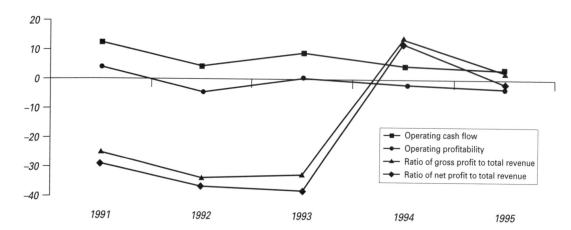

ownership. The relative weakness of the Polish stock exchange and its lack of growth (even though it was and still is one of the most successful in the region) did not support this process.

The results of the conciliation procedure in Poland were positive compared with most, if not all, of other countries in Central and Eastern Europe that underwent a banking and economic crisis. But the actual performance and real industrial restructuring of the firms that undertook workouts was less than optimal. They did not show the marked improvement that was observed in more industrial countries, such as Sweden, for example, for companies after one or another form of workout procedure. In fact, average operating profit for most of the firms that underwent the conciliation process actually fell during 1994 and 1995 (see figure 3.3). This poor showing was despite the fact that only the profitable and larger companies took part in the process and that the economy was growing by about 6 percent.

The workout process through the conciliation procedure thus achieved mixed results. But it nevertheless resulted in a relatively healthy banking sector and in faster economic growth than that of many neighbors.

Lessons Learned

Several important lessons have emerged from the recent experience with financial crises in emerging markets.

It is important to *address the underlying portfolio problems in corporations.* Dealing with systemic corporate failure is as important as addressing the potential for systemic bank failure. Public asset management companies may be useful in quickly lifting distressed debt off of banks' books, but the impact on corporate restructuring has been minimal (for example, FOBAPROA in Mexico, SDIF in Turkey, and Consolidation Bank in the Czech Republic). Korea's KAMCO was a major exception in its ability to dispose of assets relatively quickly and to put them back into circulation via market-based solutions.

As we have seen in Korea, the key is to segment the problem and address the needs of different types of firms:

- Widespread failures of small and medium businesses can have a severe impact on low-income families, particularly in the absence of an adequate social safety net. It is difficult to restructure or provide workout assistance to a large number of small and medium enterprises (Thailand tried to do so, and its workout program inevitably bogged down). One approach is simply to roll over small and medium enterprise credits, provide suitable grace periods for their repayment, and inject liquidity into the sector for working capital purposes. This could lower the failure rate, reduce bank losses, and provide an important measure of social stability in a crisis.

- Mid-cap and large companies produce much of a country's goods and services, employ large numbers of workers, and are the key to recovery, especially in economies such as Korea's and Turkey's with no base of natural resources. Distressed firms invariably require rollover and extension of bank credit. This helps them to ride out the (temporary) contraction of domestic demand during a crisis and provides the working capital needed to boost exports in the wake of a sharp currency devaluation.

- Very large firms, in contrast, must be dealt with on a case-by-case basis. These are often complex conglomerates that may own a bank (for example, Turkey's Cukrova Group) or have so-called house banks (for example, Korea's Daewoo). The failure of such groups can do substantial harm by provoking the failure of large banks or other non-bank financial intermediaries. However, simply bailing out the largest firms can be expensive, may simply postpone the problem, and may undermine credit discipline. Thus governments should aim to achieve a deep corporate restructuring, preserving as much of the firm as a going concern as possible. The involvement of private sector expertise—financial advisers, insolvency specialists, auditors, and lawyers—is likely to be necessary.

Successful out-of-court workouts depend on the ability to impose losses on participants. Restructuring of distressed companies should impose substantial losses on corporate managers, including the loss of autonomy and perhaps employment, and on shareholders, including equity dilution or loss of their investment. Restructuring also entails losses for creditors, who may be compelled to grant concessions on repayment terms, accept illiquid (and perhaps worthless) equity in exchange for their loans, or recognize the reduced value of their assets. In the absence of such loss recognition, real progress in corporate restructuring is unlikely to take place.

Preventive medicine is best. In tandem with improvements in banking supervision, there is a great need to strengthen corporate transparency. Mixed financial-industrial groups (as in Korea, Russia, and Turkey) encouraged insider lending, which was the principal reason for the intervention in 19 banks in Turkey. The lack of international accounting standards and the failure of domestic standards to require consolidated financial statements (as in Korea and Turkey) made it impossible to understand the financial situation of large complex groups. Weak disclosure and reporting standards often made it difficult to determine whether a firm could survive as a going concern. Korea's effort to establish a continuous monitoring system among the banks could be more in line with Western standards; it will be interesting to see how it progresses.

Greater capacity to manage corporate restructuring is essential. In designing a corporate restructuring program, it is important both to take account of existing capacity constraints and to invest in building restructuring capacity. Efforts to train bankruptcy judges, bank workout staff, and government employees managing the process are critical, but the scale of the problem in crisis-affected countries makes it inevitable that capacity will not be adequate to address all companies. Segmenting the treatment of corporate distress—for example, as practiced in Malaysia—makes the most sense.

It is important to use all of the tools of the trade available in a crisis. Those countries that have done well in addressing a financial crisis have shown flexibility in supporting one-off interventions or institutions, such as restructuring funds or special-purpose vehicles, to deal with real estate or debt-for-equity swaps. They have relied on a formal bankruptcy or insolvency system, but not exclusively, to avoid overwhelming the system in a crisis. They have supported the formal system with prepackaged bankruptcies (prepacks) that can reach agreements quickly and informally but still provide legal confirmation of the agreement. They have set up asset management companies to provide relief to the banks for their most distressed assets and, in some cases, relied on market solutions to divest the assets of the asset management company. Finally, they have implemented voluntary workouts in order to bring the banks and firms together and to evaluate quickly and relatively inexpensively the capacity of the firm to service its debts.

These tools of the trade—the insolvency system, asset management companies, and workouts—are complementary, but most crisis countries have not used all of them together effectively. Korea and Malaysia are exceptions, and they have performed well. Other countries (for example, Indonesia, Mexico, and Thailand) lack viable bankruptcy systems. The Mexican asset management company performed very poorly, and resolution of the crisis in Indonesia and Thailand was impeded by strategic defaults and the unwillingness of debtors to come to the table.

A systemic workout process may take a few years to complete. It is difficult to get the workout just right the first time, given the unstable economic conditions that normally exist when the workouts are concluded. Therefore, at a minimum, the process has to allow for a second round or modifications of some workouts a couple of years into the process, once economic conditions have stabilized. This reality needs to be addressed in the design of both the bank and corporate restructuring programs.

References

The word "processed" describes informally produced works that may not be commonly available through libraries.

BDDK (Banking Regulatory and Supervisory Agency). 2002. "Bank Capital Strengthening Program: Progress Report." Ankara, June 21. Processed.

Caprio, Gerard, and Daniela Klingebiel. 1999. "Bank Insolvency: Bad Luck, Bad Policy, or Bad Banking?" Paper presented at the annual conference on development economics, World Bank, Washington, D.C. Processed.

3

Davis, Raymond. 1998. "Overview of Post-Peso Crisis Mexican Corporate Restructurings and Lessons Learned." Paper presented at the conference on corporate restructuring, Lehman Brothers, Seoul, May 7–8. Processed.

Financial Supervisory Commission. 1999a. "Daewoo's CSIP Implementation." Seoul, April 27. Processed.

———. 1999b. "Evaluation and Direction of Top Five Chaebol Restructuring." Seoul, April 27. Processed.

———. 1999c. "Evaluation of 6–64 Chaebol CSIP Implementation." Seoul, April 27. Processed.

Gray, Cheryl, and Arnold Holle. 1996. "Bank-Led Restructuring in Poland: An Empirical Look at the Bank Conciliation Process." Working Paper 1650. World Bank, Washington, D.C. Processed.

Honohan, Patrick, and Daniela Klingebiel. 2000. "Controlling Fiscal Costs of Banking Crises." World Bank, Washington, D.C. Processed.

Jones, Peter. 1996. "UCABE: A Troubled Debt Restructuring Unit." Consultant's report submitted to the World Bank, Washington, D.C., February 1. Processed.

Kawai, Masahiro, Ira Lieberman, and William Mako. 2000. "Financial Stabilization and Initial Restructuring of East Asian Corporations: Approaches, Results, and Lessons." In Charles Adams, Robert E. Litan, and Michael Pomerleano, eds., *Managing Financial and Corporate Distress: Lessons from Asia*. Washington, D.C.: World Bank Institute.

Kent, Pen. 1997. "Corporate Workouts: A U.K. Perspective." Bank of England, London. Available at www.bankofengland.co.uk/londapp.htm [June 10, 2004]. Processed.

Kim, June-Dong. 2003. "Inward Foreign Investment into Korea: Recent Performance and Future Agenda." Korea Institute for International Economic Policy, Seoul, February. Processed.

Kim, Se-Jik. 2002. "Bailout and Conglomeration." Working Paper 02-10. Korea Institute for Economic Policy, Seoul, November. Processed.

Lascelles, David. 1990. "Fortunes Vary as Recession Bites." Financial Times, November 29.

Long, Millard, and Izabela Rutkowska. 1994. "The Role of Commercial Banks in Enterprise Restructuring in Central and Eastern Europe." World Bank, Washington, D.C., June. Processed.

Mako, William. 1999. "Korea's Corporate Restructuring: Initial Results." World Bank Institute, Washington, D.C., February 23. Processed.

————. 2001. "Corporate Restructuring Strategies: Recent Lessons." Asian regional seminar on financial reform and stability, Hyderbad, India, March 29. Processed.

Sherif, Khaled. 2002. "Restructuring Public Sector Banks." Paper presented at the workshop on public sector banks and privatization, World Bank, Washington, D.C., December 10. Processed.

Sohn, Chan-Hyun. 2002. "Debt Resolution, Cross-Border M&A, Governance, and Control in Korea's Post-Crisis Corporate Restructuring." Korean Institute for International Economic Policy, November. Processed.

Sohn, Chan-Hyun, Junsok Yang, and Seung Beom Kim. 2002. "Liberalization Measures in the Process of Korea's Corporate Restructuring." Korea Institute for International Economic Policy, Seoul, November. Processed.

World Bank. 1998. "Mexico: Strengthening Enterprise Finance." Report 1773ME. PSD, Washington, D.C. Processed.

————. 2003a. "East Asia Update: Progress in Financial and Corporate Restructuring." East Asia and Pacific Region, Washington, D.C., November. Processed.

————. 2003b. "Turkey Corporate Sector Impact Assessment Report." Report 23153-TU. ECSPF, Washington, D.C., March. Processed.

3

Notes

1. A billion is 1,000 million.
2. A workout is a process through which a group of creditors, often led by bank creditors, agrees to a restructuring plan with a debtor. Corporate restructuring and workouts are not synonymous. A company can decide on its own to restructure and not involve its creditors. Voluntary or out-of-court workouts take place outside the formal insolvency or bankruptcy system.
3. There is a long tradition of informal workouts between a debtor and its creditors on a case-by-case basis, primarily in Anglo-Saxon countries. In the United States, for example, all large banks maintain workout departments to deal with such cases. But the Bank of England, through what is now termed the London approach, initiated the use of informal workouts in a systemic way.

3

4. The paper does not deal with the cases of the Czech Republic, Hungary, or Slovakia, which emphasized the centralized restructuring of nonperforming assets through asset management agencies or companies (termed the Consolidation Bank in the Czech Republic).

5. This discussion of the London approach draws heavily on Kent (1997) plus discussions with a former Bank of England official who assisted in developing the workout process in Korea.

6. Demand for new corporate finance instruments (for example, hedging, leveraged merger and acquisition deals, complex syndicated facilities), which were financed with short- and medium-term facilities, resulted in high debt ratios. Therefore, at the brink of the 1989 economic downturn, many U.K. corporations experienced severe liquidity problems. Further, the multiplicity of banking relationships created management problems for borrowers attempting to develop workout solutions.

7. The rules of the London approach do not apply to banks in difficulty, because such banks present quite different problems for the central bank in its role of banking supervisor.

8. The term London approach was used until David Lascelles published an article in the November 1990 issue of the *Financial Times*, naming the Bank of England's new policy approach the London rules (Lascelles 1990).

9. In agreement with the Bank of England, the British Bankers Association published a description of the London approach in 1996 as a means to generate discussion.

10. The lead bank or steering committee is typically composed of those institutions with the largest credit exposure to the borrower. In cases where the bank group is unusually diverse, members may be designated to ensure that the divergent interests are represented. Multiple committees may be formed to represent the interest of large numbers of similarly situated lenders—that is, unsecured, secured, and bondholders.

11. In support of World Bank lending operations in Korea during the crisis, two of the authors—Ira Lieberman and William Mako—served as advisers to Korea's Financial Supervisory Commission on the design of its workout program and also analyzed the impact of the crisis on the corporate sector. Mr. Mako continued to follow up on progress in workouts and corporate restructuring until recently.

12. For an interesting discussion of guarantees, see Kim (2002).

13. The chaebols sought to increase their equity base by revaluing their assets, but this made little sense in the midst of the crisis, when asset prices presumably were falling, not rising.

14. Financial Supervisory Commission (1999c) provides an overview of progress in corporate restructuring by class of chaebol.

15. Late in 1997, as part of an initial World Bank mission to assess the need for corporate restructuring, Ira Lieberman and William Mako had lunch with Daewoo's chairman. He was basically hostile to the idea that he needed to restructure or take on advisers, especially Western advisers. He offered a simple solution: have his workers contribute one hour of extra labor a day.

16. One of the authors, Ira Lieberman, served as an adviser to the government and the other parties and helped to develop the Istanbul approach based on his direct experience in Korea. This program was tailored to Turkey's specific situation in 2001–01.

17. BRSA is often referred to by its Turkish initials BDDK, and this usage arises in cited documents.

18. See World Bank (2003b, pp. 55–60) for a detailed description of the Istanbul approach.

19. One of the authors, Ruth Neyens, has advised SDIF on market-based approaches to managing the distressed assets in SDIF's portfolio.

20. Information provided by TSKB, Istanbul Approach, Coordinating Secretariat (TSKB is a privately owned development bank, owned by a consortia of banks; it served as the coordinating secretariat for all banks that entered into restructuring cases under the Istanbul approach). An initial round of 20 workout cases had been agreed to by the banks; six additional cases had been agreed, but the corporate restructuring agreements had not been signed yet, seven cases were still in progress, and one case was rejected. The Istanbul approach will continue for some time because many of the reschedulings are intermediate in term—five to 14 years—and the corporate restructuring agreements call for legal action by the banks and other steps to be taken in the event the companies breech their agreements.

21. Loans that need to be extended but where the delay in repayment, if any, is less than 90 days and is due to reasons acceptable to the supervisory agency do not need provisioning as nonperforming loans in the balance sheet.

22. Mexico's commercial banks were nationalized during the external debt crisis in December 1982 as the last act of the outgoing president, José López Portillo.

23. World Bank (1998, p. 75) quotes a Mexican expert on the Bankruptcy Law: "In summary, we know of no one who believes that [the Bankruptcy Law] is a good law, not even a mediocre [law]."

24. UCABE can be traced back to President Ernesto Zedillo's direct experience with the external debt crisis of the 1980s, in which agreements on corporate workouts were negotiated years after the initial crisis in 1982.

25. The data are from audits by major international accounting firms carried out in 1992. Long and Rutkowska (1994) estimate nonperforming loans in the Central and Eastern European countries at 20–40 percent, with significant variation by country and bank, but equivalent to the levels experienced in crisis countries.

4

Emerging-Market and Crisis Applications for Out-of-Court Workouts: Lessons from East Asia, 1998–2001

William P. Mako

Out-of-court negotiations to restructure the finances and operations of distressed companies (known as workouts) have been widely used and frequently successful since promoted by the Bank of England in the mid-1970s. Widely known as the "London approach," workout proceedings may be used as an alternative to court-supervised insolvency or appointment of a trustee (or receiver) to administer the company. Workouts may be a preferable alternative to potentially more costly and time-consuming court proceedings[1] or the only alternative in a systemic crisis where hundreds or thousands of simultaneous cases of large corporate distress might otherwise overwhelm local courts, administrators, and other insolvency professionals.

Since the mid-1970s, workout regimes have been established during several emerging-market crises to address high volumes of corporate distress. Mexico's Unidad Coordinadora del Acuerdo Bancario Empresarial (UCABE) is one example. More recently, the 1998–2001 East Asia crisis saw the establishment of corporate workout regimes in Indonesia, Republic of Korea, Malaysia, and Thailand. These were successful to varying degrees. The East Asian crisis countries provide a wide variety of experience and afford ample opportunity to consider the effect on corporate restructuring of variations in insolvency law and creditor rights, financial sector restructuring, resolution of inter-creditor differences, and other factors.

The East Asian crisis showed how closely financial sector and corporate sector distress are intertwined, especially in countries where debt-fueled over-investment by corporations in low-margin, loss-making, or cyclical businesses encouraged the crisis. Failure to resolve underlying corporate distress through adequate "operational restructuring" risks diminishing the long-term competitiveness of the corporate sector and inducing acute corporate distress on the expiration of crisis-related "financial restructuring" concessions from creditors.

This paper is organized as follows. The first section provides an introductory discussion of corporate-financial sector linkages and issues in the operational and financial restructuring of distressed corporations. The second section summarizes key features of the workout regimes, relevant insolvency law and creditor rights, financial sector programs, and other legal and regulatory issues for Indonesia, Korea, Malaysia, and Thailand. The third section summarizes corporate restructuring results for these countries through mid-2001. Subsequent discussion of lessons from the East Asian experience separates lessons that should be relatively easy to implement (the fourth section) from lessons that directly affect the allocation of losses among debtors and creditors and can therefore be much more difficult to implement (the fifth section).

The "easy" lessons have to do with (a) London approach–type principles and processes for guiding out-of-court workouts, (b) the need to address potential tax, legal, and regulatory factors that may impede corporate restructuring, especially in a systemic crisis, and (c) the need to consider constraints in implementation capacity. These lessons are not particularly startling or profound, but they *might* provide a useful checklist for policymakers and parties at interest in a future crisis.

As for the more difficult lessons, there appear to be three potential "deal breakers," any one of which could derail an out-of-court corporate workout. Recent East Asian experience highlights the need for the following:

- In order to elicit sufficient cooperation by debtors with out-of-court workout efforts, debtors must face a credible immediate threat of total loss, for example, from foreclosure, liquidation, or receivership.
- For financial institution creditors to pursue adequate financial and operational restructuring of distressed companies, the financial supervisor must be prepared to force or induce financial institutions to recognize losses as well.

- A reliable mechanism is needed to resolve inevitable differences over loss sharing among financial institution creditors and public shareholders. The ability to convert an out-of-court workout agreement rapidly into a court-supervised reorganization (for example, a "prepackaged bankruptcy") may be the fairest method for expediting the resolution of differences.

Recent experience from East Asia suggests that there are no good alternatives to strong creditor rights and an efficient insolvency regime, careful supervision and conservative loan classification and provisioning for financial institutions, and a reliable mechanism for resolving inter-creditor differences. Without these three prerequisites, any out-of-court workout regime will almost surely fail to provide adequate resolution of corporate and financial sector distress.

Corporate-Financial Sector Linkages

Corporate and financial sector restructuring are two aspects of the same problem. The amount of debt a company can sustain—and on which lenders can expect reliable debt service—is determined by the company's cash flow. Indeed, a company cannot sustain interest payments in excess of its cash flow (that is, interest coverage of less than 1:1), let alone make any repayments on principal. Substantially higher ratios of interest coverage are most desirable.

There are a number of ways to resolve unsustainable corporate debt, some better than others. The best response is for the company to raise new equity or to undertake operational restructuring—for example, to discontinue less profitable or loss-making ("non-core") businesses, lay off excess labor, reduce other costs to increase the company's earnings and debt service capacity, and sell non-core businesses and assets (for example, real estate) to retire debt. If it appears that operational restructuring cannot reduce corporate debt to a sustainable level, financial restructuring becomes appropriate. For example, creditors could convert debt into equity or into lower-yielding convertible bonds. To avoid moral hazard, creditors should contemplate debt write-offs *only after* exhausting all other approaches and should retain some instrument (for example, equity, options, warrants) to participate in any recovery. Term extensions may be acceptable, so long as they do not have the practical effect of transforming debt into an equity-like instrument without also giving creditors the rights of shareholders. Reducing interest below the risk-adjusted rate may also be acceptable, so long as principal is repaid. Grace periods on debt service, especially on interest payments, usually just postpone the day of reckoning for nonviable companies. In cases where deferred debt service is rescheduled into a large balloon payment due after several years, it is likely that the company will relapse into distress unless it uses this breathing space to address fundamental problems through operational restructuring.

As a practical matter, operational restructuring and financial restructuring are likely to be simultaneous or iterative rather than strictly sequential. Indeed, as seen in some examples from Korea, financial stabilization and financial restructuring can "buy time" for more fundamental operational restructuring. At the outset, however, it seems important and useful *to think first* about operational restructuring and to assess whether operational restructuring alone can suffice or largely suffice in resolving unsustainable corporate debt.

Turning to the financial sector side, the distressed corporation's creditor(s) should provision—and, as necessary, further reduce its capital—to reflect (a) the present value effects of any rate reductions, term extensions, grace periods, and write-offs and (b) appropriate provisioning of remaining corporate debt based on international-standard forward-looking criteria. In cases of debt-to-equity conversions, the realizable value of the converted equity may be well below the face value of the debt before conversion, which would warrant further capital write-downs. In addition, corporate asset sales may reveal a general over-valuation of collateral, which might warrant additional provisions. If such measures as these reduce a financial institution's risk-weighted capital below some ratio (for example, 8 percent), the government may decide to close and liquidate the institution, merge it with a stronger partner, insist on additional capital from current shareholders, or recapitalize the institution and take control.

Thus corporate cash flow is linked to (a) the amount of sustainable corporate debt and (b) the cost of recapitalizing financial institutions for losses in resolving the portion of corporate debt that is not sustainable. In any case where financial restructuring of a distressed corporation involves a conversion of debt to equity, financial institution shareholders will need to make arrangements for managing and eventually selling the converted equity.

Corporate debtors and financial institution creditors will naturally seek to minimize their losses from corporate restructuring. Losses may include, in addition to monetary value, diminutions of autonomy or prestige. For example, a corporation's management and controlling shareholders will seek to avoid outside interference, loss of control, dilution of their equity interest, and sale or closure of favored lines of business and assets. A financial institution's management and controlling shareholders will seek to avoid losses on corporate debt restructuring that could necessitate capital write-downs leading to equity dilution, loss of control, and nationalization, forced acquisition, or liquidation of the institution.

The government will have to balance a variety of conflicting interests. These may include minimizing the costs of bank recapitalization; protecting workers, suppliers, and subcontractors of failed companies and minimizing ripple effects through the economy; minimizing distortions to market competition through excessive debt-rescheduling concessions; avoiding labor strife; and—last but not least—dampening public criticism enough for the government to remain in office.

From the perspective of promoting corporate turnaround and healthy companies (as distinct from preserving corporate shareholders), it is reasonable to suggest time-phased restructuring goals.

- In the *short term* (for example, three months), it will be important to achieve some financial stabilization in order to prevent the liquidation of viable albeit over-leveraged companies. Nonviable companies should be allowed to fail and exit, for example, through liquidation. In a systemic crisis, however, "strong swimmers" should not be dragged down along with the weak in the widespread liquidity crunch that typically occurs in a crisis.
- In the *medium term* (for example, six to 24 months), operational restructuring along the lines mentioned earlier should be undertaken to improve the company's profitability, solvency, and liquidity.
- Over the *longer term*, it is important to deter a recurrence of imprudent debt-fueled corporate investment. Such deterrence depends on a demonstrated quick and reliable ability by wronged creditors to foreclose on assets, liquidate nonviable companies, and seize control of viable but distressed companies from uncooperative shareholders or managers.

Recent Approaches to Out-of-Court Workouts

Recognizing that the resolution of hundreds or thousands of cases of large corporate distress through insolvency law frameworks would quickly overwhelm local courts, Korea, Malaysia, Thailand, and Indonesia all adopted local variants of the London approach that the Bank of England had promulgated in the 1980s.

Korea

In July 1998, with encouragement from the Financial Supervisory Commission, 210 local financial institutions embarked on a contractual approach to out-of-court workouts as an alternative to unsupervised "bankruptcy avoidance loans" (that is, bailouts) and court-supervised insolvency. These institutions signed a corporate restructuring accord that provided for a one- to three-month standstill (depending on due diligence requirements), which could be extended for one month; a creditors committee led by a lead creditor, typically the chaebol's lead bank; a 75 percent threshold for creditor approval of any workout agreement; a seven-person corporate restructuring coordination committee, selected by signatories, to provide workout guidelines and arbitrate inter-creditor differences in cases where creditors could not approve a workout plan after three votes; and the imposition of fines (up to 30 percent of a credit or 50 percent of the amount of noncompliance) for failure to comply with an arbitration decision (Financial Supervisory Commission 1998). Other key factors included a strong creditor rights–insolvency law system,[2] nationalization of Korea's largest banks,[3] and an increasingly active role for the Korea Asset Management Corporation (KAMCO). In the Daewoo workouts, KAMCO bought $3.8 billion in Daewoo debt from foreign creditors in late 1999 to smooth the way for agreement among domestic creditors.[4]

Malaysia

Malaysia established the Corporate Debt Restructuring Committee (CDRC) in August 1998 with secretarial support from Bank Negara Malaysia to provide a forum and framework for creditors and debtors to reach voluntary agreement. Either the debtor or its creditors could initiate a CDRC case. Eligibility for CDRC status was eventually raised to any case involving at least RM 100 million in debt and five or more financial institution creditors. CDRC also provided for a creditors committee representing at least 75 percent of credits (later reduced to 50 percent) for each company; full information sharing; appointment by the creditors committee of independent consultants to review or develop workout options; a standstill period of 60 days (extendable) to assess viability and financial needs; and 100 percent creditor approval for CDRC cases. Such a high threshold of creditor approval was consistent with the view of CDRC as a forum for facilitating purely voluntary agreements. But lower thresholds of creditor approval in other types of cases—for example, 75 percent for court-supervised reorganizations and 50 percent for workouts managed by the Danaharta public asset management company—may have given creditors an incentive to reach agreement in CDRC proceedings. CDRC acted as an adviser and mediator between debtors and their creditors. On at least some occasions, dissenting creditors were bought out by Danaharta. In addition, Bank Negara Malaysia reportedly used its influence on occasion to persuade holdout banks to accept workout plans supported by a majority of creditors.[5] Other key factors included a strong creditor rights–insolvency law system,[6] the powerful Danaharta asset management company,[7] and a thoughtful approach to segmenting corporate distress and linking corporate and financial sector restructuring. The largest corporate cases went to CDRC, Danaharta handled mid-size cases, and smaller cases remained with the workout departments of individual banks. Banks were required to sell "excess" nonperforming loans to Danaharta.[8] Subsequently, the Danamodal agency would provide bank recapitalization and promote financial sector restructuring, as necessary.

Thailand

Thailand initially pursued a purely consensual approach but soon adopted a contractual approach to out-of-court workouts. The Corporate Debt Restructuring Advisory Committee (CDRAC) was formed within the Bank of Thailand in June 1998. CDRAC, which was chaired by the Bank of Thailand's governor, included representatives of creditor and debtor interest groups. CDRAC members identified priority cases, developed a set of principles and a time line to guide voluntary workouts (the so-called Bangkok rules), attempted to facilitate and monitor restructuring negotiations, and attempted to resolve legal and regulatory impediments to corporate restructuring. By end-1998, however, only about $3.5 billion in CDRAC case debt had been restructured. This prompted Bank of Thailand to play a more active role in monitoring and to promote a more contractual approach. Bank of Thailand promulgated two model civil contracts: a debtor-creditor agreement to govern out-of-court agreements and an inter-creditor agreement to resolve differences among creditors. Signatories to the debtor-creditor agreement accepted a six- to eight-month schedule for developing and approving a corporate restructuring plan, sharing information, designating a lead creditor or steering committee, and setting thresholds for creditor approval. Approval by 75 percent of creditors was necessary to ratify a restructuring plan—the same threshold as for a court-supervised reorganization. In cases where only 50–75 percent of creditors supported the plan, it could be amended and resubmitted for another vote. In cases where creditors could not agree on a plan, the debtor-creditor agreement provided for cases to be forwarded to the courts for resolution under existing creditor rights and insolvency law. In cases of inter-creditor differences, the inter-creditor agreement provided for a three-person panel to arbitrate differences, which included an easy escape clause for concerned creditors. The two agreements empowered the Bank of Thailand to levy fines and reprimands to enforce creditor compliance, including requirements for creditors to file court petitions following a breakdown of the workout process. Other key factors included weakness in Thailand's creditor rights–insolvency law system,[9] the government's reluctance to nationalize or force the public recapitalization of Thailand's biggest banks,[10] and various legal and regulatory impediments to corporate restructuring.[11]

Indonesia

Indonesia initially pursued a purely consensual approach to out-of-court workouts but later tried a more directive approach. While the Indonesia Bank Restructuring Agency (IBRA) asset management company was expected to resolve corporate credits extended by Indonesia's largely nationalized financial sector, the Jakarta Initiative Task Force (JITF) was established in September 1998 to resolve corporate credits from foreign banks. JITF's initial focus was on advice, facilitation, and mediation and on the identification and removal of tax, legal, and regulatory impediments to corporate restructuring. The JITF was originally designed as a voluntary program under the assumption that a new bankruptcy law would provide a remedy in cases where the parties could not negotiate a workout agreement in good faith.

By end-1999, however, JITF debt workout agreements reached only $1.3 billion. Hence, in April 2000, JITF was given some ability to orchestrate regulatory relief or sanctions and to impose a time-bound mediation process. A debtor and its creditors were given an opportunity to agree on a mediation schedule. If the parties failed to agree, JITF would set a schedule for monitoring progress and mediating disputes. If it determined that a party was behaving in an uncooperative manner or that progress could not be made, JITF could terminate mediation and file a report with the government's Financial Sector Policy Committee. In turn, the committee could refer an uncooperative debtor to the attorney general for initiation of bankruptcy proceedings—an option that had not been used as of mid-2001. Other key factors included the complete lack of any protection for creditor rights,[12] the dominant role of IBRA in many corporate restructuring negotiations, and various legal and regulatory impediments to corporate restructuring.[13]

Results

The number of workout cases sometimes was not all that large (table 4.1): for instance, less than 100 cases each in Korea and Malaysia. The value of Korean cases was very large, however; in particular, the Daewoo workouts involved about $60 billion in distressed debt. Thailand was an anomaly in that more ambitious efforts were made to pursue out-of-court workouts. In Thailand, the CDRAC process was applied to almost 15,000 cases, including almost 3,000 large corporations and 12,000 small and medium enterprises, for which a "lite" version of the debtor-creditor agreement was developed. By mid-2001, restructuring agreements had been reached in more than three-quarters of the workout cases in Korea and Malaysia.[14] Completion rates were closer to half in Thailand and Indonesia. In Thailand, as of July 2001, it was expected that failed CDRAC cases would revert to the courts and that the courts would need seven or more years to resolve a combined backlog of more than 65,000 cases of nonperforming loans.

Focusing on completed workout cases, what was accomplished relative to the time-phased corporate restructuring goals suggested earlier? As the crisis developed, it became apparent that short-term financial stabilization of distressed corporations was not an immediate operational issue; instead it was a longer-term "credit culture" issue. Probably no well-run large corporation in East Asia was driven out of business by the crisis-induced liquidity crunch.[15]

Table 4.1: Overview of Workout Results, by Country

Workout result	Korea, Rep. of[a]	Malaysia[b]	Thailand[c]	Indonesia[d]
Total credits assigned for resolution				
Value (millions of U.S. dollars)	88,917	10,395	65,500	18,900
Number of assigned cases	83	54	14,917	—
Cases resolved				
Number of cases	68	46	6,345	—
Percentage of assigned credits	95	77	48	56
Ratio of financial to operational restructuring	8.1	40.5	—	13.3
New money	3,667	—	—	—

— Not applicable.

a. Includes only corporate restructuring agreement cases, as of June 2003. Ratio of financial to operational restructuring applies only to pre-Daewoo workouts agreed by July 1999.

b. Includes only cases of the Corporate Debt Restructuring Committee, as of end-June 2001. The ratio of financial to operational restructuring is for end-1999.

c. Includes cases of the post-January 1998 Corporate Debt Restructuring Advisory Committee, as of end-July 2001, including 2,859 corporations and 12,058 small or medium enterprises.

d. Under time-bound mediation of the Jakarta Initiative Task Force, as of April 2001. The term sheet is treated as qualification for resolution. In fact, only about half of debt subject to term sheets had moved forward to formal legal documentation and implementation.

e. The ratio of the dollar value of financial restructuring (for example, rescheduled or converted debt) to the dollar value of operational restructuring (for example, asset sales, cost reductions, new equity).

Source: Financial Supervisory Commission; R. Thallianathan; World Bank Bangkok office; Jakarta Initiative Task Force; and staff estimates.

Rather, the key issue was whether financial stabilization resulted from a formal standstill supported and monitored by creditors or from do-it-yourself "strategic defaulting." In Korea a company's acceptance into the corporate restructuring accord workout program immediately led to due diligence and monitoring by creditors and their advisers. All too frequently in Thailand and Indonesia, debtor companies could indefinitely resist creditor entreaties to allow due diligence or supervision or to engage in good faith negotiations. Although previous management or controlling shareholders may have remained in place at many such companies, reputations and company access to financing presumably suffered. The alternative of formal creditor standstills, due diligence, and supervision is far preferable in terms of long-term support for the development of a credit culture and business finance.

On the question of medium-term operational restructuring, it is impossible to say how much is enough without looking at individual companies. Four years after the start of the crisis, a bottom quartile of Korean corporations suffered from increasing losses, high debt, and increasingly negative cash flow. From available data on operational restructuring or other "self-help" (for example, asset sales, cost reductions, new equity) and financial restructuring concessions by creditors (for example, debt rescheduling, debt-equity conversions), however, it does appear that operational restructuring played a bigger role in Korea's corporate restructuring than in the other East Asia crisis countries. For the initial round of workouts agreed as of July 1999, the ratio of financial restructuring to operational restructuring was about 5:1. Subsequent workout agreements covering $56 billion in Daewoo debt seemed to focus almost exclusively on financial restructuring. In retrospect, however, it appears that creditors pursued near-term control in order to proceed with the follow-on sale or operational restructuring of Daewoo affiliates, which has in fact happened.[16] By contrast, the ratio of financial restructuring to operational restructuring was higher for Indonesia's JITF workouts (at 13:1) and for Malaysia's CDRC workouts (at 40:1, as of end-1999). For JITF cases at the term-sheet stage as of May 2001, 57 percent of the debt was to be rescheduled (with an average term of seven years and 2.6 years grace on principal), 36 percent was to be converted into equity or convertible bonds, and 7 percent was subject to cash settlement or debt-asset swap.[17] In Malaysia, of $3.5 billion in debt restructured as of end-1999, promised asset sales and new equity amounted to only $85 million. Two large cases involving the conversion of $2.24 billion of short-term debt into seven-year zero-coupon bonds were especially controversial.[18] Such balloon-payment arrangements appear to have featured prominently in Indonesia, Malaysia, and Thailand. The risk, of course, is that operationally flabby corporations will relapse into acute financial distress when grace periods expire and debt service demands resume. Indeed, recidivism of corporate debt default had become an issue by late 2001.

As for the long-term deterrence of imprudent debt-financed investment by corporations, Korea appears to have sustained its early success in addressing this moral hazard issue. Since 1996, at least 25 large companies involving $33 billion in debt have gone into court receivership (Kawai, Lieberman, and Mako 2000, p. 79; Lim 2002, pp. 29–30). In the Daewoo matter, creditors gained management control and displaced previous controlling shareholders in relatively short order. Following some waffling in late 2000, debt restructurings for three Hyundai "MH Group" companies (including Hynix Semiconductor) displaced family ownership interests and left creditors in control (Lim 2002, p. 14). Thus Korea sustained the lessons that no chaebol is "too big to fail" and that imprudent debt-financed investment can result in a complete loss of ownership and control. A credible and imminent threat of receivership inclined the management and controlling shareholders at other chaebols to cooperate in good faith with out-of-court workout efforts. While workouts typically imposed a loss on chaebol insiders, half a loaf was apparently better than none. In Indonesia and Thailand, where the lack of a credible immediate threat of total loss from liquidation, foreclosure, or receivership has made it easier for debtor companies to stiff their creditors, the lesson is muddled. The deadbeat corporate manager or controlling shareholder may manage to hang on, but future access to debt financing will presumably suffer for some unforeseeable period of time.

The discussion in subsequent sections suggests that differences in the quantity and quality of corporate restructuring have less to do with process or legal-regulatory impediments than with basic issues over the allocation of losses among the debtor and its creditors.

Easy Lessons

Recent experiences from East Asian workout regimes point to some easy items that need to be in place for a workout regime to succeed. These include appropriate principles and processes, resolution of tax, legal, or regulatory impediments to corporate restructuring, and responses to inevitable capacity constraints.

Principles and Processes

In each of the four crisis countries, highly qualified professionals put a great deal of thought into appropriate principles and processes to guide out-of-court workouts. One example is the improved guidelines in Malaysia, which CDRC adopted in August 2001 after the controversy over some workout agreements (see box 4.1). Another example is the standard model for memoranda of understanding for Korean workouts (see box 4.2).

These examples, along with the earlier description of creditor approval mechanisms, provide many worthwhile ideas that may well be suitable for

4

Box 4.1: Enhanced Rules for CDRC Workouts in Malaysia, August 2001

Standstill agreement

- Establish a 90-day standstill that is binding on all creditors
- Allow for appointment of monitoring accountants and special audits
- Create special debtor accounts to ensure payment of operating expenses, advisers, and debt service
- Require debtors to undertake certain tasks regarding information disclosure, inter-company lending, asset transfers, dividends, new borrowing, and investments
- Allow debtor to continue to use collateral
- Require creditors to maintain credit lines, but not allow an increase in creditor claims, acceleration, or a change in creditor priorities other than for new money
- Do not allow set-offs
- Allow standstill to be extended once.

Financial restructuring

- Require shareholders to take a bigger "haircut" than creditors

- Convert debt into equity or quasi-equity or reschedule
- Establish a common interest rate within the same class of creditor; set a maximum interest rate differential between classes of 1 percent
- Waive penalty interest
- Set a schedule for periodic payment of interest
- Designate the use of funds; include financial covenants in the agreement
- Share surplus from the disposal of unencumbered assets
- Claw back all concessions in case of failure.

Operational restructuring

- Change company management and board of directors, as appropriate
- Disclose related-party transactions
- Divest or liquidate nonviable and non-core assets
- Obtain creditor approval for asset sales
- Implement monitoring by accountants and special audits, call for regular reporting, and establish operational covenants.

Source: Thillainathan (2001).

---

workout regimes for future crises. As the ineffectual Bangkok rules showed, however, the real challenge is not to identify appropriate principles and procedures but rather to make them stick.

Legal and Regulatory Impediments

The East Asia experience highlights the number and variety of tax, legal, or regulatory issues that can impede corporate restructuring. For example:

- Gains to the debtor from financial restructuring may be treated as taxable income. Conversely, creditors may not be able to reduce their taxes by deducting losses from financial restructuring concessions.

Box 4.2: Typical Content of Workout Agreements in Korea

Commitments by the debtor

- Set five-year management targets for debt reduction, sales, and operating income
- Draw up a "self-rescue" plan for selling assets and businesses, reducing the work force, and undertaking other cost-cutting measures
- Obtain the consent of the labor union and controlling shareholders
- Agree to monitoring by management and the creditors' joint management team, including joint management team approval of the company's annual business plan, monthly unaudited financial statements, the right of creditors to replace management for failure to meet performance targets, joint management team control of cash management, and requirement for creditor approval of capital expenditures, dividends, rights offerings, or disposition of production facilities

- Accept creditors' right to appoint outside directors and an outside auditor
- Agree to equity write-downs or mergers.

Commitments by creditors

- Cooperate in implementation of agreed workout plans
- Establish a joint management team
- Reschedule debt
- Provide new credits
- Levy sanctions for noncompliance (for example, foreclosure, penalty interest, management changes, suspension of new credits, acceleration or call of existing credits, suspension from workout program, and sale of converted debt and convertible bonds)
- Set the terms for graduating from workout and ending joint management team monitoring.

Value added tax, stamp duty, or other fees may be levied on asset sales or debt-for-assets swaps. A non-cash corporate reorganization, such as a merger or spin-off, may be treated as a taxable event. Opportunities to transfer tax-loss carryforwards to a corporate acquirer or new merged entity may be limited or nonexistent.

- Corporate mergers or acquisitions may be constrained, for example, by a multi-month waiting period during which creditors may object and demand immediate repayment.
- Employees of state-owned financial institutions may be personally liable for losses in any case where their acceptance of a corporate restructuring agreement results in a loss to the financial institution.
- Banking laws or regulations may limit the amount of converted corporate equity that a financial institution can accept or may require its prompt sale.
- For a financial institution with diminished capital, acceptance of a restructuring agreement for an extra-large corporate credit may

change a de facto violation of a legal lending limit into a violation formally approved by the financial institution's management.

- The threat of local stock exchanges to delist distressed corporations or any requirement for creditors to organize a tender to buy out public shareholders may discourage conversions of debt to equity.
- Outsider public shareholders exercising their shareholder rights may oppose dilution of their equity and demand preferential terms in any debt-equity conversion.

All possible impediments should be identified at the outset of the crisis. In some cases, specific waivers (for example, on legal lending limits) or permanent or time-bound general relief (for example, on tax effects) may be appropriate. Alternatively, workout regime secretariats may pursue regulatory waivers for particular cases of restructuring. While some such secretariats—the JITF, in particular—heavily emphasized such waivers, there is no indication or reason to believe that such "carrots" ever induced debtor companies or financial institution creditors to take additional losses. While likely necessary, regulatory relief is not sufficient to induce restructuring. Public shareholder rights to oppose dilutive equity restructuring may be impossible to override in an out-of-court workout, as seen in the Daewoo spin-offs in Korea. To deal with valid protections for public shareholders, it may be necessary to link out-of-court workouts to efficient court-supervised processes (for example, "prepackaged" reorganizations).

Capacity Constraints

It is essential both to build implementation capacity and to design a resolution strategy around inevitable capacity constraints. Capacity needs are likely to include more and better bankruptcy judges and administrators, bank workout personnel, and a crisis resolution team for the government. Requirements for responding to systemic corporate and financial sector distress, however, can easily absorb all the accounting, legal, banking, and corporate turnaround expertise in a crisis country. Thus it is important to plan to work around likely capacity constraints. The assignment of almost 15,000 distressed companies to CDRAC in Thailand was probably unrealistic under the best of circumstances. Some segmentation of corporate distress—for example, placing large multi-creditor cases in out-of-court workout or court-supervised insolvency, medium-size cases in an asset management company, and small cases with the originating bank—such as followed in Malaysia, seems to make the most sense. Limiting asset management company mandates to the sale of unrestructured corporate debt (versus financial restructuring or follow-on operational restructuring) will lessen the demands on capacity of the asset management company and improve the chances of success. Joint ventures to induce professional private management of distressed corporate debt or converted equity, such as successfully used in Korea by KAMCO and corporate restructuring companies, are another way of addressing capacity constraints.[19]

Potential Deal Breakers

Workout principles and process, legal and regulatory impediments, and capacity constraints are the easy issues. Recent experience indicates that the success of an out-of-court workout scheme—measured in terms of the quantity and adequacy of corporate restructuring—will ultimately depend on the ability of creditors to impose losses on a debtor, the government's readiness to force or induce creditors to recognize losses from corporate restructuring, and the resolution of inter-creditor differences regarding the allocation of losses and risk.

Debtor Losses

Serious financial and operational restructuring of distressed companies will impose some losses (broadly defined) on corporate managers and controlling shareholders, for example, through equity dilution, creditor monitoring, diminution of managerial discretion, or forced divestiture of favored businesses and assets. Debtors involved in an out-of-court workout or court-supervised rehabilitation can be expected to resist such measures unless there is a credible timely threat of even greater loss, for example, through foreclosure, liquidation, or receivership.

Contrasts between Korea and Indonesia-Thailand are instructive. While additional operational restructuring of Korea's bottom quartile of distressed companies is still needed, the 1998–99 workouts did impose significant losses on corporate insiders from the dilution of equity, changes in management, supervision by creditors, and forced sale of assets. In Korea a low threshold for receivership gave creditors a powerful "stick."[20] The 1997 descent of 11 chaebols into receivership provided an incentive for other corporate debtors to agree in 1998–99 to lesser losses imposed by out-of-court workout agreements. In Indonesia, however, the absence of any credible threat to debtors has encouraged a dilatory and superficial approach to corporate restructuring. In Thailand, as seen in the infamous case of TPI (Thai Petrochemical), the lack of a credible threat of foreclosure, liquidation, or receivership has produced the anomalous spectacle of prolonged debtor resistance to court-supervised rehabilitation.

To elicit sufficient debtor cooperation with either an out-of-court workout or court-supervised rehabilitation, creditors should have timely access to as many sticks (for example, foreclosure, liquidation, receivership) as possible. Commencement criteria should be based on performance (for example, nonpayment of debt).[21] Procedures for converting an unsuccessful workout or court-supervised rehabilitation into receivership or liquidation should be simple, quick, and sure.

Creditor Losses

Serious financial and operational restructuring of distressed companies is also likely to cause losses to financial institution creditors. For example, interest rate concessions or grace periods may lower the present value of restructured debt, while a debt-equity conversion may leave financial institution creditors with illiquid and virtually worthless shares. In addition, sales of non-core assets or businesses may precipitate losses for financial institution creditors. The proceeds from sales may be insufficient to repay the remaining debt on the asset, for example, or a corporate acquirer may refuse to assume all of the remaining debt of the business. Such transactions may indicate that all similar collateral is over-valued. Finally, financial institution creditors may be reluctant to transfer restructured corporate debt or converted equity to a professionally managed joint venture on commercial terms if the negotiated price is below the carrying value of the credits or converted equity, in which case the transfer would force loss recognition. Such concerns seem to have discouraged some Korean banks from conveying distressed corporate assets to corporate restructuring vehicles for management by corporate turnaround professionals. Rather than risk losses and diminished capital adequacy that could prompt the regulator to insist on "prompt corrective actions," equity dilution, or intervention, financial institution creditors may settle for superficial financial restructuring (for example, balloon payments), accept slow corporate sales of non-core assets or businesses, and hang on to over-valued corporate credits or converted equity, thus leaving numerous "zombie" companies in business to depress corporate sector profits.

As noted at the outset, the resolution of unsustainable corporate debt is important for long-term corporate competitiveness. Thus, for the long-term health of the corporate sector, the government-financial supervisor should be prepared to force or otherwise induce adequate operational and financial restructuring of distressed companies. Reasonably realistic information on the financial position and performance of companies is a prerequisite for decisionmaking. This, in turn, highlights the importance of adopting international best practices in loan classification and provisioning according to forward-looking criteria. Thus informed, the authorities may intervene in financial institutions whose risk-weighted capital falls below an acceptable minimum or require sales of "excess" nonperforming loans. In Malaysia, for example, any bank with a nonperforming loan ratio above 10 percent was required to resolve the excess promptly or else sell the excess nonperforming loans to the Danaharta public asset management company.

But what if the authorities lack the financial resources or political will to intervene in additional financial institutions or force a "fire sale" of excess nonperforming loans? In such cases, the authorities may choose to provide regulatory forbearance as a way to encourage capital-weakened financial institutions to resolve unsustainable corporate debt. Forbearance, which reduces the imminence of intervention risk, may be provided on loss recognition or capital adequacy. Both were tried in the East Asia crisis.[22]

Forbearance may entail three risks. First, a financial institution may use the period of forbearance to engage in riskier lending to recover its capital position. As a result, if the institution ultimately fails, the costs will be higher. Hence, forbearance should only be allowed for financial institutions whose long-term viability seems reasonably assured, and progress toward time-bound capital adequacy goals should be closely monitored. A second risk is that some types of forbearance on loss recognition may encourage the over-valuation of restructured corporate debt or converted equity and thereby discourage follow-on operational restructuring. In Korea, for example, such forbearance discouraged loss-averse financial institutions from taking more drastic steps (for example, liquidation of non-viable companies, sale to a strategic investor, transfer of converted corporate equity to a professionally managed joint venture, or sales of possibly over-valued non-core assets or collateral) to complete the operational restructuring of distressed companies. The third risk is that forbearance on loss recognition may impede private recapitalization of financial institutions. Investors may find it difficult to undertake due diligence and feel reluctant to invest in a financial institution characterized by murky loan classification and provisioning; over-valuation of restructured credits, collateral, and converted equity; and uncertain capital.

Some observers suggest that there is always forbearance in a crisis. If so, the challenge is to minimize additional risks to the financial system and to design forbearance to meet the broader goals of corporate or financial sector restructuring. Any forbearance should be limited in applicability and duration and be carefully monitored. Moreover, any forbearance should be provided on capital adequacy instead of loss recognition.

Inter-Creditor Differences

Assuming a reasonably strong creditor rights–insolvency law system, differences among creditors may be more difficult to overcome than differences between the debtor and creditors. Due to differences in the type of credit, exposure, and capital adequacy, financial institutions may vary widely in their willingness to make financial restructuring concessions, pursue follow-on operational restructuring, or provide new money. Both Korea and Thailand tried to bind creditors to inter-creditor arbitration. The ex post facto imposition of such arbitration, however, might be open to legal challenge. Differences among creditors frequently surfaced. In Korea, for example, the Corporate Restructuring Coordination Committee provided arbitration decisions in 21 cases prior to July 1999, mostly regarding the allocation of losses from financial restructuring and additional risks from new credits. Given close linkages with the regulated financial institutions, it was perhaps natural for the financial supervisor in Korea and Thailand to play some role in enforcing workout agreements and inter-creditor arbitration decisions.[23] Such involvement, however, poses a huge conflict of interest with the financial supervisor's core function of preserving a sound financial system.

Experience with out-of-court workouts under Korea's initial framework of the corporate restructuring accord highlights a significant "free rider" problem. In some cases, while major banks were attempting to agree on a workout plan without resorting to court receivership, non-bank financial institutions held out for better terms, even though their credits were usually unsecured. If creditors could not reach at least 75 percent agreement on a

4

restructuring plan, they had to decide whether or not to put the company into court receivership. Court receivership, however, immediately required creditors to make higher loan provisions for expected losses, raising both the risks of chain bankruptcies among suppliers and subcontractors and the risks of employee layoffs. Knowing this, non-bank financial institutions sought to extract concessions from other creditors—many of which were large nationalized banks—interested in concluding a workout agreement. In many cases, large secured creditors relented and gave non-bank financial institutions a better deal in the financial restructuring of distressed companies (Lim 2002).

Difficulties in agreeing to and implementing out-of-court workouts led to development of the Corporate Restructuring Promotion Law, which replaced the corporate restructuring accord approach to workouts. The law went into effect in September 2001 and is to remain in force until 2006. Key features include the following:

- The law applies to all financial institutions (including securities companies) plus the KDIC deposit insurer and KAMCO public asset management company, not just major banks and non-bank financial institutions.
- Creditors opposed to a restructuring plan can ask those in favor to purchase their claims and, if necessary, can go to court. If creditors ask to be bought out, their credits are valued at "liquidation value" based on due diligence by an accounting firm hired by the creditors. Dissenting creditors cannot, however, just free ride and reap upside benefits without bearing downside risks (for example, from proportional participation in new credits).
- If creditors with a minimum of 75 percent of total credits cannot agree on a restructuring plan, the firm in question must proceed to court-supervised composition, reorganization, or liquidation.
- To facilitate debt-to-equity conversions, the law also lifts the ceiling on equity investments that can be held by financial institutions. Equity write-downs or write-offs, a normal step in debt-to-equity conversions in Korea, still need to be approved by at least two-thirds of voting shareholders present at a shareholders meeting.

The Corporate Restructuring Promotion Law has been used in the restructuring of three Hyundai companies (including Hynix and Hyundai

4

Engineering and Construction) and two Ssangyong companies.[24] A similar approach should be adopted before a crisis in order to avoid any concerns about its ex post facto imposition on financial institution creditors.

Other approaches to resolution of inter-creditor differences include suasion and linkages with the formal insolvency system. Reportedly in Malaysia, as earlier in London, the central bank occasionally asked hold-out creditors to reconsider their opposition to a particular workout arrangement. Out-of-court procedures in both Malaysia and Thailand mimicked creditor approval thresholds in the formal insolvency system. In Thailand, thresholds for creditor approval of a workout agreement were set at 75 percent, the same as for a court-supervised organization. Thus, in any case where a 75 percent majority of creditors could not elicit the cooperation of a hold-out minority, they could attempt to take the agreement to Thailand's bankruptcy court for ratification and imposition on hold-out creditors. In Malaysia CDRC rules required 100 percent creditor approval of any workout agreement. But lower approval thresholds in other cases—75 percent for Companies Act reorganizations and 50 percent for workouts managed by the Danaharta asset management company—may have given creditors some additional incentive to reach agreement in CDRC proceedings.

Out-of-court workouts proceed in the shadow of the law. Perhaps the best method of facilitating out-of-court workouts is to reinforce linkages with relevant law. The ability to convert an out-of-court workout agreement rapidly into a court-supervised reorganization seems the fairest and most expeditious method of dealing with hold-out creditors and public shareholders. Careful attention should be given to thresholds for creditor approval, rules for priorities among creditors and other stakeholders, and "cram down" procedures, both for court-supervised insolvencies and, by extension, out-of-court workouts.

References

The word "processed" describes informally produced works that may not be commonly available through libraries.

Brierly, Peter G. 2000. "The London Approach to Corporate Workouts." Presentation to the Bank of England, February. Processed.

Chopra, Ajai, and others. 2002. "From Crisis to Recovery in Korea: Strategy, Achievements, and Lessons." In David T. Coe and Se-Jik Kim, eds., Korea Crisis and Recovery. Washington, D.C.: International Monetary Fund; Seoul: Korea Institute for International Economic Policy.

Financial Supervisory Commission. 1998. "Corporate Restructuring Accord." July. Processed.

Franks, J. R., K. G. Nyborg, and W. N. Torous. 1996. "A Comparison of U.S., U.K., and German Insolvency Codes." *Financial Management* 25(3, Autumn): 86–101.

Haggard, Stephan, Won-hyuk Lim, and Euysung Kim. 2003. "Conclusion: Whither the Chaebol." In Stephan Haggard, Won-hyuk Lim, and Euysung Kim, eds., *Economic Crisis and Corporate Restructuring in Korea*. Cambridge, U.K.: Cambridge University.

Kawai, Masahiro, Ira Lieberman, and William Mako. 2000. "Financial Stabilization and Initial Restructuring of East Asian Corporations: Approaches, Results, and Lessons." In Charles Adams, Robert Litan, and Michael Pomerleano, eds., *Managing Financial and Corporate Distress: Lessons from Asia*. Washington, D.C.: Brookings Institution.

Lim, Won-hyuk. 2002. "Korea: Corporate Vulnerabilities and Restructuring." Korea Development Institute, September. Processed.

Lim, Youngjae. 2003. "The Corporate Bankruptcy System and the Economic Crisis." In Stephan Haggard, Won-hyuk Lim, and Euysung Kim, eds., *Economic Crisis and Corporate Restructuring in Korea*. Cambridge, U.K.: Cambridge University.

Mako, William. 2002. "Corporate Restructuring and Reform: Lessons from Korea." In David T. Coe and Se-Jik Kim, eds., *Korea Crisis and Recovery*. Washington, D.C.: International Monetary Fund; Seoul: Korea Institute for International Economic Policy.

Park, Kyung-suh. 2003. "Bank-Led Corporate Restructuring." In Stephan Haggard, Won-hyuk Lim, and Euysung Kim, eds., *Economic Crisis and Corporate Restructuring in Korea*, pp. 195–96. Cambridge, U.K.: Cambridge University.

Notes

1. For example, for a sample of cases from the United Kingdom and the United States, overall creditor recoveries averaged 85 percent in U.K.

workouts, 51 percent in U.S. court-supervised reorganizations (Chapter 11), and 34 percent in U.K. receiverships. See Brierly (2000), citing Franks, Nyborg, and Torous (1996).

2. Before the crisis, creditors could readily foreclose on collateral or (in case of two successive failures by a company to honor debts coming due) put a company into receivership. For a history of Korea's insolvency system during the 1990s, see Lim (2003, pp. 207–32). For a listing of chaebol receiverships through mid-1999, see Kawai, Lieberman, and Mako (2000, p. 79).

3. By early 2001, the government had nationalized Korea's four largest banks, merged nine, and closed more than 200 smaller institutions. Since losses had already been imposed on their shareholders and management, it might have become easier for these financial institutions to pursue follow-on operational restructuring of distressed corporations. In practice, their approach to ongoing corporate restructuring remained dilatory. Possible explanations include lack of capacity, habitual passivity, reliance on the government, and the government's difficulty in reconciling its roles as nationalized bank owner, financial supervisor, and overall crisis manager. See Haggard, Lim, and Kim (2003, pp. 312–28); Park (2003 pp. 195–96).

4. A billion is 1,000 million. Based on a briefing document prepared by KAMCO, dated May 2001. Chopra and others (2002, p. 76) report that the total buyback of Daewoo debt owed to foreign creditors, at about 40 cents on the dollar, amounted to just under $5 billion. By August 2002, KAMCO had acquired about $25 billion in Daewoo debt (based on a briefing document prepared by KAMCO, dated October 2002). See www.kamco.or.kr/eng for annual status reports.

5. Internal background study provided by R. Thillainathan to the World Bank.

6. Under the 1965 Companies Act, creditors may petition the court to appoint a receiver to "wind up" (liquidate) a corporation for failure to pay its debts. A receiver can be appointed without court involvement if the underlying document (for example, mortgage, debenture) entitles the holder to appoint a receiver. Under other provisions of the act, the court can enforce a reorganization plan that is supported by 75 percent (debt-weighted) of the company's creditors.

7. Legislation empowered Danaharta to foreclose or sell collateral without the borrower's consent (providing a 30-day notice and sale at market

value) and to appoint a special administrator to manage debtor companies.

8. Several "sticks and carrots" encouraged financial institutions to sell or convey nonperforming loans to Danaharta for management. Financial institutions whose ratio of nonperforming loans exceeded 10 percent were required to reduce the level of nonperforming loans, either by undertaking their own workout efforts or by selling such loans to Danaharta. Sellers of nonperforming loans would receive at least 80 percent of any profits realized on their subsequent sale or liquidation. Banks were given up to five years to amortize any difference between the face value of the loan and the price paid by Danaharta. Sellers had an opportunity to exchange an illiquid, non-earning nonperforming loan for an income-generating, readily marketable, and zero-risk-weighted bond from Danaharta. Conversely, a bank that declined a purchase offer from Danaharta was obliged to write down the nonperforming loans to 80 percent of the offer price and immediately recognize any loss.

9. While Thailand's bankruptcy law was revised in 1998 to include court-supervised reorganization as an alternative to liquidation, the reorganization option was underutilized. Commencement criteria were based on a balance sheet test (that is, accounting insolvency) rather than on performance (that is, actual satisfaction of debt obligations falling due). In several notorious cases, debtors claimed accounting solvency (probably based on over-valued assets) to fend off reorganization petitions. It appears that weaknesses in foreclosure-liquidation procedures (for example, long waiting times to petition, time-consuming civil code procedures, and a cumbersome disposal process), coupled with uncertainties in matters such as the appointment of an external planner, gave debtors no incentive to seek protection from a court-supervised reorganization process. Based on internal memos by Tanatat Puttasuwan, Renuka Vongviriyatham, and Michael Markels from the World Bank Bangkok Office, dated 2001.

10. Thailand closed one bank and 59 finance companies and nationalized four small and medium banks. For the remaining (large) banks, the government's August 1998 plan offered public funds (a) for Tier 1 capital to make up losses from accelerated implementation of full provisioning and prompt recognition of losses from capital restructuring and (b) for Tier 2 capital equivalent to 20 percent of new business lending. This represented a thoughtful attempt to link together corporate and financial sec-

tor restructuring. The remaining private banks were reluctant, however, to accept public recapitalization funds because controlling shareholders wanted to avoid equity dilution and diminution of control.

11. Key impediments in Thailand included the treatment of some non-cash corporate reorganizations (mergers) as a taxable event; an inability to transfer net operating losses to reduce the tax liability of a corporate acquirer or new merged entity; waiting periods of up to six months for creditor review of proposed mergers; and, according to Article 157 of the law on state-owned enterprises, personal liability for any employee of a state-owned financial institution (for example, a nationalized bank or a public asset management company) who causes any loss to the institution, including a loss from corporate debt restructuring.

12. Indonesia replaced its 1906 bankruptcy ordinance with a new bankruptcy act in 1998. While the new law was considered adequate, administration by the courts was erratic. Multi-layered appeals created opportunities for delay and anomalous judicial decisions. Creditors could not expect their rights to be protected in court.

13. Gains from debt rescheduling may be taxable to the debtor, while losses to creditors are not tax deductible. Restructuring agreements that are too slow to reduce a company's debts to single-borrower exposure limits can constitute a violation of legal lending limits. Other issues include short deadlines for financial institutions to dispose of converted corporate equity, high transfer taxes, potential delisting of restructured companies from local stock exchanges, and the possibility that a debt-to-equity conversion might require creditors to organize a public tender to buy the remaining shares from public shareholders.

14. Practically speaking, Korea's completion rate was nearly 100 percent. Companies that dropped out of the workout program typically became court-supervised insolvencies.

15. The same cannot be said for small and medium enterprises. In Korea, for example, almost 19,000 small and medium enterprises failed in 1997–98. See Kawai, Lieberman, and Mako (2000, p. 79). Greater attention should probably be paid to short-term financial stabilization and liquidity for small and medium enterprises in a crisis.

16. For example, Korea Investor Service data show that employment was cut 25–30 percent at Daewoo Heavy and Daewoo Motor Sales, 45 percent at Ssangyong Motors, and almost 60 percent at Daewoo Corporation between end-1996 and end-2001. Moreover, some affiliates were sold,

including the sale of Daewoo Motors to General Motors. Daewoo Corporation was split into three companies (two good, one bad), as was Daewoo Heavy. These spin-offs of Daewoo Corporation's trading and construction businesses and Daewoo Heavy's shipbuilding and heavy machinery businesses were somewhat delayed—first by the need to legislate tax relief for spin-offs and second by the need to negotiate preferential equity restructuring terms with public shareholders.

17. Based on a status report prepared by JITF, dated June 2001.

18. These cases, involving engineering concern UEM/Renong, saw no change in management, dilution of existing shareholders, new equity, or asset sales. Indeed, at the time, the press reported that UEM/Renong actually acquired additional assets.

19. Holders of distressed debt or converted equity, however, will first have to agree on valuations with the private investor.

20. In Korea failure on two successive occasions to honor bills coming due is grounds for receivership.

21. Experience from Thailand illustrates the undesirability of basing commencement criteria on formal determination of accounting insolvency.

22. Indonesia provided forbearance on capital adequacy by giving banks until end-2001 to raise risk-weighted capital adequacy to 8 percent. Other countries emphasized forbearance on loss recognition. In Thailand the financial supervisor allowed banks to recognize losses from corporate restructuring over a period of two and a half years in five increments and to provide loans net of (usually over-valued) collateral. In Malaysia the definition of nonperforming loans was relaxed to six months of non-payment (versus the previous three-month standard); banks were given an opportunity to reclassify restructured corporate debt promptly as performing debt, instead of waiting 12 months, as before; and banks were given five years to recognize losses on sales of nonperforming loans to Danaharta (internal background study provided by R. Thillainathan to the World Bank). In Korea, to encourage financial institutions to agree to workouts, the supervisor provided a special exemption from the general application of forward-looking criteria. Financial institutions were allowed to provision restructured corporate debt at just 2–20 percent through end-2001. In at least some cases, however, financial data and subsequent experience indicated that provisioning should have been 50 percent or higher. The financial supervisor subsequently decided to phase out this exemption to forward-looking criteria by end-2000. There

are also reasons to believe that converted corporate equity tended to be over-valued. Adoption of a lower-of-cost-or-market rule (instead of, for example, requiring illiquid shares to be valued at a nominal KRW 1 per share) may have allowed banks to carry converted equity at "market prices" that were unrealistically high as a result of thin public floats, legal protections for public shareholders, and agreements among creditor-shareholders not to sell converted corporate equity during implementation of a workout (three years, on average) without unanimous agreement among creditor-shareholders. See Mako (2002, p. 212).

23. For example, Korea's Financial Supervisory Service reportedly threatened to fine Hana Bank KRW 6 billion if it failed to provide a promised KRW 11.9 billion of emergency liquidity to Hyundai Petrochemical. See *Korea Herald*, April 21, 2001.

24. As of June 2002, the Hyundai restructurings involved KRW 5.4 trillion in debt-to-equity conversions, a KRW 1.4 trillion debt write-off for Hynix, rate reductions and term extensions, and KRW 658 billion in new credit for Hynix. Hynix creditors who were opposed to providing new credits accepted conversion of existing debt into equity or zero-coupon bonds at a loss rate of close to 75 percent. See Lim (2002).

4

Chapter 5

Are More Restructuring Regimes Becoming Like the U.S. Chapter 11 System?

James H. Zukin, with the assistance of Alan Fragen and Dorian Lowell

This paper covers three topics concerning the global market for corporate restructuring. First, it presents the basic principles of reorganizations, the enabling infrastructure, and observations regarding the use of a Chapter 11–style reorganization system. Second, it discusses progress in the reform of restructuring regimes in industrial countries. And third, it examines how a Chapter 11–style system could be used in developing countries experiencing a systemic crisis as part of a recovery plan utilizing a process of rapid sequencing. An appendix addresses questions concerning the process of corporate restructuring.

Economies are Darwinian. They compete with each other, adopt best practices, and evolve. Just as capitalism overtook communism as the better system for maximizing wealth, procedures for rescuing distressed companies should overtake systems that focus on receiverships and liquidations at the expense of lower recoveries and the disenfranchisement of creditors. The prevalence of bankruptcy systems focusing on receiverships and liquidations reflects the historical emphasis on tangible property rights, the rights of secured creditors, and the realization of assets to discharge debts. But in modern economies, we talk of cash flows and enterprise values, values that typically exceed tangible asset values. Maximizing these values when companies are in distress demands more flexible solutions than those provided by receiverships and liquidations.

The primary role of a bankruptcy regime in a modern capitalist economy should be to encourage reorganizations that maximize value based on the premise that all stakeholders—creditors, shareholders, and employees—wish to maximize their economic recoveries and, which is equally important, wish to participate collectively in the reorganization.

Chapter 11

Chapter 11 is the chapter under Title 11 of the United States Bankruptcy Code providing for the reorganization of a company; other chapters deal with case administration, liquidation, and other related procedures. Reorganizing under Chapter 11 means allowing a company to survive as a going concern, maximizing enterprise and recovery values for creditors, and discharging old debts. It allows the company to survive and to take advantage of the second chance afforded. It is not a liquidation or a receivership for the benefit of secured creditors.

Chapter 11 has seven basic objectives: (a) stabilize business operations, (b) finance the business after the commencement of insolvency, (c) maximize the value of business operations, (d) provide for the representation of unsecured creditors, (e) provide a central forum for creditors to exercise remedies, (f) allow a plan of reorganization to be proposed based on an objective valuation of the post-reorganized enterprise, and (g) provide a framework for formulating and approving a plan of reorganization. These can be summed up as efforts to "stop the madness," encourage creditor coordination, and use reasonable valuations.

The Chapter 11 process, and corporate restructuring in general, operates most efficiently when the parties involved adhere to the following basic principles: during a standstill period, (a) creditors should cooperate with each other and give the debtor time to resolve its financial difficulties, (b) creditors should refrain from taking action against the debtor, and the debtor should not take any action prejudicial to the creditors, (c) creditors should coordinate with the debtor, typically through a committee and through professional advisers appointed to assist the committee, and (d) the debtor should provide the creditors and their professional advisers with all information relevant to the process of evaluating its financial condition and any restructuring proposals. Moreover, (e) any proposal for resolving the debtor's financial difficulties should reflect applicable law and the creditors' relative positions; (f) all information should be made available to all relevant creditors and, unless public, be treated as confidential, and (g) any necessary additional funding should be accorded priority status for repayment.[1]

Chapter 11–style bankruptcy laws use four important measures to achieve efficient restructurings. A stay, or temporary moratorium, is imposed on creditor litigation and enforcement during the restructuring negotiations. Mechanisms are put in place to force responsible behavior by the debtor, in order to protect creditor interests during the period of the stay. New money is given priority for repayment, which is referred to as debtor-in-possession financing, to enable the debtor company to maintain liquidity during negotiations. Finally, to prevent a small minority of holdouts from disrupting the process, relevant creditors are bound to an agreement that has been accepted by a qualified majority, which is known as a cram down.

The Chapter 11 process has benefited from several refinements over time. Experience with repeated corporate restructurings has enabled the system to become routinized, so that much of the legal work is boilerplate. The use of standardized language and procedures improves efficiency and reduces professional fees by reducing time spent. Prearranged or prenegotiated (prepacked) bankruptcies are emerging in which debtors and creditors solicit court approval for agreed-on restructurings. Securities and Exchange Commission solicitation of a prepackaged plan of bankruptcy is also a new key technique. The sale of assets and going concerns before the resolution of inter-creditor bankruptcy issues is a key refinement of the system. A two-tier system has developed to distinguish cases on the basis of size and complexity. WorldCom is different from the insolvent corner grocery store, and its restructuring process should be different, too.

Despite these improvements, Chapter 11–style bankruptcies continue to suffer from important weaknesses. They tend to be costly. Time-based fees erode incentives for quick resolution. The legal procedures involved can be complex, which, coupled with overburdened court systems, can lead to substantial delays and encourage excess litigation by parties attempting to obstruct the process.

In many other jurisdictions, insolvency proceedings continue to emphasize receivership or liquidation, and proceedings are often dominated by politics or the courts. This suggests that business rescue is not the prevailing culture. For many countries, corporate insolvency is stigmatized as failure

5

and deserving of liquidation. It takes a fundamental change in thinking to see insolvency as an opportunity to preserve the firm as a going concern, recognizing that the value of the operating firm is usually higher than the return on selling the assets piecemeal. Essentially, the goal is to fix a bad balance sheet of a good business. Private investors in the international capital markets can help to change this approach. The distressed debt and hedge funds of today have proliferated in number and size. They see themselves as the catalysts of corporate renewal and have become highly sophisticated in using Chapter 11 to reallocate assets and capital.

A system that saves everything, such as one in which every insolvent company is recapitalized or restructured, is as problematic for an economy as one that liquidates everything. A good system clearly distinguishes between reorganization and liquidation and then provides an efficient process to guide execution of the approach taken.

Restructuring Regimes in Industrial Countries

Restructuring regimes in developed countries are diverse in their treatment of creditors and debtors, although some countries are moving toward a system comparable to Chapter 11. Of the four largest European economies, France has perhaps the least developed corporate rescue regime. Most insolvencies end in liquidation, and there is little appreciation for preserving value through corporate rescue. Employee and state interests take priority, debtor-in-possession financing is discouraged through lender liability known as *soutien abusive*, and insolvency procedures and the operations of the company are overseen by court-appointed officers. New insolvency legislation is under consideration, however. Under two proposed procedures—the *procedure de conciliation* and *procedure de saufegarde*—post-petition debt would have priority treatment over pre-petition debt, other than claims of the employees and the state. Nevertheless, the proposed law still has a long way to go to meet the basic principles found in Chapter 11 as well as the expectations of global institutional investors.

Germany passed a sophisticated insolvency act in 1999, modeled on Chapter 11, which has real potential to play a constructive role in German corporate rescues. The act provides for restructuring through a debt compromise plan (*insolvenzplan*). However, a debt-for-equity swap cannot be effected except through a decrease or increase in capital, requiring shareholder approval. Other highlights include the possibility (rarely used) of appointing a debtor-in-possession (*eigenverwaltung*), raising post-petition financing on a priority basis, imposing an automatic stay except for certain types of secured claims, establishing a creditor committee and subjecting material transactions to creditor approval, rejecting executory contracts, classifying creditors' claims and binding a class by majority voting, and providing for a cram down of impaired dissenting classes if they are not disadvantaged to a greater extent than they would be without a plan.

In Italy, the Parmalat insolvency proceeding has been a catalyst for modifying the so-called *prodi-bis* law of large corporate insolvencies governed by the *administrazione straordinaria*. Prior to Parmalat, the law was generally considered antithetical to creditor rights, due to political domination of the process and a lack of representation and transparency. Subsequent amendments provide for a *concordato* (compromise plan) with separate classification and treatment of claims, including debt-for-equity swaps and a cram-down mechanism, demonstrating the extent to which the government has sought to meet some of the concerns of the international capital markets. While the *administrazione straordinaria* is far from being as rescue-friendly as Chapter 11, the developments to date are encouraging.

Corporate restructuring in England and Wales is governed by the Enterprise Act of 2002, probably the most sophisticated regime in Europe. The regime is designed to facilitate the rescue of a company. An administrator acts for all creditors, with the objective of either rescuing the company as a going concern or achieving a better result for all creditors than through liquidation. The administrator may seek to dispose of assets for the benefit of secured creditors only if these objectives cannot be met. The act has some close parallels with Chapter 11: the company benefits from a moratorium of claims by creditors, the administrator must report regularly to a creditor meeting, and vote by a majority of creditors binds minorities. There is no provision for superpriority financing or for a cram down of holdouts, although each of these can, to some degree, be managed within the administration process.

Requirements of a Rapid-Sequencing Process in Developing Countries

An appropriate framework for corporate restructuring goes far beyond the efficient bankruptcy code afforded by a working Chapter 11–type system. To

5

promote recovery in a crisis-affected economy, it is essential to link together the restructuring and recapitalization of the financial and the corporate sectors, in what is called a rapid-sequencing restructuring of the economy. A rapid-sequencing process includes several aspects. A trained independent judiciary is necessary to adjudicate financial claims and bankruptcy. A working system of private property is required to protect creditor rights in default. Proper credit information systems are needed to enable creditors to evaluate borrowers. Banks need to base their lending decisions on creditworthiness and have a working system to monitor the solvency of debtors. A simplified Chapter 11 system should be in place. Functioning and professionally managed corporate restructuring vehicles should be available for each class of distressed assets. And, finally, countries have to be able to attract foreign direct investment. This system can be fully implemented only after a crisis, once values have stabilized.

Developing countries now subject to systemic distress vary widely in the progress made toward establishing an efficient restructuring regime. Argentina has implemented a new out-of-court mechanism, the *Acuerdo Preventivo Extrajudicial*, to facilitate the resolution of corporate bankruptcies, and the corporate sector has made progress in restructuring. Brazil has the critical economic mass and infrastructure capacity to implement a Chapter 11 system that includes all components of a rapid-sequencing process. However, the current *concordata*, a two-year moratorium on paying unsecured creditors, has not created an efficient restructuring process. Indonesia continues to suffer under enduring issues of corruption at a few large debtors, although the economic recovery indicates that systemic distress may be temporary. In the Republic of Korea, full corporate financial restructuring with significant deleveraging is just now occurring, and nonperforming loans and debt levels are rising. Mexico, an investment-grade country, is a clear emerging-market leader in restructuring. The restructuring-oriented law, *Ley de Concursos Mercantiles*, may speed up the workout process. Finally, Russia has good laws governing corporate restructuring, but they often are not used, in part due to a lack of expertise. This underlines the importance to successful corporate restructuring of adequate capacity, in addition to a reasonable legal framework.

The Merits of a Chapter 11 System for Countries

Techniques perfected in complex corporate restructurings may be transferable to sovereign debt situations. In particular, a successful process should seek to resolve all classes of creditor claims simultaneously and transparently. Any plan for restructuring sovereign debt should be feasible from a commercial point of view, should consider the country's ability to generate foreign exchange, and should take into account internal and external factors that may affect future cash flows. Such an approach works in the business world and is considerably different from the piecemeal approach typically employed to restructure sovereign obligations. The Paris Club and London Club procedures may provide the basis for such a process if they become more routine and coordinated.

The most practical and broadly acceptable reform to facilitate future sovereign debt restructurings would be a commitment by sovereign borrowers to put a package of new clauses—called collective action clauses—into all future sovereign debt contracts. The clauses are intended to create a more orderly and predictable workout process and should describe as precisely as possible what happens when a country decides to restructure its debt.

Collective action clauses would improve communication among parties, by providing for the election of a bondholder representative as interlocutor with the sovereign. The representative would be empowered to engage in restructuring discussions with the sovereign without undue delay. Collective action clauses would enable parties to change the terms on debt, without a small minority of debt holders obstructing the process. Typically, a supermajority (for example, 75 percent) of bondholders could amend the terms of payment (including an exchange of the bonds for new instruments), without counting bonds controlled by the sovereign issuer or its public sector. Properly designed, these clauses also would limit the ability of individual creditors to disrupt a workout through legal action: a minimum of 25 percent of bondholders should be required to accelerate repayments, and a majority (with a maximum of two-thirds) should be required to decelerate them; the power to initiate litigation should be granted to the bondholder representative, with individual enforcement explicitly prohibited; and any proceeds recovered by a bondholder should be distributed pro rata.[2]

Several proposals have been put forward to improve the sovereign restructuring process. The International Monetary Fund (IMF) has presented a detailed sovereign bankruptcy scheme (the sovereign debt restructuring

5

mechanism) that has played a useful role in framing the debate on alterative approaches to restructuring. The mechanism includes many admirable features, including majority rule for sovereign debt holders. However, the IMF plan would limit inclusion in the mechanism to debt held by external private creditors. This approach fails to recognize that in a sovereign debt restructuring all preexisting debt has the same legal entitlements. It is difficult to achieve a consensus among private creditors unless all similarly situated creditors, including internal debt, are subject to burden sharing.[3]

The Institute of International Finance, representing 300 lenders (including London Club members) has called on the IMF to endorse guidelines to improve the way debt is restructured once governments default. Prompt negotiations, the formation of creditor committees, and enforceable contracts would accelerate the debt restructuring process and maintain market confidence.[4] The proposal would also limit IMF involvement in country restructurings, while calling for general systemic improvements.

There is some potential to expand the role of the Paris Club in sovereign debt restructurings. This unique organization of sovereign creditors, which seeks to restructure sovereign debtors facing financial distress, is a likely candidate for the role of lead creditor in a comprehensive settlement of sovereign debts. Paris Club members, working with the IMF, have the opportunity to create incentives for global investors to abide by consensual plans that gain support from an appropriate majority. Such incentives could include honoring local laws that tax the excess profits of holdouts in certain extreme circumstances. In the future, a mediation forum could develop in Paris that would seek to resolve all classes of sovereign creditor claims simultaneously.

The Banque de France has identified six main principles that could guide a sovereign restructuring process: (a) early and regular dialogue is needed, based on trust among debtors and creditors; (b) interested parties should ensure that fair information-sharing mechanisms are in place; (c) a fair representation of creditors is critical to reaching agreement on the terms of restructuring; (d) specific procedures should ensure comparable treatment among creditors; (e) an efficient renegotiation process should primarily aim to enhance or restore, as soon as possible, a country's debt sustainability over the medium term; (f) participants should be committed to negotiating in good faith (the debtor should minimize the cost incurred by creditors and enforce contracts for as long as possible, consistent with restoring debt sustainability, while creditors should recognize that a debt restructuring might require a write-off of claims).

Conclusions

Chapter 11–type restructuring concepts are important and spreading. They are critical to effect turnarounds instead of liquidation, which can help both the company and the economy as a whole, and to attract new capital, which is required for effective restructuring. The trend toward Chapter 11 around the world is accelerating and maturing. Capacity building will be critical to the success of these new systems. The basic principles of Chapter 11 restructurings can and should be made applicable to sovereign debt restructuring.

5

Appendix 5.1: Questions and Answers on the Current Sovereign Restructuring Process

Is it feasible to create different sovereign securities for official creditors, private creditors, and new investors?

Clearly the answer is yes. A menu approach to debt restructuring is common: the Venezuela sovereign debt restructuring in 1989–90 offered discount bonds, par bonds, and "step-down, step-up bonds," and Argentina is now proposing a menu of comparable bonds (equivalent in present value terms) in different currencies, including discount bonds, par bonds with low coupons and longer maturities, and C bonds, which may capitalize interest. This menu approach suits the needs of creditors that expect different types of securities. For example, it appears that in a number of Brady bond transactions the securities designed by bank advisory committees were collateralized in ways to satisfy commercial bank regulatory requirements that non-bank investors considered unnecessary. Holders of sovereign bonds being exchanged for new bonds may be more focused on ratings, yield, secondary market pricing, and features that could improve the credit, as compared to sovereign creditors, financial institutions, and commercial banks.

Is it realistic to bring together all creditor groups for a multiparty meeting in Paris?

While sovereign lenders (the Paris Club), multilateral agencies (the IMF and World Bank), and commercial banks (the London Club) are institutionally structured to coordinate and negotiate with a sovereign debtor, the question is the extent to which bondholders and private trade and corporate creditors can be expected to participate. Bonds are widely held, difficult to organize, and suffer from an agency problem: Who will represent a group in which holders constantly change? Formation of a representative committee requires principals who would be willing to participate for a significant period of time and refrain from trading in the credit (to prevent a conflict of interest). Persuading creditors to participate in multiparty meetings may be best pursued through incentives that make a negotiated outcome more attractive than pursuing private legal actions. Such incentives could include a forum with protocols providing for transparency and due process that would seek to emulate the procedural aspects of a bankruptcy court. Over time, countries could be bound to this forum, for example, as a condition of IMF membership.

The question remains as to what pressure, if any, can be brought to bear on bondholders who are reluctant to participate in the forum. A sovereign debtor has the choice of negotiating with bondholders or presenting them with a take-it-or-leave-it offer. In 1993 Russia negotiated with a committee that included bondholders; in 1994 Ecuador set up a consultative committee to solicit views on issues relevant to an exchange offer; and in 1999 Pakistan contacted privately some of its largest eurobond holders to seek their views, and a unilateral exchange offer was then made. Argentina is now consulting with four institutional consulting groups representing institutional and individual investors. It would seem that, while a failure to attend multiparty meetings may result in less input in designing an exchange offer, precedent suggests that attendance may not be critical in effecting a successful offer (although Argentina appears to be facing significant bondholder opposition). In the final analysis, bondholder participation cannot be assured and becomes an issue related to the larger question of how to deal with holdouts, whether through treaties, domestic legislation, collective action clauses, sharing clauses, or exit consents.

Is it possible to bring new money from the private sector into a country restructuring, to be invested in sovereign securities collateralized by nonperforming loans removed from the banking sector?

The market has, to a certain extent, been conditioned by previous sovereign debt restructurings and the treatment of claims through various collateralized instruments, including debt-for-debt exchanges for Brady bonds backed by U.S. treasuries and for bonds backed by recovery rights or warrants (such as oil revenues) and debt-for-equity swaps. In theory, whether there is an appetite for new money to be placed in nonperforming loan–backed bonds will depend on the quality of the collateral and administration of the portfolio. If the portfolio of nonperforming loans is appropriately structured, valued, and administered and the securities receive an investment-grade rating and are competitively priced, then in principle the securities should be an attractive investment. However, in practice such a collateralized debt obligation may be difficult to structure and administer in an emerging-market economy without some kind of additional credit enhancement, such as a third-party guarantee (for example, from a multilateral agency) or a source of foreign exchange revenue (for example, oil).

How can the time frame to effect a sovereign debt restructuring be shortened?

Absent a forum with protocols that can impose a binding timetable, different creditors move at different speeds, and the process can only move as fast as the slowest constituency. The Paris Club is institutionally disciplined and structured to reach consensus on an expedited basis. London Club restructurings with large bank groups have taken longer, possibly because of coordination problems that arise because the portfolios are booked at face value and banks have been reluctant to take immediate write-downs. Bondholders make for a difficult group to organize and negotiate with, although they tend to be sophisticated (especially secondary market holders), can move more quickly than other creditors, and are interested in maximizing their returns in the shortest time. The factors that drive the timetable include due diligence and claims analysis, the negotiation process, dispute resolution, implementation of macroeconomic reform plans, and the formulation, documentation, and implementation of plans. A faster and more efficient approach to sovereign debt restructuring is also dependent on each creditor class negotiating in parallel rather than in sequence.

What are the prospects and pitfalls of GDP-linked debt?

Economists tend to see growth-indexed debt as a sensible way to provide insurance for a country and to facilitate international risk sharing. Government officials in Latin America at recent economic summits have promoted the idea, and the response from several members of the Group of Seven (G-7) industrialized countries, notably the United States, has been positive.

GDP-linked debt also has been discussed in the context of sovereign debt restructuring. However, investors who would have to buy the debt have tended to be cool about the idea because of concerns about the illiquidity of such markets and the reliability of statistics emerging-market countries' growth statistics.

Issuing growth-indexed bonds could help to reduce a country's vulnerability to external shocks that lead to lower growth. In a rich economy, if economic growth slows, then governments tend to reduce taxes, raise spending, or both. Emerging markets, however, can be forced to raise taxes and cut spending to maintain market confidence and to meet interest payments.

Past attempts to issue GDP-linked debt—in Bulgaria and Costa Rica, among others—had very limited success in large part because the debt contracts were poorly designed. Further information and related topics are discussed in International Monetary Fund (2004).

Reference

The word "processed" describes informally produced works that may not be commonly available through libraries.

International Monetary Fund. 2004. "Sovereign Debt Structure for Crisis Prevention." Research Department, Washington, D.C., July 2. Processed.

Johnson, Gordon. 2001. "The World Bank Principles and Guidelines for Effective Insolvency and Creditor Rights Systems." World Bank Institute, Washington, D.C. April. Available at www.worldbank.org/ifa/ipg_eng.pdf. Processed.

Notes

1. For a detailed discussion on this topic, see Johnson (2001).
2. From in-depth work undertaken by a G10 Working Group chaired by R. Quarles of the U.S. Treasury.
3. The IMF states that its own debt is excluded from the sovereign debt restructuring mechanism because the IMF lends precisely at the point where other creditors are reluctant to do so and at interest rates below those offered by the private sector. The IMF helps countries to catalyze private financing and to avoid disorderly adjustment and policies that would harm themselves, private creditors, and other countries. In the IMF's view, putting IMF claims together with commercial claims in a workout would fundamentally undermine its capacity to play that vital role in the future. However, bondholders view treating the claims of multilateral agencies differently than other claims as discriminatory and inequitable. Argentina appears to be facing this problem, to the extent

that bondholder treatment involves taking a haircut, while IMF claims are simply rescheduled.

4. Institute of International Finance statement of April 8, 2004 (www.iif. com).

5

Chapter 6

The Successful Asset Management Companies

Ruth L. Neyens, Dató Zukri Samat, Beom Choi, Yang Kaisheng, and Shinjiro Takagi

In a situation of economic and financial crisis, banks distracted by the need to manage nonperforming loans may not be able to focus on their core activities, and financial intermediation may break down. In addition, the banking landscape—fragmented banks with no special powers; the presence of one borrower, but many bankers; existing bankruptcy and foreclosure laws that slow the pace of recovery—may hinder the restructuring process. An added dimension is the existence of moral hazard: banks confronted with a systemic crisis and shrinking capital are not willing to write off losses. Asset management companies are one solution to the problem of nonperforming loans.

Asset management companies are established to acquire nonperforming loans from financial institutions with the objective of recovering value from their resolution or disposal. Most asset management companies are designed to suit the national situation, and the organization of a particular company needs to be practical and solution oriented. Usually they are set up to respond to the collapse of banking institutions or the eminent collapse of the banking system—for example, in the case of RTC and Securum. Asset management companies, together with a recapitalization agency, can contribute to banking sector restructuring.

The operations of an asset management company reflect a continuum of operations. Rapid disposition agencies are most effective when the pool of investors in nonperforming loans is large, the number of accounts is large, and a quick disposition is required. A true asset management company performs best when the number of accounts is manageable, when the non-performing loans are structural in nature, and when the asset management company has the wherewithal to resolve nonperforming loans. Asset management companies remove nonperforming loans from the banking system, minimize the side effects on the real economy, offer a holistic, organized, and focused approach to the resolution of nonperforming loans, break the links between corporations and banks, impose uniform valuation of assets, exercise special powers, and realize economies of scale. In summary, asset management companies are a potent force in dealing with nonperforming loans, provided they suit the national situation, are practical and solution oriented, and take steps to enhance their operating environment. However, a cautionary note is warranted. Asset management companies must be made finite-life organizations and not be allowed to perpetuate themselves.

In this chapter, representatives of four asset management companies—Malaysia's Danaharta, Korea's KAMCO, China's Huarong Asset Management Company, and Japan's Industrial Revitalization Committee of the Industrial Revitalization Corporation—discuss their activities. They share their experiences, including the challenges they faced, the solutions they adopted, and the results they achieved. They also evaluate what worked and what did not.

The Role and Progress of Danaharta, Malaysia, *Dató Zukri Samat*

Danaharta is neither a rapid disposition agency nor a warehouse agency. Rather, it is a nonperforming loan resolution agency created to manage logistics and resolve cases on an individual basis. Danaharta has taken over approximately 3,000 accounts with more than RM 5 million in nonperforming loans. Danaharta's objectives are to remove the distraction of nonperforming loans and maximize the recovery value of acquired assets. Danaharta has a distinct role to play in the overall strategy adopted to restructure the banking sector in Malaysia, which created complementary roles for Danaharta and Danamodal.[1]

The principles guiding Danaharta are systemwide carve-out of nonperforming loans, a market-driven approach, and a formal asset management process. Danaharta progressed through several planning phases. First, a governance structure was established; second, Danaharta generated corporate information; and, finally, the Danaharta Act of 1998 was passed, authorizing Danaharta to acquire and manage nonperforming loans and to foreclose (according to the National Land Code). The act provided the *ability to acquire* nonperforming loans through a statutory vesting process that provided for clear title and preservation of third-party claims. The act also provided the *ability to manage* nonperforming loans by sanctioning the appointment of special administrators[2] and granting a 12-month stay on claims. The special administrator takes over control and management of the company, and the resulting proposed workout is reviewed by an independent adviser and approved by secured creditors. As of February 18, 2004, Danaharta had appointed special administrators across 72 groups (123 companies), with 33 groups of companies still at various stages of special administration.

There are six stages of special administration. The Danaharta Act of 1998 provides the ability to foreclose on collateral, covering the protection of property, foreclosure through private sale, the need to give 30-day notice to borrowers, the ability to bypass the court auction process, and a transparent and market-driven process.

Danaharta is committed to transparency and disclosure in its operations. It discloses business plans and operational guidelines, issues half-yearly operational reports, and provides frequent media and analyst updates, such as press releases, parliamentary replies, and annual as well as topical reports. The act requires public announcements—for example, public notices on the appointment of special administrators and independent advisers. Finally, Danaharta maintains an updated and extensive website.

Danaharta has acquired nonperforming loans with a gross market value in excess of RM 5 million, as determined by professional appraisers. The value of secured loans is determined according to collateral value. Unsecured loans are acquired at 10 percent of the outstanding loan. Danaharta enters into a profit-sharing agreement with the financial institutions for recoveries in excess of the acquisition value, with 80 percent going to the financial institutions.

A triage process determines which loans are viable. Danaharta's objective is to restructure viable loans according to Danaharta's published loan

Table 6.1. Expected Recovery of Danharta in Malaysia, by Method

(billions of ringgit unless otherwise noted)

Method of recovery	Adjusted loan recovery rate (a)	Adjusted expected recovery (b)	Expected recovery rate (percent) (c) = (b) / (a)
Plain loan restructuring	7.63	6.11	80
Settlement	9.37	7.59	81
Schemes of arrangement	9.77	7.19	74
Schemes under special administration	5.32	2.24	42
Foreclosure	14.36	4.86	34
Others	4.74	2.64	56
Legal action	1.25	—	—
Overall	52.44	30.63	58

— Not available.

6

restructuring principles and guidelines.[3] Loan management follows a standard market-driven process.[4] The restructuring of viable loans could be informal (rescheduling, redemption, or settlement) or formal (appointment of a special administrator). The restructuring of nonviable loans resulted in the sale of collateral (foreclosure, liquidation) or the sale of the business special administrator via a bidding process. Foreign loans were invariably disposed via auction.

Danaharta's portfolio is RM 47.70 billion (RM 19.73 billion acquired and RM 27.97 managed) and involves 2,564 borrowers.[5] Danaharta's expected recovery rate is a remarkable 58 percent (see table 6.1).

Korea Asset Management Corporation: The Host of Restructuring Vehicles Tried in Korea, *Beom Choi*

Korea Asset Management Corporation (KAMCO) was established on November 23, 1997, and started operations immediately. KAMCO's role in the restructuring process had multiple objectives: to minimize the public burden and early recovery of public money, to provide liquidity to the financial sector and assist in the restructuring of financial institutions, to revitalize the Korean economy, to resolve nonperforming loans (secured or unsecured loans currently in default for three months or longer), and to restore stability to the corporate sector.

KAMCO also provided loans to companies under private workout programs, in which creditors agreed to restructure distressed assets, and to companies under court receivership or composition proceedings, whether their loans were secured or unsecured. KAMCO's portfolio consisted of classified loans (28 percent), corporate loans under court restructuring (38 percent), and corporate loans under workout (34 percent).[6] KAMCO had few residential mortgages.

KAMCO analyzed nonperforming loans according to the following principles and policies. The guiding strategy was to provide speedy and loss-minimizing resolution through efficient management, transparent procedures, and fair transactions. During rehabilitation, KAMCO suspended legal actions and foreclosure, lent working capital, engaged in debt-to-equity swaps, provided payment guarantees, and purchased discount notes.[7]

In the disposition phase, KAMCO deployed a range of financial techniques such as portfolio sales, securitization, public sales, foreclosure sales, individual loan sales, and rescheduling to facilitate recovery by the borrower. It also offered the debtor a discount on the outstanding principal balance (essentially, a write-off of debt) and a lower interest rate, extending the payment maturity.[8]

KAMCO used several structures to encourage the participation of private external equity: joint ventures, corporate restructuring companies, asset management companies (special-purpose companies), and corporate restructuring vehicles. KAMCO sold portfolios of loans to various purchasers through several financial structures: bulk sale to joint venture special-purpose companies, bulk sale to joint venture corporate restructuring companies, bulk sale to third-party special-purpose companies, sale of individual loans, sale to joint venture corporate restructuring vehicles,[9] and, finally, outright sale to third-party investors. Table 6.2 compares the three vehicles: corporate restructuring companies, corporate restructuring vehicles, and special-purpose companies (asset management companies).

Corporate restructuring vehicles, which are unique to Korea, exemplify the challenge of designing solutions to the Asian crisis.[10] The initiative was motivated by several considerations: the massive scale of distressed corporations, the desire to control the public sector costs of financial sector restructuring, and the emphasis on creating private sector infrastructure to encour-

Table 6.2: Characteristics of Three Workout Vehicles Used in Korea

Characteristic	Corporate restructuring companies	Corporate restructuring vehicles	Special-purpose companies (asset management companies)
Foundation act	Industry development law or venture capital license	Corporate restructuring investment company law, October 2000	Asset securitization law
Legal entity	Independent company	Paper company (limited life)	Paper company
Paid-in capital	KRW 7 billion	KRW 500 million	KRW 10 million
Manager role	Self-managed	Specialized manager with paid-in capital of KRW 2 billion	Specialized manager with paid-in capital of KRW 1 billion
Sponsor	None	More than three sponsors, including two or more creditors	Cash investor
Target assets	Wide portfolio: all corporate assets for restructuring	Single credit: workout company debts and swapped shares only	Wide portfolio: All pursuant to securitization law
Mandatory restructuring business	20 percent of assets to be sold within seven years	100 percent mandatory, within five-year life (one year extendable)	Optional

6

age restructuring rather than direct or enforce it. Corporate restructuring vehicles have the following features: focus on viable medium and large companies, active management of target companies, ability to raise debt or equity financing from qualified institutional investors (but not from the general public), licensing by the Ministry of Finance and the Economy, and oversight by the Financial Services Commission. Corporate restructuring vehicles were intended to offer specialists and investment managers incentives to manage and realize the value of assets acquired from the banks in a more efficient and effective manner and to combine the holdings of separate creditors to realize the benefits of concentration and control. Corporate restructuring vehicles offer private sector–funded solutions to corporate distress, flexibility for banks, investors, and regulators, and solutions that complement the traditional asset management companies.

The structure of one company per one corporate restructuring vehicle was intended to avoid complicated multi-debtor, multi-creditor status of the corporate restructuring vehicle. The corporate restructuring vehicle asset management company was expected to possess expertise and experience in mergers, acquisitions, and workouts. As a limited-life company, corporate restructuring vehicles enjoyed tax and leverage advantages. KAMCO and banks sell loans or shares (acquired by swap) and in return receive cash or shares. The joint venture between creditors and third-party investors was intended to accelerate the rate of restructuring in Korea by passing the authority for workouts from commercial banks to experts in corporate restructuring. A perceived benefit of the corporate restructuring vehicle was the ability of creditor banks to dispose of equity acquired during debt-for-equity swaps.[11]

Despite the virtues, corporate restructuring vehicles were not well received in Korea, and only three to four transactions took place. However, other countries can learn from Korea's experience. The large positive aspects—going-concern value higher than liquidation value; financial and management burden taken away from the banking sector; more efficient allocation of resources; improved prospects to realize values; supportive tax treatment of debt-equity swaps and the corporate restructuring vehicle;[12] non-cash forms of consideration (paper debt) that provide accounting flexibility—led to acceptance and commitment on the part of financial authorities, investment advisers, and investors. Yet the benefits were overshadowed by the negative aspects: a challenging new legal structure; difficulty motivating banks to realize losses on sale; loss of bank control over the restructuring process and the client relationship; difficulty of employing "transfer pricing" in terms of a valuation methodology for loans and debt; finally, in the absence of the threat of court-imposed loss, a lack of incentives for corporate debtors to agree to the draconian measures, such as asset sales, equity dilution, and diminution of management control, necessary to transfer a corporation to a corporate restructuring vehicle.

As a result, corporate restructuring vehicles did not gain wide acceptance during the restructuring. In retrospect, why were the vehicles difficult to implement, and what can other countries learn from the process? Foremost, underprovisioned creditors were reluctant to assign loans to corporate restructuring vehicles and realize loss. Further, senior creditors were reluctant to give up their seniority and be treated pari passu with other rights holders. Guarantors of loans similarly resisted the transfer of loans to a corporate restructuring vehicle as they would have had to fulfill their liabilities earlier than under the usual process of loan restructuring. Finally, it was difficult to designate a paid asset manager among multiple leading creditors. As a result of the objections, holdout creditors requested cash to exit and undermined the structure of corporate restructuring vehicles.

China's Huarong Asset Management Company, *Yang Kaisheng*

China's Huarong Asset Management Company has been resolving non-performing loans for the past three years. This is part of China's effort to develop a more efficient banking and financial system to prepare Chinese banks to compete with international banks when full integration of China into the World Trade Organization is accomplished in 2007.

China's Banking Reform

China's bank reform measures include actively reducing nonperforming loans, cleaning up balance sheets, strengthening credit underwriting, and moving toward international accounting standards. Additionally, China's banks are installing new internal rating-based credit analysis and stricter lending policies as well corporate governance practices aligned with international best practices. Although the full implementation of these will take time, China's success has been measurable. The four state-owned commercial banks reduced their ratio of nonperforming loans from 26 percent in 2002 to 20 percent in 2003. Clearly, the banks are on target to achieve the mandate of the central bank and the China Banking and Regulatory Commission (CBRC) regarding the reduction of nonperforming loans. At the end of 2003, China announced that it would inject $45 billion of its foreign exchange reserves into two of China's four largest banks. The government's goal under this pilot program is to convert both the Bank of China and China Construction Bank into joint stock banks. Each received a $22.5 billion capital injection to prepare for initial public offerings scheduled in the following two years. This is just one of the many methods that China is using to accelerate financial reforms, reduce the ratio of nonperforming loans, and bolster capital ratios so as to better compete with foreign banks.

In April 2003, the State Council created CBRC in order to separate the regulation of banks and routine management reviews from the central bank. This regulatory agency is already making positive changes. In December

6

2003, it announced that single foreign banks may have up to a 20 percent strategic interest in a Chinese bank. It announced that, beginning in 2004, all commercial banks in China are required to use a new five-category loan classification system, which is based on stricter, internationally accepted standards. These examples illustrate the most recent initiatives taken by the Chinese government to accelerate and strengthen financial system reform.

Asset Management Companies

In 1999 the four largest Chinese banks transferred $170 billion in nonperforming assets to four asset management companies. The four asset management companies have been very successful in resolving China's nonperforming loans. At the end of 2003, they had resolved 41 percent of their nonperforming loans by recovering, on average, almost 20 percent cash of book value. With headquarters in Beijing and 30 branch offices throughout China, Huarong is the largest of the four asset management companies and among the top-performing asset management companies in the world.

Established in late 1999, Huarong acquired more than $50 billion of nonperforming loans from the Industrial and Commercial Bank of China. The daily tasks are closely tied to the purchase, management, and disposal of nonperforming assets. The primary goal is to maximize the recovery value. In order to quickly implement the business plans, the Ministry of Finance injected each asset management company with paid-in capital totaling $1.2 billion.

Asset resolution and collections are the core business of an asset management company. Huarong's special legal status and broad business scope have enabled it to use various resolution strategies and collection techniques. The resolution techniques include revised repayment plans with borrowers, discounted borrower payoffs, debt-to-equity swaps, collateral sales, litigation, and sales of nonperforming loans to third-party investors (either as a single asset or as a portfolio). The most common technique is discounted pay-off with borrowers. The ability to forgive partial debt is a major legal advantage that asset management companies have over state-owned commercial banks. Presently, to prevent moral hazard, state-owned commercial banks are prohibited from granting debt forgiveness to borrowers. The law gives asset management companies special legal powers to resolve assets at less than their book value. Over the past four years, Huarong has resolved

6

more than $16.6 billion in nonperforming loans. The average asset recovery rate is 32 percent, and the cash recovery rate is approximately 21 percent.

Huarong has four key principles for managing asset resolutions:

- *Be fair, open, and transparent.* Huarong adheres to these principles in order to explain its activities, explain the market-driven approach, and remain an impartial debt collector.
- *Utilize competition to optimize recovery.* Through competition, Huarong maximizes the market pricing of its nonperforming loans. Huarong stimulates competition during the sale of nonperforming loans by bringing more investors to the market, comparing historical internal recovery rates with competitive bids, and using various joint venture deal structures.
- *Employ checks and balances in management.* To avoid technical failings and moral hazard, Huarong has standardized asset resolution procedures within the framework of government rules and regulations. For instance, it has two separate committees for managing nonperforming loans. One committee is responsible for asset evaluation and pricing, while a separate committee is responsible for final approval of the asset resolution strategy. All asset resolutions must follow established approval procedures, which are guided by collective decisionmaking and authorization.
- *Obtain an optimal balance between high recovery and fast resolution.* The four asset management companies have more than $100 billion in nonperforming loans waiting for resolution. The assets vary by type of industry, location, operating status, and availability of collateral. Huarong quickly assesses the different factors that influence asset value, such as quality, timing, market conditions, and legal issues. For example, Huarong takes measures as quickly as possible to collect assets that are likely to depreciate in value. But Huarong manages assets that have future upside potential until a reasonable market value can be obtained.

Since the loans transferred to Huarong from the Industrial and Commercial Bank of China were underwritten years ago and most of the borrowers had already defaulted, a longer holding period usually results in poor asset quality and lower recoverability. In order to increase the speed of asset resolution, Huarong embraced a strategy of bulk sale transactions beginning in 2001.

Huarong was the first asset management company in China to sell a large portfolio of nonperforming loans to foreign investors. In that transaction, it auctioned a portfolio of $1.5 billion in nonperforming loans to two groups of international investors: a Morgan Stanley–led consortium and Goldman Sachs. More important, it resolved the regulatory and policy issues that had prevented foreign investors from participating in China's nonperforming loan market. When this transaction took place in 2001, it was a pioneering effort in China's financial reform. With the momentum from this first international auction, Huarong launched a second international auction in December 2003, with a portfolio totaling $3 billion in nonperforming loans involving more than 1,900 borrowers in China. The assets were placed into 22 investment units based on geographic location to appeal to both international and domestic investors; 19 international and domestic investors registered to bid in this transaction. To date, Huarong has negotiated a memorandum of understanding on more than half of the 22 units with several international and domestic investors.

In the first half of 2003, Huarong piloted a Quasi-Nonperforming Loan Securitization Program for a portfolio of nonperforming loans with a face value of $1.3 billion. Under the structure, Huarong cooperates with a trust company in forming an asset securitization trust. With the help of a third-party appraiser and a rating firm, the assets are evaluated. Then the assets are stratified into two classes—preferred and subordinated—based on the level of expected future cash flows. Finally, through the trust company, the interest in the preferred class is transferred to investors. It is not a "true" securitization because China still faces numerous implementation challenges, including legal, accounting, and supervisory obstacles, that limit bona fide securitizations, but it has been rewarding to push the securitization concept and creatively manage a transaction within the existing legal framework. Huarong continues to explore the creative aspects of resolution strategies and methodologies with the objective of maximizing the recovery of nonperforming loans.

Restructuring Approaches Used in Japan, *Shinjiro Takagi*

The past decade of slow economic growth has had a severe impact on Japanese financial institutions: 178 financial institutions went bankrupt between April 1992 and March 2003, and nonperforming loans increased sharply. According to the National Bankers Association, total nonperforming loans of Japanese banks reached a peak of approximately ¥40 trillion in March 2002, before falling to about ¥28 trillion by September 2003. At the peak, nonperforming loans equaled less than 10 percent of total loans. Nonperforming loans in small and medium-size financial institutions (including regional banks) remain high, although the nonperforming loans of major city banks have fallen. At the end of October 2002, the Japanese government set as a goal the halving of financial institutions' nonperforming loans by the end of March 2006.

Since publication of a white paper on the economy and finance in October 2003 (which reported slow economic growth), economic news has been encouraging. Exports (particularly to the United States and China) have increased, as has cyclical demand for investment to refurbish machines and facilities. However, it is difficult to say whether the recovery is sustainable. In addition, deflation is expected to continue, although recent statistics indicate some easing of the rate of price declines. Thus the economy could return to sluggish growth, or worse, in the second half of 2004, in the absence of an effective reform of the economic structure.

Japan has taken measures to address the level of nonperforming loans in the banking system, including reforms to the rules governing corporate reorganizations, establishment of the Industrial Revitalization Corporation of Japan, and steps by major banks to improve their workout procedures.

Improvements in the Legal Structure for Corporate Reorganizations

Two statutory reorganization proceedings and an out-of-court workout scheme have been established to reorganize distressed business corporations with excessive debts:

- A civil rehabilitation proceeding enacted in 1999 (which abolished the former composition law of 1927), designed for small and middle-size enterprises[13]
- A reform of the 1951 corporate reorganization law in December 2002, designed for large corporations[14]
- An out-of-court guideline established by the National Bankers Association and other relevant organizations in 2001 referring to the INSOL-8 principles.[15]

Major differences between the civil rehabilitation and corporate reorganization concern the rights of secured creditors and the ability of debtors to continue operating the business under reorganization. Under the rules for corporate reorganization, the rights of secured creditors are stayed, and secured claims can be impaired under the reorganization plan, provided it is accepted by a majority. However, under the rules for civil rehabilitation, the rights of secured creditors are neither stayed nor changed without consent of the individual secured creditor (with some exceptions). Also, under corporate reorganizations, incumbent managers are, in principle, to be replaced by a trustee (although the court can appoint an incumbent manager, or managers, as a trustee or deputy trustee). By contrast, under civil rehabilitation, a debtor is not deprived of its right to operate the business and dispose of its assets (again, with some exceptions).

The biggest defect of both types of proceedings is that the rights of unsecured claims of trade creditors and of financial creditors have to be treated equally, in general. The "first-day" order utilized in U.S. Chapter 11 proceedings, which may allow firms to pay the claims of trade creditors in full, is not available. Failure to pay trade credit claims can severely impair the reputation of the firm and reduce the enterprise value of the debtor corporation. Thus, even if almost all banks agree to a reorganization plan through an out-of-court workout, it may not be practical to convert this agreement to a statutory proceeding (to cram down stubborn minority creditors) without causing trade creditors to accept losses pari passu with the banks. Japanese courts should be more flexible in enforcing the principle of equality of unsecured claims, to take into account the need to maintain trade finance.

The guideline for out-of-court workouts is a useful tool for reorganizing the financial structure of a debtor corporation with excessive debts owed to many banks and other financial institutions at the early stage without impairing the claims of trade creditors. Approximately 20 big cases have been resolved using the guideline so far. The biggest defect of the guideline is that the consent of all financial creditors subject to debt forgiveness or debt-for-equity swaps in the proposed plan is required. No compulsory power exists to induce creditors to accept the plan.

Along with the reform of the law, the practices involved in bankruptcy and reorganization cases are changing dramatically, led by the Tokyo and Osaka district courts. Almost all the courts in Japan are accepting reorganization cases, and the cases are being handled more expeditiously. For example, in 2002 almost 10 times as many civil rehabilitation cases were filed in

6

the Tokyo district court as composition cases under the former composition law. Previously, judges were reluctant to begin composition and corporate reorganization cases where the prospect of a successful rehabilitation was uncertain.

Corporate reorganization cases are handled more expeditiously now. In most civil cases in Tokyo, a rehabilitation plan is confirmed by court within approximately six months after a petition is filed initiating the case. Corporate reorganization cases, which are larger than civil rehabilitation cases, are dealt with more rapidly as well.

The Industrial Revitalization Corporation of Japan

The Japanese government established the Industrial Revitalization Corporation of Japan (IRCJ) in April 2003. Its purpose is to reduce non-performing and poorly performing loans by purchasing loans owed to banks other than the main bank(s) and by helping large corporations with excessive debt to restore their profitability. IRCJ purchases loans owed by distressed debtor companies that are viable and therefore likely to be successfully rehabilitated. Before deciding to help a troubled debtor corporation, IRCJ and the main bank(s) carefully review the feasibility of the reorganization plan proposed by the corporation. In order to assist them in this program, IRCJ engages suitably experienced and qualified professionals, including consultants, accountants, lawyers, and restructuring advisers. The decision to help includes IRCJ's declared intention to buy loans at a designated price from banks other than the main bank(s). Creditor banks are legally obliged neither to sell their debts to IRCJ nor to accept a proposed debt restructuring plan that provides for partial release of debts or debt-for-equity swaps.

IRCJ was established to complement efforts by the Resolution and Collection Corporation (RCC) to assist banks to reduce their nonperforming loans. RCC was established several years ago for the express purpose of buying nonperforming and subperforming loans from financial institutions and then collecting the debts purchased. In addition, RCC advises distressed debtors about restructuring their debt and business by means of out-of-court workouts, civil rehabilitation, and corporate reorganization proceedings.

While RCC may buy debts owed by small and mid-size companies, IRCJ is expected to purchase debts owed by larger corporations whose bankruptcy might have a material impact on relevant industries. IRCJ can recommend that debtor corporations reduce their size or merge with or be absorbed into

6

other corporations in order to resolve problems of excess capacity or excess supply in the relevant industries.

IRCJ has ¥10 trillion at its disposal (financed under the guarantee by the Japanese government) to purchase nonperforming and poorly performing loans from banks. All purchases must be completed before the end of March 2005, and loans and equity must be resold within three years. IRCJ has a life span of five years at the longest.

In Japan, each corporation traditionally had a "main bank" (or banks) whose function was to fund the corporation's investment and operations. The main banks used to send their employees to the corporations to serve in controlling positions as chairpersons, presidents, directors, and other high-ranking officers. Those managers and high-ranking employees who did not come from main banks were also likely to lose their "spirit of independence" under the protective umbrella of the main banks. The main banks continue to supply loans, producing excessive exposure, even after secondary banks have eliminated theirs. IRCJ tries to resolve the "main bank problem" by stipulating a debt restructuring plan involving only three parties: IRCJ, the main bank, and the debtor corporation. IRCJ was expected to be the last realistic opportunity that the government had to resolve, once and for all, the seemingly insurmountable problem of nonperforming and poorly performing loans in Japan.

ICRJ uses the following procedures to assist distressed debtors.

First, companies that are struggling due to excessive debt draft a reorganization plan with their main bank(s). Staff of the company and the banks develop this plan with help or backing from certified public accountants and restructuring advisers. The reorganization plan should encompass both financial and business reorganization, the first achieved by using debt forgiveness and debt-for-equity swaps to cut interest-bearing debt and increase or decrease capital and the latter by closing and cutting unprofitable businesses in peripheral divisions, strengthening profitable core divisions, and even splitting up the company, by means of mergers, affiliations, and business transfers. Preparing the draft plan usually takes two to three months and involves more than 20 staff, including bank and company staff and external specialists. Financial advisers provide help, and staff look for sponsors and corporate recovery funds.

Second, the main bank and the company hold preliminary discussions with IRCJ's professional office. The office uses external sources such as restructuring advisers and follows the advice of members of the IRCJ Commission, as necessary, to review the accuracy of the financial data and the draft's validity, feasibility, and economic rationale. Revisions are made, as necessary, and the office calls on the advice of certified public accountants, tax accountants, and lawyers, as necessary. The office also performs a due diligence process to set the appropriate market value for the purchase price of debt. This process requires about 20 staff and a two- or three-month period.

Third, once a reorganization plan with high feasibility is completed, the company and its main bank(s) officially apply to IRCJ for aid. After consulting with the relevant ministers, the IRC Commission decides whether to offer revitalization support. Based on this decision, IRCJ makes its own decision on support and distributes the plan to the non-main banks, requesting a temporary stay on collections. IRCJ also asks the banks to decide within a maximum of three months whether to apply for debt purchase or to accept the reorganization plan. The detailed reports prepared by the restructuring advisers and specialists are used by the relevant ministers in their consultation and by the commission in making their decision regarding the prospects for the company's successful revitalization. In other words, a great deal of preparatory work is done out of sight during the period beginning with the prior consultations and ending with the application for revitalization support. Most plans that do not seem likely to succeed, despite revisions made at the review stage, never make it to the official application stage. IRCJ does not publicly release information on plans that make it to the application stage and are not accepted.

Fourth, with the exception of a few creditors that can be excluded without impeding revitalization, IRCJ purchases the debt when the non-main banks apply for debt purchase or agree to the reorganization plan. IRC withdraws from the decision process if it does not gain the cooperation of the necessary financial institutions, and in this case the companies are likely to go through statutory reorganization procedures. IRCJ sells the purchased debt within three years of purchase, and during this time it monitors the progress of the plan with the main bank. Any breakdown in the revitalization process is likely to trigger statutory reorganization procedures.

IRCJ Activities during the First Year

The Industrial Revitalization Corporation of Japan started business operations on May 8, 2003. After intensive due diligence of debtors' assets and investigation of the feasibility of the draft reorganization plans made by professional staff of IRCJ, the Industrial Revitalization Commission decided to assist the reorganization of the following debtor corporations before the end on January 2004:

- Kyushu Industrial Transportation Corporation with its subsidiaries operates passenger and cargo transportation and other business, including travel agencies and hotel operations. Kyushu Industrial Transportation is an unlisted company with approximately 4,700 employees. If it had declared bankruptcy, the adverse impact on the regional industry would have been severe.
- DIA Construction is a condominium developer with about 3,700 employees doing business all over Japan and listed on the Tokyo Stock Market.
- Usui Department Store is a local department store in Koriyama, Fukushima, whose shutdown would have caused a serious decline in the shopping arcade in Koriyama, the biggest city in Fukushima Prefecture.
- Mitsui Mining had been in the coal mining business since 1911 and was the biggest coal mining company in Japan before exiting the business several years ago. Mitsui Mining and its subsidiaries engage in many kinds of business, including trading of coal, production of coke, manufacture of machinery, operation of cement plants, transportation of cargo, and development of land. Mitsui Mining is a listed company with more than 800 employees.
- Meisei Shokai is a trading house for chemicals, electronics, and other products.
- Matsuya Appliances is a chain store with 1,000 employees.
- Tsumatsubishi Department Store is located in Tsu, the capital city of Mie Prefecture. Its closing might have had a severe impact on many retail stores in the city.
- Yagami Medical Supplies is a wholesaler of medical supplies with nearly 200 employees.
- Kimmon Manufacturing is a listed company group and the top manufacturer of meters for natural gas, liquefied petroleum gas, and water in Japan, with approximately 2,500 employees.
- Fuji Yugyo is a wholesale business of oil and oil products.
- Osaka Marubilu is a well-known hotel located just in front of Osaka station.

6

Journalists criticized the selection because the number of targeted companies was small and the companies were smaller than expected in size. They questioned whether IRCJ could help Japan to regain its prosperity, when it was not given the opportunity to reorganize the largest, most influential corporations with excessive debts. The difficulty was that ICRJ could select only those cases requested by the banks. The largest Japanese banks (the main banks) were reluctant to bring large, influential cases to IRCJ because they were concerned about losing control of the valuation process. The main banks tend to assume the largest responsibility for maintaining finance to distressed companies (the smaller banks often refuse to roll over loans when they become due, and the main banks, which may have indirectly controlled the debtor corporations for years, find it difficult to persuade other banks to share losses on a pro rata basis in a workout process based on the out-of-court guidelines) and prefer to keep control over the reorganization process.[16] However, the main banks saw their financial strength deteriorate during the prolonged economic recession and thus have little room left to help corporations with large debts. Banks are gradually changing their attitude toward IRCJ and have brought more cases this year.

Differences between Asset Management Companies in Foreign Countries and IRCJ

Several countries have established asset management companies to purchase the nonperforming loans of financial institutions. In 1989 the Resolution and Trust Corporation was established in the United States. As a number of savings and loan associations and savings banks, whose main business was housing mortgage loans, went bankrupt as a result of the fall in real estate prices, many nonperforming loans of bankrupt institutions were transferred to the Resolution and Trust Corporation and disposed. In 1992 and 1993, two asset management companies were established in Sweden, where the amount of nonperforming loans rose when the real estate bubble burst, and two of the four major banks were nationalized after going bankrupt. By taking over the nonperforming loans in each bank, two asset management companies were established. Elsewhere, two successful examples are KAMCO, which was established in Korea, and Danaharta, which was established in Malaysia, both in 1998 in response to the currency crisis in Asia. Asset management companies were also established in Finland, Indonesia, Mexico, the

Philippines, Spain, and seven African countries including Ghana, but they are not known to be successful.

The biggest difference between asset management companies in foreign countries and IRCJ is that, in Japan, there is no enforcement power, and financial institutions do not have to bring cases to IRCJ. In the asset management corporations in foreign countries, enforcement is effective, and nonperforming loans must be brought to the asset management companies directly or indirectly. Officials in financial institutions have an obligation to collect debts owed by debtor corporations as much as possible. IRCJ, however, determines whether a revitalization plan is feasible from the viewpoint of a neutral third person and, after inspecting the details, decides whether to support it or not. It is natural that officials of financial institutions are concerned that IRCJ may request a greater haircut than the institution expected. In fact, the staff member in IRCJ who specializes in revitalization not only reduces the cost but also draws up a future plan by proposing a new business model; for this reason, the expected future income is more accurate, and the assessment of the corporation's value is appropriate. Professional staff of IRCJ assume that the requested haircut is even smaller than that of a conservative business plan, but it took a long time for people to understand this fact.

Second, foreign asset management companies sold their purchased assets rapidly using several schemes, including securitization and foreign vulture funds, or resold assets after revitalizing debtor corporations whose business was relatively simple, such as real estate developers and hotels. On the contrary, IRCJ does more than revitalization; it also is available for any kind of business, including manufacturing. IRCJ must carry out a difficult task without any compulsory power.

Establishment of Bank Subsidiaries to Revitalize Debtor Corporations

The large banks have also taken independent actions to promote restructuring of debtor corporations. After the establishment of IRCJ in May 2003, Mizuho bank group, UFJ bank group, and Sumitomo Mitsui bank group established decentralized bank subsidiaries to revitalize customer debt corporations and affiliates one by one. They established these subsidiaries by making a partnership with investment banks, such as Cerberus, Merrill Lynch, Morgan Stanley, and Goldman Sachs, to tap their expertise in revitalizing businesses.

Mizuho and UFJ established consolidated subsidiaries (as holding companies in the group obtained a majority of the stock), while Goldman Sachs owns 51 percent of the Sumitomo Mitsui affiliate. All of these subsidiaries and affiliates were established to revitalize debtor corporations with nonperforming or poorly performing loans by transferring debts to the specialized subsidiaries. Although the receivables of several thousand companies have been transferred to these affiliates, transfer to a consolidated subsidiary is not a significant off-balance transaction. Still, these special revitalization corporations may assist with the process of conducting due diligence and drafting restructuring plans for debtor corporations, which have a reasonable prospect of restoring their profitability. These subsidiaries establish a "bad bank" to manage the debts, similar to the asset management companies, like Securum and Retriva in Sweden. One of the reasons why mega bank groups create these specialized revitalization corporations might be to exercise their own banks' control and initiative in disposing of nonperforming loans without involving IRCJ. Moreover, the debtor corporations might benefit from loans to maintain operations.

Care must be taken that affiliates of the main banks pay sufficient attention to debtors' profitability and cash flow. The negotiation of restructuring plans between the debtor corporation and its main banks can be difficult. The debtor may be forced into agreeing to a restructuring plan that fails to restore financial viability. Involving a neutral third party, like IRCJ, can be helpful in reaching agreement on a sustainable plan. Reaching such an agreement is in the interest of the bank as well, to avoid having to provide additional financial support or incur further losses.

Human Resources for Corporate Restructuring

Japan might yet be seen as having effective reorganization laws and out-of-court solutions as a result of the enactment of an effective civil rehabilitation law, corporate reorganization reform law, and out-of-court workout guidelines. IRCJ and RCC may be good schemes to restore the Japanese economy. Japan now has effective tools to reorganize troubled businesses. However, having the right tools in place is not enough. Japan also needs highly skilled human resources—that is, restructuring advisers and turnaround managers, who are capable of reconstructing and regenerating the business of troubled corporations. The past few years have seen the establishment of organizations, including the Japanese Association for Business

Recovery, the Education Center for Restructuring Advisers, and Japanese Association of Turnaround Professionals, to foster, educate, and train more specialists in the field of insolvency and business recovery.

Revolutionary cultural changes are required to restore the Japanese economy. In January 2003, the Ministry of Economy, Trade, and Industry proposed guidelines to restore the health of troubled business corporations, based on the advice of a committee organized for that purpose. Among other things, the guidelines include proposals to abandon the main bank system and amend the life-long employment system, which had been instituted to build up company loyalty but impeded outside monitoring.

Conclusions

This review of the experience of asset management companies reveals common principles that were central to their success. First, asset management companies need effective policies and procedures for the disposal of assets. These processes must be transparent and designed within the framework of appropriate governance structures. Ensuring that they are short-lived agencies helps to establish the right incentives for rapid disposal of assets and for corporate reorganizations that address underlying problems.

Second, time is of the essence. Asset management companies are rarely in a position to manage the ongoing business operations of distressed corporations. Without effective management, assets will deteriorate due to lack of maintenance; lack of employee, supplier, and customer commitment; and inability to respond to changes in the business environment.

Third, asset management companies must acquire assets at a realistic price and be prepared to dispose of assets at market prices, without regard to historical cost. If asset management companies purchase distressed assets at book value (for example, to assist in the recapitalization of the banks), then their managers must not be held accountable for losses relative to this (inflated) purchase price.

Fourth, asset management companies should engage the private sector in the process of asset disposition. The papers presented in this chapter describe innovative measures by Korean and Chinese asset management companies to use private expertise, for example, through joint ventures with investment banks.

6

Finally, asset management companies need to be flexible. No single financial technique is appropriate for each situation, and a menu of instruments is necessary to deal with distressed corporations.

6

Appendix 6.1: Civil Rehabilitation Proceeding in Japan

The civil rehabilitation law was enacted to cure the defects of the composition law. According to the composition law, a secured creditor was free to enforce or foreclose its secured right, even after commencement of the case; a debtor had no weapon to induce a secured creditor into accepting an arrangement or an extension. Under the civil rehabilitation law, a secured creditor is still able to enforce its secured rights, but a debtor is eligible for a temporary stay order prohibiting enforcement of that secured right for a certain period. The purpose of the stay order is to create a reasonable time frame during which the debtor and secured creditor can negotiate an acceptable compromise.

According to the Japanese civil code, which is based on the Napoleonic code, a secured right is not limited to the value of the collateral. In other words, a secured creditor can refuse to relinquish its secured right, even if a debtor has paid the part of the secured debt that is equivalent to the value of the collateral. The secured right cannot be extinguished without the consent of the secured creditor unless the debt has been paid in full. Under the new civil rehabilitation law, however, a secured right is extinguished when the debtor pays enough of the claim to be equal to the value of the collateral. If the secured creditor objects to the debtor's valuation, the court determines the amount, based on the assessment made by a court-appointed appraiser. Due to this provision, an undersecured creditor cannot insist on full payment even if the underlying debt exceeds the value of the collateral.

Other reforms made by the civil rehabilitation law include mitigation of the majority requirement, court permits for sale of the debtor's business, and reduction of capital without shareholders' resolutions. A plan may only alter the rights of unsecured creditors if it is accepted by a simple majority of creditors holding more than half of the total amount of unsecured claims. The main reason why the civil rehabilitation law mitigated the majority requirement is that government or other state-owned financial institutions, which are usually creditors with large numbers of claims, are reluctant to accept plans that alter their claims. These institutions tend to stick to the conservative standards set in their manuals. However, in order to alter the rights of secured creditors, the consent of each secured creditor is required.

When a debtor is insolvent, a court can permit a sale of all or a part of its business without a shareholders' resolution. A plan can also reduce a company's capital without a shareholders' resolution when the debtor is insolvent, but a shareholders' resolution is still required to increase capital. However, this is inconsistent with the corporate reorganization law, where both reductions and increases in capital can be accomplished without a shareholders' resolution.

Appendix 6.2: Corporate Reorganization Proceeding in Japan

The corporate reorganization law was modeled after the old U.S. Bankruptcy Act of 1898, as amended in 1938. The Japanese law was enacted in 1952 and partly amended in 1967. The old Japanese reorganization law was revised and updated with the enactment of the corporate reorganization reform law in 2002.

The corporate reorganization proceeding provides a debtor corporation with strong weapons to enable it to reorganize its business. Even secured creditors cannot enforce or realize their secured rights pending a proceeding, and a reorganization plan that is accepted by majority can alter the rights of secured creditors. When the commencement order is given to open a corporate reorganization proceeding, government organizations are stayed from collecting even sovereign debts. Moreover, a reorganization may be exempt from various provisions of the commercial code that would otherwise govern the debtor corporation, such as requirements concerning the reduction of capital, the issue of new shares, the sale of the debtor's business, and the merger and formation of new corporations.

A distinctive feature of the earlier corporate reorganization law is that it did not adopt a U.S.-style debtor-in-possession (DIP) system. On an opening order issued by a court, the incumbent managers of a debtor corporation were deprived of their power to operate the business and dispose of its assets. There were further differences. For instance, unlike the former U.S. law, the old Japanese corporate reorganization law provided that managers of every reorganizing debtor corporation must be removed and a court-appointed trustee or administrator be vested with all of their powers. Moreover, the Japanese fair and equitable rule required that all shares of a debtor corporation had to be retired when the debtor was insolvent. A reorganization plan that altered the creditors' rights had to provide for 100 percent dilution of capital, and all rights of the debtor's owner were eliminated completely.

In theory, the corporate reorganization proceeding was supposed to be suitable for larger corporations, while the civil rehabilitation proceeding was better for middle- or smaller-size corporations. But even large corporations, such as the large Japanese retail stores Sogo and Mycal, filed petitions for civil rehabilitation instead of the corporate reorganization proceeding. After the civil rehabilitation law became effective in April 2000, many large corporations filed petitions under it and not under the corporate reorganization law. The principal reason why even large corporations did not file for corporate reorganization proceedings might be attributable to the lack of a U.S.-style DIP system.

In civil rehabilitation proceedings, a debtor may continue in possession of the business under the loose supervision of a court-appointed supervisor. A trustee may be appointed in rare cases, but only under exceptional circumstances. Indeed, the new corporate reorganization reform law made it clear that a court may appoint existing executives as a trustee or deputy trustees in some cases. Consequently—due partly to this DIP system—when managers who were unable to resolve the problems of the distressed corporation were replaced by turnaround managers before filing a petition, a court might appoint the turnaround managers as trustees or deputy trustees. A corporate reorganization proceeding, with its stronger weapons, was more useful than civil rehabilitation for larger corporations. It is hoped that a pre-arranged corporate reorganization proceeding will be used far more widely in Japan now that the new corporate reorganization reform law has come into effect in April 2003.

In short, the corporate reorganization reform law of 2003 made a lot of changes to the old corporate reorganization law. Modifications introduced by the new reform law include improvement in the transparency of proceedings, greater disclosure of information, clear and simplified valuation standards for assets and the collateral of secured rights, mitigation of the majority requirement, expedited procedures, simplified proceedings for filing and fixing of claims, shortening of the payment term for the balance of partly released claims, and many more. In addition, the new reform law adopted a current-value standard for valuing assets and collateral, instead of the more complicated going-concern basis. Other changes to streamline the corporate reorganization proceeding were made in the new reform law. However, the new law did not change the rule that mandates the retirement of shares when the rights of creditors are altered and the debtor corporation is insolvent.

According to the new reform law, the reorganization plan is accepted by unsecured creditors if the plan is accepted by a simple majority of unsecured creditors who attend the creditors meeting and who together hold more than half of the total amount of unsecured claims, a plan that provides for deferred payments only for secured debts is accepted by the secured creditors holding more than two-thirds of the total amount of secured claims, and a plan that provides for partial release of secured debts is accepted by the secured creditors holding more than three-fourths of the total amount of secured claims. A reorganization plan must be proposed within one year after commencement of the case.

Appendix 6.3: Out-of-Court Workout in Japan

The National Bankers Association, Federation of Economic Organizations, and other relevant organizations associated with the Financial Services Agency, the Ministry of Finance, the Ministry of Economy, Trade, and Industry, the Bank of Japan, and the Deposit Insurance Corporation established a committee, which introduced the Guideline for the Out-of-Court Workout. The guideline, which makes reference to the INSOL-8 principles for international multi-creditors, was designed to clear out the huge number of nonperforming loans owed to multiple banks and financial institutions and to restore the debtor corporations to viability.

The procedure established by the guideline begins with the debtor corporation applying with a "main bank" for a multibank out-of-court workout in cases where a number of banks have a lending exposure. The application must be accompanied by financial documents that explain the reasons why the debtor became financially distressed and by a proposal for a reorganization plan. The proposal should include a business restructuring plan as well as a debt reorganization plan. The main bank then investigates the financial documents and reorganization plan to determine whether the statements are accurate and the plan is both feasible and reasonable. If they are persuaded that these criteria are indeed met, and they agree that the plan is likely to be acceptable to all banks whose debts are to be impaired under the reorganization, then the main bank issues a notice of standstill to all the relevant banks and convenes the first meeting of creditors. This meeting must be held within a week after the notice of standstill is issued.

At the first meeting of creditors, the unanimous consent of the creditors must be obtained to continue the standstill period. If they all agree, then a creditor committee may be elected. The committee can designate professionals (including lawyers and accountants) to examine the accuracy of financial statements and the reasonableness and feasibility of the proposed reorganization plan. During the standstill period, the relevant creditors should refrain from any collection efforts, enforcement or realization of secured rights, or improvement of their exposure relative to other relevant banks and must maintain the original balance of their claims. Before the end of the third month after the first meeting, a second meeting must be held at which all relevant creditors must indicate whether they accept the plan or not. If all creditors whose rights will be affected by the debtor's rehabilitation consent to the proposed plan, the reorganization plan can proceed, and the rights of the relevant creditors will be amended according to the provisions contained in the plan. If one or more of the creditors refuses to agree to the plan, then the out-of-court workout procedure is terminated. The debtor must decide whether to file a petition with a court to begin statutory insolvency proceedings.

The guideline is designed to facilitate multibank workouts to rehabilitate larger corporations burdened with huge amounts of claims and applies only in exceptional cases. Therefore, contrary to the INSOL-8 principles, the Japanese guideline specifies the requirements for a business restructuring plan, which can become part of any proposed plan. If the debtor has a negative net worth, the plan must eliminate this problem within approximately three years. If the debtor has a net loss, the plan must indicate how that loss will be transformed into a profit within the three-year period. The plan should provide that the interests of the debtor's controlling shareholders should, in principle, be divested, and the proportional interest of the existing shareholders should be reduced or eliminated altogether through a capital reduction and subsequent capital increase. The plan should, in principle, also require that the debtor's present managers retire on the creditors' acceptance the proposed plan.

Many practitioners have criticized the arrangements under the guideline, contending that the requirements are too severe. In contrast, the Japanese Federation of Economic Organizations supports the rigid requirements included in the guideline, because members would like to resolve excess competition in certain industries by reducing the number of poorly performing companies in those segments.

6

By the end of 2003, more than 20 corporations had been reorganized through an out-of-court workout using the guideline. The practicing committee of the guideline discussed how to make the guideline more popular, including allowing for some reasonable exceptions. The guideline is a good tool for reorganizing the financial structure of a debtor with excessive debts at an early stage without impairing debts owed to trade creditors. But to obtain the unanimous consent of all relevant financial institutions is almost impossible.

Notes

1. Danamodal was formed to recapitalize banks.
2. Special administrators are appointed only if Danaharta is satisfied that the borrower is unable or is likely to be unable to pay its debts, the survival of the borrower as a going concern is threatened, or a formal restructuring of the debts of the borrower would be more advantageous than a winding-up. All appointments of special administrators are approved by the Oversight Committee.
3. The publication outlines the following loan restructuring principles: a proportionately larger haircut for shareholders than for creditors, fair treatment to secured and unsecured creditors, no dilution of inadequate security, only one opportunity for restructuring, and the requirement that borrowers work for lenders. It also details the following guidelines: maximize the overall recovery value and return to Danaharta, minimize the involvement of taxpayers' money, ensure the fair treatment of all stakeholders, and use, where appropriate, Danaharta's special powers to leverage and benefit the banking system as a whole.
4. Asset restructuring involves the sale of business or collateral and applies the principles of competitive bidding, the preservation and enhancement of the value of the business or collateral, and the orderly disposition of assets through a transparent process.
5. RM 1 = US$0.263.
6. Corporate loans under court restructuring are loans to companies under court receivership or composition proceedings, whether they are secured or unsecured. Corporate loans under workout are loans to companies under private workout programs, which have been agreed by creditors for restructuring distressed assets.

7. The Korean government supported debt-to-equity swaps by a special law (the Corporate Restructuring Promotion Act). Debt-to-equity swaps were exempt from limitations on banks' stock purchase limits. Similarly, by commercial law, the price of the new issue must be higher than par (5,000 won). The new issue price under par value is up to the court's approval. In the case of debt-to-equity swaps, shareholders' approval was sufficient and did not require court approval. Debt-to-equity swaps and convertible debt were used as well in corporate reorganization and workouts. Debt-to-equity swaps involved considerable risks for the creditor. The converted equity lost value if the debtor was liquidated, and values and controls were diluted if there was a subsequent swap.

8. By extended debt maturity, the present value of debt was reduced and became an effective debt write-off. During a grace period, only interest was repaid.

9. As a workout vehicle, corporate restructuring vehicles need to have a simple creditor status, meaning a single debtor rather than a portfolio.

10. Corporate restructuring vehicles are special-purpose vehicles that assist the restructuring process by relieving banks of the burden of managing nonperforming assets and by improving the efficiency of the process.

11. The volume of these equities held on the books of banks has been growing since the workout initiatives were introduced.

12. Accounting forbearance was discussed but not introduced in the legislation.

13. See appendix 6.1 for the detail.

14. See appendix 6.2 for the detail.

15. See appendix 6.3 for the detail.

16. Although the main bank system was pervasive for a long time in Japan, the financial environment is changing. Corporations with a good financial reputation are able to raise funds in the capital market and no longer rely on the main banks. Nevertheless, corporations that are unable to raise money from the market have continued to rely on the main banks.

6

Chapter 7

Progress toward the Resolution of Nonperforming Loans

Jack Rodman

Since Ernst & Young issued the *Nonperforming Loan Report: Asia 2002* (Ernst & Young 2002), Asian banks and financial institutions have made substantial progress in reducing their stock of nonperforming loans. The 2002 report estimated that Asian economies had accumulated $2 trillion of nonperforming loans (about twice the official estimate); however, recent figures indicate about $1 trillion of nonperforming loans at year-end 2003 (table 7.1). Despite the seemingly large reduction in nonperforming loans, most of the decrease was through simplified or artificial means such as write-offs and transfers to government agencies rather than through active debt resolution. Although write-offs mathematically reduce the amount of nonperforming loans on the banks' balance sheets (and allow them to refocus their attention on current business), the volume of write-offs does not indicate true progress in the resolution of nonperforming loans. The loans remain on the bank's balance sheet at a reduced face value and may be subject to future write-downs.

Emerging markets now offer perhaps the best opportunity for investors to make money purchasing nonperforming loans (see table 7.2). More mature markets, such as Japan, Republic of Korea, and Taiwan (China), have been selling distressed assets for some years now; the market is highly competitive, and the risk of resolving nonperforming loans has stabilized. But the

Table 7.1: Official Estimates of Nonperforming Loans in Select Markets

(billions of U.S. dollars)

Economy	Nonperforming loans in financial institutions	Nonperforming loans in government-related asset management companies	Gross reduction in nonperforming loans since the Asian financial crisis
Japan	330	112	600
China	307	107	200
Germany	300[a]	—	—
India	30	—	—
Taiwan (China)	19	—	50
Thailand	19	5	95
Indonesia	17	5	37
Korea, Rep. of	15	45	125
Philippines	9	—	—
Total	1,046	274	1,107

— Not available.

a. Not official government estimate

Source: Ernst & Young (2004).

7

emerging markets, like China, Germany, the Philippines, and Turkey, present a unique opportunity for investors to invest capital and earn high returns because these countries need outside capital to sustain economic development. In new investment markets, both domestic and foreign investors believe that purchasing nonperforming loans can be highly risky, so both the discount applied to the purchase price of nonperforming loans and the returns to be gained from the investment can be quite high. However, as the markets become more established over time, both risk and the rate of return decline (table 7.3).

The Resolution of Nonperforming Loans

Despite the progress made over the past two years, nonperforming loans remain a substantial problem in many countries. This paper discusses issues affecting the resolution of nonperforming loans, including the importance of strong government leadership, the willingness of government to use tax-

Table 7.2: Characteristics of Markets for Nonperforming Loans, by Status of the Market

Current status of the market	Investment potential (U.S. dollars)	Region	Characteristic
Tapering off	Less than $250 million	Indonesia, Malaysia, Thailand	Limited potential; small markets
Gearing up	Up to $500 million	Czech Republic, Philippines, Poland, Russia, Turkey	Opportunistic; warrant further study; the next emerging markets, significant unknowns; mid-size markets; limited competition
Emerging	Up to $1 billion	China, Germany, India	Fewer barriers to entry; strong investor interest; huge market potential; no dominant players; new legislation on nonperforming loans
Mature	Over $1 billion	Japan, Korea (Rep. of), Taiwan (China)	High barriers to entry; larger deals; mature markets; highly competitive; existing legislation on nonperforming loans

Source: Ernst & Young (2004).

Table 7.3: Definition of and Annual Return in Markets for Nonperforming Loans, by Status of the Markets

Current status of the market	Definition	Example	Annual return
Emerging	Large problem of nonperforming loans; limited progress beyond identification of nonperforming loans; minimal legislation governing asset management companies; efforts that are new or unproven over the long term; additional resources needed	China, Czech Republic, Germany, India, Philippines, Russia, Turkey	25–30 percent or more
Established	Well-established market for nonperforming loans developed over several years, with experienced investors; predictable pricing and valuation of nonperforming loans based on actual experience; low pricing volatility; many established players in the market; high barriers to entry; clearly understood legal system for enforcement of creditor rights; capital available to finance nonperforming loan transactions	Indonesia, Japan, Korea (Rep. of), Malaysia, Taiwan (China), Thailand	20 percent
Normalized	Same as in established markets	France, Italy, Mexico, Spain, Sweden, United States	Local market rates

Source: Ernst & Young (2004).

173

payers' money to resolve bad debts, the need for realism in evaluating the magnitude of nonperforming loans, the attitude toward foreign investors and financial advisers, and the role of multinational agencies.

Strong government leadership is essential to reducing a country's supply of nonperforming loans. The provision of government capital to special asset management companies, like the Asset Recovery Corporation (ARC) in India, the Thai Asset Management Corporation (TAMC) in Thailand, the Korea Asset Management Corporation (KAMCO) in Korea, or the Agency for Restructuring Credit Organisations (ARCO) in Russia, is an important indicator of government commitment to resolving the problem. Countries without such commitment have not made real progress in reducing their stock of nonperforming loans. Nevertheless, simply transferring nonperforming loans into an asset management company—that is, just moving the asset from one balance sheet to another—is not enough. If real progress is to be made in the battle against bad debt, governments (and the financial institutions they oversee) will have to push for better internal collections, accurate write-offs, and a flow of sales transactions to third-party investors (who bear the ultimate risk of resolving the loan).

Governments can substantially lower the costs of resolving nonperforming loans by clarifying the legal structure for transactions, strengthening creditor rights and the role of the court system, and opening the market to foreign competition. These steps reduce market risks, increase competition among investors, and minimize the loss that governments and banks must incur to remove nonperforming loans from their books. Economies with policies that encourage stronger capital markets and increased investor interest, such as Japan, Korea, Taiwan (China), and others, have a wider range of instruments for selling nonperforming loans, such as asset-backed securitizations and joint ventures. Specifically, joint ventures are used to bridge the price gap between buyers (with international expertise) and sellers, as nonperforming loans commonly sell at large discounts below book value due to their risky nature. That is, joint ventures can provide some protection that the investor will get his capital back (by purchasing at a large discount) but also ensure that the seller will participate in the recovery on bad debts. For example, KAMCO (in Republic of Korea) and Huarong Asset Management Company (in China) have been very successful in using joint venture structures to resolve nonperforming loans. During the 1980s, the U.S. Resolution Trust Corporation reduced the estimated cost of bailing out the savings and loan industry from more than $300 billion to about $150 billion.[1] This cost savings of 50 percent was achieved simply by embracing joint ventures that allowed sellers to participate in the proceeds of resolved debts.

The legal rules and the effectiveness of the courts also have a great influence on how nonperforming loans are resolved. In China, for example, from 65 to 75 percent of all nonperforming loans are resolved through discounted pay-offs or negotiated settlement.

In Japan, nonperforming loans are also resolved through discounted pay-offs and foreclosure settlements. However, these foreclosures are accomplished through the Japanese court system, which is more efficient and reliable than the Chinese court system. In Taiwan (China), 70 percent of defaulted debt is cleared through the courts, and in Korea, most nonperforming loans are resolved using the country's effective foreclosure system.

Governments must also be *willing to make strong regulatory decisions.* Taiwan (China) used to have difficulty finalizing the sale of nonperforming loans. Most third-party transaction sales were negotiated, but few were ever successfully finalized. Then, President Chen Shui-Bian imposed stringent rules (the 2-5-8 Plan) for the disposition of nonperforming loans. In two years, all banks were to reduce their bad loans to below 5 percent and to achieve an 8 percent risk-adjusted capital ratio. Banks that failed to achieve these goals were subject to a series of restrictions, including no new branches, lower salaries for directors and supervisors, and limited hiring, long-term investment, and loans to related parties. Banks that continued to miss the plan's targets could be subjected to fines, replacement of management, and revocation of their banking license. At the same time, tax holidays were implemented, while other regulations were eased or removed. This carrot-and-stick approach and its decisive execution by the government was a huge success: in the 18 months after initiation of this program, 25 market sale transactions to third-party investors were completed.

Governments need to be *willing to use taxpayers' money to achieve progress* in reducing nonperforming loans. Often a lack of fiscal resources leads governments to adopt artificial solutions that do not address the underlying problem. For example, a decade ago, the Japanese resisted using government funds to resolve nonperforming loans because they did not want to bail out the banks. Instead, they transferred the banks' nonperforming loans to the Cooperative Credit Purchasing Company. The banks received a tax deduction, but they were still obligated for losses on the nonperforming loans that remained on the purchasing company books 10 years later. At the same time, Japanese banks continued to harbor bad loans to avoid recognizing losses. In some cases, banks would lend money to a company on March 30, a day before the end of the fiscal year. The company would use the loan to make the service payment due on March 31 and would have an even bigger nonperforming loan the next day. In the absence of progress on resolving nonperforming loans, the Japanese economy did not recover for almost 13 years, and nonperforming loans ballooned from $300 billion to $1.2 trillion.

Japan's nonperforming loan problem remained unresolved until the government took strong measures and finally used taxpayer monies. Under the leadership of the Financial Service Agency director, Heizo Takenaka, regulators scrutinized bank balance sheets to identify impaired loans. Banks were forced to recognize their losses and accept an injection of taxpayer capital, the size of which was closely tied to measured progress in cleaning up the balance sheet. Banks that did not meet their goals faced the possible replacement of their management. By 2005, banks will have to reduce their nonperforming loans by 50 percent. This program encouraged accountants to review thoroughly the value of loans, essentially improving accounting discipline for the banking system. A problem that had festered for a decade is now being addressed because of strong leadership and the willingness to commit taxpayers' money to its resolution.

One of the greatest obstacles to reducing nonperforming loans is *hostility to the participation by foreign investors* in such transactions. In theory, countries are amenable to foreign money, but they are often reluctant to approve sale transactions that would enable foreign investors to buy distressed assets. Domestic investors often complain that foreign investors calculate huge profits into their purchase of nonperforming loans. At the same time, however, few domestic investors are willing to commit their own money because doing so is too risky and the capital investment in nonperforming loans is sizable. Critics fail to realize that foreign investors are usually the best option for resolving a seller's nonperforming loans. Most foreign buyers of distressed debt have teams of people dedicated solely to the purchase of bad debt, high levels of risk tolerance, access to large amounts of investment capital, and a commitment to hiring local workers and educating them about recovering from delinquent borrowers. Without foreign investment and an open, transparent, and secure environment for foreign investors, the local market for nonperforming loans will never develop.

Financial advisers are overlooked and underappreciated participants in the process of resolving nonperforming loans. On the one hand, sellers are

7

reluctant to hire their services under the assumption that they themselves can manage resolution strategies without external guidance. On the other hand, buyers are quick to criticize the financial adviser for any mistakes, delays, or other transaction difficulties. But without these advisers, deals do not get done. External advisers are vital to guiding the overall resolution process. The valuation gap between what sellers think their assets are worth and what investors are willing to pay is usually significant. Financial advisers manage the process by lowering the seller's price expectations and raising the buyer's purchase price by building confidence in the bad loans. In other instances, financial advisers are necessary to ensure fair and transparent negotiations between buyer and seller. Financial advisers are usually hired after both parties fail to agree on a deal; the independent adviser becomes a brokering intermediary to comment on the proposals and bring the parties together.

Sellers of nonperforming loans need *greater realism about risk-based market pricing of nonperforming loans and the capacity to absorb losses*. Banks may be unwilling to sell a dud loan for 20 cents on the dollar when they can potentially collect 40 cents. But the problem is that collecting the 40 cents takes time—often years—and significant effort. The collection process requires staff, office space, legal and appraisal expenses, and other resolution costs. Banks forget that keeping the nonperforming loan impairs its ability to make other loans because bad debt negatively weighs on the balance sheet and hurts their ability to raise new capital. As time passes, the market value of a pledged collateral asset that backs the loan continues to deteriorate. Buildings fall into disrepair, tenants move out, and projects stagnate. President Yang of China's Huarong Asset Management Company said, "Nonperforming loans are like an ice cream cone. If you don't get rid of them, they melt all over your hands and you don't have anything left to sell." The key issue for the seller is the price it is willing to accept today to avoid the wait and the commitment of resources required for potential collection. The present value of the expected collection of 40 cents on the dollar may be only 20 cents, after costs. The problem is that sellers of nonperforming loans do not properly embrace a discounted cash flow valuation methodology that duly considers the time value of money and the costs involved in collections. Moreover, many banks lack the expertise required to collect loans efficiently.

Regulators, the government, and the general public also need to recognize that nonperforming loans must be sold at their market value.

Programs in China, Indonesia, the Philippines, and Thailand to dispose of nonperforming loans were impeded because government did not want to be perceived as selling assets too cheaply. Thailand's program was initially stalled because no employee wanted to take responsibility for recognizing a loss at the state banks. An employee who approved the sale of a bad loan could potentially be charged with defrauding state assets. In China, the book value of loans transferred to the asset management companies was on the order of 80 cents on the dollar, while recoveries were perhaps 30 cents on the dollar. As a result, it took a long time to obtain approval for transactions, which significantly limited the pace of dispositions. President Yang of Huarong was a China pioneer, accomplishing deals in the face of extremely complex tax and legal regulatory requirements. But there should have been more deals. The key is that professionals hired to dispose of nonperforming loans, as in China's four asset management companies, should not be held accountable for loan losses that existed before they themselves acquired the bad loan from the originating bank. The performance of asset management companies must be judged relative to the market value of loans once they are received, not the face value.

Korea's strategy for resolving nonperforming loans was successful, in part, because the government created KAMCO with a more realistic view of the value of loans. KAMCO's job was not to make a profit, at least relative to the price it paid for the loans. KAMCO's basis in the nonperforming loans was probably around 60–66 cents, but recovery prices ranged from 20 to 40 cents. Had it been mandated to make a profit, KAMCO would not have made any sales or resolutions. Rather, its goal was to maximize the recovery value of assets as quickly as possible. Rather than establish a value for each nonperforming loan, the government transferred all the loans with a single journal entry. If the government had attempted to look at all the loans, their value would have deteriorated during the process. In their early sales, recoveries were quite low: one was for only 12 cents on the dollar. But this attracted investors and fostered the development of the asset-backed securities market in Korea. The government was proactive: it published a schedule of sales so that investors knew that a steady flow of deals would be available, and it ensured a process of rapid government approval. In the next three years, the volume of sales expanded rapidly, and by the end of the process these sales resolutions had reached 50 cents on the dollar. The overall average recovery was 40 plus percent—twice the original estimates.

Multinational agencies need to play a more useful role in assisting govern-ments with nonperforming loans. Typically, the assistance of agencies such as *the World Bank, the International Finance Corporation, the International Monetary Fund, and the Asian Development Bank* is in the form of studies or advisers. But more studies are not needed. Rather than provide a technical development grant of $10 million to pay for new studies, governments could use assistance from multinationals to underwrite a few small transactions that pioneer new financial products and establish a positive reputation for resolving nonperforming loans. Countries such as India, the Philippines, or Vietnam that are struggling with their nonperforming loans could use $10 million to hire a much needed financial adviser with the expertise necessary to close deals. Multinationals could be repaid from the proceeds of the transaction. Essentially, the multinationals need to focus on transac-tion-oriented projects and services. It is important to note, though, that the International Monetary Fund did play a positive role in convincing both the Thai and Korean governments to move forward with an effective restructur-ing program.

Some of these agencies recently have formed joint ventures to acquire nonperforming loans from banks. In essence, they are going to compete with the private sector funds to purchase nonperforming loans. This is a mistake. Hundreds of investment companies worldwide have the ability to acquire and successfully resolve nonperforming loans. These same companies have an abundance of investment capital seeking to buy nonperforming loans. The world needs the funds of multinational agencies to remedy the lack of deal flow by seeding underdeveloped markets, not competing in them.

Finally, despite the progress made in resolving existing nonperforming loans, we have to be *vigilant about the risks of new nonperforming loans.* The Asian financial crisis led analysts to think of nonperforming loans as the result of extreme situations. But today it may be more appropriate to think of the growth of nonperforming loans as an institutional issue, the expected result of cyclical booms that are accompanied by high rates of lending and bubbles for pledged collateral value. For example, the rapid growth of loans in China has contributed to the mathematical reduction in the ratio of nonperforming loans to total loans from 30 percent in 2001 to about 20 percent in 2003. The problem is that, with loans growing at more than 20 percent a year, Chinese banks should have larger loan loss reserves just in case the newly issued loans should falter. Historically, markets with explo-sive growth of loans eventually generate substantial losses as banks become less selective in their underwriting criteria. The urge for local bank branches to participate in a country's overall economic upswing usually overpowers underwriting and due diligence standards prior to issuing the loan. The issue is that the accounting profession does not record a loan loss reserve unless it can confirm that the bank has incurred a loss; that is, it does not allow reserves for an anticipated or potential loss. This is an extremely risky strategy in markets with rapid growth of loans. Still, some Chinese banks remain very profitable and have made excellent progress in reducing nonperforming loans. Specifically, Chinese banks have been able to write off about $200 billion in nonperforming loans while continuing to generate sufficient profits to maintain capital adequacy ratios. But the new spate of bad loans in Korea from personal credit card debt and the increase in auto loan default rates in China should clearly signal that exponential growth will result in a higher incidence of nonperforming loans.

Recommendations

In conclusion, I offer the following advice to all participants in the market for nonperforming loans.

Sellers of nonperforming loans need to view the problem realistically, accept that nonperforming loans sell for substantially less than face value, and close transactions at market-clearing prices. Multiple strategies should be used to resolve nonperforming loans, depending, in part, on the effectiveness of legal and regulatory institutions. Sellers should welcome foreign investment and use financial advisers to guide transactions, ensure transparency, and carry out due diligence.

Governments need to create resolution-friendly nonperforming loan regulations, including market-clearing principles for the disposition of nonperforming loans, and to enforce them through strong political leadership. Capital and bailout monies are required to make the process work, along with efforts to promote transparency and support the development of capital markets.

Investors should recognize that the market for nonperforming loans is vast—an estimated $1.3 trillion worldwide—and represents a significant opportunity for investment banks, opportunity funds, and other global investors. Financial advisers can play a role in supporting due diligence, obtaining information on local markets, and serving as intermediaries for negotiated purchases.

The World Bank, the International Monetary Fund, and the Asian Development Bank must play a more useful role in assisting governments with nonperforming loans. To develop the market for nonperforming loans, these agencies need to focus on transaction-oriented projects and services that stimulate the flow of deals.

References

Ernst & Young. 2002. *Nonperforming Loan Report: Asia 2002.*
———. 2004. *Ernst & Young Global Nonperforming Loan Report 2004.*

Note

1. A billion is 1,000 million.

7

Part II
War Stories from the Crises

Restructuring in Weak Legal and Regulatory Jurisdictions: The Case of Indonesian Restructurings

Ray Davis

The restructuring process in the emerging markets is somewhat different from that in the developed world, particularly in countries with weak legal and regulatory environments. In Japan, the United Kingdom, the United States, and many other countries with a credible legal system, the process for recovering defaulted debt is known and, from the creditors' point of view, reasonably reliable. Restructuring can be in-court or out-of-court, and the out-of-court restructuring is influenced by the deterrence of courts. In the emerging markets, outcomes depend on the relative negotiating strength of the counterparties, influenced by external forces, such as the government. The desire of the debtor to seek a reasonable result, so as to have continuing access to credit, also is a major factor.

My experience in the emerging markets has been principally in Mexico, after the peso crisis, and in Southeast Asia, in the period from 1997 to 2002, where I worked in several countries, notably Indonesia, advising several of the largest companies undergoing restructuring. These included Asia Pulp and Paper (APP), the largest of the emerging-market defaulted debtors. I was one of the financial advisers to APP from January 2001, when a contemplated exchange offer for APP's maturing debt was abandoned, until August 2002. It is important to acknowledge that I can only speak to what is available in the public domain. My colleagues and I played a key role in convincing the creditors to keep APP out of the Singapore court system and to pursue an out-of-court consensual restructuring. We obtained an informal standstill among the creditors and developed and presented the first plan, which set the overall framework for the restructuring. However, over this period our role diminished, following the release of year 2000 financial results for APP's Indonesian subsidiaries, which we had urged the company to publish on a timely basis. The subsidiaries admitted to irregularities in prior-year financial statements, and they also wrote off substantial receivables at the Indonesian mills, owed by private Singapore-based trading companies (which the *Wall Street Journal* suggested were controlled by APP management). The situation worsened when these disclosures led to class action lawsuits; eventually, the investigative arm of the Singapore Monetary Authority launched an inquiry. Ultimately, my efforts to have APP maintain an open, constructive dialogue with the creditors going forward led APP's management to believe that I was too close to the creditors. While on vacation in August 2002, I received word that APP no longer wanted me to be part of its advisory team.

The following observations on corporate restructuring reflect my experience with numerous restructuring negotiations.

Distressed companies in the emerging markets usually achieve successful debt restructurings. Most companies reach consensual restructurings with their creditors in a reasonable period of time. The most difficult situations are those, such as APP, where value and debt are impaired and the existing owners and management are determined to maintain control of the debtor.

The efficacy of local courts is more important than the law itself in providing the backdrop for a consensual restructuring. Consensual restructurings typically are negotiated with creditor rights under local law, and potential outcomes from resorting to a court petition are reflected in the negotiations. If both debtors and creditors are uncertain about the court outcome, there is mutual fear of a negative court result and a desire to reach a balanced, consensual out-of-court arrangement. In contrast to the experience in most other countries, in Indonesia it soon became clear that the courts were easily manipulated, altering the negotiating balance strongly in favor of the debtors.

Creditor organization and leadership are critical to a successful outcome for both debtors and creditors. It is important for the creditors to be organized and to speak with a single voice to the debtor, even where they have different institutional structures and are lenders to different legal entities of the debtor. In the absence of strong leadership, both smaller creditor groups and the debtor can exploit the situation to their own advantage. Moreover, in times of turmoil, preserving the ongoing enterprise is of critical importance. Creditors may have to temper their normal instincts to take a strong stance against a debtor, even one that appears to be only minimally cooperative. In order to preserve the value of the business, it may be important for the debtor to appear to be in control.

The presence of local creditors, or other interested parties, whose interests are aligned with those of foreign creditors is an important factor in achieving an orderly restructuring. Local creditors whose interests are aligned with those of foreign creditors can help to organize the local regulatory environment and the local community to put sufficient pressure on all sides to move forward in negotiations.

Laws passed at the time of crisis can have an unexpected and complicating effect on corporate restructurings. Laws passed in Indonesia just after the crisis gave the Indonesian Bank Restructuring Agency (IBRA) extraordinary powers to seize the assets of bank owners, and this worked to the disadvantage of creditors in more senior structural positions.

Government involvement in the restructuring process, either formal or informal, can expedite the restructuring. In Malaysia and Mexico, government involvement was a key factor in resolving large complex restructurings. The experience in Indonesia was mixed. IBRA, in most cases, was focused on its own exposure. Early after the crisis, the Indonesian government set up a process for debtors and creditors to meet and discuss their differences, but this process had no ability to pressure the parties to move forward in restructuring negotiations.

Where publicly held debts of emerging-market issuers are governed by U.S. law, the requirement for a U.S. legal process to complete the restructuring adds difficulty and complexity. Public debt of foreign issuers, using U.S. law–style documents, is governed by the U.S. Trust Indenture Act. This debt is not considered discharged, under U.S. law, unless each individual creditor agrees or a U.S. bankruptcy court issues an order. To address this requirement, a number of Latin American companies have filed U.S. prepackaged bankruptcy petitions, but to my knowledge no Asian debtor has made such a filing.

Successful Indonesian Restructurings

Prior to commencing work with APP, I had been involved as a financial adviser to numerous Indonesian companies. Bimantara, Danareksa, Gajah

Tunggal, GT Petrochem, Indocement, Kalbe Farma, Sampoerna, and Satelindo were all clients that successfully restructured their debt. Astra, where we represented an unsuccessful bidder, restructured successfully twice—the second time under new ownership. Each of these companies had debt issued predominantly in dollars. Their major creditors were principally foreign banks or distressed investors who bought the foreign bank claims, and their credits were generally in the form of bank loans and commercial paper. Their assets were located in Indonesia. One exception was Polymax, controlled by the Salim Group, which held only Indocement shares as collateral for Polymax's public debt. The public debt was governed by U.K. law and was restructured together with the debt of Indocement.

The Impediment of a Weak Court System

Basic creditor protections, such as covenants, have little meaning where courts or regulators do not enforce creditor rights. One of the early deputy directors of IBRA questioned us about a company we were offering to IBRA as part of a settlement. There was a covenant against a change of control without the banks' consent. The company had already busted a bigger covenant: timely payment of interest. We told the deputy director that it was only a covenant, giving the banks the right to accelerate, not a prohibition. Covenants are like traffic lights: if the enforcers are not watching or can be co-opted, they only have meaning to people who agree voluntarily to observe them.

Most observers point to the lack of a dependable court system in Indonesia as the principal factor contributing to the lack of progress with APP's restructuring. One client of mine owned a bank in the United States and a bank in Indonesia. The U.S. bank prospered and was sold at a substantial profit. The Indonesian bank was shut down by the government after the crisis. The reason given was that the vast majority of the loans were to his businesses, relatives, and business counterparties. When I asked how this came to be, he told me that these were the only people he could rely on to repay their debts. Other than personal relationships, there was no enforcement mechanism.

Dató Param Cumaraswamy, United Nations special investigator on the judiciary, was quoted in mid-2002 as saying that Indonesia was the worse situation he had seen, comparable only to Mexico. The difference, in my experience, is that in Mexico, after the peso crisis, creditors, principally

Mexican banks, avoided the courts.[1] In Indonesia, after the Asian monetary crisis, some practitioners went straight to the courts when debtors were initially uncooperative.

Creditors found that the Indonesian courts could be worse than useless. They could be outright dangerous. Manulife learned that lesson when a Rp 5.1 billion bankruptcy suit was filed in an Indonesian court because of a disputed Rp 50 million life policy. In a second case, a commercial court found Manulife's Indonesian subsidiary bankrupt, and its local manager was jailed. The reason given was that the company did not pay dividends, although the board had voted to skip the dividend payment and the company was solvent. The second case was reversed, but only after direct intervention of the Canadian government.

Indonesia passed a new bankruptcy law at the insistence of the International Monetary Fund. Based on Dutch law, the new law improved the legal framework, but the court system was not changed. Problems for foreign creditors in the courts persist today. A recent case filed by the foreign creditors of Danareksa Jakarta International, the company owning the Jakarta Stock Exchange building, turned the tables on them through a lawsuit claiming that the owners were owed $75 million in damages and an additional $100 million for depression and pressure caused by the creditors' demands for repayment of the $240 million owed. Foreign creditors were not alone in their frustration with the courts. On many occasions, IBRA sought to refer cases to the prosecutors, or their lawyers sought and failed to obtain judgments against debtors.

Like the case of war, issuing threats in emerging-market restructurings is often more effective than taking action. Unfortunately, early on in Indonesia, American Express Bank found its bankruptcy petition for PT Ometraco, a defaulted debtor, rejected by the court. The International Finance Corporation also felt it necessary to file a bankruptcy petition for PT Dharmala Agrifoods in a Jakarta court. The court, once again, rejected this petition, demonstrating the lack of leverage of foreign creditors in negotiations. Given the uncertainty for both sides, a court outcome is an ineffective tool for bringing debtors and creditors together.

Effect of Weak Courts on the Rights of Secured Creditors

Laws in most jurisdictions give secured creditors the right to seize their security through a simple court process. (Indonesia's new bankruptcy law actually weakened to some degree the rights of secured creditors, allowing their claims to be stayed for 90 days from the filing of a bankruptcy petition.) In Indonesia, local practitioners distinguished between types of securities. If a security consisted of shares of a public company, the holder could ask the stock exchange to cross the shares. Land pledged as security could, in theory, be realized by going through the local land registry office. Security in the form of plant and equipment would need to be realized through a court process.

However, the difficulty of realizing corporate assets in court led to less differentiation between secured and unsecured creditors in restructurings involving foreign creditors. In most of the Indonesian cases in which I was involved, the creditors were unsecured and received, in return, unsecured restructured debt. In Indocement's case, we treated secured and unsecured creditors alike. Indocement provided a security package, consisting of some assets to be shared equally among all of the creditors. APP, in the original plan circulated to the creditors, offered the same economic outcome to both unsecured and secured creditors. The secured creditors objected to that treatment and brought litigation in U.S. courts and in Sumatra.

Strong Creditor Organization and Leadership

Strong leadership by creditors, speaking in one voice, was a critical element of success in many of the 40 or so large restructurings on which I have worked. In Indonesia, the lack of effective coordination among all creditors was one reason for the lengthy and still-inconclusive process required to negotiate the restructuring of APP (see box 8.1). As APP began to experience financial difficulty, the Chinese banks, the bondholders, and the export credit agencies, together with the remaining commercial banks, formed three creditor groups. The non-Chinese creditors subsequently formed a combined steering committee that met frequently. The bondholders were represented on that committee but maintained separate legal counsel and a separate subcommittee.

The Chinese banks were organized and well led. However, a single leader never emerged among the institutions forming the combined creditors committee. The commercial banks that were co-lenders with the export credit agencies, in the beginning, were jockeying for control, but none had large exposure. Although some of the bondholders had large positions, apart from

---

Box 8.1: Asia Pulp and Paper

APP is the largest of the emerging-market restructurings, with an extremely complex structure. Its most significant assets were pulp mills and paper mills in Indonesia and four brand-new paper mills in China. The company also had a small operation in Singapore. The parent company, controlled by the Wijaya family of Indonesia, was based in Singapore and had myriad subsidiaries, including a few that were not consolidated for financial reporting. Two of the four principal Indonesian subsidiaries were public companies. Both the Indonesian operations and the Chinese operations were held through intermediary holding companies. The Indonesian subholding company was an Indonesian legal entity. The Chinese holding company was a Bermuda company. Debt was issued at all levels of the company and totaled approximately $13.9 billion, a large percentage denominated in U.S. dollars.

APP's largest creditor group consisted of public debt holders, with notes denominated in U.S. dollars, holding approximately $6 billion in public securities. (Public debt was issued at the parent company, or finance subsidiaries of the parent company, at each of the four Indonesian mills, and at the Bermuda subholding company.) IBRA was the largest single creditor, holding the equivalent of $1 billion in debt acquired from the Wijaya family–controlled bank, Bank International Indonesia. The remaining large groups of creditors were 12 government export credit agencies, a group of Japanese trading companies, which had close business ties to APP, and Chinese commercial banks, which had lent to the Chinese mills. The export credit agency debt had been structured so that a certain percentage of each loan was held by a commercial bank.

APP is an anomaly in Indonesian restructurings. Most large Indonesian corporations that required restructuring finished negotiations within a reasonable time frame. The more complex cases took three to four years. Almost all of these Indonesian cases ended in reasonably acceptable results for the creditors. The debtors typically maintained a constant and generally open dialog with creditors and ultimately reached a consensual agreement. Although they understood the weakness of the legal system, most were motivated to treat creditors fairly. The Salim Group, for example, continued to top up the required shares pledged as collateral for their Polymax issue, which had Indocement shares pledged as collateral. They continued to contribute the shares even after Indocement defaulted on its debt.

However, APP's size, mix of international creditors, multinational legal jurisdictions, and asset base place it in a class separate from other Indonesian cases. APP's restructuring has been ongoing for three years and will continue for some time. One difference between APP and some of the earlier Indonesian cases is the level of impairment. Many of the companies that successfully restructured were over-leveraged, but the value of the company roughly equaled or slightly exceeded the debt. Initial valuations based on the existing and projected cash flow indicated that the enterprise value of APP (the potential value of restructured debt plus equity) was potentially significantly less than the aggregate debt. A conventional restructuring would have converted a large amount of debt to equity. Unless this equity was carefully structured, the Wijaya family would lose control.

APP will eventually successfully restructure. A tried-and-true method of dealing with creditors, where they have weak recourse, is to wear them down. Recent press reports suggest that unsecured bondholders are unhappy but realize that they have no alternatives. APP management always expressed the desire to repay their debts, particularly to the export credit agencies and banks, but not at the expense of APP's agenda. According to APP's chief executive officer, the restructuring must be "win-win." That may have to change a little to complete the restructuring and settle all litigation. My experience is that consensual restructurings occur when all parties are unhappy but willing to compromise.

8

their legal representative, they had no local presence in either Singapore or Indonesia. I approached representatives of one of the largest creditors, a Japanese bank, and urged them to assume the role of chairman of the combined steering committee. They refused, saying that they did not have the language skills or experience. Coordination was impaired because the Chinese banks, in the beginning, attended some of the meetings but rarely met with the other creditors.[2] The Chinese banks thwarted the early efforts by foreign creditors to be active members of the Chinese creditors committee, instead insisting that they would develop a plan and share it with the non-Chinese creditors for approval.

Apart from IBRA, local creditors consisted of small commercial banks with drawn lines of working capital and public debt in the form of rupiah bonds issued by the Indonesian subsidiaries. The rupiah bondholders were well organized and insisted from the outset that they be paid in full. They agreed to extend maturities but demanded current interest. I attended some of the meetings of rupiah bondholders and put forth the foreign creditors' position that all pari passu creditors should be treated the same. At my last meeting at the Dusit Mangga Dua Hotel in Jakarta, the bondholders vehemently asserted that they be treated differently because the trees harvested to supply APP's mills were a national asset. After that meeting, APP's management worried that the rupiah bondholders might organize and seek to damage the local mills if they did not receive current interest. APP rolled over the lines of the local Indonesian banks for fear that they would trigger another bank failure and adverse publicity in Indonesia. The non-Chinese foreign creditors (who held roughly $10.5 billion of APP's total $14 billion debt) effectively acquiesced. IBRA became the only Indonesian creditor with nonperforming debt.

The creditors failed to respond to the APP plan proposed in February 2002. They insisted, until May, that they would not make a counterproposal until the committee's financial adviser released its findings, including the forecasted amount of debt that the Indonesian operations could sustain. APP suddenly made a major issue of the size of the creditors' financial advisory bill. This occurred at the same time that IBRA was demanding the first installment of $100 million, under a settlement with the Wijaja family. With no leadership of the creditors, no single creditor oversaw the interaction between APP and the creditors' adviser or was in a position to pressure APP to provide timely information and to control the adviser's costs. They had assigned a large team to review APP and were sometimes required to wait for data to be provided, lessening their efficiency and causing costs to mount. APP also insisted that all requests for information be submitted in writing, adding to the cost.

Vewing the challenge to their adviser's fees as a delaying tactic, two institutions broke ranks with the combined steering committee and filed a petition in a Singapore court asking that a judicial manager be appointed to oversee the restructuring negotiations. In the absence of strong coordination, dissident creditors can use the legal system to the disadvantage of the broader creditor group. I provided testimony in both of the attempts by individual creditors to petition the courts in Singapore concerning the APP negotiations. The first case was an action, brought by an individual small creditor, seeking to receive favorable treatment ahead of the other creditors. The second case was entered by these two institutions, out of frustration, when APP was viewed as deliberately delaying progress.

Singapore law allows the creditors of an insolvent company to petition the courts to appoint a judicial manager to take control of the reorganization or disposition of assets. I strongly believed that APP did not belong in a Singapore court. I had doubts that a Singapore court-appointed judicial manager could control the Indonesian and Chinese operations or that, if the subsidiaries filed in Indonesia, an Indonesian court-appointed administrator would coordinate with the Singapore judicial manager. The Indonesian mill managers would most likely not have taken instructions from a Singapore-based court appointee, resulting in chaos.

The second judicial management case was a more serious challenge to the consensual restructuring. Apart from the bondholders (whose legal adviser's fees were unpaid), the remaining members of the creditors committee did not support the dissident creditors. The judge pointed to my testimony and my experience, among other elements, as critical factors in letting APP's management continue to pursue an unsupervised restructuring.

The dismissal of the second judicial management petition was a major turning point in the case. Winning emboldened APP's management to cut off the bondholders from any discussion for some period of time and exacerbated the lack of leadership of the combined steering committee. The case distracted the creditors from the issue of their financial adviser, allowing APP to undermine the adviser's effectiveness. The consensual process, in which all creditors were in a dialogue with the debtor, ended. At this point, my role also ended.

8

Cash Controls

Cash controls are a typical feature that creditors seek to impose on a debtor in a capital-intensive industry. Indocement agreed to cash sweeps and control over annual budgets as part of its restructuring. In the Asia Pulp and Paper negotiations, members of the creditor group saw cash controls as a critical element of the restructuring. APP's Chinese banks had installed financial representatives in each of APP's Chinese mills and controlled even relatively small cash disbursements. Creditors' concerns grew when the Indonesian mills' year 2000 financial statements disclosed (among other items) that cash balances at Pindo Deli, one of the Indonesian subsidiaries, were actually deposits in a private, Cook Island–based, single-purpose bank controlled by the Wijaya family. The asset side of the private bank balance sheet consisted of illiquid, undeveloped real estate, adjacent to the Pindo Deli paper mill. The prior-year consolidated financial statements, audited by the local Arthur Andersen affiliate, had mischaracterized the deposits as being in a branch of Bank International Indonesia (BII), a large public bank with a similar name, also controlled by the Wijaja family. The financial authorities in Indonesia investigated the Indonesian subsidiaries, after disclosure of their financial statements for 2000. Each of the four Indonesian subsidiary companies paid fines, but no sanctions were levied against officers or directors. The Singapore-based parent company never published consolidated statements after 1999. No regulator has apparently demanded that the parent company publish subsequent consolidated financial statements or correct prior-year statements.[3]

On September 11, 2001, at the creditor meeting in Shanghai, APP management promised the creditors that they would agree to and actively pursue some form of controls on APP cash. We arranged for a subsequent meeting, in Hong Kong (China), with the bondholders' representative to discuss this topic. He was to invite one or two other creditors. APP's chief executive officer expected to attend a small meeting where he could have a frank discussion about how this structure would affect his decisionmaking and control. Instead, all of the steering committee showed up, with some 40 people present. He felt ambushed, and from that moment forward he was suspicious of the creditors' motives. Indeed, APP subsequently fired Hendrik Tee, the chief financial officer, who had proposed a structure in which the family would remain in control of operations and independent parties would control the Indonesian sales, marketing, and cash disbursements.

Following the Hong Kong (China) meeting, some of the bondholders reported that large amounts of publicly traded APP parent-company and Indonesian mill debt were being bought by Indonesian-based brokerage firms. The creditors strongly believed that the family was using cash flow from the Indonesian operations to purchase the companies' debt, including U.S.-registered publicly traded debt. APP management vehemently denied that the family was buying the debt.[4]

Much later, in an attempt to address the creditors' concerns, IBRA announced that it had installed financial controllers in APP's Indonesian operations. Foreign creditors continued to press for a structure in which independent parties controlled the cash, but IBRA, in subsequent negotiations with the export credit agencies, categorically rejected any external control of APP's cash at the Indonesian mills.

Unexpected Effect of Laws Passed at the Time of the Crisis

A complicating factor in the APP restructuring arose from an agreement entered, before the standstill, between IBRA and the Wijaya family to settle the debts of the family-controlled bank, BII. Under the agreement, the Indonesian mills agreed to repay, over four years, debts owed by APP subsidiaries to IBRA for BII debts transferred to IBRA. The Wijaya family members were also liable for these debts.

At the time of the crisis, in an effort to stabilize the banking system, the Indonesian central bank made advances to banks to replace lost deposits. Subsequently, in many cases, the controlling shareholders were found to have violated legal lending limits by providing more credit to related parties than allowed under central bank regulations. Consequently, shareholders of the banks were held personally liable to the Indonesian government for these advances. Nonperforming loans, such as the APP debt, were removed from the banks and held by IBRA. The former bank owners were liable to IBRA for these debts.

Under laws passed at the insistence of the International Monetary Fund after the crisis, IBRA had the right to seize assets of any company controlled by a debtor owing IBRA. This law allowed IBRA to seize and sell unsecured assets ahead of other creditors at either the parent or the subsidiary level. This was apparently true even where non-IBRA debt at a subsidiary level was

8

structurally senior to IBRA's claims. IBRA could also seize and sell secured assets but was required to recognize and deal with the secured claim.

This law was reflected in the settlement agreement and resulted in IBRA demanding and receiving better treatment than the other creditors in the restructuring subsequently negotiated by IBRA with the export credit agencies.[5] The law was developed, in part, to dilute the economic power of the wealthy families in Indonesia. The law effectively altered the credit standing of debts that were in place at the time the law was passed. It had the unintended effect of deepening foreign creditors' negative perception of the Indonesian credit environment.

IBRA demanded and ultimately received the first installment of debt from the Indonesian mills at the point where the foreign creditors were in a standstill and awaiting their adviser's report. IBRA's demands occurred at the same time that APP challenged and withheld the fees of the creditors' advisers. This added to the anxiety of the creditors, leading to the second judicial management case.

Role of Government Interventions in Restructuring Negotiations

In Indonesia, some creditors that (based on the experience in Mexico or Malaysia; see boxes 8.2 and 8.3) expected government pressure to reach a comprehensive solution in large complex cases have been disappointed. Early in the Asian crisis, the government of Indonesia established a forum, called the Jakarta Initiative, mandated to facilitate out-of-court restructurings in recognition of the lack of reliability of the court system. This was to be modeled on the London rules, which were informal guidelines that the Bank of England had used to facilitate out-of-court restructurings in the United Kingdom. Unfortunately, Indonesia never empowered the Jakarta Initiative in a way that enabled the government to force debtors and creditors to compromise. The Jakarta Initiative was relatively ineffective in larger, complex cases.

Foreign Government Intervention

Following dismissal of APP's second judicial management petition, the export credit agencies attempted to fill the leadership void among the

---

Box 8.2: Role of the Mexican Government in Restructuring

In Mexico, numerous out-of-court restructurings of large companies were successful and completed quickly following the Mexican peso crisis. Mexico, in 1995, differed from Indonesia in that Mexican banks were the largest creditor group of the failed companies. Some of the Mexican bank debt had been acquired by Fondo Bancario de Protección al Ahorro (FOBAPROA), the Mexican equivalent of IBRA. FOBAPROA was formed, after the peso crisis, to hold the debts of failed Mexican banks and the nonperforming debt of surviving banks. Unlike the experience in the earlier Latin American crisis in 1982, where foreign commercial banks were large lenders to failing Mexican companies, foreign commercial banks had little exposure to failing Mexican corporates in 1994–95. Tight credit controls imposed following the 1982 crisis were effective. Wall Street firms, in contrast, held some of the largest foreign exposures to the failing Mexican corporates at the time of the peso crisis.

In contrast to Indonesia, Mexican creditors, with the support of the government through FOBAPROA, were very proactive in instituting changes in the management of companies where debt was impaired. For example, the Mexican banks and FOBAPROA held $1.1 billion of the total $1.2 billion of the debt of Aeroméxico and Mexicana de Aviación. The banks were able to force the chief executive officer to resign and converted all of their debt holdings to equity (leaving original holders with 2 percent of the equity of the combined companies).

The largest of the Mexican companies to be restructured was Grupo Sidek, a hotel management, property developer, and steel company. Its corporate structure was almost as complex as that of APP, although all of its assets were in Mexico. Most of Sidek's debt was to Mexican banks and to FOBAPROA, the government entity holding the bad debts of Mexican banks. (The Mexican government had insisted that Mexican banks, including government-owned Nacional Financiera, lend some $220 million to Sidek in early 1995 to stabilize the company during rescue discussions with the U.S. Treasury. Proceeds of this loan were used to pay off maturing debt, mostly owed to foreign institutions. In the subsequent restructuring, the lenders attempted to have this debt repaid ahead of the debts of other creditors. We rejected their request in that there was no basis in Mexican law for such priority treatment.) The creditors forced the family to resign from management after 18 months of negotiation proved fruitless. A new chief executive officer was selected, some financial irregularities were discovered, senior officials, including one family member, were arrested for fraud, and Lehman Brothers, my employer at the time, was appointed as financial adviser. We reached an agreement with creditors 13 months later. At my final meeting with Sidek's board of directors, the board asked for the resignation of Jorge Martínez Guitrón from the position of nonexecutive chairman of Sidek's steel subsidiary, Grupo Simec, even though he had not been involved in running the real estate development group, Grupo Situr, where the irregularities had occurred. Nevertheless, the board no longer wanted the family to be associated with the company in any way.

8

---

non-Chinese foreign creditors and sought to advance the restructuring discussions without the other creditors. Export insurance claims filed against Nippon Export Insurance (NEXI) focused the Japanese government on the first large insurance claim paid in many years, and NEXI officials became impatient with the progress of the discussions. NEXI began to assume a more proactive role among the export credit agencies. The U.S., German, and Japanese governments each sent letters to the government of Indonesia, ask-

---

Box 8.3: Role of the Malaysian Government in Restructuring

Like Mexico, the Malaysian government took a significant and proactive approach to finding an attractive solution for high-profile cases. Most notable was the case of Renong Berhad and its affiliate UEM, the largest of the Malaysian restructurings, with a total of approximately M$25 billion ($6.1 billion) combined debt at all levels. Approximately one-third of this debt was at the Renong and UEM parent-company levels, which were the subject of the restructuring.

Renong, which subsequently faced restructuring again, relied on the credit of its toll road subsidiary—Plus—to rescue the parent company. Plus issued new zero-coupon debt, which was to pay cash once the bank debt of the toll roads matured. This debt was sold to Malaysian institutions and issued to unsecured creditors. Secured creditors were paid in full from the proceeds of the securities sold. The Malaysian govern-

ment supported this arrangement by allowing this debt to have certain features that made it attractive for institutions to hold, including satisfying requirements imposed on banks to encourage new lending.

The Corporate Debt Restructuring Committee (CDRC), a Malaysian government entity set up to facilitate restructurings, played the most critical role in reaching agreement on the Renong restructuring. The CDRC chairman, Datuk Chellappah Rajandram, participated in creditor meetings. Issuing new debt to repay creditors left the company highly leveraged, but it avoided the conversion of debt to equity and left management temporarily in place. Renong soon faced a second restructuring, and the chief executive officer was forced to resign. As was the case in Mexico, local Malaysian institutions were significant lenders to Renong Behard and UEM.

---

ing that it intercede and force IBRA to work jointly with the other governments. At APP's request, I visited the U.S. embassy to offer my perspective on the situation. This was apparently the first time in any country that a group of governments had joined together to intercede at the highest levels in a purely commercial issue.

Under pressure from the foreign governments, IBRA and a group of export credit agencies entered a memorandum of understanding to act as a team in bringing the APP settlement to a conclusion. I was encouraged by this direct government involvement and, as one of my last acts as adviser, urged the bondholders to allow the export credit agencies to lead the negotiations.

The export credit agencies ended up negotiating with both IBRA and APP, not as a team with IBRA. They sought to have cash controls and shares of the Indonesian subsidiaries placed in trust as protection against future defaults. IBRA sought to accelerate the pace of the restructuring to meet the deadline to cease operating imposed by its enabling legislation and refused to support the more stringent provisions sought by the foreign creditors. At one point in the negotiations, the creditor governments asked the Indonesian government to intercede with IBRA and were turned down.

They eventually reached an agreement that lacked many of the terms sought by the foreign creditors. The U.S. EXIM Bank broke ranks with the other export credit agencies and rejected the agreement, filing a suit in the United States. In early 2004, IBRA sold its debt to a single purchaser for an average price of 24 cents.

Preserving the Value of the Enterprise

At a time of crisis numerous forces can be at play that are rarely encountered in developed markets. A lack of law and order, or lawless entrepreneurial behavior, can threaten the value of the company under restructuring. In both Mexico and Indonesia, after the crisis, enterprising journalists threatened disruptive disclosures unless compensated. In one case, where I was the adviser, virtually every street corner of Jakarta had a magazine vendor hawking a brand new publication accusing a prominent businessman of corruption, while the publisher was approaching the businessman with an offer to cease publication.

At the commencement of the APP restructuring, there was considerable potential for destruction of the Indonesian APP operations if the Wijaya family was not seen as firmly in control. I was concerned that APP's pulp mills, located in Sumatera, would become another Dipasena.[6] A major structural factor in APP is ownership of the rights to harvest the trees to make pulp. The Wijaya family owned the concession to the forests in Sumatera and had agreed under their credit documents to sell the harvested trees to APP's Indonesian mills at cost. Soon after local press reports of APP and the Wijaya family's problems circulated in Indonesia in early 2001, problems started in the Sumatra forests controlled by the family. Perceiving the family's weakness, rogue traders set up a well-equipped large camp, deep in the forest, and began to steal wood and sell it to competitors. Once the press speculation on the weakness of the family subsided, the problems in the forest died down.

Complexity of Public Debt

In a restructuring where only bank debt and commercial paper are outstanding, it is relatively easy to identify and approach each creditor to obtain consent to a restructuring. In most of the successful Indonesian restructurings, outlined earlier, there was no public debt. In situations where there are public bonds, particularly in the emerging markets, almost invariably less than 100 percent of the bondholders can be reached. In cases where it is possible to identify all the holders, often some neglect to vote or vote against the restructuring.[7]

Indocement's affiliate, Polymax, had debt governed by a trust deed under U.K. law.[8] A supermajority of the bondholders voted to accept a recovery of 82 cents that was binding on all of the bondholders. APP, in contrast, had debts at the parent company and at the Indonesian subsidiaries governed by U.S. law.[9]

This adds more complexity to the restructuring in that such debt is governed by the U.S. Trust Indenture Act, which theoretically offers strong protection to creditors. Under U.S. law each individual creditor has the right to be repaid unless a court orders otherwise (to be absolutely certain, most lawyers would say unless a U.S. court so orders). If APP were to restructure its Indonesian debt, without bringing the case to a U.S. bankruptcy court, APP's management runs the risk that a dissident creditor, not joining the restructuring, could obtain a judgment from a U.S. court. (However, from a practical point of view, it might be difficult for the dissident creditor to obtain a recovery. If a company restructures, obtaining an order from a foreign court without the U.S. proceeding, a disgruntled creditor could not sue in that foreign country. The creditor could obtain a U.S. judgment but would still need to get that judgment enforced in a jurisdiction where a court recognizes the judgment and the debtor has assets.)

This increased complexity adds to the time and cost of the restructuring. Creditors who are wary of the lack of control, costs, or disclosure and antifraud provisions of U.S. bankruptcy law can delay a restructuring or seek to have the debt purchased by parties supporting the debtor so U.S. proceedings can be avoided. It is ironic that the greater protection afforded by the U.S. law can cause behavior that might lead to delays and possibly lower recoveries.

No company issuing new debt is concerned about the ease or complexity of a future restructuring. Subsequent purchasers of that debt are concerned about the ease or difficulty of reorganizing the company when there is a default. In the emerging markets, where local courts are unreliable and U.S. courts present complexity, the ability to restructure public debt without a court, through a vote of the creditors, is a great benefit.

A number of Latin American companies have been restructured through prepackaged U.S. bankruptcies because of this U.S. law requirement. To my knowledge, no Asian company has yet to file in a U.S. bankruptcy case.

Summary

In emerging markets, companies restructure their debts, despite the lack of reliable court systems. In places like Mexico in past periods and Indonesia today, where the court systems are not reliable, government intervention in large, complex restructurings can be helpful. Governments should act particularly if there is a concern about the effect of delayed or failed high-profile restructurings on future foreign investment. In most emerging markets, local institutions often have exposures similar to those of foreign creditors, and they will lobby regulators and governments to intervene. The worse situations are those such as APP, where debt is impaired in value, the controlling shareholders are determined to maintain control, and only foreign creditors have nonperforming debt.

Notes

1. Apart from concern about the court system, inadequacies in the old Mexican bankruptcy law made it difficult to use in a complex case. The most important cases in Mexico, following the peso crisis, were the restructurings of Grupo Sidek and those of the two airlines, Aeroméxico and Mexicana de Aviación. These restructurings were completed out-of-court, and the results mirrored the rights of creditors under Mexican law. Mexico recently passed a new bankruptcy law correcting shortcomings in the older law. To date, there have been few major cases involving foreign creditors under the new law.

2. The Chinese creditors continued to receive interest payments during the restructuring. Some of the export credit agencies, related banks, and Japanese trading companies had debt at the Chinese mill level pari passu with the Chinese banks but were paid on a delayed basis. The banks related to the export credit agency debt initially made a tactical error by insisting that the Chinese banks had to use the financial adviser selected by the combined steering committee. The representatives of the Chinese

banks, who had the most exposure to the Chinese operations, rightfully wanted to select their own adviser or at least have a say in the choice of advisers.

3. The Singapore Monetary Authority did launch an investigation after Mark Mobius, senior executive of Franklin Templeton, voiced his concerns. It recently announced that it had completed the investigation and was considering what actions to take. One of the possible factors in the relatively gentle treatment by local regulators is the lack of any local financial institution, in either Singapore or Indonesia (apart from IBRA), with a large nonperforming exposure.

4. In June 2004 in an interview reported in the Financial Times, a family member admitted that companies related to the family had, in fact, been purchasing APP debt.

5. In addition to repayment of the installments agreed between IBRA and the family, the restructuring agreement treated IBRA's debt at the intermediate holding company pari passu with debt at the Indonesian operating company.

6. Early after the onset of the financial crisis, I represented the Nursalim family in their preliminary negotiations with IBRA to settle claims of their closed bank. Under the preliminary terms, Samsjul Nursalim agreed to relinquish control of Dipasena, a shrimp farm in Sumatra, to IBRA. Perceiving Nursalim's weakness, labor organizers stirred up emotions among the farmers, who were angry over loans they owed in dollars (frozen shrimp were exported and sold in dollars), which had grown fivefold following the collapse of the rupiah. The farmers attacked him when he went to discuss the loans and first wounded and later dragged his bodyguards from the local infirmary and killed them. The shrimp export operations at Dipasena never restarted.

7. An example is Aeroméxico, which had $135 million of public debt subject to U.S. law. We identified the bondholders and had almost 100 percent participation, with 97 percent accepting the restructuring. We had set a 95 percent threshold. Holders of the 3 percent sued Aeroméxico in a U.S. court and were paid in full. In the cases in Asia, where I was involved with trust deeds under U.K. law, participation was lower. Approximately 75 percent of the holders responded to the solicitations in both Polymax and the case of Renong in Malaysia. In some cases—for example, Polymax—we failed to have a quorum at the initial meeting.

8. A typical trust deed requires a 75 percent positive vote at a meeting to alter the economic terms of the notes. A quorum of 66.7 percent of note holders is required, but quorum requirements drop to 33.3 percent at an adjourned meeting. If exactly 33.3 percent submit proxies to attend the adjourned meeting, as few as 28 percent of the creditors can approve the plan. The vote is binding on all of the note holders of that issue. No court involvement is necessary.

9. APP's China subholding company is a Bermuda company. APP recently completed a restructuring of this company in a Bermuda court, filing for a scheme of arrangement requiring that a majority in numbers of the holders owning 75 percent of the debt approve the plan. The plan, converting virtually all of the debt to equity, was approved, but the agent hired to solicit votes (who apparently had not been paid by APP) subsequently reported to the court that a number of the bondholders had failed to collect their shares, and an investigation found that they were employees of APP's Indonesian mills.

8

Chapter 9

Government Policy Responses in Korea

Hogen Oh

In this paper, I briefly address my experience as chairman of a corporate restructuring committee during the economic crisis in Republic of Korea. For quite some time, Korea had been practically a state-managed economy.[1] The transformation of that state-managed economy into something that resembles a market economy began toward the late 1980s, around the time of the Olympics in Seoul. The economic crisis was the result of a number of factors, including the introduction of market forces.

When the crisis hit in November 1997, Korea was undergoing a political transition. In December, a new president was elected, and he confronted a tripling of the exchange rate, a doubling of interest rates, and the possible bankruptcy of hundreds of corporations because of the liquidity crisis.

The first thing the new government did was to create a financial supervisory commission. Previously, supervision of the financial sector had been divided among boards for the banks, the securities industry, and insurance. These were run more or less like an old boys' club. A civil servant nominally acted as one of the senior figures, but issues were settled among insiders within the club. Thus a financial supervisory commission was a totally new concept. A powerful government agency was created to oversee banking, securities, and insurance and to exercise authority over accounting firms, the setting of standards, and similar issues.

9

The first, and in my view the most important, of the many policy measures taken was to force the supervised firms (particularly the banks) to be audited according to international accounting standards. The board's authority over the banks also led corporations to adopt international accounting standards, which enabled a series of measures. Without this requirement, many of the policy responses to the crisis would not have been possible.

The financial supervisory commission tightened the supervision of the financial industry, particularly banks. The banks typically had been allowed to carry huge nonperforming loans on various pretexts, excuses, and exceptions. For example, banks did not write off their losses in the value of a security unless it dropped below 30 percent of its acquisition value. This changed overnight, and banks had to face reality. In turn, Korean corporations, and especially the chaebols, were forced to delete all their cross-guarantees.

The groundwork for some of these policies was laid in my office. For example, the financial supervisory commission borrowed a couple of my talented staff, and this team worked 24 hours a day for more than two weeks to come up with a formula for restructuring. However, in the end, a financial supervisory commissioner declared in the press that chaebols had to reduce their debt-to-equity ratio to 200 percent by the end of the year, period. There was a real uproar among chaebols and corporations. In reality, he lacked the legal power to impose specific leverage limits on corporations. However, the commission could force the banks not to lend to anybody or to renew their loans, unless their debt-to-equity ratio came down to the standard. This was a highly controversial, high-profile measure that was not expected to be fully enforced. With an average debt-to-equity ratio of 400 percent, it was impossible to reach 200 percent within a year. Nevertheless, this measure had a large impact on the way business leaders thought about financing and how they rationalized their balance sheet.

The next important step was to introduce the London approach to corporate restructuring. In my view, the government was partly forced, partly encouraged, and partly ready to adopt the London approach to corporate restructuring. The government encouraged financial institutions to develop a special accord for corporate restructuring, which all 230 financial institutions of note had signed by June 1998.

The goal of the London approach was to facilitate agreements on corporate restructuring, which was a considerable task given the creditor structure of Korean corporations. The typical medium-size Korean corporation, with a financial exposure of $1.5 billion, would usually have anywhere between 40 and 60 institutions lending to it in one form or another. With so many creditors, it could be difficult to achieve the 75 percent threshold for agreement provided for in the accord. Therefore, the accord provided for a corporate restructuring committee, with an executive chairman, which would review proposals for corporate restructuring. If 75 percent of the creditors could not reach agreement, the restructuring proposal would be submitted to the committee, which then issued a binding judgment on the proposal.

It was very difficult for the government to find someone independent, who was not related to either a political party or the chaebols. Thus they chose me, a retired academic and merchant banker; I agreed to take on the task for one year. Unfortunately, the media promoted the view of me as the overlord of hell for business. Nevertheless, the process was private and voluntary, which helped to make the task and my role more acceptable.

In any event, the proof of success is in the results. We managed workouts for about 102 corporations, including Daewoo companies. My committee rejected six of them for the workout, two others failed after the workout, and the rest appear to be healthy. The accord was extended for another year, and I agreed to stay on for that period.

Some of the workouts were an outstanding success, like Daewoo Group companies. The Daewoo Corporation as a single corporation had the largest financial exposure, just over 30 trillion won. The construction company that we spun off from Daewoo became the number one construction company in Korea within two years of the workout, while the trading company is probably the only truly international trading company in Korea and is making good profits.

Where we have not succeeded, in my view, is in addressing the problems of the largest chaebols (other than Daewoo). The policymakers still believe that the largest chaebols are too big to fail. Thus they were allowed to undertake voluntary restructuring among themselves—the so-called Big Deals. Seven Big Deals were proposed, and they went nowhere after months of talk. I was asked to be the judge on these Big Deals, but I initially refused. The government expected big returns for the economy, the chaebols expected to pass on their losses to the banks, and the banks felt that it was a government-chaebol conspiracy to hit them. At the end of the day, I took the position, but I rejected six of the seven deals. They were basically designed to siphon money off of the banks.

In short, one of the mistakes, albeit an understandable one, is that we should have addressed the need for corporate restructuring regardless of the

9

size of the corporation. Nevertheless, we achieved considerable success in addressing the corporate crisis. I do not know if anybody else in the world has confronted $100 billion in financial exposure of hundreds of corporations on the brink of bankruptcy or at least insolvency. The know-how and methodology are not written out. You just have to face the task and do what you can; you have to go back to the basics.

The greatest factor in Korea's successful corporate restructuring is that the government created an appropriate environment for voluntary restructuring. At the same time, the government never meddled in the details of restructuring itself; the creditors and my committee handled all of that. And the government did not name which industry or which company it wanted to survive. That was critical to our success. The government found the fiscal resources to support the restructuring process, but let the process proceed by itself.

Note

1. As a young professor of economics in the early 1970s, I wrote a paper comparing the Korean economic system to that under Hitler, which got me into a lot of trouble.

9

Chapter 10

Malaysia's Experience with Corporate Restructuring

Dató Zainal Abidin Putih

This paper emphasizes how efforts made in stabilizing and restructuring the banking sector set the stage for future corporate reform in Malaysia. For this purpose, the 1997–98 Asian financial crisis is the pivotal point, since it catalyzed many of the major initiatives implemented in Malaysia.

Before the Crisis

When the Asian financial crisis descended on Malaysia in the second half of 1997, the country was in a position of strength. During the early to mid-1990s, Malaysia was one of the fastest-growing East Asian economies. Together with Indonesia and Thailand, Malaysia experienced high economic growth rates of between 7 and 12 percent annually, while China's economy expanded between 9 and 14 percent annually. Other countries such as Singapore, Republic of Korea, and Taiwan (China) were also growing rapidly.

The economic indicators of these countries, often loosely referred to as the East Asian newly industrialized economies, suggested impressive macroeconomic performance and strong economic fundamentals. Generally, the countries had moderate inflation, no significant fiscal imbalances, high savings, and a large skill base.

Malaysia practiced the free market system diligently by promoting trade and investment, practicing fiscal discipline, implementing only a few subsidies, undertaking tax reform, liberalizing the financial system, ensuring a competitive exchange rate, embarking on privatization, introducing deregulation, and safeguarding property rights.

As reported by the Malaysian National Economic Action Council, during the five years leading up to 1996, Malaysia's real GDP growth averaged 8.7 percent a year, inflation was low, at around 3.8 percent, and the unemployment rate was only 2.5 percent (in 1996). As of June 1997, Malaysia had a relatively low external debt of $45.2 billion or 42 percent of gross domestic product. The debt service ratio was only 6.1 percent of exports in 1996.

The country was prospering. Its saving rate, at 38.5 percent, in 1996 was one of the highest in the world. Its stock market, the fifth largest in terms of market capitalization in Asia, peaked on December 13, 1996, with the Kuala Lumpur Stock Exchange Composite Index recording 1,188 points. The ringgit was stable at around M$2.52 to the U.S. dollar. The banking sector was in good health, with a capital adequacy ratio of 12.2 percent. Nonperforming loans were only 2.2 percent of total loans in June 1997, although there was concern about the rapid expansion of credit to the private sector, especially during the period from 1994 to 1996, when credit grew at an annual rate of 24 percent.

Michael Camdessus, managing director of the International Monetary Fund at the time, stated in a speech on June 17, 1997, that he had a lot of confidence in Malaysia, in its economic fundamentals, and in the management of its economy: "Malaysia is a good example of a country where the authorities are well aware of the challenges of managing the pressure that results from high growth and of maintaining a sound financial system amid substantial capital flows and a booming property market." These policies helped to integrate the Malaysian economy with other regional and global blocs, earning the country prominent spots on the radar screen of investors.

Impact of the Crisis

The crisis hit swiftly and severely. It started when the Thai baht experienced a series of speculative attacks following investors' concerns about the health of Thailand's banks and finance companies, eventually resulting in the flotation of the baht on July 2, 1997. Other regional economies were quickly affected and came under tremendous pressure. On July 8, 1997, Malaysia intervened in the foreign exchange market to defend the ringgit but withdrew after about a week when it was unable to cope with the pressure on the currency.

Between July 11 and August 14 of the same year, Indonesia and the Philippines were forced to float their respective currencies. By October, the contagion reached China (Taiwan and Hong Kong), and by November, Korea was also infected. By December, Korea had to seek financial support from the International Monetary Fund, following in the footsteps of Indonesia and Thailand.

The crisis brought about the collapse of stock markets and asset prices. Almost immediately after Malaysia was forced to float the ringgit, the Kuala Lumpur Composite Index dropped to a 30-month low of 880 points. It slid further to 574 points in December 1997, before hitting 262 points on September 2, 1998. This was a decline of more than 70 percent within a period of 15 months.

The deteriorating stock market created panic among investors, resulting in capital flight, severely depleting Malaysia's reserves, and sharply weakening the ringgit. The ringgit fluctuated wildly in the range of M$3.52 and M$4.71 against the U.S. dollar. This dire situation forced the Malaysian government to impose selective exchange controls, one of which was to peg the ringgit at M$3.80 to the U.S. dollar, effective at 11.00 a.m., September 2, 1998.[1]

In 1998 alone, the economy contracted 7.4 percent, while private investments shrank 55 percent. In short, the crisis hit businesses hard, undermined the financial system, choked the banking system with bad loans, and caused a major economic upheaval in its wake.

Factors Contributing to the Crisis

The crisis destabilized the Malaysian financial system, making comprehensive restructuring efforts necessary for both the banking and corporate sectors.

Although the economy showed signs of recovery by early 1999, the contagion had taken its toll on the financial sector. External factors not-

10

withstanding, the problems were caused, at least partly, by the sector's own weaknesses. For example, during the high-growth years before the crisis, banks exuberantly extended credit to borrowers, with a high percentage of loans going to the booming construction and property sectors.[2] Many of these loans were secured against properties or proposed real estate projects as well as quoted shares.

However, in the banks' eagerness to increase their loan assets, many of the loans were approved, as discovered later, without proper assessment of the borrowers' viability and without adequate valuation of the collateral. Some companies amassed debts beyond their capability to service the loans, while some of the properties pledged as collateral were valued using unrealistic assumptions with fantastic yield projections. Therefore, when the stock market deteriorated and the construction and property sector contracted 23 percent in 1998, borrowers defaulted, the value of loan collateral plummeted, and nonperforming loans hit the roof. As a result, properties formed 43 percent of the collateral for the nonperforming loans taken over by Danaharta, while shares constituted 20 percent (Danaharta 2000: app. 2).

Bank Negara Malaysia, the central bank, had always cautioned banks to exercise prudence in their lending activities. In fact, in April 1997, Bank Negara introduced measures to curb excessive lending to the real estate sector for the purpose of dealing in shares.

The booming economy also encouraged many companies to embark on business expansion drives. Unfortunately, some expanded beyond their means and capability, while quite a number ventured into areas unrelated to their principal business and in which they had very little, or no, expertise and experience at all. Back then, a plastic manufacturing company would venture into township development, or a road construction company would buy into a stock brokerage firm. Typically, a majority of the over-expansion and indiscriminate diversification was funded through bank borrowings. Excessive leverage, lack of management expertise, and deteriorating market conditions led to the failure of many such ventures.

In addition, the crisis exposed the fact that Malaysian corporations were heavily dependent on short-term borrowing from banks to fund long-term corporate needs, such as funding for project development. This usually led to a mismatch between the cost of funds and the maturity of the project, especially where the project had a long gestation period. When that happened in a crisis scenario, more often than not the corporate borrower would stop servicing the loan, which raised the level of nonperforming loans.

10

At the peak, bad loans in the banking system reached 9 percent, based on a six-month net nonperforming loan classification, or 14.9 percent on a three-month net classification, compared with 2.2 percent six-month net nonperforming loans just before the crisis. The high rate of nonperforming loans weakened the banks' capital base and distracted the financiers from their core business, which was lending to viable businesses and borrowers. Bankers were reluctant to lend because of the high probability that these loans would turn bad. This led to a liquidity problem, where businesses faced a drought in funding sources, further aggravating the economic situation.

Essentially, the crisis, apart from inflicting its own damage on the economy, exposed an environment of complacent corporate governance in the banking and corporate sectors. Despite a well-developed legal framework and active monitoring and enforcement by the regulatory bodies, the boards of directors and audit committees of the banks and companies were not monitoring their businesses in an effective manner. Furthermore, by being passive, minority and institutional shareholders did not contribute toward improving the situation.

The government realized very early in the crisis that corporate restructuring and recovery were necessary precursors to economic recovery. Companies must be given a chance to continue as going concerns and expand or diversify, thus generating multiplier effects that expand the economy. This recognition is clearly reflected in the policy response to the crisis.

The National Economic Recovery Plan

In January 1998, the Malaysian cabinet established the National Economic Action Council (NEAC). The council has 26 members, is chaired by the prime minister, and includes the deputy prime minister, representatives of ministries with economic portfolios such as finance and international trade and industry, the NEAC executive director, the chief secretary of the government, the governor of Bank Negara Malaysia, representatives from industries, banking and finance, trade unions, and consumer associations, and select resource persons. The council serves as a consultative body to the government, especially in the following areas:

- Formulating measures that could effectively pull Malaysia out of the crisis and minimize the adverse impact on the economy

10

- Changing policies and measures quickly to respond to the changing situation
- Fine-tuning measures and removing any obstacles to implementation.

Once established, NEAC worked swiftly and intensively. A working group met with more than 250 groups and individuals within two months to gather information and feedback in order to determine the causes and impact of the crisis. From the feedback received, NEAC identified a number of important tenets to guide the formulation of the recovery plan. One of the tenets was that the crisis served as an opportunity to address issues in the finance and corporate sectors that were found to be wanting in a number of instances. It was also agreed that the entire framework of corporate governance had to be reviewed in order to prepare the economy for a rapid return to the growth path. Therefore, there was a clear agenda for comprehensive restructuring of the banking and corporate sectors.

The findings were then documented as the National Economic Recovery Plan and launched on July 23, 1998. The plan had six objectives:

- Stabilize the ringgit
- Restore market confidence
- Maintain financial market stability
- Strengthen economic fundamentals
- Continue the equity and socioeconomic agenda
- Revitalize affected sectors.

Banking Restructuring

The six objectives were to be achieved by way of more than 500 detailed measures. This section focuses on the third objective: maintaining financial market stability. Several key measures were identified for this objective.

One was to establish agencies along the lines of the Resolution Trust Corporation or the Federal Deposit Insurance Corporation in the United States. Danaharta was set up as an asset management company with functions similar to those of the Resolution Trust Corporation. Meanwhile, Bank Negara Malaysia began developing a deposit insurance scheme for the banking system (Bank Negara Malaysia 2002).

Another key measure was to recapitalize the banking sector, especially to assist banks whose capital base had been eroded by losses. Danamodal Nasional Berhad was set up to undertake this task.

Meanwhile, the integrity of the whole banking system was at risk due to rising nonperforming loans. There was an urgent need to restructure corporate debts in order to reduce stress on the banking system and to repair the financial and operational positions of the corporate borrowers. This measure was to be implemented by the Corporate Debt Restructuring Committee (CDRC).

How were these three agencies linked? A bank in trouble because of huge amount of bad loans in its books would see Danaharta to sell its nonperforming loans. Thereafter, if the bank was still in a bad financial position and the shareholders could not recapitalize, the bank would seek financial assistance from Danamodal, at a cost. Effectively, new money would be injected into the bank, diluting the original shareholders. This meant that Danamodal could facilitate the consolidation of the sector by selling its stake to a stronger bank and thereby fostering mergers. Meanwhile, CDRC acted as an informal mediator, facilitating dialogue between borrowers and their creditors to achieve voluntary restructuring schemes. If CDRC could achieve this, then nonperforming loans would be resolved voluntarily. If not, Danaharta would be asked to take over the bad loans.

The three entities were coordinated via a steering committee chaired by the governor of the central bank, Bank Negara Malaysia.

Danaharta

Danaharta was established in June 1998 with two objectives: to remove nonperforming loans from the banking system and to maximize the value recovered from the nonperforming loans. To ensure that Danaharta could perform its task effectively, efficiently, and economically, the parliament of Malaysia approved the Danaharta Act, which gave Danaharta special powers to deal with nonperforming loans.

Under the Danaharta Act, Danaharta was able to acquire nonperforming loans from banks via statutory vesting, which sped up the transfer process. Danaharta completed its primary acquisition of loans by June 1999, six months ahead of schedule. Danaharta also had the ability to foreclose on property collateral without going through the court process, which significantly reduced the time and costs involved in recovering

10

nonperforming loans. Another special power was the ability to appoint a special administrator over a company that could not settle its debts with Danaharta. Throughout his appointment, the special administrator was given full control and responsibility over the assets and affairs of the company. He was required to prepare a workout proposal outlining how the company would pay off its creditors. This could include securing a white knight, or new investor, to take over the business, selling assets, changing management, or undertaking operational restructuring to unlock values and offload liabilities.

Danaharta did not take over *all* nonperforming loans. It only purchased those with face values of M$5 million or more at discounted prices based on the value of the underlying collateral. In the case of unsecured loans, Danaharta paid the bank a price equivalent to 10 percent of the loan amount outstanding. There was no compulsory acquisition of loans. All transactions were conducted at arm's length on a "willing buyer, willing seller" basis. To encourage banks to sell their nonperforming loans, Danaharta even agreed to a profit-sharing scheme for recovering nonperforming loans over and above Danaharta's purchase and holding costs with the selling bank (80 percent for the bank; 20 percent for Danaharta). As payment for these acquisitions, Danaharta issued government-guaranteed zero-coupon bonds to the banks.

Danaharta now has nonperforming loans of M$52.44 billion, roughly equivalent to $13.8 billion, within its portfolio. This includes loans it acquired from banks as well as the bad loans of two defunct banking groups that it manages on behalf of the Malaysian government. The smaller loans, which were more manageable, were left for the banks to recover.

Once the nonperforming loans were vested with Danaharta, the agency identified a recovery strategy for each and every loan. The recovery methods ranged from softer options, such as plain loan restructuring for viable enterprises, to harsher methods, such as foreclosure of loan collateral or legal action where a borrower failed to restructure his loan or where the enterprise was not viable to begin with.

Throughout its life span, Danaharta expects to recover M$30.63 billion, or 58 percent of its total portfolio of nonperforming loans. It has already received 73 percent of the expected recovery amount and is now in the midst of collecting the balance of M$8 billion, which it expects to complete by the time it winds down its operation in 2005.

10

Proceeds from the recovery of nonperforming loans will be used mainly to redeem Danaharta zero-coupon bonds with a total face value of M$11.14 billion issued to banks as payment for the purchase of nonperforming loans. At the end of 2003, Danaharta had redeemed M$2.61 billion of the bonds, with the balance maturing every quarter up to March 31, 2005. At the same time, recoveries from the nonperforming loans under management were distributed to the government. As of December 31, 2003, the government had received M$12.9 billion in the form of cash. Meanwhile, M$425 million in cash and 66.47 million units of securities had been distributed to selling banks under the surplus sharing arrangement.

By transferring their nonperforming loans to Danaharta, the financial institutions were able to refocus on their core business, which was to extend loans to viable borrowers. It also helped to reduce the level of nonperforming loans in the system to the present 6.8 percent on a six-month net basis or 9 percent on a three-month net basis.

Danamodal

Danamodal's task was to recapitalize banking institutions that failed to restore their capital adequacy ratio to 9 percent. Candidates for recapitalization were selected based on the results of stress tests conducted by Bank Negara Malaysia.

The "first loss" principle, by which the equity of original shareholders is written down, was strictly applied to all transactions. Institutions requesting capital injections had to submit recapitalization plans and were subject to monthly reporting of performance against a list of identified targets. Danamodal exercised control over management by appointing at least two representatives to the institution's board of directors, one of whom was to be an executive director or chairman of the board.

Since its establishment, Danamodal has injected a total of M$7.59 billion in the form of debt-to-equity convertible instruments or subordinated loans or both into 10 banking institutions. Danamodal has almost completed its mission, pending the divestment of its holding in the last bank.

Danamodal has also redeemed its entire M$11 billion (nominal value) five-year zero-coupon unsecured redeemable bonds, which matured on October 21, 2003. Danamodal issued these bonds in 1998 to fund the recapitalization exercise.

10

Corporate Debt Restructuring Committee

CDRC was established in July 1998 to mediate voluntary out-of-court restructuring of large debt cases involving borrowers with multiple major creditors. It was based on the London approach model that was successfully employed to deal with the secondary banking crisis in the United Kingdom in the 1970s.

Debt restructuring under CDRC was reserved for viable businesses, not for those in receivership or liquidation. Aggregate bank loans had to be in excess of M$50 million, with at least three lending institutions participating. The creditor committee had to represent at least 75 percent of total debt of all creditors.

CDRC had no legal status and was not backed by any special legislation. However, the debt restructuring negotiations were facilitated by a joint public-private sector steering committee appointed by Bank Negara Malaysia, assisted by a secretariat.

Although the progress initially was slow, new guidelines issued in August 2001 enabled CDRC to complete corporate debt restructuring and activate operational restructuring, which could include disposal of borrowers' non-core assets and separation of ownership and management. By the time CDRC closed down at the end of July 2002, it had helped to resolve all 48 cases it had accepted for mediation, involving M$52.5 billion of total debt outstanding.

Corporate Restructuring

Although the three agencies were established to maintain financial market stability, they also contributed, directly or indirectly, toward corporate restructuring.

Danaharta encouraged viable borrowers to restructure their loans, because more often than not, loan restructuring generates higher recovery value of nonperforming loans than other recovery methods. However, all borrowers had to comply with Danaharta's published loan restructuring principles and guidelines. The guidelines required that, in restructuring a company's nonperforming loans, shareholders of the company must take a proportionately larger haircut than creditors; the borrower must treat secured and unsecured creditors fairly; inadequate security must not be diluted; and, most important, every borrower is given only one opportunity to restructure a loan. This motivates borrowers to work hard to sustain the viability of their businesses, because once a borrower fails to comply with the guidelines or his business is found to be not viable, the penalty can be harsh. Danaharta may not have any other choice but to step in to foreclose and dispose of the borrower's assets or to dispose of his business to another party.

Meanwhile, Danamodal played a crucial role in restructuring the banking sector. With banks being important intermediaries in the economy, the recapitalization exercise restored confidence in the safety and soundness of the banking sector, thus preventing systemic failure and setting the foundation for stronger recovery. Danamodal also set the stage for consolidation of the banking sector by accelerating bank mergers. From a highly fragmented industry structure made up of 71 institutions prior to the crisis, there are now only 30 banking institutions under 10 domestic banking groups.

As for CDRC, its role in mediating for voluntary debt workout between borrowers and creditors paved the way for operational restructuring, such as through the disposal of assets or the sale of non-core business.

It is also important to note that all three are finite-life agencies. This was a deliberate policy decision to avoid moral hazard. Their establishment and respective roles may be relevant and justified during a period of economic crisis, but to have these agencies as permanent organizations would defeat the aim of developing healthier banking and corporate sectors.

Conclusions

With the banking restructuring efforts going well, the Malaysian government has now set its sights on improving the environment of corporate governance. In essence, the broad objectives of the reform agenda, which aim to rectify the weaknesses exposed by the crisis, are as follows:

- To provide fair treatment to all shareholders and protect minority shareholder rights, with particular emphasis on enhancing the rights and remedies of minority shareholders
- To promote transparency through the timely disclosure of adequate, clear, and comparable information concerning corporate financial performance, corporate governance, and corporate ownership
- To enhance the accountability and independence of the board of directors

10

- To promote training and education at all levels to ensure that the framework for corporate governance is supported by the necessary human and institutional capital
- To strengthen regulatory enforcement.

Significant progress has been made.

In 2001, the Malaysian government announced the Finance Committee Report on Corporate Governance and the Capital Market Master Plan, which collectively provided a comprehensive blueprint for the corporate reform agenda over the following 10 years. The overall approach represents a mix of self-regulation by the market and regulatory discipline by the relevant regulators, in addition to the laws that are already in existence or to be enacted.

For example, under new rules introduced by the Malaysian Stock Exchange Berhad, board members and shareholders shoulder more responsibilities and accountability on the conduct of listed companies, including in the areas of disclosure and reporting, internal controls, and protection of minority shareholders. Company directors are now compelled to undergo intensive training as a means to enhance their professionalism and promote better governance. The legal and regulatory frameworks that have supported corporate governance in Malaysia are constantly reviewed and improved to ensure continuing relevance and effectiveness. To ensure proper, timely, and transparent financial reporting, all companies are required by law to comply with the Malaysian accounting standards.

These are only a few of the positive changes that have taken place, and we can expect to see more in the future. In essence, the stage has been set for the corporate sector in Malaysia to undertake serious reform. The government has played a significant role in resolving problems besetting the financial system during the crisis, which could have caused severe, permanent damage to the corporate sector. It is now up to the private sector to take up the challenge of reforming itself.

References

Bank Negara Malaysia. 2002. *Annual Report 2002.*

Danaharta. 2000. *Operations Report for the Sixth Months Ending 30 June 2000.*

Mahani, Zainal Abidin. 2003. *Rewriting the Rules: The Malaysian Crisis Management Model*. Petaling Jaya: Prentice-Hall.

Notes

1. The peg rate was the prevailing ringgit exchange rate on the day selective capital controls were implemented. On September 1, 1998, the day the controls were implemented, the rate was M$4.22 to the U.S. dollar. However, following the announcement, the ringgit strengthened 10.5 percent against the U.S. dollar to M$3.82 and appreciated further to M$3.80, after which the peg rate was fixed. The peg rate of M$3.80 was also within the range in which the ringgit was traded between February and mid-June 1998 (M$3.60 to M$3.80 to the U.S. dollar). There was no plan to peg the ringgit at the pre-crisis level (M$2.50 to the U.S. dollar) because that would be unrealistic and out of line with other regional currencies.

2. Refer to Mahani (2003). Dr. Mahani, an economist, was actively involved with the National Economic Action Council.

10

Chapter 11

An Alternative to Government Management Companies: The Mellon Approach

Richard H. Daniel

For many years, the international banking community has been dealing with an overabundance of loans that are not being properly serviced by those obligated to do so. These business and real estate loans have been defined variously as bad, problem, or nonperforming. Not included are those that should have been identified as nonperforming but were not for several reasons. The international community manages these assets as performing loans, often with direct governmental assistance.

I spent most of my 40-year career in banking working as a commercial lender, as a loan portfolio manager, and, for the last sixteen years, as a manager of problem commercial loan portfolios in three major U.S. banks: Security Pacific in Los Angeles, Crocker Bank in San Francisco, and Mellon Bank in Pittsburgh, where I was also the chief credit officer. During that period of time, I became convinced that it was absolutely necessary to take the really bad loans away from the lenders who made them. They were not able to acknowledge that they had made a bad loan, let alone admit it to themselves. I was one of the first in the country to set up and run a full-fledged commercial loan workout department at a bank. At Security Pacific I demonstrated that it takes a different mentality to be in loan workouts and that we could succeed if we had the proper tools and were supported by senior management. The bank acknowledged that we had a problem and

223

that dealing with it required a paradigm shift. This realism started the ball rolling. It got us into the credit-monitoring process, which allowed us to find all the problem loans, to separate them from the marketing function, and to deal with them differently. As a result of our success, I was made the first executive vice president to run a commercial workout department in any major bank in the country. While at Security Pacific, I was a director of Robert Morris Associates and founded and moderated for seven years its Senior Workout Officers' Roundtable, representing the 15 largest banks in the country. I was also chairman of the unsecured creditors committee in the bankruptcy of Wickes Companies, the largest of its kind at the time. Finally, when I got to Mellon Bank, I was in charge of both the credit-granting and the loan workout departments—the front end and the back end of the total credit process. As a result of all this experience, I know and understand the administration of bank loan workouts in the United States.

Since my retirement, I have consulted in Hungary and Republic of Korea with banks trying to deal with their problem loan portfolios. My experience in these countries has shown that it is very difficult to solve this problem when the country is trying to move from a state-managed to a free market economy. Until the countries that perpetuate noneconomic businesses through bank loans that cannot be serviced decide to stop doing so, their governments will have to continue pouring money into their banking systems, either directly or indirectly, to lower their nonperforming loans. And bad loans will continue to be made. To stop the continual inflow, the decision will have to be made to stop making and renewing bad loans, which is very difficult to do in a state-managed economy. That, however, is just the first step. Then they will have to bifurcate the portfolio and move the bad loans into a new environment, in which the task is to collect loans, not make them. This requires a different kind of loan officer, one who knows when a loan is bad, who knows how to get the most out of the situation as fast as possible, and who has the unqualified support of senior management.

In my experience, a bank must have five basic attributes in order to deal with an excessive problem loan portfolio:

- A validated and properly functioning system of credit quality control and asset classification
- The needed reserves to write off all portions of the identified losses

- The removal of these assets from the line organization that underwrote them and their transfer to a specially trained group of collectors
- The use of a well-functioning legal system to help force collection
- The stoppage of making, or renewing, bad loans.

To illustrate my point, I use the Mellon National Bank in Pittsburgh, which in 1987 was experiencing a temporary lack of control over credit quality, a burgeoning number of nonperforming loans, and an increase in its loan charge-offs. It solved these problems without direct government assistance. A year earlier, in 1986, Mellon Bank hired me as vice chairman and chief credit officer to determine the health of the bank's credit process. My first task was to determine the soundness of the process and the expertise of the people running it. Soon I was spearheading an aggressive effort to identify all of the nonperforming loans that had not been identified by the existing loan-monitoring system. On the basis of a closer examination of the portfolios, and a more accurate classification of the assets, we found that, by the end of 1986, nonperforming assets were up 77 percent from the prior year's end, and we were still finding new ones. At that time, we began adding "acquired assets" into the reported totals. Year-end nonperforming assets went from $600 million in 1985 to $1 billion in 1986 and to $1.6 billion in 1987, all after writing off more than $700 million of perceived losses. Mellon clearly had a credit crisis, the extent of which would not have been known were it not for this effort to assess more accurately the amount of risk in the loan portfolio. The establishment of realistic loan risk assessment helped us to understand the problem.

I turn now to what we believed needed to be accomplished, the solution we came up with, and the outcome of our efforts. In July 1988, Mellon announced a two-prong capital financing and asset restructuring program. The first task was to raise $525 million of new equity capital from the investment firm of Warburg Pincus. This provided the reserves needed to take the next step in the process.

Later that year, we established Grant Street National Bank (In Liquidation). The sole purpose of Grant Street was to acquire a $640 million written-down portfolio of low-quality assets, to liquidate them, and then to dissolve the entity. Grant Street was spun off to the Mellon shareholders, with a non-Mellon board to distance the control of these assets from Mellon and its customers. The Mellon board supported the whole structure

11

of Grant Street. Grant Street then approached Drexel, Burnham, Lambert and raised $513 million of junk bond financing, which it used to purchase the written-down assets, with Mellon taking $97 million of preferred stock. Grant Street had already entered into a contract with Collection Services Corporation, a subsidiary of Mellon, for the management of the liquidation process. As its chief executive officer, I staffed Grant Street with Mellon workout people and outsiders, all with experience and training in the areas of expertise we needed. The customer relationships were transferred to this group. The marketing line organization was no longer in the picture. That, in and of itself, did wonders for our collection efforts. The borrowers were now dealing with "the last stop." It was made clear to them that we wanted cash, and only cash, and would go to the mat to get it. They had nowhere else to go. The buck had finally stopped.

The liquidation process proceeded very closely to the forecasted cash flows used to make up the discounted values. The business loans were collected faster than anticipated; however, the real estate loans and assets, which made up half of the portfolio, took a bit longer. In most cases, when we came to an impasse with a borrower, we had the potential to use our legal system to force either bankruptcy or foreclosure. These options were used, first as a threat and then as the final action if the threat did not produce the required result. It gave us the ability to push the collection process to a timely conclusion, which is not possible in countries where the legal system can take years and years to reach a final outcome, if at all. The United States legal system really works.

By 1988, we had successfully identified all of our nonperforming assets. We also had provided the needed reserves to write down our loans to their perceived values. We had removed the targeted problem assets from Mellon's balance sheet and the line organization, and we had begun an aggressive effort to collect the maximum cash we could from the assets as fast as possible.

The final and crucial step was to stop renewing problem loans and creating new ones. To accomplish this, we thoroughly overhauled the credit-granting process. A more centralized and dynamic procedure was installed, with a higher level of quality oversight. We needed to demonstrate to the financial community that we had solved our credit problems. The proof of having done so was that we went from a net loss of $844 million in 1987 to a net profit of $437 million in 1992, with continued increased profits thereafter.

11

The success we experienced at Mellon would not have been possible had we not strictly adhered to each and every one of the five attributes that a bank must have. Once again, they are (a) a validated and properly functioning system of credit quality control and asset classification, (b) the needed reserves to write off all portions of the identified losses, (c) the removal of these assets from the line organization that underwrote them and their transfer to a specially trained group of collectors, (d) the use of a well-functioning legal system to help force collection, and (e) the stoppage of making, or renewing, bad loans.

It is very difficult to carry out this process in any country that is trying to move from a state-managed to a free market economy. My experience indicates that this includes any economy in which one group controls both the business and the banking functions. Loan granting is driven by politics and connections, rather than commercial considerations, and loans wind up on the books without establishing the company's ability to service the debt. This inability to service the debt is usually hidden because good data are scarce on which to make intelligent credit decisions. The banks do not push the companies deeply enough to be able to validate that the companies' cash flows are adequate to service the debt. Consequently, the loans get made for the wrong reasons.

According to the *Wall Street Journal*, China's nonperforming loan ratio in the banking sector is close to 45 percent (as opposed to the reported 18 percent), and it will cost upward of $500 billion to clean up the balance sheets. We are all aware of the problems of nonperforming bank loans in Japan and Korea, and it looks as though China's probably will be even worse.

As long as countries continue to perpetuate noneconomic businesses through bank loans that cannot be properly serviced, they will have to continue pouring money into their banking systems or fund the asset-purchasing entities that relieve the banks of their bad loans. Either way, the government is bailing out the banks. The decision must be made either to bite the bullet, to clean up the banks, and to stop supporting noneconomic entities or to accept the fact that they are greatly shackled by having a state-managed economy. The process will not be easy and undoubtedly will take many years, but every journey begins with the first step.

11

Chapter 12

Corporate Restructuring Funds: The Lessons from Korea

Christopher Vale

This paper offers a perspective on why corporate restructuring funds were established in the Republic of Korea and then provides details regarding them, with specific examples from the fund managed by State Street/ Rexiter. And because the crux of the matter is to make the implementation of these funds effective, I discuss some of the problems we encountered with the structure of the funds in Korea.

Background

The objective of corporate restructuring funds must be seen in the context of the objectives of the Korean government in the aftermath of the crisis at the end of 1997. First, in the crisis, while big companies experienced problems, smaller companies fell off a cliff. Korea could have ended up with a few very large chaebols. Small and medium enterprises were the largest employers, and rehabilitating them was one of the priorities. Another objective was to improve corporate governance. Korea's systemic corporate crisis was an accident waiting to happen, in particular because typical debt-to-equity levels were at 400 percent across the entire market. Trying to get management to believe that anything over about 100 is risky, we found, was quite

12

difficult. In historical context, the leverage was understandable, because the chaebols were controlled by families. They did not have that much equity, and they did not want to dilute the equity they had. Moreover, they did not want to pay taxes, so they wanted to limit reported profits. They accomplished this by borrowing. The crisis also motivated a dramatic opening up of the market. For instance, foreign ownership was highly restricted in the banking system until May 1998, when regulations eliminated the 4 percent cap on foreign ownership of banks, starting in 1999.

Corporate Restructuring Funds

Corporate restructuring funds had two objectives: a policy objective and a performance objective. If the investment guidelines are clear, and the fund can be run as a performance-oriented fund, it can be marketed internationally, which allows it to mobilize money from international institutions. International capital markets are hard-nosed and interested only in performance. In Korea there was little appetite for funds with policy objectives, and the government was not able to raise money internationally from pension funds or endowments in the United States. Therefore, corporate restructuring funds mobilized domestic funding from 23 Korean financial institutions, which contributed a total of $1.3 billion.

Two points are notable. First, these were the first mutual funds in Korea and, as such, were governed by the rules applicable to mutual funds. Second, this was the first time that Korea had appointed foreigners to manage domestic funds. Given endemic conflicts of interest, bringing international best practice, especially in corporate governance and the encouragement of smaller companies, had a salutary effect.

Three funds had balanced mandates. Effectively, they had equity mandates, because, by the time they began to invest, interest rates had fallen and fixed-interest investments were not attractive. Although they were permitted to have up to 30 percent debt, various instruments (convertibles, bonds, and bonds with warrants) counted as debt. The funding was received on November 1, 1998, and 50 percent had to be invested by April 1999. Obviously, from a performance point of view, it is clearly bad to follow such a rapid investment process.

The funds had detailed investment guidelines. First, they could only invest in newly issued debt or equity. So, every investment was privately

12

negotiated. Some hindrances were associated with this. For example, a fund might want to buy the old debt at a distressed price and restructure the balance sheet in bonds with longer-term maturities or in equities. However, the funds were not allowed to buy old debt.

Second, the funds were not required to do workouts, which one would have thought was the main objective. They were encouraged to provide expansionary capital and some venture capital. Although it is good to support venture companies, the mandate was too broad. The funds subsequently had to do workouts, when the minister of finance ordered all four managers to undertake restructuring.

Third, workouts take a long time. The fund managed by State Street/Rexiter made 40 investments in Korea in about three years, of which 25 were made in the first year. One of the workouts had 41 creditors and took 18 months to complete. It clearly was impossible to undertake 21 or 25 workouts in one year.

Fourth, the Korean authorities did not define investment sectors per se. But Korea places considerable emphasis on exports in technology markets, and the Korean authorities wanted to promote technology exporters.

Fifth, the funds were limited to 50 percent of the equity in the chaebol and 10 percent of the equity in any one company. Given the size of the funds—$250 million—the largest investment was $25 million. The other rule was to set the minimum number of investments at 25, or $10 million per investment. That rule was hard to meet. The provisions inhibited investments in the 6–64 largest chaebols, which had in excess of a billion dollars of debt. So, again, that had key implications for the nature of the investments.

Sixth, there was an aversion to paying fees for private equity investments. Although there were performance fees, management fees were geared to the standards of compensation for publicly listed securities. And given the amount of effort that State Street/Rexiter put into this, and the number of people involved, the management fees were not profitable at the proposed level. Structurally, the design was also wrong and ended up benefiting the managers because the performance fee was paid on an annual basis, not an internal rate of return basis over a long horizon. Moreover, the fund had to employ a legal advisory firm, so the fund was paying out 30 percent of the fees.

Finally, State Street/Rexiter had a two-year contract. This was the first time the Korean authorities had appointed foreign managers, but clearly,

12

with a private equity mandate, a longer engagement period is warranted. Five to seven years are needed to allow investments to mature.

Therefore, if a country is considering setting up corporate restructuring funds, it needs to think carefully through the objectives and the design.

Considerable resources were needed to manage this mandate and give the Korean authorities best practice. Therefore, State Street/Rexiter entered a joint venture with a local investment advisory firm and hired four analysts. A four-man investment committee met in Korea every two months and was chaired by the vice chairman of State Street.

The Investment Process

We encountered problems because restructuring funds were structured as mutual funds. Mutual funds in Korea have to list within 12 months of being established. We were asked to list, and we refused. We argued that closed-end funds trade at a discount and experience peculiar periods of trading. One of the funds did list, raised a lot of money from retail investors, and, within two weeks, went to a 40 percent discount. So the investors immediately lost 40 percent of the value of the balance sheet.

Second, the fund was managed by a board of directors, chaired by Korea Development Bank. The board of directors was formed with senior representatives from each of the banks that had invested in the fund. But the investors had effectively been coerced into investing, and they were mostly interested in getting their money back. As a result, the board was not involved in operations of the funds.

Another provision called for Korea Development Bank to be the custodian, the administrator, and the client. The Financial Supervisory Commission pointed out that, under mutual fund law, a company is not allowed to be both the custodian and the administrator. So after two years, a separate administrator had to be appointed.

Due diligence during the investment process was accomplished with the help of merger and acquisition companies, Korea Development Bank, and the banks themselves. Boutique merger and acquisition companies were the most helpful for providing leads to potential investments. The funds were quite well publicized at launch, and Korea Development Bank offered to introduce us to the companies. The banks themselves provided numerous

12

introductions; State Street/Rexiter received seven introductions from banks. We were approached quite a lot.

We saw more than a thousand companies. Once we got interested in one, we visited it at least five times, and we met with or had conference calls with its customers. We established the financial projections, which were fairly standard. But, in our experience with smaller companies in Korea, actually getting three-year projections of a profit-and-loss account, a cash flow account, and a balance sheet was not as easy as it sounds, and quite often the accounts did not add up. We had to go back many times and verify our assumptions.

At the end of the process, we invested in around 40 companies. There were 10 venture companies and 13 dot-com companies, as well 11 companies listed on the Korea Stock Exchange. Of the 16 companies that were unlisted, six issued initial public offerings. We did two major workouts. We also did exit investments and then reinvested some of the money, because the idea was to help smaller companies. We made capital distributions from profits. In retrospect, making those capital distributions was a bad idea. When we realized a profit of $100 million in May 2000, the capital distributions were taxable, and we had to sell another investment to pay the $17 million tax bill.

As of now, the internal rate of return is probably only about 7 percent. But given the dual objectives of the fund and the nature of bailouts, this is a respectable result.

Positives and Negatives

There were both good and bad aspects of the corporate restructuring funds. I begin with the positives.

In Korea the liquidity and turnover of the market are very high, and we could exit relatively easily from large investments. That is a huge benefit for a fund that needs an exit strategy.

The objective of the funds was to provide much-needed capital to many smaller companies in a crisis situation. This goal was reasonably well achieved, and our fund certainly encouraged that sector. Other funds also raised money to do that, and a virtuous cycle started. We met the policy goal of improving company balance sheets.

12

The efforts to improve investor relations also were quite successful. Ararang and the other funds conducted a large amount of due diligence, and other investors in Korea knew where we had invested and that we had performed the due diligence. This improved their confidence.

Another key point is that a lot of people were worried that there would be directed investments, but there were none. We had discretion, and we were never pressured by Korea Development Bank, or anybody else, to invest in companies that we did not find attractive.

Now for the negatives. First, the mutual fund structure was not desirable, given Korea's mutual fund laws. It would have been much better to have an offshore fund and to operate under international standards for private equity funds. Having to make distributions every year did not work either, and the fee structure was not right.

Second, an active board is needed to provide support for operations, and the funds did not receive enough support from the boards.

Third, the range of investments clearly was too wide. From venture to bailout is an extremely wide mandate that requires diverse professional expertise, and venture investments should have been included in this sort of fund.

Finally, the legal background, obviously, was not good. Foreign law firms are not allowed in Korea, expertise is limited, and advice is opaque. Legal services are expensive, too, and that was not helpful.

Part III
Technical Issues

Debt and Firm Vulnerability

Jack Glen

Debt and capital structure hold a prominent place in the finance literature, reflecting their importance in corporate finance more generally. Most of the research to date, however, concentrates on the determinants of capital structure and ignores the credit implications of debt. This paper takes a different approach by largely ignoring the stock of debt outstanding and concentrating on interest service and the relationship between interest service obligations and cash flow generated by operations.

Little research has concentrated on this obviously important subject. There is a relatively well-developed literature on the topic of predicting default on fixed-income securities, a large part of which is centered on the ideas incorporated into the Z score, as summarized in Altman (1984). That literature, however, concentrates exclusively on default and does not consider the impact of external factors on firm performance. Specifically, in that framework there is no link between the firm and the economic environment in which it operates.

Much of the literature on international finance has concentrated on measuring vulnerability in the correlation between exchange rate movements and stock prices. The literature has emphasized the idea that the exchange rate exposure of firms either with debt denominated in foreign currency or with export-import market exposure is an important determinant of firm value through its impact on earnings or the cost of debt. A recent example of this approach is Bodnar and Wong (1999). In addition to having considerable difficulty identifying any impact, this framework makes no explicit attempt to measure the relationship between firm performance, as proxied by earnings or cash flow, and the economic environment in which the firm operates.

In an innovative analysis of the relationship between capital structure and risk, Mulder, Perrelli, and Rocha (2002) examine the extent to which increased leverage on corporate balance sheets can exacerbate macroeconomic imbalances and increase the likelihood of a macroeconomic crisis. They find that corporate balance sheet variables have a significant impact on both the likelihood and the depth of crisis. Higher levels of debt and shorter maturities are associated with higher probability of a macroeconomic crisis. Their analysis does not, however, look beyond balance sheet measures or examine the implications of a crisis for firm vulnerability.

The currency and debt crises of the 1990s spawned a large literature on the causes of crises and how to predict them. Goldstein, Kaminsky, and Reinhart (2000) provide a good overview of this literature. Largely missing, however, is any mention of the corporate sector. One exception is Stone (2000), who examines corporate sector dynamics during systemic financial crises. Stone documents the extent to which the crises were amplified in the corporate sector through exchange rate and interest rate effects. His evidence, however, is limited to a few crisis events and is based entirely on aggregate corporate statistics, which do not permit him to examine the reaction of corporate cash flows to the crises.

The East Asian crisis of 1997 and its apparent origins in the corporate sector generated interest in corporate behavior up to, during, and after the crisis. Claessens, Djankov, and Klapper (1999) examine the extent to which distressed firms exploit bankruptcy in order to resolve their problems and the factors, both corporate and institutional, that influence their decision. They find that ownership structure and creditor rights are important determinants of the use of bankruptcy. Their analysis provides considerable insight into the nature of bankruptcy in several countries and the conditions under which firms enter into that process, but they provide little insight into the factors, either within or outside the firm, that cause firms to become distressed in the first place.

Claessens, Djankov, and Nenova (2001) examine measures of corporate risk globally and relate them to a variety of firm-level, institutional, and macroeconomic factors. One attractive feature of this work is its global nature. Included in their list of corporate risk measures is the ratio of operating cash flow to interest expense, which makes some of their analysis close in spirit to this one. They find that legal origin, creditor rights, and the nature of the financial system all play an important role in determining the level of risk that a firm is willing to hold. Their analysis, however, is largely cross-sectional in nature and so does not address the impact of aggregate demand or other macroeconomic conditions on their measures of firm risk, which is the emphasis in this work.

Unlike most analysis that has followed the 1997 crisis, Allayannis, Brown, and Klapper (2003) decompose the capital structure of a sample of Asian firms by currency denomination. This enables them to compare the performance of firms that had significant foreign currency–denominated exposures during the crisis with that of other firms. Remarkably, they find that firms with higher foreign exchange exposure were also more likely to have foreign currency–denominated revenues, allowing them to perform reasonably well during the crisis. They also examine the ratio of cash flow to interest expense and find that the use of foreign currency–denominated debt did not result in additional distress for the borrowers. Once again, however, their analysis is cross-sectional only and so does not permit an examination of the impact of time-varying economic factors on the cash flow and debt service of firms.

Closest to this paper in some ways is the work done in Bernanke and Campbell (1988), which examines corporate debt levels and interest service for a sample of U.S. firms over the period 1969–86. In addition to documenting the level of interest coverage for each of those years, they also simulate the impact of a recession on liquidity, as measured by the ratio of interest payments to operational cash flow. They find that this ratio is tied to the level of overall economic activity and that illiquidity increases during recessions. They do not, however, specifically measure the correlation between GDP growth and liquidity or incorporate other economic factors, such as interest rates or inflation, into the analysis.

This paper differs from those cited in three important ways. First, it covers both a large number of countries and firms as well as a reasonably long period of time. This panel data approach has the advantage of allowing one to follow firms over time in order to see the extent to which changes in the economic environment have an impact on operational performance. Second, it does not concentrate on a single event, such as a currency crisis, or restrict itself to firms that are obviously vulnerable. By applying the analysis to both healthy and distressed firms and economies, this approach may elicit more general conclusions from the data than would be possible with a more biased sample. Third, although the analysis uses a reduced-form model, the result is an estimate of the sensitivity of firm interest coverage to changes in the macroeconomic environment, which was not previously available and should be of considerable interest to investors concerned about the impact of recessions and other macroeconomic events on debt or fixed-income portfolios.

This is a purely empirical paper, but the conceptual issues involved are consistent with general economic principles that link aggregate demand and firm-level cash flow. The basic idea is to examine the relationship between cash flow generated by operations and interest obligations in the form of an interest coverage ratio (ICR), a concept that is well recognized by financial analysts.[1] The ICR then provides a measure of firm viability: firms that generate sufficient cash to maintain the ratio above 1 can service their debt, whereas firms that maintain a ratio below 1 do not generate adequate cash flow to service their debt.

Failure to generate enough cash flow from operations to service debt does not, of course, necessarily force the firm into default. Alternative sources of cash, through the issuance of new securities, the sale of assets, or the consumption of cash balances, all can be used to save the firm temporarily from default. Ultimately, however, an ICR ratio of 1 or greater is needed if the company is to avoid default. For that reason, this paper concentrates on the ICR and its relationship to firm and environmental factors.

Several factors have an impact on the ability of a firm to service its debt. An obvious one is the amount of debt that, combined with the interest rate involved, determines the total amount of interest expense. It is for this reason that academic interest in capital structure has been so strong. But debt vulnerability extends beyond the amount of debt outstanding. Also important are the expected level and volatility of cash flow generated from operations.

Among the determinants of cash flow and its volatility are the level of sales, the margin on those sales, and the amount of capital invested. To some extent, these factors reflect the sector in which a firm operates, the technology it employs, and market conditions at any point in time. Market conditions, of course, include the level of aggregate demand, as measured by GDP growth, the level of interest rates, and the level of inflation.

The remainder of this paper examines the ICR for a large number of firms in a broad cross section of countries during the period from 1994 to 2001. After controlling for firm, sector, and country fixed effects, the analysis shows a very strong economic and statistical link between the macroeconomic environment and a firm's ability to service its debt. As one would expect, debt service becomes problematic when economic conditions deteriorate. The contribution of this analysis is to identify how much deterioration one should expect from any given level of change in the economic environment. Given the distribution of ICR across firms, one can then use the analysis to calculate how many firms one would expect to have an ICR with a value below 1 for a given set of macroeconomic conditions.

The main finding is that GDP has a strong impact on debt service ability. For every 10 percentage point decline in GDP growth, the ICR drops about 1 percentage point. Globally, such a decline in the ICR would increase

Figure 13.1: Median Interest Coverage Ratio and GDP Growth Rate in Thailand, 1994–2001

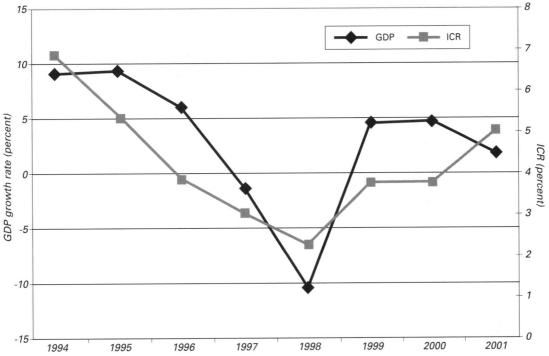

Source: Osiris database.

the percentage of firms with an ICR less than 1 in 2000 from about 20 to about 28. As a more specific example, given that GDP dropped about 16 percentage points in Thailand between 1996 and 1998, one would expect that, in 1998 and given the distribution of ICR for Thai firms in 1996, the percentage of Thai firms with an ICR of less than 1 would have increased from about 12 percent to about 25 percent of firms. Figure 13.1 summarizes this impact for the median Thai firm. The figure clearly shows a deterioration in the ICR as GDP growth slowed in the years leading up to 1997, with recovery in both GDP and ICR in 1999. Notably, the impact of economic growth does not differ significantly for developed and developing countries.

The analysis also suggests that monetary policy has an important role to play. Both inflation and interest rates have a negative correlation with ICR, independent of their impact through GDP growth. In the case of a crisis similar to what was experienced in Thailand in 1997, this means that the deterioration in the ICR for firms was even worse than suggested by looking only at business cycle effects. The analysis does suggest, however, that these interest rate effects are most pronounced in developing countries, possibly because their interest rates are both higher and more volatile generally than in more developed countries. By decomposing firm cash flows into margins and sales, the analysis also suggests that these macroeconomic developments largely affect sales rather than margins, but additional analysis is needed to clarify this effect.

The analysis also suggests that specific country factors play a role in determining the average level of ICR across firms within a country. Creditor rights, in particular, play a significant role in determining the average level of ICR.

The remainder of the paper is organized as follows. The next section describes the data and provides relevant summary statistics. This is followed by a section presenting the results of a set of regression analyses that relate the ICR to firm, sector, and country factors. Concluding remarks are offered in the final section.

Data Description

The data consist primarily of corporate financial statement data from the commercial database Osiris. Only firms in manufacturing sectors are included, which limits the number of firms in some countries but precludes the

Table 13.1: Number of Firms, by Economy and Year, 1994–2001

Economy	1994	1995	1996	1997	1998	1999	2000	2001
Argentina	6	6	9	6	7	13	16	14
Australia	34	36	38	42	46	49	83	125
Austria	25	25	28	37	42	39	38	32
Belgium	26	26	33	48	53	62	59	51
Brazil	—	3	29	43	77	89	149	136
Canada	98	117	140	142	197	213	203	208
Chile	42	42	53	57	59	56	55	1
Colombia	4	3	6	31	12	8	38	33
Czech Republic	11	11	38	67	79	61	57	33
Denmark	55	53	61	66	69	69	66	57
Finland	26	26	31	39	59	67	68	68
France	140	142	189	221	274	311	300	267
Germany	184	186	225	265	323	362	337	269
Greece	20	26	35	41	44	59	72	75
Hong Kong (China)	39	49	58	62	67	76	92	95
Hungary	1	1	4	3	7	11	10	7
India	44	44	85	140	140	284	279	223
Indonesia	21	21	24	26	21	11	5	34
Ireland	14	13	17	19	20	22	20	18
Israel	8	8	12	16	27	32	35	8
Italy	18	18	43	45	49	63	67	59
Japan	324	377	933	1,037	1243	1,269	1,199	1,234
Korea, Rep. of	517	636	683	752	794	853	860	890
Malaysia	57	82	94	91	102	120	125	123
Mexico	21	32	16	21	28	43	46	48
Netherlands	40	43	61	69	75	71	66	58
Norway	23	23	32	43	49	47	34	35
Pakistan	1	1	3	5	8	12	9	5
Peru	—	1	1	50	48	52	46	44
Philippines	3	2	3	2	4	3	9	8
Poland	1	1	4	9	21	23	26	25
Portugal	9	9	10	13	16	17	15	14
Singapore	12	12	18	19	26	24	27	26
South Africa	5	6	10	11	10	14	18	20
Spain	19	19	29	29	40	42	46	40
Sweden	52	64	85	92	111	108	94	84
Switzerland	61	62	86	89	103	99	98	94
Taiwan (China)	6	7	17	33	55	58	71	59
Thailand	31	42	48	35	27	19	76	73
United Kingdom	327	356	369	408	408	401	377	348
United States	986	1,171	1,323	1428	1,526	1,637	1,605	1,442
Total	3,311	3,802	4,983	5650	6,430	6,869	6,896	6,483

— Not available.

Source: Osiris database.

difficulties associated with the financial sector and utilities, both of which are highly regulated. Annual financial statement variables for the period 1994–2001 are included in the analysis. Data prior to 1994 are available for some countries and firms, but the number of firms in the sample is significantly smaller. Similarly, data for 2002 are available for some firms, but delays in reporting imply that the number of firms in the sample is significantly smaller, and so the year is excluded.

The number of firms by country is presented in table 13.1. Globally, the number of firms varies from a low of 3,311 in 1994 to a high of 6,896 in 2000, with a total of 44,424 firm-years in the sample. A total of 41 countries are represented in the sample. The United States has the largest number of firms, with Japan a close second. A few countries—for example, Pakistan and the Philippines—have only limited representation.[2]

Table 13.2 presents the sector composition for 2000. For convenience, firms are classified into eight sectors on the basis of the NAICS (North American Industry Classification System). Globally, the largest number of firms by far is in the general manufacturing sector, which includes a variety of manufactured products. The chemical sector is the second most represented sector, with the other sectors having far fewer firms. In what follows, sector effects are often important.

The median ICR by country and year is presented in table 13.3. Given the sectoral composition by country described in table 13.2 and the importance of sector factors in determining capital structure, the ratios in table 13.3 need to be interpreted with caution, but they provide interesting insight into both country differences and the apparent impact of economic conditions. Globally, the average ICR was in the range of 4.4–5.3, with no obvious trend, but there were large differences across countries. In the United States the average was close to the global average, but with an obvious downward trend over time. In contrast, in Japan, where the economy was slow throughout the sample period, ratios were in excess of 10 in four of the years, suggesting that either institutional features or accounting differences between Japan and the United States were substantial. The impact of the 1997 crisis is evident in both Republic of Korea and Thailand (as illustrated in figure 13.1). In Korea firms entered the crisis with much lower levels of ICR and then recovered quickly to levels well above pre-crisis levels. In Thailand ICRs were well above the global mean at the beginning of the sample period but deteriorated rapidly through 1998, with only limited recovery in 1999–2000. The impact of the crisis in Argentina in 2001, and

Table 13.2: Number of Firms, by Economy and Sector, 2000

Economy	Chemicals	Food and beverages	General manufacturing	Nonmetallic	Plastics	Metals	Pulp and paper
Argentina	4	3	5	2	—	2	—
Australia	16	14	32	12	2	2	5
Austria	4	7	23	1	1	1	1
Belgium	9	10	25	3	5	3	4
Brazil	36	17	63	5	3	14	11
Canada	27	34	98	13	6	10	15
Chile	7	16	16	7	—	7	2
Colombia	5	13	4	9	2	2	3
Czech Republic	5	4	36	6	3	1	2
Denmark	11	8	35	4	3	1	4
Finland	5	5	42	3	5	2	6
France	30	48	177	10	14	11	10
Germany	34	34	218	15	15	12	9
Greece	8	13	32	6	2	8	3
Hong Kong (China)	11	9	61	3	2		6
Hungary	3	2	2	1	2		
India	107	17	92	24	14	21	4
Indonesia	1	1	1	1	—	—	1
Ireland	3	8	5	4	—	—	
Israel	4	—	29	1	—	—	1
Italy	7	3	41	7	2	4	3
Japan	152	110	698	62	63	60	54
Korea, Rep. of	133	49	540	30	26	53	29
Malaysia	12	11	65	11	9	9	8
Mexico	6	15	11	5	1	4	4
Netherlands	6	11	37	1	7	1	3
Norway	2	3	25	—	—	—	—
Pakistan	4	3	1	1	—	—	—
Peru	9	17	9	4	2	3	2
Philippines		5	3	1	—	—	—
Poland	5	5	10	1	2	3	—
Portugal	2	2	4	3	—	—	—
Singapore	3	2	17	—	2	1	2
South Africa	—	2	8	1		1	6
Spain	8	12	10	7	1	3	5
Sweden	8	3	65	—	2	4	12
Switzerland	17	8	58	4	1	5	5
Taiwan (China)	11	3	43	4	3	6	1
Thailand	15	18	25	9	1	5	3
United Kingdom	50	43	230	19	12	8	15
United States	289	93	1,061	18	41	44	59
Total	1,069	681	3,957	318	254	314	303

— Not available.

Source: Osiris database.

13

Table 13.3: Median Ratio of EBITDA to Interest Expense (ICR), by Economy and Year, 1994–2001

Economy	1994	1995	1996	1997	1998	1999	2000	2001
Argentina	1.84	1.84	4.57	5.52	5.66	2.36	2.24	2.13
Australia	6.67	6.79	5.23	5.33	5.51	6.29	4.55	3.71
Austria	4.64	4.82	4.70	6.72	6.41	5.99	6.80	5.98
Belgium	3.18	3.18	3.95	5.07	4.25	3.75	3.56	2.53
Brazil	—	0.96	1.72	1.79	1.55	1.41	1.55	1.34
Canada	6.12	5.06	5.56	6.29	4.44	3.90	4.36	3.80
Chile	8.26	8.26	5.84	5.12	4.67	3.56	4.78	14.25
Colombia	5.17	2.26	4.73	1.52	2.24	1.20	2.09	4.83
Czech Republic	2.68	2.68	2.20	1.84	1.56	1.26	2.08	2.09
Denmark	3.98	4.26	4.42	5.53	5.62	6.11	5.11	3.30
Finland	3.28	3.28	4.57	6.15	7.46	6.63	6.96	6.42
France	5.11	4.91	6.35	6.43	6.67	7.01	5.24	5.11
Germany	6.09	6.09	6.89	7.09	7.90	7.62	7.20	5.32
Greece	3.78	5.18	5.71	6.08	6.22	7.11	6.14	6.56
Hong Kong (China)	5.93	4.36	5.58	6.37	6.26	6.65	5.67	5.42
Hungary	6.00	6.00	9.52	8.56	3.69	3.87	5.74	4.92
India	4.39	4.39	3.27	3.03	2.68	3.14	2.85	3.56
Indonesia	5.49	5.49	4.13	2.17	1.42	2.32	0.88	2.10
Ireland	6.04	5.94	5.98	6.89	5.83	7.74	4.76	3.43
Israel	6.67	5.20	5.82	7.07	4.82	5.68	3.86	3.32
Italy	2.58	2.58	4.01	5.24	5.04	5.97	4.86	3.83
Japan	3.96	5.81	9.14	10.10	8.92	11.03	13.33	10.97
Korea, Rep. of	1.58	1.63	1.65	1.67	1.39	2.79	3.49	2.29
Malaysia	8.10	5.31	5.99	4.46	2.74	4.28	8.14	7.06
Mexico	2.81	1.65	3.81	4.59	3.76	3.73	4.06	3.66
Netherlands	6.75	6.82	7.83	8.64	9.06	8.65	7.03	6.06
Norway	4.76	4.76	5.05	4.65	4.65	3.93	3.13	3.21
Pakistan	6.35	6.35	7.58	3.07	3.02	3.05	6.44	10.44
Peru	—	3.18	3.05	2.60	2.84	2.72	2.89	3.68
Philippines	11.62	25.32	7.18	2.85	2.30	2.85	4.75	2.53
Poland	3.51	1.16	3.75	1.43	2.42	2.83	2.49	1.67
Portugal	2.51	2.51	3.20	4.16	7.47	7.29	4.95	4.46
Singapore	11.58	6.53	5.25	4.21	3.47	8.15	6.62	2.61
South Africa	9.85	10.58	5.27	3.95	5.66	3.97	4.42	6.33
Spain	4.59	4.59	6.73	8.26	8.40	9.84	6.95	5.79
Sweden	6.30	7.59	7.71	7.06	6.75	6.77	6.97	5.16
Switzerland	5.01	5.35	6.89	6.90	6.66	7.66	7.66	5.64
Taiwan (China)	8.11	7.93	6.57	6.81	3.62	4.72	4.32	2.40
Thailand	6.85	5.41	3.85	3.00	2.24	3.75	3.76	5.26
United Kingdom	10.02	9.50	10.15	9.40	7.56	7.47	5.75	5.2
United States	5.12	4.44	4.53	4.44	3.45	3.35	3.07	2.65
Total	4.54	4.48	5.30	5.31	4.76	5.31	5.09	4.43

— Not available.

Source: Osiris database.

the years of economic downturn that led to it, is also evident. Also notable are the generally low levels of ICR in Brazil, a country that experienced much turbulence over the years as well as relatively low levels of growth and high interest rates.

While the median values in table 13.3 provide insight into the behavior of the ICR, these median values do little to reveal the considerable variation across firms in the sample. To give a feel for that variation, figure 13.2 presents a histogram of the ratio for all firms globally for 2000. Globally, for that year, the mean value of the ICR was 8.6, well above the median value of

Figure 13.2: Histogram of Interest Coverage Ratio (ICR) for All Countries and Firms, 2000

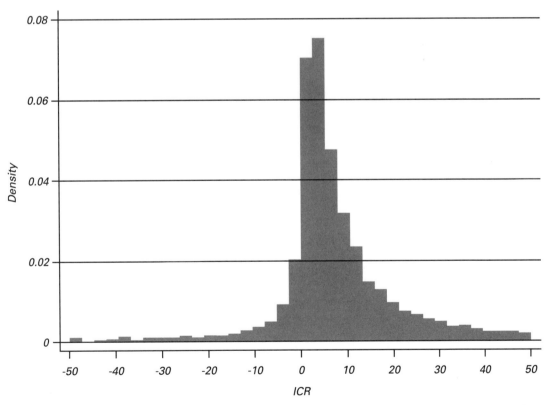

Note: The sample has been limited to observations within the range [-50, 50] in order to improve the visual appearance of the figure by eliminating the long tails.

Source: Osiris database.

13

Figure 13.3: Interest Coverage Ratio (ICR) for All Brazilian Firms in the Sample, 2000

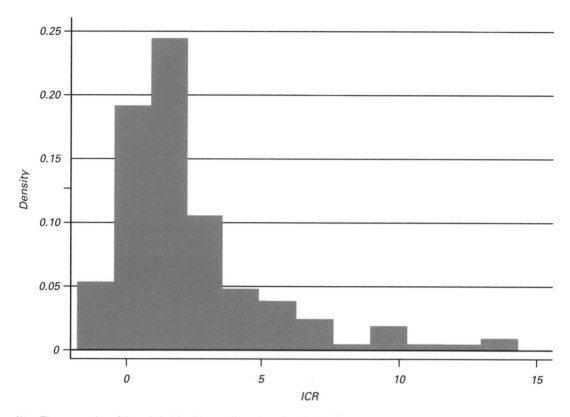

Note: The mean value of the ratio is 2.3, with a median value of 1.5. In the population, 25 percent has a ratio less than 0.52; 35 percent has a ratio of 1 or less.

Source: Osiris database.

5.1, which is also reflected in the somewhat asymmetric nature of the graph. Both of these values are comparable to the values obtained for the pooled sample for all years. About 15 percent of the sample in this year had an ICR less than zero, and about 20 percent had an ICR below 1. Those percentages do not differ much from the values for the total pooled sample for all years. There was considerable variation across countries in the distribution, as is evident in figure 13.3, which presents a histogram of the ICR for Brazil in 2000. The distribution of the ICR in Brazil has a much lower mean and median than the global sample, and about 35 percent of Brazilian firms had an ICR at or below 1 in 2000.

Regression Analysis

The summary statistics suggest that there is considerable variation in the ICR across countries, sectors, and time. This section employs a regression framework in order to identify some of the factors that are correlated with the variation in the ratio and its constituent components. The analysis is based on a regression of ICR on a set of firm-specific, industry, and country factors. Mathematically, the regression equation is as follows:

$$(13.1) \quad ICR_{ijkt} = \alpha + \beta_i CPI_{kt} + \beta_2 IntRate_{kt} + \beta_3 GDP\%_{kt} + \beta_4 IntCV_{it} + \beta_5 EBITDACV_{it} + \\ \beta_6 TLTASS_{it} + \beta_7 CATASS_{it} + \beta_8 LNTASS_{it} + \gamma Sector_j + \delta Country_k + \varepsilon_{ijkt}.$$

In the equation four subscripts are used to express variation across time (t), firm (i), sector or industry (j), and country (k). Following the constant term, the first three variables are country factors measuring the level of inflation, the level of interest rates, and the rate of growth of GDP. Both the rates of inflation and GDP growth are obtained from the World Bank's global development finance database, whereas the annual year-end interest rate is obtained from the International Monetary Fund's international financial statistics database. Each is meant to capture a particular aspect of macroeconomic activity. Higher levels of inflation are associated with more volatility of interest rates, lower economic activity, more uncertainty generally, and negative implications for firms.[3] Because the dependent variable—ICR—is the ratio of cash flow to interest expense, the inclusion of countrywide interest rates is obvious, as is the growth of GDP, which is a major determinant of domestic aggregate demand. One shortcoming in this context is that the relevant interest rate is firm specific. Given that such detailed information is not available, we are forced to look at the impact of aggregate interest rates on the firm-level ratio.

The use of aggregate GDP growth is meant to capture the implications of fluctuations in aggregate demand on the generation of cash flow, the numerator in the ICR. Two potential problems arise from this. First, while both the ICR and GDP figures are annually reported, they are not necessarily synchronized, and there may be some lag in the relationship between changes in GDP and changes in cash flow at the firm level. A second issue is the extent to which firm sales are directed outside of the domestic economy and, therefore, the extent to which firm cash flows are somewhat immune from the domestic business cycle. Both of these potential problems merit further research but are outside the scope of this exercise.

The factors associated with regression coefficients β_4 to β_8 relate to firm-specific characteristics. The first two of those (IntCV and EBITDACV) are the coefficients of variation (standard deviation/mean) of interest expense and EBITDA (earnings before interest, taxes, and depreciation allowance), the two constituent components of ICR. These are calculated variables derived from the firm's financial statements over the sample period and are intended to incorporate into the analysis two firm-specific sources of risk: volatility in interest expense and cash flow. Although it would be preferable to calculate these measures from pre-sample data, data shortages require the use of in-sample calculations.

The next three factors reflect firm-specific characteristics: size (as measured by the natural log of total assets in U.S. dollars), capital structure (ratio of total liabilities to total assets), and asset structure (ratio of current assets to total assets). All three factors have been shown in previous research to be closely related to firm performance and capital structure.[4]

The analysis also incorporates fixed effects for both industry and country. In addition, one specification of the model includes an interaction term between GDP growth and the industry fixed effect.

The results for the basic model are reported in table 13.4.[5] The first version of the model illustrates several points. First, with a large number of observations, the model explains very little of the total variation in the dependent variable. In every case, total explained variation (R^2) does not exceed 12 percent. Second, all three of the macroeconomic variables (interest rates, inflation, and GDP growth) are statistically and economically significant. Interest coverage is negatively related to inflation and interest rates, but positively related to GDP growth. Third, neither of the coefficients of variation risk measures is significant. And fourth, each of the firm-specific balance sheet factors is highly significant and has an intuitively understandable sign.

To put some economic content to the macroeconomic factor coefficients, the inflation coefficient translates into a decline of 1 percentage point in the ICR for every 10 percentage point increase in inflation. In both Korea and Thailand, the 1997 crisis was associated with an increase in inflation of about 3 percentage points, suggesting a decline in the ICR for firms in those countries of about 0.3. The order of magnitude of the interest rate variable is just slightly smaller, suggesting that in Korea, where interest rates as

Table 13.4: Regression Models

Variable	Model 1 Coefficient	Model 1 t-statistic	Model 2 Coefficient	Model 2 t-statistic	Model 3 Coefficient	Model 3 t-statistic	Model 4 Coefficient	Model 4 t-statistic
CPI	-0.1046	-2.93	-0.1098	-3.08	-0.2698	-3.18	-0.0294	-0.95
IntRate	-0.0833	-3.06	-0.0859	-3.17	-0.1051	-1.45	-0.0737	-3.06
GDP%	0.1080	3.71	0.2352	5.96	0.2109	4.38	0.2122	2.07
IntExpCV	0.4445	1.10	0.4381	1.09	-0.0015	-0.00	5.868	7.18
EBITDACV	0.0036	1.79	0.0037	1.82	0.0036	1.79	0.031	0.88
TLTASS	-17.45	-36.47	-17.43	-36.40	-16.90	-32.54	-20.78	-19.37
CATASS	3.7632	5.84	3.773	5.85	3.8593	5.44	4.333	3.57
lnTASS	1.5437	30.32	1.548	30.42	1.6427	30.21	0.0809	0.71
R^2	0.121		0.121		0.120		0.220	
Number of observations	43,638		43,638		38,921		4,717	

Note: The dependent variable is the ratio of EBITDA to interest expense (ICR). Independent variables include consumer price index inflation (CPI), interest rate (IntRate), GDP growth (GDP%), the coefficient of variation of interest expense (IntExpCV), the coefficient of variation of EBITDA (EBITDACV), the ratio of total liabilities to total assets (TLTASS), the ratio of current assets to total assets (CATASS), and the natural logarithm of total assets (lnTASS). Estimated coefficients and *t*-statistics are reported, with standard errors adjusted for heteroskedasticity. All models include fixed industry- and country-effect dummy variables, which are not reported. Model 1 includes no interaction between GDP% and the industry dummy variables; all other models include these interactive terms. Model 3 includes OECD and high-income countries only. Model 4 includes low-income, lower-middle-income, and upper-middle-income countries only.

measured here increased about 3 percentage points in 1997, the ICR would have declined by about 0.5; Thailand experienced a much smaller decline of 0.08.[6] GDP growth rates were associated with increases in the ICR of an amount almost exactly opposite the inflation effect. In this case, GDP growth dropped 13.4 percentage points in Korea from 1996 to 1998, suggesting a decline in the ICR of about 1.5; in Thailand, which experienced a more severe recession, the ICR declined about 1.8. Collectively, these three shock effects of the crisis would have been associated with a decline in the average ICR of about 2.3 in Korea and about 2.2 in Thailand. Given the distribution of the ICR for firms in Korea in 1996, these changes suggest an increase in the percentage of firms with an ICR less than 1 from about 25 percent of firms in 1996 to about 75 percent in 1998. For Thailand the share of firms with an ICR less than 1 increased from about 12 percent in 1996 to about 35 percent in 1998.

The reality is that the deterioration in the ICR for both countries was less than predicted by the model. In Korea only about 38 percent of all firms had an ICR less than 1 in 1998, and only 22 percent of firms in Thailand fell into that category. One reason for the difference is apparent in the second model of table 13.4, which allows for an interactive term between the industry dummy and GDP growth. In this case, the base industry is general manufacturing, with the other industry coefficients representing deviations from this base. In this model, the base industry coefficient jumps to 0.23, more than twice the level of the first model. Note, however, that all of the other industries, with the exception of primary metals, have coefficients (not reported) that are significantly negative and that, when added to the base-case coefficient, have a net coefficient that is economically insignificant. These industry differences reflect two factors. First, within a closed economy, we know that some industries are more highly correlated with the business cycle than others. Second, we also can imagine that some industries are more prone to international trade than others. Collectively, these two effects determine the net impact of domestic GDP growth on firm cash flow. What the data do not allow us to identify is which of these effects determines the net outcome. Given that no information on exports or import competition exist for these firms, disentangling the two effects is not possible in this sample.

Other factors also intervened to offset the deterioration in Korea, in particular. Firms in that country managed to reduce the total amount of debt on their balance sheets by 5 percentage points over 1996–98. Given a large and negative coefficient on that factor in the regression model, the lower level of debt would have moderated considerably the reduction in Korea's ICR forecast by the model.

The third and fourth columns in table 13.4 present estimated coefficients for the model (with an industry/GDP interactive term) separately for developed- and emerging-market countries.[7] A number of interesting points emerge from these two models. First, the explanatory power of the model is much higher for the emerging-market sample than for the developed-market sample. Second, the base GDP growth coefficient is nearly identical in the two models, although some of the other industry coefficients do differ. Third, the inflation coefficient is highly significant for the developed-market sample but is insignificant for the emerging-market sample, whereas the opposite is true for the interest rate coefficient. And finally, whereas neither of the (coefficient of variation) risk measure coefficients (IntCV and EBITDACV) is significant for the developed-market sample, the interest rate risk factor is very significant for the emerging-market sample. Apparently, although firms in both groups of countries are similarly sensitive to domestic economic growth, emerging-market firms are much more sensitive to interest rates and interest rate risk than are their developed-market counterparts.

Constituent Components: Sales Margins and Turnover Effects

As the ratio of cash flow to interest expense, movement in the ICR reflects the impact of changes in demand in a firm's product markets as well as the level of interest paid. In this section I concentrate on the numerator—cash flow—in order to determine the extent to which different product market factors contribute to movement in the ICR. In order to avoid undesirable statistical properties, cash flows (EBITDA) are divided by total assets, giving a sort of cash flow return on assets (CFROA). This is then further decomposed into two components.

$$(13.2) \qquad \frac{EBITDA}{TotalAssets} = \frac{EBITDA}{Sales} \times \frac{Sales}{TotalAssets}.$$

In this framework we can examine the extent to which changes in the ICR, as reflected in changes in the CFROA, are themselves a consequence of changes in the margins that firms receive for their products (EBITDA/Sales, MARGIN) or a consequence of changing levels of turnover (Sales/Total Assets, TURNOVER). Which of these factors plays the dominant role will reflect competition in the product market and the nature of the product. The analysis is performed through a set of regressions similar to those in table 13.4, except that CFROA is the independent variable.

The regression results for each of the three variables (CFROA, MARGIN, and TURNOVER) are presented in table 13.5. The emphasis in this discussion is on the GDP growth factor, which, for CFROA, is statistically positive, with only one sector (food and beverages) showing a net coefficient that is statistically zero. Apparently, cash flow generation is closely linked to the business cycle, which is intuitively appealing. The second and third regressions, however, suggest that the main reason for this correlation is related not to movements in margins (and pricing) but to turnover. Margins show no significant correlation with GDP growth in this sample, whereas turnover in general manufacturing is highly correlated with GDP. Once again, most other sectors—the exception being primary metals—are

13

Table 13.5: Regression Models

Variable	Model 1		Model 2		Model 3	
	Coefficient	t- statistic	Coefficient	t- statistic	Coefficient	t- statistic
CPI	0.0075	1.70	0.0054	3.52	0.0661	2.17
IntRate	-0.0011	-0.79	-0.0011	-0.97	-0.0380	-1.76
GDP%	0.0035	2.84	0.0061	4.55	-0.0136	-1.00
IntExpCV	-0.3397	-1.45	-0.183	-16.8	-0.7133	-1.47
EBITDACV	0.0001	1.33	0.0001	2.11	0.0002	0.60
TLTASS	-0.1726	-5.08	0.432	22.75	-1.357	-1.79
CATASS	0.126	1.04	0.9067	23.57	0.7053	1.18
lnTASS	0.0414	3.90	-0.0308	-8.27	0.6103	4.61
R^2	0.003		0.159		0.006	
Number of observations	43,638		43,505		43,337	

Note: The dependent variable varies by model. For model 1, it is the ratio of EBITDA to total assets; for model 2, it is the ratio of sales to total assets. For model 3, it is the ratio of EBITDA to sales. Independent variables are the same as in models 2–4 in table 13.4. Estimated coefficients and their t-statistics are presented. Standard errors are corrected for heteroskedasticity

at odds with the general manufacturing sector and have near-zero correlation with GDP. However, the failure to identify any statistical link between GDP and margins reflects the low explanatory power of the regression. In fact, the estimated coefficient on GDP in the margin regression is quite large but, given the large standard errors involved, statistically insignificant. Clearly, additional analysis is justified in order to understand better the link between margins and the business cycle.

Country Effects

Not shown in table 13.4 in order to conserve space is a set of 41 country fixed-effect coefficients that tell us something about the impact of country-specific factors on firm-level ICRs. Qualitatively, those coefficients suggest relatively low levels of ICR for the United States and higher levels for other countries. Further direct interpretation of the fixed effects is difficult. Nevertheless, in this section I analyze the correlation between those coefficients and other fixed institutional features that are constant across the sample period. Although the number of potential candidates for inclusion in the regression is large, I concentrate on just three: creditor rights, origin of the legal system, and average level of interest rates over the sample period.[8]

Following the definition in La Porta and others (1998), I use legal origin and creditor rights to differentiate the investment climate in the cross section of countries. As they explain, creditor rights and legal origin have material implications for the treatment of creditors, accounting standards, and the efficiency of contract enforcement. With stronger creditor rights, one would expect both firms and lenders to adjust their behavior and to behave more conservatively regarding debt. Along these lines, Levine and Demirgüç-Kunt (2001) show a significant link between legal origin and financial sector development, whereas La Porta and others (1998) show a link between creditor rights and finance. Interest rates are included in the model to account for the broad range of other factors—for example, monetary policy—that could influence the behavior of the firm's capital structure.[9]

The results of the estimation are presented in table 13.6. With a cross section of just 41 countries in the sample, the three factors have only limited ability to explain the country fixed effects. Creditor rights, however, have a coefficient that is economically very large and positive and is statistically significant at the 7 percent level. Bear in mind that this variable is defined as an index ranging from 1 to 4, with higher values indicating better creditor rights. In this case, movement in a country by one unit increases the average ICR in that country by 0.83, which is economically significant. Apparently, better creditor rights induce firms to be more conservative in their capital structure. Also notable, however, is the lack of any correlation between the country fixed effect and legal origin.

Table 13.6: Country Fixed-Effects Regression

Independent variable	Coefficient	t-statistic
Legal origin	-0.406	-0.75
Creditor rights	0.840	1.87
Interest rate	0.020	0.48
Constant	3.985	2.46
R^2	0.01	
Number of observations	41	

Note: The dependent variable is the set of 41 country fixed effects from regression model 2 in table 3.4. The independent variables include indexes of creditor rights and legal origin (both taken from La Porta and others 1998) and a measure of aggregate interest rates.

13

Conclusions

Traditionally, debt finance has been viewed as less expensive than equity and has been used both to decrease the average cost of capital and to enhance shareholder returns. There is also a dark side to debt, however, as interest payments must be met regardless of market conditions, and this vulnerability is an important factor that firms must consider when making decisions concerning their capital structure. This paper has examined the issue of firm vulnerability to interest payments by analyzing the ratio of cash flow to interest payments for a global sample of firms from 1994 to 2001. The findings suggest that a number of factors play a role in determining the average level of ICR chosen by firms as well as the vulnerability of firms to ICR volatility as a result of changes in the economic environment.

Perhaps the major contribution of this analysis has been to document the nature of the link between the business cycle and the ability of firms to service their debt. By employing a large sample of firms spanning 41 countries and controlling for firm and industry factors, the analysis documents the extent to which the rise and fall in aggregate demand translate into higher and lower levels of ICR. From these estimated relationships, one can extrapolate the impact of a given economic shock on the distribution of firms and their ICR.

As in much research of this type, many questions remain unanswered. First are the reasons for differences in the apparent exposure to GDP movements in the various sectors. At first glance, these differences are not intuitively understandable, but, as noted, perhaps the explanation lies as much in the composition of the sample regarding the extent to which firms in certain industries are export oriented. An alternative issue pertaining to the sample is the extent to which these results are driven by the specific sample period, although this is perhaps less intuitively obvious given the similarity in results for the developed- and developing-market samples.

The failure of either firm-level risk measures—the coefficients of variation for cash flow and interest expense—is also distressing. It is intuitively appealing that firms should recognize their vulnerability to volatility in either cash flow or interest expense and adjust the average level of their debt accordingly. That these measures fail to capture this effect suggests either that better measures are needed or that something peculiar to this sample period is not yet understood.

13

Finally, this type of analysis always raises the question of the extent to which any reduced-form equation can capture the nature of the decision-making process that takes place within firms and in markets more generally and, therefore, can be used effectively to predict what will happen in the next crisis. Obviously, much additional work is needed.

References

The word "processed" describes informally produced works that may not be commonly available through libraries.

Allayannis, George, Gregory Brown, and Leora Klapper. 2003. "Capital Structure and Financial Risks: Evidence from Foreign Debt Use in East Asia." *Journal of Finance* 58(6, December):2667–710.

Altman, Edward. 1984. "The Success of Business Failure Prediction Models." *Journal of Banking and Finance* 8(2):171–98.

Bernanke, Ben, and John Campbell. 1988. "Is There a Corporate Debt Crisis?" *Brookings Papers on Economic Activity* 1.

Bodnar, Gordon, and M. H. F. Wong. 1999. "Estimating Exchange Rate Exposures: Some Weighty Issues." NBER Working Paper 7497. National Bureau of Economic Research, Cambridge, Mass. Processed.

Claessens, Stijn, Simeon Djankov, and Leora Klapper. 1999. "Resolution of Corporate Distress in East Asia." Policy Research Working Paper 2133. World Bank, Washington, D.C. Processed.

Claessens, Stijn, Simeon Djankov, and Tatiana Nenova. 2001. "Corporate Risk around the World." Working paper. University of Amsterdam, Faculty of Economics and Econometrics. Processed.

Fan, P. H. Joseph, Sheridan Titman, and Garry Twite. 2003. "An International Comparison of Capital Structure and Debt Maturity Choices." Working paper. University of Science and Technology, Hong Kong; University of Texas at Austin, Department of Finance; and Australian Graduate School of Management. Processed.

Glen, Jack, and Ajit Singh. 2003. "Capital Structure, Rates of Return, and Financing Corporate Growth: Comparing Developed and Emerging Markets, 1994–2000." In Robert Litan, Michael Pomerleano, and V. Sundararajan, ed., *The Future of Domestic Capital Markets in Developing Countries*. Washington, D.C.: Brookings Institution Press.

13

Goldstein, Morris, Graciela Kaminsky, and Carmen Reinhart. 2000. *Assessing Financial Vulnerability*. Washington, D.C.: Institute for International Economics.

La Porta, Rafael, Florencio López-de-Silanes, Andre Shleifer, and Robert Vishny. 1998. "Law and Finance." *Journal of Political Economy* 106(6):1113–55.

Levine, Ross, and Aslı Demirgüç-Kunt. 2001. "Bank-Based and Market-Based Financial Systems: Cross-Country Comparisons." In Ross Levine and Aslı Demirgüç-Kunt, eds., *Financial Structure and Economic Growth*. Cambridge, Mass.: MIT Press.

Mulder, Christian, Roberto Perrelli, and Manuel Rocha. 2002. "The Role of Corporate, Legal, and Macroeconomic Balance Sheet Indicators in Crisis Detection and Prevention." IMF Working Paper WP/02/59. International Monetary Fund, Washington, D.C. Processed.

Stone, Mark. 2000. "The Corporate Sector Dynamics of Systemic Financial Crises." IMF Working Paper WP/00/114. International Monetary Fund, Washington, D.C. Processed.

Summers, Lawrence. 1981. "Inflation and the Valuation of Corporate Equities." NBER Working Paper 824. National Bureau of Economic Research, Cambridge, Mass. Processed.

Notes

1. ICR is defined as the ratio of earnings before interest, taxes, and depreciation allowance (EBITDA) to interest expense.

2. Osiris contains data for several additional countries, but often only for a few firms in those countries. Given the need to calculate country fixed effects in the models employed here, those countries were excluded from the analysis. China was excluded on the basis that most of the Chinese companies in the Osiris database were state-owned enterprises and their behavior toward capital structure and debt might be fundamentally different from that of purely private firms.

3. See Summers (1981) for a discussion of the impact of inflation on firm valuations.

4. See Glen and Singh (2003) for empirical evidence on the links among debt levels, performance, and these three factors.

5. The number of observations in the regression is less than the number reported in table 13.1. The difference reflects the fact that some companies had incomplete data for some years. In addition, some companies were dropped owing to inordinately large values of either the dependent variable (ICR) or one or more of the independent variables. Dropping outliers from the regression, which effectively deals with mean values, is much more important than in the case of the median values reported in the summary statistics.

6. Undoubtedly, some will argue that interest rates increased much more than the relatively small amounts mentioned here. That is, of course, true for short-term rates and for a short period of time. But given the drop in demand for credit and the end of the initial currency crisis, interest rates in both countries dropped back quickly to reasonable levels. Using year-end rates, or even annual averages, does not capture this short spike in interest rates. For borrowers with fixed-interest-rate contracts, which were prevalent in these countries, such a spike would have had limited impact.

7. Developed-market countries include all Organisation for Economic Co-operation and Development countries and countries classified as high income by the World Bank; all other countries are considered to be emerging markets.

8. Fan, Titman, and Twite (2003) examine the role of institutional factors in the capital structure of firms globally. They find a significant role for legal system, among other factors.

9. Additional variables to measure macroeconomic volatility, including trade relative to GDP as a measure of openness, the standard deviations of GDP, and consumer price index, were also tried, but they had no impact and actually reduced the statistical significance of the main variable of interest: creditor rights.

Chapter 14

The Contingent Claims Approach to Corporate Vulnerability Analysis: Estimating Default Risk and Economywide Risk Transfer

Michael T. Gapen, Dale F. Gray, Cheng Hoon Lim, and Yingbin Xiao

Many studies have documented the importance of monitoring weaknesses in the corporate sector and their impact on the wider financial system. The motivation for close monitoring derives from the fact that corporate failures are usually expensive in terms of lost employment, lost output, and banking sector distress (in cases where the corporate sector is heavily dependent on bank financing). Moreover, to the extent that the banking sector enjoys full or partial financial guarantee from the government, the losses incurred by the banking sector could translate into a higher debt burden for the public sector as the government issues bonds to cover the cost of recapitalizing banks. In cases where the transmission of risk among sectors is magnified by the linkages between sectors, problems that appeared isolated in the corporate sector could have far-reaching consequences, triggering severe economywide financial crises—what we refer to as macrofinancial risk. The cost of corporate failures tends to be more acute in emerging markets than in mature markets because corporate financing is less diversified and more vulnerable to sudden outflows of capital and sharp changes in both world interest rates and exchange rates. Moreover, fewer avenues are available to hedge or absorb financial losses.[1] Developing an effective approach to detect corporate vulnerabilities before they become severe is essential to minimize macrofinancial risks, thereby protecting the stability of the financial system and the overall economy.

The contingent claims approach was developed from modern finance theory and has been widely applied by financial market participants to measure the probability of default based on the market prices of a firm's debt and equity.[2] In this chapter we apply the contingent claims approach on an aggregated level to estimate corporate sector credit risk and evaluate the potential costs of macrofinancial risk transfers. In particular, we examine the ability of the contingent claims approach to estimate the probability of default within the corporate sector, assess and value the potential for risk transfer, and serve as an early-warning indicator.

Since market prices represent the collective views and forecasts of many investors, the contingent claims methodology is forward looking—unlike analysis based only on a review of past financial statements—and improves the predictive power of the estimates of default risk. The ability to translate continuously adjusting financial market price information into estimates of current market value of assets is especially important given the speed with which economic conditions change relative to the time span between the release of consolidated accounting balance sheet information. In contrast, accounting-based approaches to assessing corporate credit risk rely on historical balance sheet information, which arrives with a significant lag, usually 90 days after the end of the quarter or annual period.[3] Furthermore, the contingent claims approach takes into account the volatility of assets when estimating default risk. The volatility of assets is crucial in this process because firms may have similar levels of equity and debt, but very different probabilities of default if the volatility of underlying assets differs.

We use the contingent claims approach to estimate risk indicators at the aggregated industry level for the nonfinancial corporate sector, including distance to distress and probability of default. This is the first and central purpose of the chapter. However, focusing solely on the corporate sector ignores important possibilities for transferring risk across the consolidated balance sheets of the corporate, financial, and public sectors. Therefore, the second purpose is to extend the contingent claims methodology to a multisector framework in which linkages between the corporate, financial, and public sectors can be examined. A multisector analysis allows for a more thorough understanding of the potential feedback effects between sectors and the implications, if any, for the health of the financial and nonfinancial corporate sectors.

Through two historical case studies, we apply the contingent claims approach using Moody's macrofinancial risk (MƒRisk) model to assess the potential value of such models to act as early-warning indicators of vulnerability.[4] We apply the framework to assess retroactively the likelihood of corporate failure at the industry level and compare the results with actual events. We then extend the framework to a multisector analysis to estimate the level of risk transmitted transmission at the macro level among the corporate, banking, and public sectors. We conclude with a discussion of the results, including potential measures to mitigate risk through enhanced surveillance and policy design.

Contingent Claims Analysis

Initial theoretical work on contingent claims focused both on the pricing of options and the application of option theory to the analysis of corporate capital structure.[5] Since the total value of the firm is equal to the sum of the value of securities in the capital structure, these securities can be viewed as contingent claims on the underlying value of the firm.[6] The contingent claims approach can be used to analyze how the value of the contingent claim changes as the value of the firm changes through time. Therefore, contingent claims analysis should be viewed as a generalization of option pricing theory, with the aim of specifying a framework within which all contingent claims can be valued.

Contingent claims analysis is based on three simple principles: (a) the value of liabilities flows from assets, (b) liabilities have different seniority (and thus different risks related to their seniority), and (c) there is a random element to the way asset value evolves over time. Debt is a senior claim on the asset value, and equity has a junior or residual claim on the asset value. Debt is risky because asset value may not be sufficient to meet the promised debt payments. The value of risky debt, therefore, can be seen as having two components, the *default-free value* of the debt (promised payment value) and the *expected loss* associated with default when the assets are insufficient to meet the promised payments on the debt. The value of the junior claim (equity in the case of firms) is derived from the residual value after the promised debt payments have been made.

If the value of assets has a random component (for example, price changes, shocks, and other factors affect asset value), higher asset volatility means a greater probability that assets will fall below the level necessary to meet the senior debt payments over the horizon period. Consequently, higher volatility means higher expected loss and a lower value of risky debt, other things equal. Financial techniques—namely option pricing relationships—have been developed to measure the expected losses as a function of the asset value, asset volatility, the default-free value of debt, and the time horizon. Similarly, the value of equity and junior claims can be measured as a function of the same variables. The expected loss in risky debt is an implicit put option. Equity and junior claims are implicit call options.[7]

The essence of the contingent claims approach is that changes in observed variables—the value of securities in the capital structure—are used to infer changes in unobserved variables—the value of the firm. The application of the contingent claims approach to the capital structure derives from the seniority of liabilities in the capital structure and the balance sheet identity that the total market value of debt plus equity must equal the current market value of the firm.[8] Since equity represents a residual claim with limited liability, there is a correspondence between equity and a call option. In other words, the equity holder can simply walk away if the value of the firm drops below the face value of debt. The payoff on debt at maturity is equivalent to the difference between the default-free value of the debt and a put option on firm value, with the strike price equal to the book value of the debt and the expiration date equal to the maturity of the debt. The put option represents the limited liability claim written by the debt holder to the equity holder, which gives the equity holder the freedom of surrendering firm assets and walking away when firm value falls short of the promised payment to the debt holder at maturity.

The Contingent Claims Methodology

In this section we briefly illustrate the contingent claims methodology as applied to a simplified corporate balance sheet comprised of senior debt and junior equity.[9] At any point in time, the total market value of assets, A, of a firm financed with debt, D, and equity, E, is equal to the market value of equity plus market value of risky debt. Fundamental analysis dictates that firm asset value is derived from the stochastic discounted present value of income minus expenditures, with the potential for asset value to decline below the point where scheduled debt payments can be made. If assets fall to a level where debt cannot be serviced, then default is the result. This level is often referred to as the distress barrier, *DB*, and is equal to or close to the default-free value of debt.[10]

Equity holders have a junior contingent claim on the residual value of assets in the future. In this manner, the value of equity can be viewed as an option where holders of equity receive the maximum of either assets minus the distress barrier or nothing in the case of default. The value of equity, therefore, is

(14.1) $E = max [\ A - DB,\ 0\ ].$

The standard option pricing formulas can then be used to relate changes in the price of firm assets to changes in equity. Given the relationship between firm equity and firm assets, changes in the value and volatility of traded equity can be used via option pricing relationships to infer changes in the market value and volatility of firm assets.

The case of risky debt, however, is slightly more complex. Holders of debt are obligated to absorb losses in the event of default, and the guarantee of repayment by the lender can be modeled as an implicit put option since debt holders receive assets of the defaulted firm (or, equivalently, the assets of the firm get "put" to the debt holders). Thus holders of risky debt receive the minimum of the default-free value or, in the event of default, the senior claim on assets. Since the value of default-free debt is equal to the distress barrier and the implicit put option on the assets of the firm yields *max* [*DB* – A, 0], the market value of risky debt can be modeled as

(14.2) $D = min [A,\ DB] = DB - max [DB - A,\ 0].$

Inserting these option pricing relationships into the economic balance sheet identity results in a market value of firm assets at time *t* of

(14.3) $A = D + E,$

and

(14.4) $A = DB - max [DB - A,\ 0] + max [A - DB,\ 0].$

The option pricing formula is used in a two-step process. First, the observed market value of equity and the distress barrier are used with the call option formula to derive the value of firm assets. The value of firm assets and the distress barrier are then used with the put option formula to derive the implied market value of risky debt. Thus the contingent claims approach uses call and put option pricing formulas to develop a market-value balance sheet based on observed financial market variables and financial statement information.

Distance to Distress and Probability of Default

Two useful indicators of credit risk that arise from implementation of the contingent claims approach are the distance to distress and the probability of default.[11] The option pricing formulas applied in the contingent claims approach to estimate credit risk rely on only a few select variables: the value and volatility of equity, the distress barrier, the risk-free interest rate, and time. These variables can be combined into a measure of default risk, called the distance to distress, which computes the difference between the implied market value of firm assets and the distress barrier scaled by a one standard deviation move in firm assets. In applying the contingent claims approach to the capital structures of actual firms, most practitioners compute the distress barrier as the sum of the book value of total short-term debt and half of long-term debt plus interest on long-term debt. This computation is used since historical instances of firm defaults have shown that it is possible for the value of firm assets to trade below the book value of total debt for significant periods of time without a default if most of the debt is long term. Short-term debt, however, is more binding since the firm faces rollover risk in a shorter period of time. Thus an adjustment is made to reduce the weight of long-term debt in the distress barrier.

The distance to distress combines into one measure the difference between assets and distress barrier and the volatility of assets,

$$(14.5) \qquad \frac{Market\ value\ of\ assets - Distress\ barrier}{Market\ value\ of\ assets\ x\ Asset\ volatility},$$

which yields the number of standard deviations of asset value from distress. The distance to distress for a hypothetical firm is illustrated in figure 14.1. The numerator measures the distance between the expected one-year-ahead market value of firm assets and the distress barrier. This amount is then scaled by a one-standard-deviation move in firm assets. Lower market value

Figure 14.1: Distance to Distress

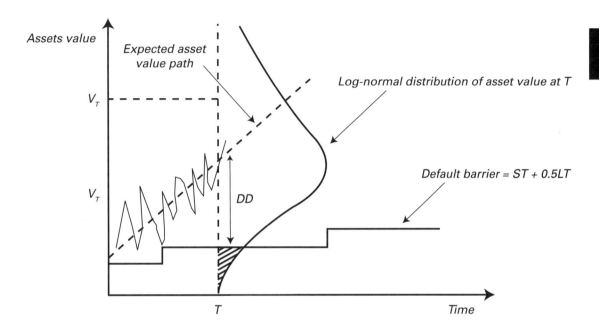

of assets, higher levels of leverage, and higher levels of asset volatility all serve to decrease the distance to distress.

The final step to the probability of default consists of a mapping between the distance-to-distress measure from equation 4.5 and the actual probabilities of default based on historical data.[12] Using historical information on a large sample of firms and given a distance-to-distress measure, Moody's KMV is able to estimate the proportion of these firms that actually defaulted in a one-year-ahead time horizon.

Moody's M*f*Risk Model: Contingent Claims Analysis in a Multisector Framework

While the contingent claims approach as applied to individual corporate balance sheets has become a useful and widely applied tool in risk analysis, the focus on the corporate sector alone is too narrow to fully assess vulnerabilities. The corporate, financial, and public sectors are linked, and changes in value in one sector can transmit risk from one sector to another. Changes in the value of assets of one sector lead to changes in the value of liabilities of that sector, which, in turn, affect the value of assets and liabilities in other sectors. For example, a decline in the assets of the corporate sector leads to a decline in the value of risky corporate debt as the expected losses increase. The lower value of debt held by banks lowers bank assets and causes the value of bank liabilities to fall, which increases the likelihood of financial difficulties in the banking sector. Since governments frequently provide explicit or implicit financial guarantees to banks and large financial institutions out of concerns of systemic risk, the guarantee to the financial sector is a contingent liability on the sovereign balance sheet and a contingent asset on the financial sector balance sheet. As recent history has shown, these guarantees can become very large—from 20 to 70 percent of GDP in recent emerging-market crises. These guarantees can be modeled as implicit put options (see Merton 1977, for example).

The existence of these linkages via risky debt and guarantees allows for risk transfer across balance sheets, which means that corporate sector vulnerabilities may come from "inside" the business environment or from "outside" if the value of the guarantee were to change suddenly. Therefore, a complete analysis of corporate sector vulnerabilities and the potential for risk transfer requires a set of interrelated balance sheets across the corporate, financial, and public sectors (Gray 2002; Gray, Merton, and Bodie 2003). The ability to recognize and price both the expected losses in corporate debt and implicit guarantees is essential for conducting a full assessment of corporate sector vulnerabilities.

Moody's MfRisk model applies the contingent claims approach to the major sectors of a national economy in order to measure and analyze macro-financial risks.[13] The model constructs market value balance sheets of assets, debt liabilities, and junior claims for the aggregated corporate, financial, and public sectors to measure risk exposures and analyze risk transmissions between sectors. Hence, the MfRisk model builds on previous methods of assessing credit risk using contingent claims by analyzing the probability of private and public debt defaults, currency crises, convertibility risk, cross-balance-sheet vulnerability, and the values of government guarantees provided to the financial and corporate sectors. Like Moody's KMV, Moody's MfRisk uses the same approach to calculate distance to distress, default probabilities, and other risk indicators.

Assessing Corporate Sector Vulnerabilities

To assess the ability of contingent claims methods to predict corporate sector vulnerabilities, we apply Moody's M*f*Risk model to calculate retroactively the distance to distress and estimated actual default probabilities of the nonfinancial corporate sector for two case studies: Brazil and Thailand.[14] The contingent claims approach can be applied at the sector level in one of two ways. The sector can be built up from contingent claims models of individual firms (for example, Moody's KMV), or the principles of the contingent claims approach can be applied to the aggregate balance sheet for each of the main industry sectors of the nonfinancial corporate sector. Under the second approach, the contingent claims approach treats each industry sector as if it were one large firm. A disadvantage of aggregating across industry sectors is that the process of aggregation may mask the weakness of individual firms because the ability of any one firm to affect the market-value balance sheet of the industry is dependent on firm size relative to the industry as a whole. However, the aggregation process should indicate possible systemic vulnerabilities because a critical mass of firms is needed to influence the balance sheet of the overall industry sector. Aggregation maintains the fundamental premise underlying the contingent claims approach: (a) the value of sector liabilities flows from sector assets, (b) the liabilities have different seniority, and (c) there is a random element to the way sector asset value evolves over time.

The next sections describe the application of Moody's M*f*Risk model to the corporate sectors in Brazil and Thailand during 2002 and 1997, respectively. Historical information on industry balance sheets is combined with actual market price information to compute distance to distress and probability of default. The resulting indicators of vulnerability across industry sectors are then compared with the results of actual corporate sector defaults to test the ability of the aggregated contingent claims approach to serve as an early-warning indicator of corporate sector vulnerabilities.

The Brazilian Corporate Sector

Demand for capital in Brazil during the 1990s was spurred by large-scale privatizations accomplished through the use of leverage, and, in some cases, existing leverage was sold with the asset itself. Consequently, corporate sector leverage increased during this time in the form of dollar-denominated,

14

short- and medium-term securities (figure 14.2).[15] The sectors that were most leveraged were transportation, metals and mining, food and beverage, pulp and paper, and vehicles and parts (table 14.1). Official data indicate that the overall corporate sector had a sizable negative foreign exchange position on its balance sheet before hedging through derivative operations.[16]

Some industry sectors are naturally hedged since they have export proceeds. However, the export base of Brazil is fairly small—at the time, merchandise exports of goods and services amounted to about $70 billion (15 percent of GDP)—in relation to total external debt.[17] While foreign exchange debt ratios were high in the metals, mining, and pulp and paper sectors, these sectors have the ability to generate foreign exchange revenues and, consequently, were better positioned to weather foreign exchange shocks. However, currency mismatches were likely present in sectors that operate primarily in the domestic economy, such as electric utilities, telecommunications, and retail trade. Foreign exchange hedging was accomplished by the use of foreign exchange derivatives intermediated through the

Figure 14.2: Indicators of Corporate Sector Leverage in Brazil, 1995–2002

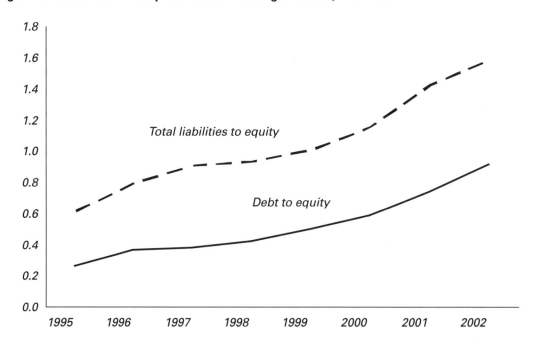

Table 14.1: Leverage and Debt Structure of Nonfinancial Companies, Brazil, December 2001

Sector	Debt to equity	Liabilities to equity	Current liabilities to liabilities	Short-term debt to total debt	Foreign exchange debt to total debt	Short-term foreign exchange debt to short-term debt	Long-term foreign exchange debt to long-term debt
Basic and fabricated metals	1.50	2.44	0.39	0.43	0.76	0.76	0.75
Chemicals	0.75	1.74	0.48	0.32	0.62	0.81	0.52
Construction	0.64	1.84	0.42	0.66	0.15	0.00	0.44
Electronic goods	0.75	2.27	0.59	0.72	0.63	0.70	0.47
Electric power	0.58	1.15	0.33	0.23	0.70	0.48	0.76
Food and beverage	1.34	2.39	0.50	0.48	0.61	0.61	0.61
Industrial machinery	0.61	1.35	0.70	0.68	0.61	0.75	0.34
Mining	0.75	1.18	0.38	0.32	0.93	0.87	0.96
Oil and gas	0.34	1.51	0.60	0.52	0.63	0.89	0.35
Pulp and paper	1.09	1.47	0.43	0.42	0.78	1.76	0.07
Telecommunications	0.55	1.10	0.45	0.25	0.61	1.23	0.40
Textiles	0.66	1.35	0.56	0.58	0.44	0.55	0.30
Trade	1.00	2.59	0.69	0.49	0.72	0.75	0.69
Transportation services	-41.22	-82.84	0.37	0.21	0.29	0.13	0.33[a]
Vehicles and parts	1.05	2.51	0.70	0.66	0.64	0.49	0.91

a. This value was the result of a large loss incurred on a small negative shareholders' equity.

Source: Economatica; International Monetary Fund staff estimates.

14

financial system and facilitated by the provision of foreign exchange–linked domestic public sector debt.[18]

The Contingent Claims Approach and Financial Market Uncertainty in Brazil in 2002

Applying the contingent claims framework retroactively to the aggregated industry sectors of publicly listed companies on the Brazil stock exchange suggests that this approach would have provided an accurate view of the pending financial difficulties within Brazil's corporate sector. Using the historical balance sheet capital structures in conjunction with historical

Figure 14.3: Distance to Distress in Brazil, by Sector, March 2002

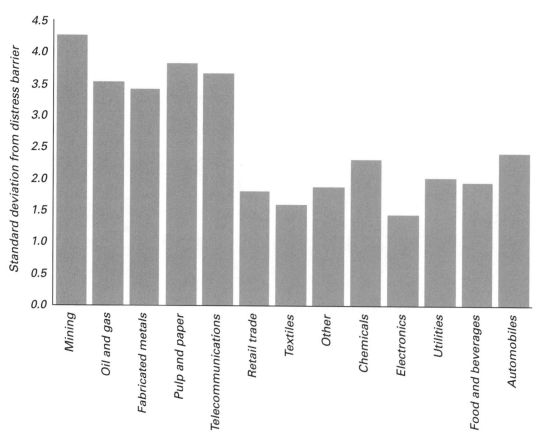

traded equity prices as inputs, the option pricing framework relates these to the value of industry assets. Prior to the financial market volatility, most industries of the corporate sector were two or more standard deviations away from the sector distress barrier, correlating to a relatively low probability of default over a one-year-ahead time horizon (figure 14.3).[19] During the second half of 2002, fears over policy continuity following the upcoming presidential elections, combined with weakening sentiment in external capital markets, caused financial market conditions to deteriorate in Brazil. Access to international capital markets by both the public and private sectors came to a halt beginning in July 2002, and pressure on the currency intensified. Brazil's currency, the real, depreciated from R$2.3 per U.S. dollar in April 2002 to nearly R$4.0 in October, before ending the year at R$3.5.

Equity valuations began to decline in April 2002 and continued to decline steadily before bottoming out in October. As equity valuations declined significantly, the distance to distress decreased for many firms, and resulting probabilities of default were at their highest at end-September 2002 (figure 14.4), when financial uncertainties peaked. Despite the high volatility of asset prices and capital outflows, equity markets remained selective. In particular, while the ensuing market uncertainty affected all industries, equity price declines were more concentrated in industries that had operations primarily in the domestic economy as opposed to export-led sectors. Industries that operated in the domestic economy, such as retail trade, textiles, home appliances (electronics), utilities, and food and beverages, were more likely to have dollar liabilities on their balance sheets versus local currency revenue streams. At the height of the crisis, the distance to distress for these industries ranged from −0.3 standard deviation for home appliances to 0.4 standard deviation for chemicals, indicating high levels of balance sheet distress (when distance to distress turns negative, the contingent claims approach suggests that some firms in the industry sector are in default). In contrast, the main export industries—mining, oil and gas, steel, pulp and paper, and petroleum chemicals—were less affected because currency mismatches between assets and liabilities were less prevalent. Distance to distress for these sectors averaged 1.1 standard deviations, well below their levels in March, but well above the distance to distress of their nonexport-based counterparts. Therefore, markets discriminated against nonexport sectors more heavily when weighing the impact of the depreciation and economic slowdown.

Figure 14.4: Distance to Distress in Brazil, by Sector, September 2002

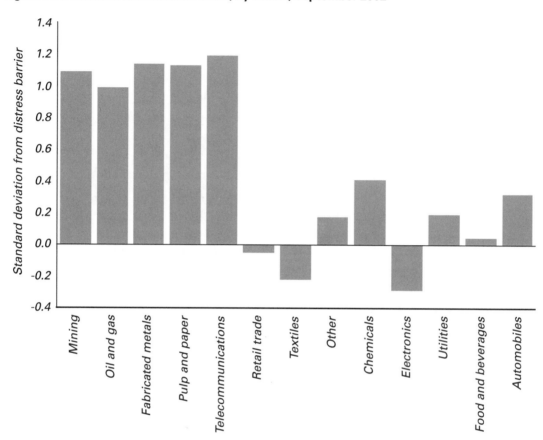

The electric utility industry is an example of an industry that operates primarily in the local market, with revenues in local currency and some liabilities in foreign currency. The electric utility sector raised large amounts of funds during 1998–99 in dollar loans related largely to privatization efforts. The subsequent devaluations in the currency in 1999 and 2002, along with the rationing of power in 2001, resulted in weak balance sheets. As shown in figure 14.5, the distance to distress in the utility sector narrowed steadily and reached its lowest level at end-September. Prior to the financial market volatility, the utility sector had a distance to distress of slightly above 2 standard deviations. The subsequent mapping of this distance to distress into probability of default indicated that the aggregated industry had a one-year-ahead probability of default equal to 5 percent (figure 14.6). In September, when equity price declines were largest and implied that asset volatility had reached its peak (figure 14.7), the distance to distress for the sector had fallen to a standard deviation of 0.2 at its lowest recorded level and averaged a standard deviation of 0.6 for the entire month. This average standard deviation was equivalent to a one-year-ahead probability of default of around 30 percent for the sector as a whole.

The highest-profile case of distress within the electric utility sector was Eletropaulo, Latin America's largest power distributor and a subsidiary of AES Corporation. On August 26, 2002, Eletropaulo was placed in selective default by Standard and Poor's after missing a debt payment and approached holders of R$700 million ($223 million) in debt with a plan to extend payments by two years. Other instances of weakness in the utility sector were

Figure 14.5: Assets Relative to Distress Barrier in the Utility Sector in Brazil, 2002

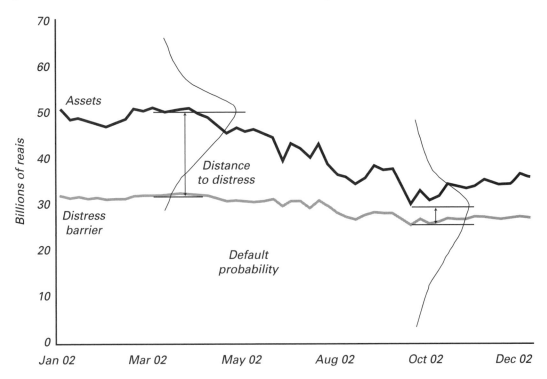

Figure 14.6: Estimated Actual Default Probability Versus Distance to Distress in the Utility Sector in Brazil, March–December 2002

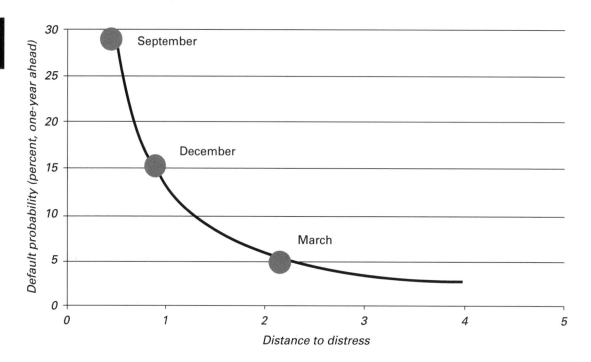

partially resolved by an infusion of government lending or an infusion of capital by the parent company. In addition to the utility sector, other high-profile cases of corporate defaults confirm the level of distress indicated in the MfRisk model output. For example, BCP Telecommunications, the wireless unit of BellSouth and Safra Group, defaulted on a $375 million loan in late March. Globopar, Latin America's largest media company, defaulted on $1.5 billion worth of debt in October 2002. This decision also pushed one of its subsidiaries, Globo Cabo, into default on nearly $100 million of debt in early November. Varig, the largest airline carrier in Latin America, agreed with creditors in September to reschedule debt payments after returning some of its leased aircraft and renegotiating more favorable terms on remaining leases.

Outside of some systemic weakness in utilities and media-telecommunications, Brazil's corporate sector weathered the financial volatility in 2002

Figure 14.7: Implied Asset Volatility in the Utility Sector in Brazil, 2002

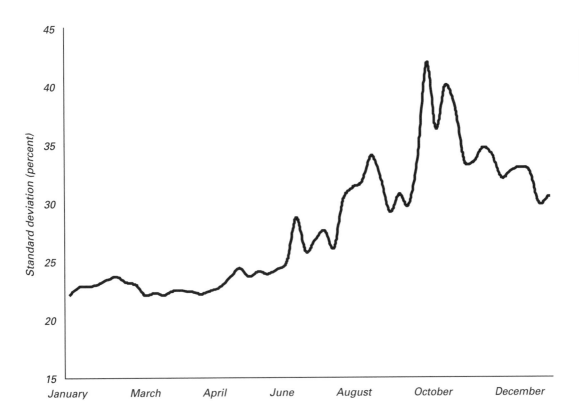

14

relatively well due to, in part, the rapid improvement in the economic environment after the election-related uncertainties passed. There were instances of capital infusion from parent entities or public sector sources, but this process was more the exception than the rule, and widespread corporate defaults were avoided. In Asia in 1997–98, in contrast to Brazil, bankruptcies of highly leveraged companies eventually posed systemic vulnerabilities to the financial and public sectors. The next section uses the MfRisk model to assess retroactively the aggregated contingent claims approach on the Thai corporate sector during the Asian crisis.

The Thai Corporate Sector

Strong economic growth, along with a fixed nominal exchange rate and capital account liberalization, contributed to a surge in capital inflows in Thailand and most of Southeast Asia from 1992 to 1996. Private sector investment in manufacturing and real estate was complemented by public sector investment, especially in infrastructure relating to transportation, telecommunications, and utilities. Private sector capital inflows into the five economies most affected by the Asian financial crisis increased from $30 billion in 1992 to $73 billion in 1996.[20] Unlike in Latin America, the bulk of capital inflows into Asia came in the form of bank lending, which accounted for $120 billion (51 percent) out of $234 billion in total private capital flows.

Much of the bank lending went to the nonfinancial private sector in the form of short-term U.S. dollar-denominated loans. About 65 percent of all external borrowing was conducted by the nonfinancial corporate sector from 1992 to 1996 (table 14.2), and the majority of this debt was contracted at short maturities. Nearly 75 percent of all short-term debt had original maturities of less than six months, with one to three months being the most popular time horizon (table 14.3). Successive years of heavy reliance on debt relative to equity financing resulted in a debt-to-equity ratio of nearly 160 percent in 1996, the highest in Asia at that time.[21] Even with increasing quantities of short-term U.S. dollar-denominated debt on corporate sector balance sheets, the widespread perception that the peg would remain stable contributed to low hedging positions. While data on overall corporate sector hedging practices are not available, studies are available that provide insight into hedging behavior. For example, one study examined 29 large nonfinancial firms and found that 85 percent of the total foreign debt positions were unhedged.[22]

The real estate and asset price bubble came under pressure beginning in 1996 as growth began to slow significantly in the second half of the year. Successive years of capital inflows and an appreciating U.S. dollar after 1994 caused an appreciation in the real exchange rate (International Monetary Fund 2002; Radelet and Sachs 1998). A higher real exchange rate combined with decreasing external demand led export growth to decline sharply from 25 percent in 1995 to −2.0 percent in 1996. Manufacturing output, especially in the areas of durable goods and associated inputs, fell sharply. Declines were also registered in beverages and textiles. Overall, measures of capacity utilization in the manufacturing sector declined from 80 percent in 1995 to 76 percent in 1996.

14

Table 14.2: Gross External Borrowing by the Non-Bank Sector, Thailand, 1992–96

Sector	1992 Short term	1992 Total	1993 Short term	1993 Total	1994 Short term	1994 Total	1995 Short term	1995 Total	1996 Short term	1996 Total
Total	14,870	17,730	16,076	18,816	14,757	18,061	16,606	22,064	18,228	25,943
Non-bank financial institutions	4,632	4,807	6,578	6,900	6,169	6,569	8,528	9,685	7,338	8,745
Nonfinancial sector	10,238	12,923	9,498	11,916	8,588	11,492	8,078	12,379	10,890	17,198
Trade	3,832	3,982	4,099	4,264	3,251	3,394	3,147	3,460	3,806	4,148
Construction	151	199	156	194	91	185	110	145	200	791
Industry	5,195	7,035	4,478	6,167	2,917	4,414	3,331	6,174	4,178	6,216
Food	348	506	173	262	180	286	87	352	84	414
Textiles	257	362	302	594	237	309	145	282	125	252
Metals	388	531	447	592	296	472	316	523	235	492
Electrical appliances	1,425	1,692	1,139	1,319	619	744	1,101	1,402	1,172	1,548
Machinery and transportation	2,025	2,209	1,392	1,488	1,054	1,099	937	1,079	1,990	2,015
Chemicals	257	358	313	604	221	374	237	922	264	906
Petroleum products	145	595	515	634	123	528	219	562	107	292
Others	350	783	197	684	187	602	289	1,052	201	297
Services[a]	111	162	152	215	83	190	157	504	294	623
Others	949	1,545	613	1,076	2,246	3,309	1,333	2,096	2,412	5,420

Note: Gross external borrowing includes borrowing from affiliates but excludes commercial banks and Bangkok international banking facilities.

a. Excludes real estate.

Source: Reprinted with permission from International Monetary Fund (2002). Data provided by the Thai authorities.

14

Table 14.3: Borrowing Terms of Private External Loans, Thailand, 1992–96

(millions of U.S. dollars unless otherwise noted)

Term	1992 Amount of borrowing	1992 Percent of total	1993 Amount of borrowing	1993 Percent of total	1994 Amount of borrowing	1994 Percent of total	1995 Amount of borrowing	1995 Percent of total	1996 Amount of borrowing	1996 Percent of total
Total	17,730	100.0	18,816	100.0	18,061	100.0	22,064	100.0	25,943	100.0
Short term	14,870	83.9	16,076	85.4	14,757	81.7	16,606	75.3	18,228	70.3
Less than 1 month	375	2.1	721	3.8	2,698	14.9	4,486	20.3	4,546	17.5
1–3 months	10,922	61.6	11,051	58.7	9,200	50.9	8,495	38.5	9,604	37.0
4–6 months	2,605	14.7	3,481	18.5	1,727	9.6	1,980	9.0	2,522	9.7
7–11 months	59	0.3	25	0.1	54	0.3	61	0.3	216	0.8
12 months	909	5.1	798	4.2	1,078	6.0	1,584	7.2	1,340	5.2
Long term	2,860	16.1	2,740	14.6	3,304	18.3	5,458	24.7	7,715	29.7
No age	237	1.3	263	1.4	276	1.5	621	2.8	892	3.4
More than 1–3 years	689	3.9	809	4.3	1,224	6.8	1,893	8.6	2,994	11.5
More than 3–5 years	748	4.2	619	3.3	818	4.5	1,461	6.6	1,994	7.7
More than 5–10 years	1,097	6.2	725	3.9	863	4.8	1,002	4.5	1,243	4.8
More than 10 years	89	0.5	324	1.7	123	0.7	481	2.2	592	2.3

Note: Gross external borrowing includes borrowing from affiliates but excludes commercial banks and Bangkok international banking facilities.

Source: Reprinted with permission from International Monetary Fund (2002). Data provided by the Thai authorities.

The Contingent Claims Approach and the Asian Financial Crisis

While the generalized slowdown should have signaled an increase in the probability of an economic adjustment from built-up imbalances, traditional signals of vulnerability did not register much forewarning.[23] However, aggregated contingent claims provide some indication of weakness prior to the severe financial market volatility that ensued. Equity prices began to decline in early 1996, nearly 18 months before the floating of the baht, decreasing the distance to distress for many firms. Since much of the accumulated debt during previous years was short term and dollar denominated, the distress barrier became more binding since firms were vulnerable to both rollover and exchange rate risk.[24] By the end of 1996, the distance to distress had fallen in three of the four main nonfinancial industry sectors. Manufacturing, trade and services, and real estate and construction all registered lower dis-

Figure 14.8: Assets Minus Distress Barrier in Thailand, 1992 and 1996

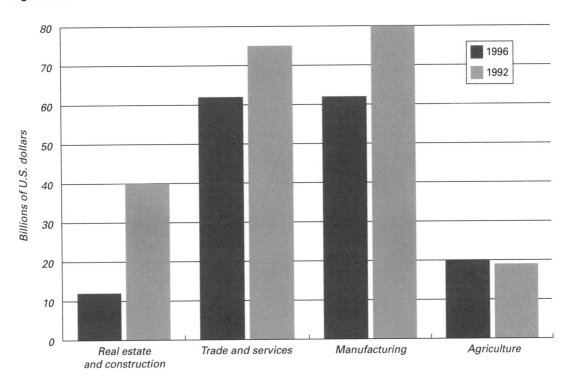

14

tance to distress relative to their 1992 positions, while agriculture registered a slight increase. Industry-level assets relative to distress barriers in 1992 and 1996 are displayed in figure 14.8. The distance to distress was lowest in the real estate and construction sectors, reflecting the increasing likelihood of a boom-bust cycle.

Serious pressures on the foreign exchange market began in early 1997 with the release of poor fiscal and export data. Concerns over increased monetization, a deteriorating current account, and proliferation of non-performing assets in the financial sector caused foreign investors to begin unwinding their carry-trade positions.[25] The default by Samprasong Land in February and rising short-term interest rates in developed economies further fueled capital flight and foreign exchange pressures. Extensive intervention

Figure 14.9: Distance to Distress in Thailand, by Sector, July 1997

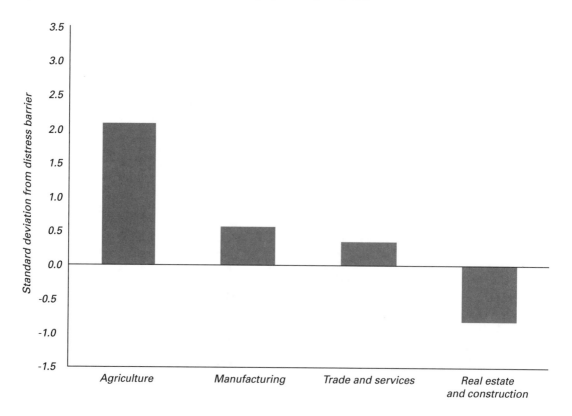

Figure 14.10: Distance to Distress in Brazil, by Sector, October 1997

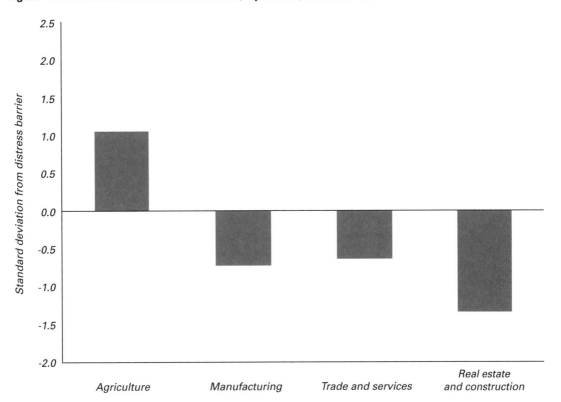

14

by the Bank of Thailand in support of the currency and the imposition of capital controls in May failed to stem capital flight and speculative positions by market participants. The baht was subsequently floated on July 2, 1997.

By the end of July, the baht had depreciated nearly 24 percent, and equity prices had depreciated 20 percent relative to their end-1996 levels. The depreciation substantially raised distress barriers for firms with dollar-denominated liabilities, and equity prices continued to reflect a worsening economic outlook and capital outflows. By the end of July, distance-to-distress indicators showed a disturbing picture for the real estate and construction sectors and substantial strains on the manufacturing, trade, and service sectors. As shown in figure 14.9, standard deviations from the distress barrier were significantly negative for real estate and construction. Manufacturing and trade and services were all within 0.5 standard deviation of the distress barrier.

Following the initial turbulence, Thailand agreed on a $17 billion stabilization program with the International Monetary Fund (International Monetary Fund 1998). However, the currency continued to depreciate, and equity prices continued to fall. By the end of October, the baht had fallen 58 percent from 25 to 40 baht per U.S. dollar and the SET Index stood at 447, or 46 percent below its end-1996 value. At these levels, contingent claims analysis implies a very serious crisis with widespread corporate defaults, as the distance to distress became negative for all corporate sectors except agriculture (figure 14.10). The contingent claims approach effectively predicts the widespread corporate defaults experienced after the floating of the baht. According to reports by financial institutions to the Bank of Thailand, around $5 billion of corporate debt, or 3 percent of GDP, was engaged in restructuring in June 1998. This amount rose to around $19 billion, or 16 percent of GDP, in June 1999. Of this total, an estimated two-thirds was held by domestic commercial banks, with the balance evenly split between foreign banks and finance companies.

Multisector Contingent Claims Analysis

While the examples of the corporate sectors in Brazil and Thailand highlight the usefulness of contingent claims analysis as a tool in risk analysis, the focus on the nonfinancial corporate sector alone may be too narrow to fully assess vulnerabilities. As previously indicated, third-party guarantees like implicit government guarantees of the financial system are present or implicit across the balance sheets of the public sector, financial sector, and nonfinancial corporate sector. Therefore, a complete analysis of corporate sector vulnerabilities and potential for macrofinancial risk transfer requires a set of interrelated balance sheets across the corporate, financial, and public sectors.[26] The following sections discuss two examples of the application of contingent claims analysis to a multisector framework. First, the example of Brazil illustrates risk transfer from the public sector to the corporate sector balance sheet. Second, the example of Thailand illustrates risk transfer from the corporate sector to the balance sheets of the financial and public sectors.

Multisector Contingent Claims Analysis: Brazil

In the context of Brazil, the multisector contingent claims framework can be used to analyze the transmission of risk between the public sector and the corporate sector during 2002 through explicit guarantees. The public sector provided interest rate and currency hedges to the corporate sector through the regular issuance of domestic public sector debt with returns linked either to short-term interest rates or the *real* per U.S. dollar exchange rate. The financial market instability during 2002 caused some market participants to call into question the sustainability of the public sector debt and, in turn, the value of the interest rate and currency hedges provided to the corporate sector.[27] Through the provision of an explicit guarantee, any severe public sector distress is transmitted to the asset side of the balance sheet of the corporate sector.[28]

The liabilities of the public sector include external debt, domestic debt, financial guarantees, and base money. In addition to providing liquidity and being a medium of exchange, domestic money is also valued because it can be exchanged for foreign currency. As domestic currency is exchanged for foreign currency, foreign exchange assets of the public sector decline. If sovereign external debt payments have first claim on foreign currency assets in the public sector balance sheet, then only residual foreign currency reserves in excess of scheduled external debt payments are available for conversion from domestic to foreign currency holdings. Therefore, the holders of domestic currency have a claim on the residual foreign currency assets of the public sector above what is necessary to service public sector external debt.

This claim can be viewed as a call option on government foreign currency assets. The payoff is equal to the maximum of residual foreign exchange reserves or zero if (a) foreign exchange reserves fall below the costs of external debt service or (b) capital controls are put in place to restrict convertibility. Restrictions on the ability to convert local currency to foreign currency would prohibit the ability of the corporate sector to service external debt. The contingent claims approach can be applied to determine the probability of an "inconvertible" event, which is an important measure of corporate sector vulnerability.[29]

At end-2001, Brazil had gross international reserves of $36 billion, and external debt of the nonfinancial public sector amounted to $93 billion. External debt service costs in 2002 were estimated at $7.4 billion of interest and $6.5 billion of principal. The public sector also had outstanding domestic dollar-linked debt and foreign exchange swaps of $65 billion at the end of 2001, much of which was short term. However, these instruments were denominated and payable in domestic currency, easing the government's foreign currency constraint. Reserve coverage, therefore, appeared adequate to cover one-year-ahead hard foreign currency requirements of the public sector.

In contrast, the private sector had significant foreign currency liabilities. At end-2001, total external debt of the financial and nonfinancial corporate sector amounted to $117 billion, much of which was short term. External debt service costs for the private sector were estimated at $8 billion in interest and $30 billion in principal. The private sector hedged this foreign exchange exposure through government-issued dollar-linked debt and foreign exchange swaps, intermediated through the financial system.[30] While denominating these instruments in the local currency eased the government's foreign exchange constraint, it did not ease the hard currency constraint on the private sector. The hedge position was a domestic currency asset of the private sector versus a foreign currency liability. The holders of the hedge still had to convert reais into foreign currency, mainly U.S. dollars, to complete the transaction.

During the financial market volatility in 2002, the contingent claims approach indicates that market perception of convertibility risk increased. As access to international capital markets dried up and rollover rates on external debt fell, demand for dollars increased and public sector international reserves fell. The result was an increased perception of convertibility risk as a subset of public sector assets (international reserves) approached an implicit distress barrier (one-year-ahead foreign currency liabilities of the public sector). Local markets were not seen as providing an effective hedge partly because all local contracts were settled in the domestic currency. As shown in figure 14.11, the probability that restrictions would be placed on currency convertibility rose from 5 percent in March to 30 percent in September.[31] As the perception of convertibility risk increased, some firms either stopped rolling over foreign exchange hedges or even sold existing hedges in order to purchase dollars in the spot market.[32] This withdrawal of hedges coincided with prepayments and capital outflows of nearly $7 billion during the same time period.[33] As uncertainties subsided, both convertibility risk and capital outflows declined rapidly by year-end. Overall, the use of contingent claims to estimate convertibility risk appears to explain some of the rationale behind the capital outflows and corporate sector behavior during the second half of 2002.

Figure 14.11: Convertibility Risk and Capital Outflows through CC5 Accounts in Brazil, 2002

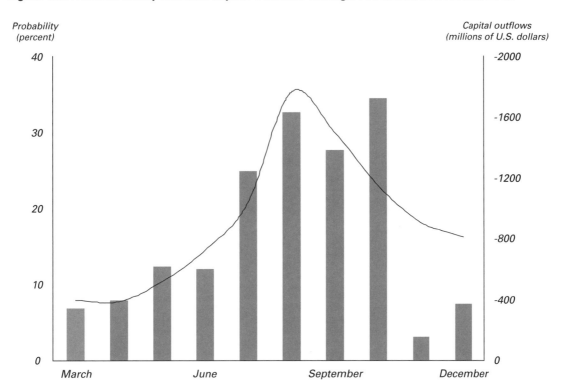

The Brazilian government took many steps to address the market uncertainty, focusing on a set of core policies that maintained discipline and restored market confidence. The government increased the primary surplus and gave tax and pension reform priority in the reform agenda. Consistent policy implementation and improving fundamentals led to a rapid normalization of financial markets. For example, nine months after external access was halted and six months following the peak of financial market turbulence, the sovereign once again accessed external capital markets in April 2003. Widespread access by the corporate sector to external markets returned shortly thereafter.

Multisector Contingent Claims Approach: Thailand

In the context of Thailand and the Asian crisis, the multisector contingent claims framework can be used to analyze the transmission of risk from the

14

corporate sector to the financial sector to the public sector. The size of the risk transfer across the balance sheets is captured in two steps. First, equity of the financial sector is modeled as a call option on total financial sector assets, yielding estimates of changes in the market value of financial sector assets over time. Second, the financial guarantee from the public sector is modeled as a put option based on the derived market value of financial sector assets. The value of the put option also requires an assumption about recovery rates, which are normally less than full. For this analysis, a recovery rate of 80 percent is assumed for the banking sector and 60 percent for nonbank financing companies. Based on this structure, declines in the value of financial sector equity from the depreciation of the baht and increases in loan delinquency rates caused the market value of assets to decline, increas-

Figure 14.12: Financial Sector Distance to Distress in Thailand, 1997

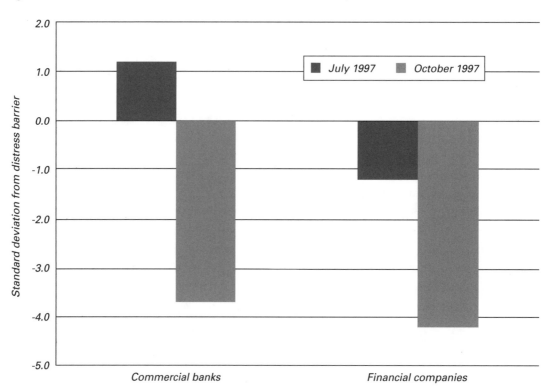

ing the probability of default. As the probability of default rose, the value of the government guarantee adjusted for recovery rates increased.

As discussed above and displayed in figures 14.9 and 14.10, distance-to-distress indicators for the industry sectors were low or negative by end-July 1997, especially in real estate and construction. By the end of October, corporate sector distance-to-distress measures were negative for all sectors except for agriculture, implying a high probability of widespread corporate defaults. Corporate sector weakness was transferred to the balance sheet of the financial sector, reflected in lower equity prices, increased asset volatility, and decreasing distance to distress. As shown in figure 14.12, distance to distress for financing companies was already significantly negative in July 1997. In August 1997, around the same time Thailand agreed on the stabilization program with the International Monetary Fund, the Bank of Thailand suspended operations in 42 financial companies. By October, the distance to distress for both commercial banks and financial companies was negative. The problems in the balance sheets of the financial companies became so severe that the Bank of Thailand closed 56 finance companies in December 1997.

The decreasing market value of financial sector assets relative to the distress barrier increased the value of the financial sector guarantee. Figure 14.13 plots the evolution of the one-year-ahead estimate of the value of the financial sector guarantee throughout 1997. The value is listed as a percentage of 1996 nominal GDP for scale purposes. As shown in the figure, the value of the guarantee was relatively small during early 1997 but had already increased to nearly 10 percent of GDP prior to the float, representing the building vulnerabilities on the balance sheets of the financial companies in particular. After the baht was floated in July and subsequent turbulence, according to the contingent claims approach, the value of the financial sector guarantee was between 30 and 40 percent of GDP by October 1997.

Subsequent restructurings in the financial sector indicate that the one-year-ahead estimated value of the financial sector guarantee was relatively accurate. In October 1998, reports by private sector specialists estimated that 45 percent of loans were nonperforming and that loan losses amounted to 27 percent of GDP or 350 percent of financial sector capital (Armstrong and Spencer 1998). The slow pace of the restructuring process meant that the actual number of restructured loans was not known until several years later. Fortunately, the Bank of Thailand has published extensive data on the debt restructuring carried out by financial institutions after the 1997 finan-

Figure 14.13: Value of the Financial Sector Guarantee in Thailand, 1997

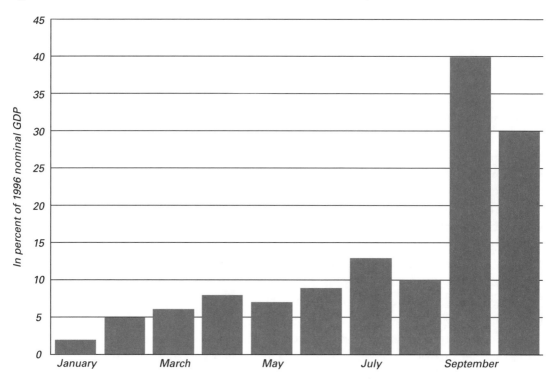

cial market crisis.[34] The database includes number of cases and amounts restructured in total and by type of loan. Based on these data, financial sector debt equivalent to 23 percent of GDP had completed the restructuring process by end-1999. By end-2000, this value had reached 40 percent of GDP. Both numbers correspond roughly to model estimates.

Conclusions

In this paper, we have examined the application of the contingent claims approach to identifying corporate sector and macrofinancial vulnerabilities. In doing so, we applied the Moody's MƒRisk model, which uses principles of aggregated contingent claims, to assess vulnerabilities retroactively in the corporate sector as well as in a multisector setting through two historical cases. The results presented here indicate that the method holds promise for identifying corporate sector vulnerabilities and estimating the associated value of macrofinancial risk transfer across interrelated balance sheets of the corporate, financial, and public sector.

The main output of the contingent claims approach is an estimated probability of default, which is a function of the capital structure of the balance sheet, the volatility of asset returns, and the current asset value. Since the information contained in the firm balance sheet and equity price can be translated into a probability of default, the contingent claims approach underpins the development of credit risk and risk management techniques. In particular, the contingent claims approach is used by (a) major credit rating agencies to monitor and assign credit ratings, (b) financial institutions to inform interest rate pricing on loans and set adequate levels of regulatory capital, and (c) investment banks and insurance companies to assess value-at-risk. For example, when applied across a portfolio of firms, the probability of default multiplied by weighting within the portfolio creates a value-at-risk (VaR) indicator, which is then used in conjunction with other VaR indicators to adjust capital adequacy or allow the firm to offset risk exposure by entering into offsetting financial transactions.

Although the contingent claims approach has been applied most often to the balance sheets of individual firms, this chapter has used the Moody's MfRisk model to demonstrate how the contingent claims approach also can be applied to aggregated sector balance sheets or across balance sheets in a multisector framework. The evolution of the contingent claims approach to a multisector framework incorporates the potential for risk transfer across balance sheets, providing an additional avenue for vulnerability analysis. The conclusions presented here show that such analysis is warranted in the event of (a) a full or partial financial guarantee from the government to the financial sector, (b) government provision of guarantees such as interest rate and currency hedges to the corporate sector, and (c) the presence of a high degree of correlation across firm balance sheets (the chaebol structure in Korea is an example of the potential for increased interconnectivity across firm balance sheets).

Advantages of the Contingent Claims Approach

The advantages of the contingent claims methodology are numerous, only some of which are discussed here. The main advantage is that it uses observable balance sheet and financial market data along with volatility to construct a measure of default risk. The ability to translate continuously adjusting financial market price information into current market-value estimates of asset value is especially important given the speed with which economic conditions change relative to the time span between releases of consolidated accounting balance sheet information. Furthermore, balance sheet information arrives with a significant lag, usually 90 days after the quarter or annual ending period. The contingent claims approach combines the capital structure of the balance sheet with current price information from financial markets to construct a market-value estimate of the current balance sheet along with forward-looking indicators of vulnerability. In addition, it distinguishes itself from other vulnerability analysis by recognizing the important role that volatility has in determining default probabilities. Increases in volatility raise the option value and benefit equity holders at the expense of bondholders. By capturing volatility, the contingent claims approach accounts for the fact that firms with the same capital structure may have different distance-to-distress and default probabilities.

While not explicitly detailed in this chapter, the contingent claims methodology incorporates nonlinearities that yield significant improvements in vulnerability analysis over traditional linear relationships. In option pricing theory, the value of the option is dependent on changes in the underlying asset. The rate of change in the price of the option relative to changes in the underlying asset is referred to as the *delta*. The equivalent measure in bond pricing is *duration*: how much the bond price changes in response to a change in interest rates. However, the duration measure is only accurate for small changes in the interest rate. In fact, duration changes as the interest rate changes, and this measure is referred to as *convexity*. The same is true with option prices. The option delta is only accurate over small changes in asset price. The equivalent measure to convexity in option pricing is called the option *gamma*, or the rate at which the option delta changes as the price of the underlying asset changes. Therefore, the nonlinearity of the Black and Scholes methodology allows for a more accurate description of changes in vulnerabilities from large changes in asset prices just as both duration and convexity are needed to compute accurate changes in bond prices from large movements in interest rates.[35] Linear relationships that ignore higher orders could dramatically underestimate potential vulnerability and, consequently, fail to be adequate indicators for surveillance purposes.

Hurdles to Overcome

There are several hurdles to overcome when implementing the contingent claims methodology, but most can be mitigated. First, the approach uses on-balance-sheet information to construct the capital structure of the balance sheet and may not include off-balance-sheet items like hedging or derivative positions. This fact, however, is not a disadvantage of the contingent claims approach alone; it is a shortcoming of all vulnerability indicators that rely on balance sheet information. Rather, the contingent claims approach relies heavily on financial markets to synthesize the current economic situation and its potential impact on the balance sheet and reflects this in current equity or junior claim prices. Thus, with respect to off-balance-sheet positions, the contingent claims approach implicitly assumes that financial markets are the best source for information regarding the current value of a firm. This is not an unrealistic assumption since industry analysts, equity specialists, and other local market participants are likely in the best position to assess current trends and developments. However, the contingent claims approach does not assume that market forecasts are always correct. Financial markets can be taken by surprise, and the degree to which this happens limits the ability of the contingent claims approach to accurately forecast vulnerabilities.

Option pricing relationships in the contingent claims approach derive a risk-neutral default probability based on cumulative normal distributions that must be mapped into actual expected default probability. The use of risk-neutral default probabilities generally overstates the actual probability of default, requiring a mapping of the estimated actual probability of default based on historical data. Fortunately, Moody's KMV has been able to use historical observations of public and private company defaults to map risk-neutral default probabilities into actual expected default probabilities. The resulting distribution has slightly fatter tails than a cumulative normal distribution. The mapping, however, is mainly representative of U.S. firms, although it has been used successfully in a wide variety of applications. Some emerging markets have poor-quality information and many unlisted firms. Moody's has tried to address this problem with a blended approach using an option model and financial data (Riskcalc). Comparative studies have shown that the models related to the contingent claims approach are much more accurate than Z-score accounting ratio models or accounting ratios in predicting default (around 70 percent accuracy ratios for the contingent claims–type models and about 50–56 percent for the Z-score and accounting ratio models; Sobehart and Stein 2000).

Finally, application of contingent claims to the financial sector and public sector balance sheets is still a relatively new phenomenon. Credit risk within financial institutions is often difficult to disentangle given the problems inherent in analyzing and pricing illiquid loan portfolios and understanding true liability positions. However, equity markets understand these issues well, and results from this analysis and Moody's KMV suggest that the contingent claims approach does well in assessing vulnerabilities within the financial sector. With respect to applying the contingent claims approach to the public sector balance sheet, sovereign defaults are rare, making testing and calibrating the model on sovereign balance sheets difficult. Moody's-MfRisk has overcome this problem by correlating the public sector risk indicators with credit spreads instead of a pool of defaults, allowing for calculation of sovereign spreads and default probabilities for a variety of different scenarios. Therefore, while application of the contingent claims approach to the public sector is new, early results indicate that this application holds promise.

Implications for Macroeconomic Risk Management

At a minimum, application of the contingent claims approach in a multisector setting allows for the ability to value the potential for risk transfers across balance sheets and, in particular, the ability to value the public sector guarantee to the financial sector, as shown in the case of Thailand. However, just as the private sector uses contingent claims to analyze risk and implement risk management strategies, policymakers can use contingent claims in a multisector framework at the public sector level. The multisector setting in the Moody's MfRisk model provides an interconnected framework within which policymakers can analyze potential policy mixes and evaluate which may be more adept at countering vulnerabilities.

Policymakers can follow several strategies in order to transfer or mitigate risk, including (a) a direct change in the balance sheet through policy action (for example, increasing the primary surplus increases the assets of the public sector relative to the distress barrier), (b) management of implicit or explicit guarantees (for example, providing or withdrawing credit guarantees to the banking sector or currency hedge to the corporate sector), (c) risk transfer strategies (for example, signing contracts with foreign banks or insurance companies), (d) institutional changes in markets (for example, capital requirements, Basel core principles, payments systems, mark-to-market requirements), and (e) mitigation of risk by diversification, hedging, or insurance. Any of these strategies, either individually or in a combination, can be analyzed in a multisector framework to manage risk in a dynamic economy. While not the subject of this chapter, it is a useful avenue for further study.

References

The word "processed" describes informally produced works that may not be commonly available through libraries.

Altman, Edward I. 1968. "Financial Ratios, Discriminant Analysis, and the Prediction of Corporate Bankruptcy." *Journal of Finance* 23(4, September):589–609.

Altman, Edward I., Robert G. Haldeman, and P. Narayanan. 1977. "A New Model to Identify Bankruptcy Risk of Corporations." *Journal of Banking and Finance* 1(1, June):29–54.

Armstrong, Angus, and Michael Spencer. 1998. "Will the Asian Phoenix Rise Again?" Emerging Markets Research–Global Emerging Markets. Deutsche Bank Research, October. Processed.

Black, Fischer, and Myron S. Scholes. 1973. "The Pricing of Options and Corporate Liabilities." *Journal of Political Economy* 81(3, May-June):637–54.

Crosbie, Peter J., and Jeffrey R. Bohn. 2003. "Modeling Default Risk." Moody's KMV [online]. Available at www.moodyskmv.com. Processed.

Crouhy, Michel, Dan Galai, and Robert Mark. 2000. "A Comparative Analysis of Current Credit Risk Models." Journal of Banking and Finance 24(1–2):59–117.

Dasri, Tumnong. 2000. "Out-of-Court Corporate Debt Restructuring in Thailand." Presented at the International Conference on Systemic Resolution of Corporate and Bank Distress in Crisis-Affected East Asian Countries, World Bank, Asian Development Bank Institute, and Japan Ministry of Finance, Tokyo, Japan, January 11–12. Processed.

Geske, Robert. 1979. "The Valuation of Compound Options." *Journal of Financial Economics* 7(1):63–81.

Gray, Dale F. 2002. "Macro Finance: The Bigger Picture." *Risk Magazine*, June 6, pp. 18–20.

Gray, Dale F., Robert C. Merton, and Zvi Bodie. 2003. "A New Framework for Analyzing and Managing Macrofinancial Risks of an Economy." M*f*Risk Working Paper 1-03. Available at www.moodys-mfrisk.com. Processed.

International Monetary Fund. 1998. *International Capital Markets: Developments, Prospects, and Key Policy Issues*. World Economic and Financial Surveys. Washington, D.C., December.

———. 2002. "Thailand: Selected Issues and Statistical Appendix." IMF Country Report 02/195. Washington, D.C., September. Processed.

Jarrow, Robert A., and Stuart M. Turnbull. 1997. *Derivative Securities*. South-Western College Publishing.

Merton, Robert C. 1973. "Theory of Rational Option Pricing." *Bell Journal of Economics and Management Science* 4(1, Spring):141–83.

———. 1974. "On the Pricing of Corporate Debt: The Risk Structure of Interest Rates." *Journal of Finance* 29(2, May):449–70.

———. 1977. "An Analytic Derivation of the Cost of Loan Guarantees and Deposit Insurance: An Application of Modern Option Pricing Theory." *Journal of Banking and Finance* 1:3–11.

———. 1998. "Applications of Option Pricing Theory: Twenty-Five Years Later." *American Economic Review* 88(3):323–49.

Pomerleano, Michael. 1998. "The East Asia Crisis and Corporate Finances: The Untold Microeconomic Story." *Emerging Markets Quarterly* (Winter):14–27

Radelet, Steven, and Jeffrey Sachs. 1998. "The Onset of the East Asian Financial Crisis." NBER Working Paper 6680. National Bureau of Economic Research, Cambridge, Mass. Processed.

SBC Warburg Dillion Read. 1997. "Valuation Issues: Reality Check 2." November. Processed.

Sobehart, Jorge R., and Roger M. Stein. 2000. "Moody's Public Firm Risk Model: A Hybrid Approach to Modeling Short-Term Default Risk." Moody's Rating Methodology. March. Processed.

Notes

1. In the Asian crisis during the 1990s, widespread bankruptcies of highly leveraged companies contributed to sharp declines in output and significant losses in the banking sector. Eventually, the public sector was forced to recapitalize the banking sector at a significant fiscal cost.

2. See Crouhy, Galai, and Mark (2000); Merton (1998). Perhaps the most widespread application of the contingent claims approach has come from Moody's KMV, whose products are used by more than 2,000 leading financial institutions and firms in more than 80 countries. Utilizing 30 years of historical data for more than 6,000 public and 70,000 private company default events for a total of 70,000 public and 1 million private companies, both healthy and distressed, around the world, Moody's KMV uses firm asset value, future asset distribution, asset volatility, and the level of the default barrier to derive the firm-specific probability of default, which they refer to as the Expected Default Frequency.

3. The accounting-based approach maps a reduced set of financial accounting variables to a risk scale to discriminate between repayment and nonrepayment. A prominent accounting-based approach developed by Altman (1968) uses a linear combination of five accounting and market variables to produce a credit score—the so-called Z-score. A subsequent seven-factor "Zeta model" was later introduced by Altman, Haldeman, and Narayanan (1977).

4. The MfRisk model was developed under a joint research effort between Moody's and Macro Financial Risk, Inc. Access to MfRisk is only available through subscription.

5. Black and Scholes (1973) and Merton (1973, 1974) use no-arbitrage principles to derive the theoretical valuation formula for options commonly known as the Black and Scholes option pricing model. The authors also discuss the application of option pricing to corporate liabilities. In subsequent work, Geske (1979) shows how options on equity are really compound options on firm value and expands the formula of Black and Scholes to cover such cases.

6. The general definition of a contingent claim is any asset whose future payoff is contingent on the outcome of an uncertain event. In this context, a contingent claim is the right to obtain the residual value of the asset or the obligation to receive (residual) value of an asset.

14

14

7. Government guarantees to the banking and financial sector increase with the volatility of assets in that sector. The government guarantees are also implicit put options, which are a function of the banking and financial sector asset value, the associated asset volatility, the associated deposits and debt obligations, and the time horizon.

8. Securities on the liability side of the corporate balance sheet could also include senior collateralized debt, convertible securities, and preferred equity.

9. See appendix I (available from the authors) for additional detail on contingent claims analysis and the application of the Black and Scholes option pricing formula.

10. Analysis by Moody's KMV shows that from an empirical point of view the distress barrier is approximated by short-term debt plus interest on long-term debt plus half of long-term debt.

11. Although not explicitly discussed here, a third useful indicator of credit risk that can be obtained from the contingent claims approach is the credit spread, or the additional risk premium required by bondholders to compensate for expected loss.

12. This step is necessary since the option pricing formula used to derive the distance to distress generally overstates the actual probability of default. The Black and Scholes option pricing formula results in risk-neutral probabilities of default since the formula is derived from no-arbitrage conditions. Using historical instances of default, Moody's KMV has demonstrated that the actual probability distribution has fatter tails than the normal distribution applies. See Crosbie and Bohn (2003) and Jarrow and Turnbull (1997) for additional information.

13. See appendix II (available from the authors) for additional information on the MfRisk multisector model and consolidated balance sheets.

14. Unless otherwise indicated, all reported values from applying the contingent claims approach to the country cases are obtained from the MfRisk model.

15. Data for the corporate sector represent quoted companies on the São Paulo stock exchange (BOVESPA) from Economatica, a private data provider. The companies in the sample hold about 70 percent of the overall nonfinancial private sector external debt and include some public sector companies, but Petrobras has been excluded.

16. Official data indicate that the corporate sector had $63 billion in assets at end-2001 against a debt level of about $90 billion. Corporate sector

assets included $51 billion registered as direct investment abroad and were likely less liquid.

17. A billion is 1,000 million. The ratio of total external debt to total exports of goods and nonfactor services was about 300 percent.

18. Foreign exchange hedging via derivatives is widespread, and Brazilian firms hedged foreign exchange risk, mainly by the use of foreign exchange derivatives. The public sector provided the corporate sector with interest rate and currency protection through the highly indexed structure of public debt. Banks acted as intermediaries by buying the dollar-linked bonds or foreign exchange swaps issued by the public sector and then selling the foreign exchange hedge to the corporate sector. Firms also hedged themselves on the BM&F, the local derivatives market, which is very active.

19. Private sector credit risk analysts and Moody's M*f*Risk associates view a one-year-ahead distance-to-distress measure below 0.5 as an indication of severe stress.

20. International Monetary Fund (1998). The five economies are Indonesia, Republic of Korea, Malaysia, the Philippines, and Thailand. Capital flows are measured as net foreign direct investment plus net portfolio investment plus net other investment.

21. Pomerleano (1998) shows that debt-to-equity ratios increased from 70 percent in 1992 to 155 percent by end-1995.

22. SBC Warburg Dillion Read (1997). The level reported is the weighted average of unhedged short-term and long-term debt and should only be viewed as an indicative measure of hedge since firm-by-firm statistics in the sample varied widely. The firms in the sample accounted for $16 billion in U.S. dollar-denominated debt, of which 15 percent was classified as short term.

23. Radelet and Sachs (1998) examine a wide variety of macrofinancial indicators for the Asian crisis countries. According to their analysis, indicators were highest in Korea and Thailand, but alarms were few in Indonesia, Malaysia, and the Philippines.

24. Recall that the distress barrier is the sum of the book value of short-term debt plus half of long-term debt and interest. Higher ratios of short-term debt to total debt imply a more stringent barrier.

25. A carry trade is a short-term position put in place to take advantage of persistent interest rate differentials and a fixed exchange rate. See International Monetary Fund (1998: 44) for additional details.

26. The composition of the consolidated balance sheets is detailed in appendix II, which is available from the authors, with special emphasis on application of the contingent claims approach to the public sector.

27. Spreads on external Brazilian public sector debt tripled to above 2,400 before rallying to 1,400 at year-end. The rollover rate on domestic public debt fell below 50 percent, and average maturity of newly issued debt fell to 12 months, causing a decline in the average maturity of the stock of domestic public debt from 36 to 32 months.

28. To the extent that the corporate sector holds government debt directly, changes in the value of these assets would appear on the balance sheet. As discussed below, currency hedge is typically intermediated through the financial system.

29. Convertibility risk can also be measured through the differential between the nondeliverable forward offshore contract and the implied onshore foreign exchange forward.

30. Risk transmission from the corporate sector to the banking sector is relatively mild. Private sector credit is only 25 percent of GDP, and foreign exchange exposure is only intermediated from the public sector to the private sector. Therefore, net foreign exchange exposure remains on the public sector balance sheet as opposed to the banking sector.

31. The convertibility risk measure in figure 14.11 is displayed as a monthly average.

32. The notional value of outstanding hedge positions registered on the CETIP, a securities clearing registry, declined from $50 billion as of end-May 2002 to $37 billion at end-October. Amounts on CETIP include financial companies and trading within own accounts and indicates hedging practices as opposed to actual amounts.

33. Capital outflows are registered flows through so-called CC5 accounts and were obtained from the Central Bank of Brazil. See www.bcb.gov.br/?ECONOMIA.

34. See the website of the Bank of Thailand (www.bot.or.th/) and Dasri (2000) for additional information.

35. Advances in option pricing methodology also include the option vega, which can allow for changing volatility of the underlying asset. This feature is important since volatility of assets often increases significantly during periods of financial stress. Traditional linear relationships are, therefore, significantly inferior to their nonlinear counterparts.

Chapter 15

Developing an Effective Framework for Insolvency and Credit Rights

Gordon W. Johnson

15

The emerging-market crises of the late 1990s gave rise to an unprecedented international effort to promote global standards for financial stability. This joint World Bank/International Monetary Fund (IMF) effort, encompassing some dozen areas, aims to strengthen financial systems at both the international and domestic levels and to improve the ability of countries to respond to crises and to identify and address systemic vulnerabilities. The main purpose of country diagnostics is to support reforms that help systems to comply with international best practices.[1] The standards and codes used in these country assessments are divided into categories aimed at transparency, financial sector systems, and market infrastructure systems.

The *transparency standards*—data dissemination, fiscal transparency, and monetary and financial policy—are based on codes developed by the IMF, which undertakes these assessments. In addition, the World Bank and the IMF have jointly developed the public debt management guidelines to assist countries in regard to good debt management practices. The *financial sector standards*—banking supervision, payment and settlement systems, insurance supervision, securities regulation, and anti–money laundering—address core financial systems within a market. Financial sector assessments are undertaken jointly by the IMF and World Bank. The *market infrastructure standards*—accounting and auditing, corporate governance, and insolvency

15

and creditor rights systems—represent the bedrock systems for commerce and play a fundamental role in promoting and sustaining confidence in commercial relationships. These assessments are conducted by the World Bank.

The Role and Significance of Enforcement and Insolvency Systems

The challenge under the Insolvency and Creditor Rights Initiative is to develop effective and efficient credit and corporate recovery systems to mitigate the impact of corporate financial distress and insolvency. An effective framework for insolvency and creditor rights will also strengthen the investment climate and promote private sector development.

Experience with financial crises has shown that effective systems of enforcement and insolvency are critical to promoting commercial confidence before, during, and after crises. Such legal systems constitute the backdrop against which corporate restructuring takes place; facilitate asset resolution in a way that reduces the deterioration of asset values and promotes greater access to credit; operate as a safety valve for corporate distress by enabling parties to salvage viable businesses and transfer assets more efficiently to better uses; and serve as a disciplinary effect to promote good corporate governance.

Meeting the Challenges of Business in a Global Market

Credit is the lifeblood of commerce. Credit and its accessibility require willing lenders and investors who have at their disposal a wide array of lending and investment options supported by the law. Lenders and investors also operate on the basis of reasonable, manageable risks, which are more easily gauged when the rights of the parties are clearly established by law. Credit protection and corollary enforcement mechanisms play an important role in this regard. Collateral has become increasingly significant and quite varied in modern lending practices, enabling businesses to tap into the potential, underutilized value of business assets to access much-needed capital. Modern security laws and systems can facilitate this process. When businesses fail—a natural consequence of competition in today's capital markets—the interests of the credit community must be balanced against sovereign policies encouraging investment, growth, and employment. This balance seeks the equilibrium between reliable enforcement of creditor rights and revitalization of business.

Promoting Sound Investment Climates and Commercial Confidence

Enforcement and insolvency systems help to foster commercial confidence and predictability by enabling market participants and stakeholders to price, manage, and resolve default risk more accurately. Where these systems function effectively and efficiently, prompt response minimizes asset deterioration: parties are able to resolve disputes quickly and to maximize recovery through efficient bargaining and restructurings or through auctions and sales. They also have a disciplinary effect on commercial relationships, encouraging responsible conduct of business through rules by which management can be held accountable, replaced, or penalized if it steps outside the boundaries of reasonable and fair behavior. In this way, effective and efficient legal frameworks can promote access to credit by establishing more reliable measures of credit risk.

Enforcement and insolvency systems also function as a safety valve for corporate distress. When businesses get into financial difficulty, there is a mechanism for salvaging them efficiently and quickly. For businesses beyond salvage, there is a mechanism for transferring the assets to more efficient market users. And consequently, these two elements—corporate rescue and liquidation procedures—serve a natural and necessary function within the market economy. They facilitate good credit risk management and responsible behavior within the financial sector in regard to lending and credit by giving creditors a set of tools for managing their portfolio and for taking corrective action as necessary in order to minimize the impact on their portfolios. These concepts are the foundation for the World Bank's principles and guidelines for effective insolvency and creditor rights systems (see appendix 15.1 for the text of the principles).

The Risk Assessment Continuum

In developing the principles, the World Bank first considered the natural life cycle of a typical commercial transaction from the inception of the credit or investment relationship through the stages of distress, default, or demise.

15

Figure 15.1: The Risk Assessment Continuum

Credit access	Financial distress	Enforcement/resolution
• Information • Security • Negotiation (pricing) • Contracting • Registration of rights • Monitoring	• Information • Identification of options • Negotiation (pricing) • Amendment of contracts • Registration of rights • Monitoring	• Information • Security options • Negotiation (plan) • New contracts or agreements • Registration of rights • Monitoring of implementation

Source: World Bank.

This can be plotted along a risk assessment continuum (see figure 15.1). At the beginning of the credit relationship—the *credit access phase*—a lender engages in a series of conventional steps in deciding whether to extend credit, including research into the creditworthiness of the borrower and the risks associated with extending credit to a particular borrower. Depending on the risks identified, the creditor may request credit protection or enhancement through collateral and other forms of securities. The credit risk is also reflected in the price of the credit negotiated. In the best of all possible worlds, the banker has little to do other than monitor the credit to ensure that repayment is made timely and properly. Unfortunately, we do not live in a world with perfect markets.

As part of the natural order, businesses frequently encounter financial problems and default in the performance of obligations—the *financial distress phase*. Businesses may become financially distressed for a number of reasons—bad management, fraud, litigation, changes within the market, or business products that become obsolete or less competitive—whatever the cause, a credit provider, a prudent lender, or an investor will need to reevaluate the credit risk in light of the changed circumstances in which the business finds itself. The main question at this stage is whether the risk is manageable so as to justify a debt rescheduling or restructuring of the business and, if so, on what terms. Questions of specific regulations governing the treatment of nonperforming loans and provisioning, or taxation with respect to debt relief and transfers, may enter into the equation. Improving the protection afforded to the creditor is likely to be required—for example, by taking pledges over new collateral or restructuring contracts. If the lender or the investors conclude that the business is not viable or the debt cannot be restructured, they may opt instead to collect the debt through individual action, such as by executing on the collateral, or through formal systems for collective resolution, such as bankruptcy—the *resolution and recovery phase.*

The risk assessment continuum reveals a direct connection between credit risk at the front end of the relationship and the downside risk at later stages, when the business faces financial decline or a default in performance. The efficacy of the legal mechanisms and systems that serve to protect creditors and provide recovery in the event of a default can increase or decrease the risk to the lender or investors. If one concludes that the enforcement or insolvency procedures will yield little or no return, then the chance of nonperformance carries a higher risk of loss that must be factored into the cost of the credit at the front end of the transaction. This is typically reflected in higher interest rates and higher lending costs, which restrict access to credit by making it less accessible or accessible only at greater cost to the market.

The World Bank Principles and the Risk Assessment Continuum

The World Bank's framework for assessing insolvency and creditor rights systems is based on this spectrum of commercial risk. The principles were developed specifically to help policymakers to assess the effectiveness of systems that enable stakeholders to manage and mitigate risk along the continuum of a commercial relationship (see figure 15.2).

Systems that support access to credit include those governing credit information, credit protection (for example, guarantees, mortgages, and pledges), and registries. Rights without the ability to enforce them, however, are meaningless; thus enforcement procedures must also be evaluated, including the efficiency of the court procedures by which collection and enforcement actions typically take place. At the stage of financial distress, a number of other systems become particularly relevant, including director and officer liability for trading the business during insolvency, credit risk management practices, resolution and informal workout mechanisms, and the broader environment that facilitates restructurings, such as corporate and tax laws that may create incentives or disincentives to write off debt and

Figure 15.2: The World Bank Principles/ROSC Assessment Framework

Credit access	Risk management	Enforcement/resolution
• Credit information systems	• Director, office liability	• Corporate exit mechanisms
• Collateral systems	• Risk management practices	• Liquidation procedures
• Registries (notice)	• Informal workouts	• Reorganization procedures
• Enforcement systems	• Enabling environment	• Quasi-formal restructuring
• Auction procedures	• Tax treatment on bad debt or restructured debt	• Implementation through courts and regulation

Source: World Bank.

undertake restructuring. Finally, the more formal systems for resolution and recovery—bankruptcy and reorganization or their quasi-formal cousins—are also examined. These systems cannot be measured properly on the basis of the law alone; they must also be examined with respect to implementation through the courts and regulation of the professionals.

The Commercial Insolvency Framework

Commercial insolvency is a collective process for resolving and adjusting the rights and interests of stakeholders in a failed business. Invariably, the system includes three primary pillars: the legal, institutional, and regulatory frameworks.

The law embodies the rules that reflect a number of potentially diverging policies and interests that must be balanced and harmonized to make the system function in a manner that fits within the unique context of a country's values, culture, legal heritage, and other factors. Given the wide disparity in sovereign cultures, legal heritage, values, and policy choices, it is nearly impossible to design a model law that works for every country. At the same time, an insolvency law generally contains the various procedures by which the process is to be handled and with respect to which there is generally a much higher degree of commonality, as all proceedings must have a start and a finish. Many of these common features can be designed on the basis of best practices that have been tested and shown to work more effectively in light of modern business needs. What is important to maintain commercial confidence is that the rights created under the wider commercial framework be harmonized and balanced with the goals and objectives of the insolvency process. Accordingly, in designing the law itself, one must often look to the rights governing the interests of other stakeholders doing business with the debtor.

The *institutional framework* addresses the sufficiency of the implementation of the law and examines basic elements of the court's role in the overall process, such as the qualifications and appointment of judges, the specialization of courts and judges, the efficiency of administration procedures, and the ability of government to make decisions concerning the restructuring or liquidation of companies in a responsive and fair manner. There are two main approaches to designing the institutional framework for insolvency. A few countries—for example, Colombia, Peru, and until recently the Philippines—have opted for an agency model, where insolvency hearings are held before a specialized agency of the government. Most countries adopt a judicial approach to insolvency procedures, however, where hearings are held in courts of general jurisdiction or, in some cases, in more specialized courts dealing with commercial law. In evaluating the effectiveness of the courts, the World Bank considered the ability of judges to respond in a way that inspires commercial confidence. Even in the presence of bad laws, good courts can interpret the laws in a consistent manner, which provides reasonable reliability to the markets and thus less risk for commercial players.

Finally, there is the *regulatory framework*. In most systems, insolvency or restructuring is supervised by a specialized practitioner. Thus the practitioner must be qualified to carry out his duties, ensuring efficient administration of the business and its assets, with a view to maximizing the value of recovery for the benefit of creditors. The administrator's role is of paramount value and should be appropriately regulated.

In looking at the total picture, it is important to keep in mind that there are other important linkages and interrelationships between a country's insolvency system and other parts of the commercial framework. Rules and regulations pertaining to corporate governance in the period leading up to and during insolvency are important. Accounting and auditing rules have an impact on the balance sheet of businesses, the valuation of assets, cash flow, and forecasts. Monetary and fiscal policy may affect the treatment of taxes or fiscal claims and the treatment of nonperforming assets from a lender's perspective. These and other linkages must be considered carefully to ensure that the insolvency system is designed properly.

15

Are the World Bank Principles Pro-Creditor or Pro-Debtor?

Labels such a pro-creditor and pro-debtor attempt to simplify what tend to be complex systems that are not susceptible to these facile stereotypes. Nevertheless, a number of factors can be used to evaluate the degree to which a system falls on the pro-creditor or the pro-debtor side of the scale.[2]

The factors used to measure the orientation of the system consider a number of key areas where the insolvency law could interfere with or alter the contractual rights of creditors in the context of insolvency. Arguably, the insolvency law in pro-creditor systems does not infringe significantly on a creditor's contractually bargained-for rights. At the other end of the scale, the law in pro-debtor systems tends to erode those rights and expectations to achieve rehabilitation of the business.

Notably, in the past decade, the trend has been toward convergence, with pro-creditor systems becoming more debtor friendly and pro-debtor systems tilting back toward stronger creditor rights. Thus in countries like Germany, Japan, and the United Kingdom, the trend is toward amendments to promote corporate reorganization, while in other countries, like the United States, the trend is toward going-concern sales or assets sales at earlier stages of the proceedings. This gradual convergence toward the midpoint of the continuum can be attributed in part to the impact of globalization (global business and financial markets), which increasingly forces countries to adopt a set of rules and systems conducive to investment and competition both domestically and globally. The World Bank principles reflect this balance, based on best practices. This is not to say that every country will strike the same balance as reflected in the principles or aim for the middle of the pro-creditor/pro-debtor scale. Each country's approach will reflect its history, policy choices, and the issues affecting a particular market at a particular time and must evolve with the changing needs of business, commerce, and society.

Experience with the World Bank Principles under the ROSC Framework

The World Bank principles serve as the basis for benchmarking country systems globally under a joint IMF–World Bank program to prepare Reports on the Observance of Standards and Codes (ROSCs). This section examines the results of ROSCs for eight emerging-market countries and six European Union (EU) member countries.[3]

Creditor Rights Systems

The area of creditor rights benchmarks the treatment of collateral and registry systems and secured and unsecured enforcement. In the sample of eight emerging-market countries, these systems are substantially weak but still performing. About half of the countries are operating more or less at a functional level. The rest are not working well at all, meeting the applicable principles only in a few areas, mostly falling below compliance in regard to effective enforcement. By contrast, in the EU sample of countries, creditor rights systems function reasonably well.

Insolvency Systems

In general, the emerging-market sample scores slightly worse on insolvency law frameworks than on creditor rights systems: most of the laws in the emerging-market sample fail to match up to the principles in a number of material respects. That is, their scores do not indicate functionality, much less efficiency. Many of these countries have undertaken significant reforms on insolvency in the past decade as part of their transition effort. Not surprisingly, these efforts have paid off in some countries. Others are still attempting to get the balance right.

Contrast that with the EU sample of countries, where the results reflect systems largely compliant and functional (fully or largely observed), with Greece and Spain being the exceptions. Spain recently adopted a new insolvency law in July 2003 that will be assisted by new specialized courts, and the new law is a substantial improvement over what was previously the oldest insolvency law in Europe. Greece also has insolvency reform on the agenda, as do France and Italy.

Rehabilitation and Reorganization of Businesses

The developing-country sample scores worse in the area of rehabilitation and workouts than on the general insolvency and liquidation frameworks. In actuality, reorganizations are not common practice, and there has been little experience outside the context of privatization. Reorganizations either are not happening or happen at such a slow pace that the process ultimately leads to the demise of the patient. Similarly, in most of the developing countries, the enabling framework and the process for workouts are essentially nonfunctional in all of these countries.

By contrast, among countries in the EU sample, the results are somewhat mixed, with half functioning well (Denmark, Germany, United Kingdom) and the other half functioning poorly (France, Greece, Spain). The most curious results come from France. Although French law is often associated with a very strong bias toward rehabilitation, under the EU study, the French system scores rather poorly. It would seem that, in their efforts to save everything, the French model succeeds in saving little. The French are now in the process of evaluating their system to introduce reforms that will improve the prospects for rehabilitation, while at the same time shifting the balance to encourage swift liquidations and better protection for creditors.

Institutional and Regulatory Frameworks

The developing-country sample on the whole receives the lowest ratings for compliance with the World Bank principles, although clearly there are pockets of compliance and some countries score better than others. The problems identified include enormous delays in the efficiency of the courts, poorly organized courts, and little or no transparency in decisionmaking. Enforcement is also generally below standard. Almost no countries have performance standards by which to measure the activities or qualifications of judges. The integrity of the courts in many of these countries is called into question, as is the integrity of participants, insolvency trustees, and practitioners.[4] Compliance with the regulation principles is the weakest link in the chain for all systems in the developing-country sample: as a general rule, there is no regulation of the quality of practice and skills of practitioners who play a fundamentally important role in administering the case, developing business solutions, and facilitating the resolution of disputes.

In contrast, performance within the courts and regulation of the process are significantly better in the EU countries, with substantial compliance in most areas of the principles. Of course, most countries within the EU have a much longer history than emerging-market countries of dealing with insolvency through the courts.

Lessons and Experience in Applying the Principles

Although significant progress has been made in reforming the laws in emerging markets, an enormous amount of work remains to be done to develop modern laws and efficient procedures dealing with insolvency. Weak creditor rights and slow enforcement limit recoveries and raise the risk of lending, thus reducing access to credit. Many countries lack rescue procedures, so potentially viable companies are forced into liquidation. Judicial capacity is frail, making it difficult for courts to respond promptly and efficiently, which is particularly problematic where a strong and prompt response is crucial to preserving the business and its assets. The importance of these problems is highlighted when considering workouts, corporate rescue, and their interaction with the social safety net provided by employee rights and the tax system.

The treatment of employee rights and social protection of labor is particularly weak in many emerging markets and often is the greatest obstacle to successful corporate restructuring. It is extremely difficult to establish a healthy balance sheet without reducing costs, and this often means laying off employees. This can be difficult to accomplish and can result in excessive hardship in the absence of effective rules to enforce a fair process and to protect redundant workers. Rampant layoffs are not always the best solution, as we have seen in countries like Indonesia during the early stages of its financial crisis. One approach to protecting workers is to establish a protection fund, or a guarantee payment fund, that sets priorities for access by employees laid off during corporate restructuring. The German model most closely reflects the model that is consistent with the objectives of the World Bank principles: in Germany, a guarantee fund pays out employees at an early stage of the process in order to minimize the impact on restructuring.

Another area where workouts are hampered has to do with tax and provisioning laws that penalize parties for engaging in a debt rationalization process. For example, creditors may want to write off or rationalize debt or convert their debt into an equity interest in the debtor company. The tax laws may impose heavier tax burdens on such transactions, however, forcing the creditors to adopt alternative measures that are tax safe, but that lead to unnecessary litigation, execution, or liquidation of the debts and business. Alternatively, parties may be forced to carry artificially valued assets on their books to avoid the incurrence of taxes or the burden of provisioning for losses. Such laws create disincentives to restructuring.

Corporate Restructuring: Common Implementation Goals

In today's global economy, there is an important need to stabilize distressed but viable businesses and avoid unnecessary liquidation. At the same time, losses must be properly apportioned among creditors. Equity restructuring offers a solution, by allowing creditors to convert debt in the business to equity and encouraging subsequent operational restructuring, as necessary. Equity restructuring also provides a means for accessing new financing for working capital or essential investment needs, possibly giving the new lenders preferred rights or priorities in repayment. As a safety measure, these systems should enable parties to convert unsuccessful workouts efficiently into formal procedures.

Corporate Rescue Approaches

Corporate rehabilitation models range from the purely informal approaches, which are contractual in nature, to the most formal models involving court-administered reorganization procedures, with hybrids that contain elements of both. However, they all share some common features, as reflected in figure 15.3.

Figure 15.3: Corporate Rescue Approaches

Credit access	Risk management	Enforcement/resolution
• No forum	• Application to court	• Application to court
• Lead bank, committee	• Lead bank, committee	• Committee nominated
• Contractual standstill	• Stay, moratorium	• Stay, moratorium
• Establish cash flow and liquidity	• Cash flow and liquidity	• Cash flow and liquidity establish
• Information	• Information	• Information, disclosure
• Evaluate options	• Evaluation of options	• Evaluation of options
• Negotiate restructure agreement	• Negotiation, vote on plan	• Negotiation, vote on plan
• Binding effect limited (signatories)	• Binding effect limited (class)	• Binding on all creditors

Source: World Bank.

In the context of an informal workout, there is no established forum for resolving disputes, although parties may have negotiated a forum with respect to mediation or arbitration. The lead bank or a standing committee will often take command in prompting the discussions and negotiating a contractual standstill. As a matter of first importance, cash flow must be available to sustain the business during the period of negotiations, either by negotiating new financing or by selling assets to establish interim liquidity. To reasonably evaluate options and successfully engage in fair negotiations, the parties must have access to current, accurate, and sufficient information on the business to make decisions about whether the restructured business will be viable and capable of repaying the restructured obligations. Assuming that negotiations are successful, the parties enter into a restructuring agreement. In the informal process, the restructuring agreement or settlement binds only those parties that sign the agreement (although a majority action clause can bind other banks in a syndicated lending arrangement or based on an inter-creditor arrangement). Creditors outside the agreement are free to pursue enforcement individually or to apply for the commencement of formal insolvency proceedings, as applicable. Thus, in the purely informal process, holdout creditors can pose a serious risk to the achievement of successful restructuring.

The formal workout—that is, a quasi-formal rescue procedure—can be, but is not necessarily, a court-supervised procedure. It has some features of the formal system, such as application to the court, a formal moratorium or stay of proceedings imposed by law, and a binding effect that is potentially broader than the purely informal process in that it may, by law, encompass some dissenting creditors in a class of creditors where the majority has accepted the restructuring.

Formal Proceedings

The purely formal process involves formal commencement of the procedure in the court, with the court or another institution overseeing the process. A committee of creditors may be nominated, or rules will govern the general assembly with respect to decisions and voting. The formal rules will typically impose a stay on creditor actions and a moratorium on the repayment of pre-petition claims. As in the less formal proceedings, cash flow and financing play an important role in the court-supervised procedure. Disclosure and access to timely, current, and accurate information are crucial to evaluate properly the options for the business and to develop a plan of reorganization. The main differences between the formal process and the less formal or informal procedures are—not surprisingly—the degree of formality and structure and the extent to which the restructuring, when approved by the court, binds the creditors. In the formal case, it is *binding on all creditors* in the case, while in the quasi-formal process, only select classes or groups of creditors may be bound. In the informal process, the restructure agreement binds only those who signed the agreement.

Comparative Tax Consequences for Debt Write-offs

Tax issues play an important role in the dynamic of the negotiation in a number of ways. Tax considerations can be the main factor in the restructuring of a company. Favorable tax treatment on the write-off or restructuring of debt can enable creditors to write off more debts or create a structure that is better suited to a restructuring of the business or to a reallocation of the risks and wealth. Conversely, unfavorable tax treatment can be a deal breaker and prevent restructurings from taking place on rational terms. In short, tax laws can affect the write-off of debt in many ways, whether it be a straightforward write-off, a partial write-off for interest or some portion of the principal, a write-off of debt based on discounting or rescheduling, a write-off based on a sale of the assets at discount, or a write-off based on an exchange of debt for debt or debt for equity. In debt-equity swaps, tax implications could arise where the nominal value of the debt differs from the value of the equity received in exchange for the debt.

From the debtor's perspective, income tax treatment or income revenue treatment has an impact on debt that has been written off: outside of the formal bankruptcy process, such write-offs may constitute income to the debtor, while in the formal insolvency process, the obligation to declare forgiven debt as income may be waived. A number of common law systems (for example, Australia, United Kingdom, United States) tend to have more comprehensive and favorable tax treatment for debt write-offs, making the business environment more conducive to restructuring, while the civil law countries studied (for example, France, Germany, Japan) tend to have tax regimes that are less favorable to the writing off of debt and hence tend to create less friendly restructuring environments. In the civil law systems in the study, the questions on tax treatment are not addressed, or the system makes it difficult to gain the desired tax treatment.

Social Protection Systems

Essentially four models are in use worldwide to deal with employee rights and claims. The most pro-employee approach is characterized by China, where the employees are accorded a higher priority in repayment even than secured creditors, at least with respect to the restructuring of state-owned enterprises.[5] Under this approach, other creditors are effectively forced to underwrite the employee losses at their own expense; in China, the state banks have been the primary underwriters for the restructuring process and have served as a de facto social safety net.

The second model is referred to as the bankruptcy priority model. This approach is characterized by Mexico, which gives employees priority during bankruptcy but no insurance protection or guarantee of payment from a fund established for the purpose of repaying employee claims in the context of insolvency. The employee would get a priority on repayment ahead of other creditors in the case, possibly over secured creditors or only over a certain unsecured class of creditors.

The third model combines the bankruptcy priority with the guarantee payment fund; it can be found in Denmark and other countries. This model is perhaps the most favorable for employees, because they enjoy two forms of protection. First, they have priority over other creditors in the bankruptcy, which reduces their risk relative to other creditors in the proceeding; second, a guarantee fund provides an option for them if a distribution does not take place.

The fourth model contains no priority for employee claims but ensures repayment of those claims from the guarantee fund. This model is represented by Germany, where the fund pays the employee directly before distribution in the case. In my view, this is the ideal solution because employees have maximum protection through up-front repayment early in the case: they do not have to wait until the end of the proceeding to get paid. They get paid from the guarantee fund, and the guarantee fund then subrogates to the rights of the employee to receive repayment, which is likely to amount to only a partial repayment. At the same time, the relative priority of secured creditors is respected so that commercial expectations are preserved. How one establishes and capitalizes the guarantee fund is an important issue in addressing the challenges of downsizing the work force in the context of restructuring.

And, finally, other issues are of key importance to the restructuring process, such as financing and how to deal with institutional weaknesses. The increasing international trend is to try to bypass institutional weaknesses by creating hybrid models that incorporate features of the U.S. concept of a prepackaged bankruptcy. And that is where parties negotiate the out-of-court resolutions and agree to and vote on the restructuring before commencing the formal proceeding in court. This minimizes the amount of time and cost of the court proceedings and typically takes from two to four months. Similar fast-track solutions are being utilized elsewhere. Turkey adopted this approach in 2003.

The Way Forward

The World Bank principles and the assessment program have proven to be an important developmental tool for promoting the Bank's goals of assisting client countries to achieve sustainable development. The principles are a functional diagnostic tool with which countries can better appreciate the impact that their creditor rights and insolvency systems have in establishing a sound investment climate and with which to consider how domestic systems measure up to an international set of norms based on best practice. Assessments also reveal how weaknesses in country systems can distort market behavior and produce incentives or disincentives that affect the behavior of business owners, lenders, and other creditors. The country assessment is not an end in itself. Rather, it is a tool for legislators and policymakers to take decisive action to adapt their systems to maximize commercial confidence and economic growth by creating responsive systems.

Appendix 15.1: World Bank Principles and Guidelines for Effective Insolvency and Creditor Rights Systems

The principles and guidelines were prepared by Bank staff in collaboration with the African Development Bank, Asian Development Bank, European Bank for Reconstruction and Development, Inter-American Development Bank, International Finance Corporation, International Monetary Fund, Organisation for Economic Co-operation and Development, United Nations Commission on International Trade Law, INSOL International, and the International Bar Association (Committee J). This appendix is reproduced from World Bank (2001: 7–12).

15

Focus	Principle
Legal framework for creditor rights	
1. Compatible enforcement systems	A modern credit-based economy requires predictable, transparent, and affordable enforcement of both unsecured and secured credit claims by efficient mechanisms outside of insolvency, as well as a sound insolvency system. These systems must be designed to work in harmony.
2. Enforcement of unsecured rights	A regularized system of credit should be supported by mechanisms that provide efficient, transparent, reliable, and predictable methods for recovering debt, including seizure and sale of immovable and movable assets and sale or collection of intangible assets such as debts owed to the debtor by third parties.

3. Security interest legislation

The legal framework should provide for the creation, recognition, and enforcement of security interests in movable and immovable (real) property, arising by agreement or operation of law. The law should provide for the following features: (a) security interests in all types of assets, movable and immovable, tangible and intangible, including inventory, receivables, and proceeds; future or after-acquired property, and on a global basis; and based on both possessory and non-possessory interests; (b) security interests related to any or all of a debtor's obligations to a creditor, present or future, and between all types of persons; (c) methods of notice that will sufficiently publicize the existence of security interests to creditors, purchasers, and the public generally at the lowest possible costs; (d) clear rules of priority governing competing claims or interests in the same assets, eliminating or reducing priorities over security interests as much as possible.

4. Recording and registration of secured rights

There should be an efficient and cost-effective means of publicizing secured interests in movable and immovable assets, with registration being the principal and strongly preferred method. Access to the registry should be inexpensive and open to all for both recording and search.

5. Enforcement of secured rights

Enforcement systems should provide efficient, inexpensive, transparent, and predictable methods for enforcing a security interest in property. Enforcement procedures should provide for prompt realization of the rights obtained in secured assets, ensuring the maximum possible recovery of asset values based on market values. Both nonjudicial and judicial enforcement methods should be considered.

Legal framework for corporate insolvency

6. Key objectives and policies

Though country approaches vary, effective insolvency systems should aim to (a) integrate with a country's broader legal and commercial systems, (b) maximize the value of a firm's assets by providing an option to reorganize, (c) strike a careful balance between liquidation and reorganization, (d) provide for equitable treatment of similarly situated creditors, including similarly situated foreign and domestic creditors, (e) provide for timely, efficient, and impartial resolution of insolvencies, (f) prevent the premature dismemberment of a debtor's assets by individual creditors seeking quick judgments, (g) provide a transparent procedure that contains incentives for gathering and dispensing information, (h) recognize existing creditor rights and respect the priority of claims with a predictable and established process, and (i) establish a framework for cross-border insolvencies, with recognition of foreign proceedings.

7. Director and officer liability

Director and officer liability for decisions detrimental to creditors made when an enterprise is insolvent should promote responsible corporate behavior while fostering reasonable risk taking. At a minimum, standards should address conduct based on knowledge of or reckless disregard for the adverse consequences to creditors.

8. Liquidation and rehabilitation

An insolvency law should provide both for efficient liquidation of nonviable businesses and those where liquidation is likely to produce a greater return to creditors and for rehabilitation of viable businesses. Where circumstances justify it, the system should allow for easy conversion of proceedings from one procedure to another.

9. Commencement: Applicability and accessibility

(a) The insolvency process should apply to all enterprises or corporate entities except financial institutions and insurance corporations, which should be dealt with through a separate law or through special provisions in the insolvency law. State-owned corporations should be subject to the same insolvency law as private corporations.

(b) Debtors should have easy access to the insolvency system upon showing proof of basic criteria (insolvency or financial difficulty). A declaration to that effect may be provided by the debtor through its board of directors or management. Creditor access should be conditioned on showing proof of insolvency by presumption where there is clear evidence that the debtor failed to pay a matured debt (perhaps of a minimum amount).

(c) The preferred test for insolvency should be the debtor's inability to pay debts as they come due—known as the liquidity test. A balance sheet test may be used as an alternative secondary test, but should not replace the liquidity test. The filing of an application to commence a proceeding should automatically prohibit the debtor's transfer, sale, or disposition of assets or parts of the business without court approval, except to the extent necessary to operate the business.

10. Commencement: Moratoriums and suspension of proceedings

(a) The commencement of bankruptcy should prohibit the unauthorized disposition of the debtor's assets and suspend actions by creditors to enforce their rights or remedies against the debtor or the debtor's assets. The injunctive relief (stay) should be as wide and all-embracing as possible, extending to an interest in property used, occupied, or in the possession of the debtor.

(b) To maximize the value of asset recoveries, a stay on enforcement actions by secured creditors should be imposed for a limited period in a liquidation proceeding to enable higher recovery of assets by sale of the entire business or its productive units and in a rehabilitation proceeding where the collateral is needed for the rehabilitation.

11. Governance: Management

(a) In liquidation proceedings, management should be replaced by a qualified court-appointed official (administrator) with broad authority to administer the estate in the interest of creditors. Control of the estate should be surrendered immediately to the administrator except where management has been authorized to retain control over the company, in which case the law should impose the same duties on management as on the administrator. In creditor-initiated filings, where circumstances warrant, an interim administrator with reduced duties should be appointed to monitor the business to ensure that creditor interests are protected.

(b) There are two preferred approaches in a rehabilitation proceeding: exclusive control of the proceeding by an independent administrator or supervision of management by an impartial and independent administrator or supervisor. Under the second option complete power should be shifted to the administrator if management proves incompetent or negligent or has engaged in fraud or other misbehavior. Similarly, independent administrators or supervisors should be held to the same standard of accountability to creditors and the court and should be subject to removal for incompetence, negligence, fraud, or other wrongful conduct.

12. Governance: Creditors and the creditors committee

Creditor interests should be safeguarded by establishing a creditors committee that enables creditors to actively participate in the insolvency process and that allows the committee to monitor the process to ensure fairness and integrity. The committee should be consulted on non-routine matters in the case and have the ability to be heard on key decisions in the proceedings (such as matters involving dispositions of assets outside the normal course of business). The committee should serve as a conduit for processing and distributing relevant information to other creditors and for organizing creditors to decide on critical issues. The law should provide for such things as a general creditors assembly for major decisions, to appoint the creditors committee and to determine the committee's membership, quorum and voting rules, powers, and the conduct of meetings. In rehabilitation proceedings, the creditors should be entitled to select an independent administrator or supervisor of their choice, provided the person meets the qualifications for serving in this capacity in the specific case.

15

15

13. Administration: Collection, preservation, disposition of property

The law should provide for the collection, preservation, and disposition of all property belonging to the debtor, including property obtained after the commencement of the case. Immediate steps should be taken or allowed to preserve and protect the debtor's assets and business. The law should provide a flexible and transparent system for disposing of assets efficiently and at maximum values. Where necessary, the law should allow for sales free and clear of security interests, charges, or other encumbrances, subject to preserving the priority of interests in the proceeds from the assets disposed.

14. Administration: Treatment of contractual obligations

The law should allow for interference with contractual obligations that are not fully performed to the extent necessary to achieve the objectives of the insolvency process, whether to enforce, cancel, or assign contracts, except where there is a compelling commercial, public, or social interest in upholding the contractual rights of the counterparty to the contract (as with swap agreements).

15. Administration: Fraudulent or preferential transactions

The law should provide for the avoidance or cancellation of pre-bankruptcy fraudulent and preferential transactions completed when the enterprise was insolvent or that resulted in its insolvency. The suspect period prior to bankruptcy, during which payments are presumed to be preferential and may be set aside, should normally be short to avoid disrupting normal commercial and credit relations. The suspect period may be longer in the case of gifts or where the person receiving the transfer is closely related to the debtor or its owners.

16. Claims resolution: Treatment of stakeholder rights and priorities

(a) The rights and priorities of creditors established prior to insolvency under commercial laws should be upheld in an insolvency case to preserve the legitimate expectations of creditors and encourage greater predictability in commercial relationships. Deviations from this general rule should occur only where necessary to promote other compelling policies, such as the policy supporting rehabilitation or to maximize the estate's value. Rules of priority should support incentives for creditors to manage credit efficiently.

(b) The bankruptcy law should recognize the priority of secured creditors in their collateral. Where the rights of secured creditors are impaired to promote a legitimate bankruptcy policy, the interests of these creditors in their collateral should be protected to avoid a loss or deterioration in the economic value of their interest at the commencement of the case. Distributions to secured creditors from the proceeds of their collateral should be made as promptly as possible after realization of proceeds from the sale. In cases where the stay applies to secured creditors, it should be of limited specified duration, strike a proper balance between creditor protection and insolvency objectives, and provide for the possibility of orders being made on the application of affected creditors or other persons for relief from the stay.

(c) Following distributions to secured creditors and payment of claims related to costs and expenses of administration, proceeds available for distribution should be distributed pari passu to remaining creditors unless there are compelling reasons to justify giving preferential status to a particular debt. Public interests generally should not be given precedence over private rights. The number of priority classes should be kept to a minimum.

15

15

17. Design features of rehabilitation statutes	To be commercially and economically effective, the law should establish rehabilitation procedures that permit quick and easy access to the process, provide sufficient protection for all those involved in the process, provide a structure that permits the negotiation of a commercial plan, enable a majority of creditors in favor of a plan or other course of action to bind all other creditors by the democratic exercise of voting rights (subject to appropriate minority protections and the protection of class rights), and provide for judicial or other supervision to ensure that the process is not subject to manipulation or abuse.
18. Administration: Stabilizing and sustaining business operations	The law should provide for a commercially sound form of priority funding for the ongoing and urgent business needs of a debtor during the rescue process, subject to appropriate safeguards.
19. Information: Access and disclosure	The law should require the provision of relevant information on the debtor. It should also provide for independent comment on and analysis of that information. Directors of a debtor corporation should be required to attend meetings of creditors. Provision should be made for the possible examination of directors and other persons with knowledge of the debtor's affairs, who may be compelled to give information to the court and administrator.
20. Plan: Formulation, consideration, and voting	The law should not prescribe the nature of a plan except in terms of fundamental requirements and to prevent commercial abuse. The law may provide for classes of creditors for voting purposes. Voting rights should be determined by amount of debt. An appropriate majority of creditors should be required to approve a plan. Special provision should be made to limit the voting rights of insiders. The effect of a majority vote should be to bind all creditors.

| 21. Plan: Approval of plan | The law should establish clear criteria for plan approval based on fairness to similar creditors, recognition of relative priorities, and majority acceptance. The law should also provide for approval over the rejection of minority creditors if the plan complies with rules of fairness and offers the opposing creditors or classes an amount equal to or greater than would be received under a liquidation proceeding. Some provision for possible adjournment of a plan decision meeting should be made, but under strict time limits. If a plan is not approved, the debtor should automatically be liquidated. |

15

| 22. Plan: Implementation and amendment | The law should provide a means for monitoring effective implementation of the plan, requiring the debtor to make periodic reports to the court on the status of implementation and progress during the plan period. A plan should be capable of amendment (by vote of the creditors) if it is in the interests of the creditors. The law should provide for the possible termination of a plan and for the debtor to be liquidated. |

| 23. Discharge and binding effects | To ensure that the rehabilitated enterprise has the best chance of succeeding, the law should provide for a discharge or alteration of debts and claims that have been discharged or otherwise altered under the plan. Where approval of the plan has been procured by fraud, the plan should be subject to challenge, reconsidered, or set aside. |

| 24. International considerations | Insolvency proceedings may have international aspects, and insolvency laws should provide for rules of jurisdiction, recognition of foreign judgments, cooperation and assistance among courts in different countries, and choice of law. |

Informal corporate workouts and restructurings

25. Enabling legislative framework

Corporate workouts and restructurings should be supported by an enabling environment that encourages participants to engage in consensual arrangements designed to restore an enterprise to financial viability. An enabling environment includes laws and procedures that require disclosure of or ensure access to timely, reliable, and accurate financial information on the distressed enterprise; encourage lending to, investment in, or recapitalization of viable financially distressed enterprises; support a broad range of restructuring activities, such as debt write-offs, reschedulings, restructurings, and debt-equity conversions; and provide favorable or neutral tax treatment for restructurings.

26. Informal workout procedures

A country's financial sector (possibly with the informal endorsement and assistance of the central bank or finance ministry) should promote the development of a code of conduct on an informal out-of-court process for dealing with cases of corporate financial difficulty in which banks and other financial institutions have a significant exposure, especially in markets where enterprise insolvency has reached systemic levels. An informal process is far more likely to be sustained where there are adequate creditor remedy and insolvency laws. The informal process may produce a formal rescue, which should be able to quickly process a packaged plan produced by the informal process. The formal process may work better if it enables creditors and debtors to use informal techniques.

Implementation of the insolvency system

27. Role of courts

(a) Bankruptcy cases should be overseen and disposed of by an independent court or competent authority assigned, where practical, to judges with specialized bankruptcy expertise. Significant benefits can be gained by creating specialized bankruptcy courts.

(b) The laws should provide for a court or other tribunal to have a general, non-intrusive, supervisory role in the rehabilitation process. The court/tribunal or regulatory authority should be obliged to accept the decision reached by the creditors that a plan be approved or that the debtor be liquidated.

28. Performance standards of the court, qualification and training of judges	Standards should be adopted to measure the competence, performance, and services of a bankruptcy court. These standards should serve as a basis for evaluating and improving courts. They should be enforced by adequate qualification criteria as well as training and continuing education for judges.
29. Court organization	The court should be organized so that all interested parties, including the administrator, the debtor, and all creditors, are dealt with fairly, objectively, and transparently. To the extent possible, publicly available court operating rules, case practice, and case management regulations should govern the court and other participants in the process. The court's internal operations should allocate responsibility and authority to maximize resource use. To the degree feasible, the court should institutionalize, streamline, and standardize court practices and procedures.
30. Transparency and accountability	An insolvency system should be based on transparency and accountability. Rules should ensure ready access to court records, court hearings, debtor and financial data, and other public information.
31. Judicial decisionmaking and enforcement	Judicial decisionmaking should encourage consensual resolution among parties where possible and otherwise undertake timely adjudication of issues with a view to enforcing predictability in the system through consistent application of the law. The court must have clear authority and effective methods of enforcing its judgments.
32. Integrity of the court	Court operations and decisions should be based on firm rules and regulations to avoid corruption and undue influence. The court must be free of conflicts of interest, bias, and lapses in judicial ethics, objectivity, and impartiality.
33. Integrity of participants	Persons involved in a bankruptcy proceeding must be subject to rules and court orders designed to prevent fraud, other illegal activity, or abuse of the bankruptcy system. In addition, the bankruptcy court must be vested with appropriate powers to deal with illegal activity or abusive conduct that does not constitute criminal activity.

15

34. Role of regulatory or supervisory bodies	The body or bodies responsible for regulating or supervising insolvency administrators should be independent of individual administrators and should set standards that reflect the requirements of the legislation and public expectations of fairness, impartiality, transparency, and accountability.
35. Competence and integrity of insolvency administrators	Insolvency administrators should be competent to exercise the powers given to them and should act with integrity, impartiality, and independence.

References

Wood, Philip R. 1995. *Principles of International Solvency*. Sweet and Maxwell.
World Bank. 2001. "Principles and Guidelines for Effective Insolvency and Creditor Rights Systems." Washington, D.C., April. Available at http://www.worldbank.org/gild. Processed

15

Notes

1. As of January 2004, some 500 assessments had been conducted in approximately 100 countries.
2. These factors were adopted by Dr. Philip Wood in his treatise on international insolvency (Wood 1995).
3. The emerging-market sample includes eight transition economies: Argentina, Brazil, Czech Republic, Lithuania, Philippines, Russia, Slovakia, and Turkey. The EU countries include Denmark, France, Germany, Greece, Spain, and the United Kingdom. The study was undertaken by experts from the EU and not by the World Bank; accordingly, the Bank takes no position with respect to the accuracy of the results.
4. According to a local practitioner in one country, "There would be no corrupt lawyers if there were no corrupt judges (and vice versa)."
5. China has been developing a new insolvency law that would apply to businesses in the private sector. Notably, the latest drafts of the proposed new law have maintained the priority for employees relative to other unsecured creditors but do not preempt the rights of secured creditors, as under the state-owned enterprise bankruptcy law.

Financial Restructuring: Techniques and Negotiating Dynamics

Alan D. Fragen

This appendix illustrates various techniques for restructuring balance sheets to resolve financial distress, using examples of a debt-for-debt and debt-for-equity exchange by a hypothetical company.

To a restructuring practitioner, a business enterprise is often categorized as either a good or a distressed company with either a good or a problem balance sheet. In this very simplified view, a good company produces positive cash flow before debt service (that is, the company has positive free cash flow margins); a distressed company consumes cash to maintain its operations. A good balance sheet is one where the company can meet its debt service obligations (scheduled payments of interest and principal on outstanding funded debt obligations) using the free cash flow it generates.[1] The greater the cushion, measured by the ratio of free cash flow to debt service, the better the balance sheet.

Figure A.1 illustrates this simplified view. Companies to the right of the Y axis generate positive free cash flow from operations; companies to the left consume cash to either build or maintain a business.

The author would like to give particular thanks to his colleague James Zukin for his valuable perspectives and to Christopher Wilson, Alya Hidayatallah, and Christian Digemose for their material assistance in preparing this appendix.

Figure A.1: The Restructuring Practitioner's Evaluation of a Business Enterprise

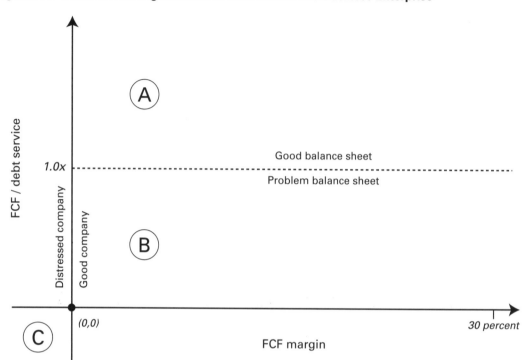

In the figure, sector A includes good companies with good, or appropriate-size, balance sheets. In general, these enterprises are not candidates for restructuring. A restructuring indicates some element of distress; it is a forced event created by the breach of one or more incomplete financial contracts. Because companies in sector A have positive free cash flow after debt service, the owners of the company either have no need to reprofile the company's debt obligations or have some measure of flexibility (measured as the time before the enterprise becomes liquidity constrained) in refinancing the company's outstanding debt obligations without completely compromising their equity ownership.

Sector B contains good companies with problem balance sheets. These enterprises generate positive cash flow from operations but cannot afford their debt service obligations. If the situation persists, a company in sector B will be starved for capital and enter a cycle of distress. In general, the cycle of distress is caused by owners or managers who seek to avoid a default at nearly any cost. While extreme, this behavior is entirely rational if the presumed cost of default is a complete disenfranchisement of ownership rights. The cycle begins with a period in which the company services debt with capital that should be invested internally to maintain the base of productive assets. Over time, the underinvestment will be manifest. Margins will erode, suppliers will be stretched, and the reputation and performance of the enterprise generally will degrade.

If unchecked, this distress will drive an enterprise from sector B into sector C. Sector B contains going-concern enterprises, with both tangible and intangible value. Sector C contains marginal enterprises, where the cost of maintaining the going-concern value (that is, of funding the negative cash flow from operations) rapidly consumes the underlying asset (or liquidation) value.[2] The transition from sector B to sector C destroys value (at a minimum, all intangible value is lost); restructuring regimes that count preservation and maximization of economic value as a top priority would do well to create incentives to avoid these situations.

Companies in sector B are good candidates for restructuring. By definition, they have positive free cash flow; they employ fixed assets and human resources in a manner that generates a positive return. Before considering the capital structure, these enterprises add value to the overall economy. Preserving these good companies as going concerns through either a stand-alone reorganization or a going-concern sale should be considered as part of a national policy that seeks to maximize the general economic welfare. Even if the reorganization creates foreign equity ownership, it would still maximize the "resident" value by preserving a host of benefits, including, among others, demand for domestic jobs and services (for example, facilities and communications).

A stand-alone reorganization basically reconstructs the problem balance sheet of a good company. A balance sheet becomes a problem balance sheet when the value-generating enterprise cannot meet its contractual payments of principal and interest. In this circumstance, the balance sheet (the mix of debt and equity capital) needs adjustment to reflect the firm's ability to generate free cash flow. To reconstruct the balance sheet (that is, to change the mix of debt and equity), a restructuring banker employs a technique generally known as an exchange offer. Generically, an exchange offer is an offer to exchange an existing claim against a company for some other consideration. In a debt-for-debt exchange, old claims against a company are settled for new debt securities. In a debt-for-equity exchange, old claims against a company are settled for an ownership interest. And in a debt-for-cash exchange (really a tender offer), the company uses cash (either existing cash or newly invested capital) to retire debt obligations at a discount to the amount of their claim. This appendix focuses on hypothetical examples of the debt-for-equity and debt-for-debt exchange. Other cases, as well as analyses of actual examples, can be found in the longer version of this paper, which was submitted for the conference.

Debt-for-Debt Exchange

Any restructuring transaction must begin with an analysis of the subject company. For this case study, I created OpCo, a company facing a significant debt repayment.

Situational Overview

OpCo is engaged in a reasonably asset-intensive manufacturing business that requires regular reinvestment in order to maintain its asset base. As the historic income and cash flow statements indicate (tables A.1 and A.2), OpCo has produced positive but declining earnings and cash flows from operations. These results are consistent with a mid-size manufacturing concern experiencing pricing pressure that may be the result of any number of factors, including, potentially, increased competition from larger-scale enterprises, a concentration or reduction in its customer base, higher costs of raw materials, or, if OpCo is an exporter, foreign currency issues. The pressure on the revenue line has caused too little absorption of fixed costs, and margins have eroded.

OpCo's projected results indicate a sustained period of slow growth and improving gross profit margins. To rebuild operating income, management made modest, but important, cuts to selling, general, and administrative (S,G&A) expenses during 2003 and intends to increase these costs at a rate less than the rate of sales growth. All in all, OpCo's operating projections are assumed to be reasonable relative to the existing and expected operating environment and are not inconsistent with historic results.

In each of the first two years, OpCo generated enough cash from its operations to meet payments of contractual interest and principal and accumulated enough extra cash over the time frame to meet its most recent

Table A.1: Historic and Projected Income Statement, OpCo, Fiscal Year Ended December 31, 2000–07
(millions of dollars unless otherwise noted)

Item	Actual			Estimated	Projected			
	2000	2001	2002	2003	2004	2005	2006	2007
Revenue								
Amount	300.0	291.0	279.4	273.9	280.7	291.9	303.6	315.8
Percent growth	5.0	-3.0	-4.0	-2.0	2.5	4.0	4.0	4.0
Cost of sales	190.5	189.2	187.2	186.2	186.7	192.7	198.9	205.2
Gross profit								
Amount	109.5	101.9	92.2	87.6	94.0	99.3	104.7	110.5
Percent margin	36.5	35.0	33.0	32.0	33.5	34.0	34.5	35.0
Selling, general, and admin- istrative costs	69.0	71.8	74.6	73.1	73.1	74.6	76.1	77.6
Operating income	40.5	30.1	17.6	14.5	20.9	24.7	28.7	32.9
Interest expense								
Secured term loan	(4.1)	(3.7)	(3.4)	(2.9)	(2.2)	(0.9)	n.a.	n.a.
10.5 percent senior notes due in 2003	(10.5)	(10.5)	(10.5)	(10.5)	n.a.	n.a.	n.a.	n.a.
New senior notes	n.a.	n.a.	n.a.	n.a.	(12.0)	(12.0)	(12.0)	(12.0)
Interest income	0.0	0.2	0.2	0.2	0.1	(0.5)	(2.7)	(1.9)
Pretax income	26.0	16.0	3.9	1.2	6.7	11.2	13.9	19.0
Less taxes (40 percent)	(10.4)	(6.4)	(1.6)	(0.5)	(2.7)	(4.5)	(5.6)	(7.6)
Net income	15.6	9.6	2.3	0.7	4.0	6.7	8.3	11.4

n.a. Not applicable

335

A

Table A.2: Historic and Projected Cash Flow Statement, OpCo, Fiscal Year Ended December 31, 2000–07
(millions of dollars unless otherwise noted)

	Actual			Estimated	Projected			
Item	2000	2001	2002	2003	2004	2005	2006	2007
Cash from operations								
Net income	15.6	9.6	2.3	0.7	4.0	6.7	8.3	11.4
Adjustments								
Depreciation and amortization	14.6	14.7	14.8	14.9	14.8	14.8	14.7	14.7
Net working capital	(1.1)	0.7	0.9	0.4	(0.5)	(0.8)	(0.9)	(0.9)
Net cash from operations	29.1	25.0	18.0	16.0	18.4	20.7	22.2	25.2
Cash from investing activities								
Capital expenditures	15.8	15.9	16.0	14.3	14.2	14.2	14.1	14.1
Net cash from investing activities	15.8	15.9	16.0	14.3	14.2	14.2	14.1	14.1
After-tax cash from operations	13.3	9.1	2.0	1.8	4.1	6.5	8.1	11.1
Cash from financing activities								
Repayment of secured term loan	(4.9)	(4.9)	(6.5)	(8.1)	(13.0)	(27.6)	n.a.	n.a.
Repayment of 10.5 percent senior notes due in 2003	n.a.	n.a.	n.a.	(100.0)	n.a.	n.a.	n.a.	n.a.
Proceeds from new notes	n.a.	n.a.	n.a.	100.0	n.a.	n.a.	n.a.	n.a.
Repayment of new notes	n.a.	n.a.	n.a.	n.a.	n.a.	n.a.	n.a.	n.a.
Net cash from financing activities	(4.9)	(4.9)	(6.5)	(8.1)	(13.0)	(27.6)	n.a.	n.a.
Cash								
Increase in cash	8.5	4.2	(4.5)	(6.4)	(8.9)	(21.1)	8.1	11.1
Cash at beginning of period	2.0	10.5	14.7	10.2	3.8	(5.0)	(26.2)	(18.1)
Cash at end of period	10.5	14.7	10.2	3.8	(5.0)	(26.2)	(18.1)	(7.0)

n.a. Not applicable.

payment of secured debt principal. OpCo has continued to make the capital investments necessary to maintain the earnings power of its business.

A close inspection of OpCo's estimated balance sheet reveals the nature of its problems (table A.3). As indicated, OpCo has had two types of debt outstanding: traditional secured bank debt (in the form of a term loan) and a senior unsecured bond issue. As is common, the bank-type debt is a senior secured obligation that requires regular payments of both interest and principal. It is likely to be secured by most, if not all, of OpCo's assets. If OpCo were domiciled in a sophisticated legal jurisdiction, it would also be common for the bank debt contract to name all of OpCo's primary operating subsidiaries as either co-borrowers or guarantors.

OpCo also had an outstanding $100 million issue of 10.5 percent senior notes due in 2003. These notes paid interest at a relatively high rate; in OpCo's financial results, the annual interest rate on the secured bank debt and on the notes due in 2003 was 6.5 and 10.5 percent, respectively. Contrary to the bank debt that was structured with periodic (and escalating) payments of principal, the notes due in 2003 had a "bullet" maturity. In other words, the entire contract came due on a single date. Bullet maturity or other back-end weighted amortization schedules are fairly common. These contract structures implicitly incorporate the assumption that, as long as a borrower maintains its creditworthiness, market-priced capital will be available to refinance the maturing obligation.

OpCo was aware of the maturity and, as the estimated results indicate, expected to refinance the obligation with a new series of unsecured notes. Prior to year-end, OpCo hired an investment banker to market and arrange the debt placement. Because of the generally difficult capital market conditions, OpCo budgeted a significant increase in financing costs. Unfortunately, despite offering a very attractive interest rate, the investment banker was unable to arrange the new financing. On December 31, 2003, OpCo did not have the cash to pay the notes maturing in 2003 and declared a payment default. With no compelling reason to make the $5.3 million semiannual interest payment that was also due on the notes, OpCo decided to retain the cash and preserve its operating flexibility. As of January 1, 2004, OpCo was in payment default on its notes due in 2003 and had the actual balance sheet shown in table A.4.

A restructuring is a forced event that occurs when an obligor to a contract cannot perform. In this case, OpCo was in breach of its bond indenture contract when it failed to pay the principal and interest that came

A

Table A.3: Historic and Projected Balance Sheet, OpCo, Fiscal Year Ended December 31, 1999–2007
(millions of dollars unless otherwise noted)

Item	Actual				Estimated		Projected		
	1999	2000	2001	2002	2003	2004	2005	2006	2007
Assets									
Cash and equivalents	2.0	10.5	14.7	10.2	3.8	(5.0)	(26.2)	(18.1)	(7.0)
Other current assets	50.9	53.4	51.8	49.7	48.8	50.0	52.0	54.1	56.2
Net property, plant, and equipment	175.0	176.2	177.3	178.5	177.9	177.3	176.7	176.2	175.6
Total assets	227.9	240.1	243.9	238.5	230.5	222.3	202.6	212.1	224.8
Liabilities									
Accounts payable	18.0	18.9	18.3	17.6	17.3	17.7	18.4	19.1	19.9
Accrued expenses	11.4	12.0	11.6	11.2	11.0	11.2	11.7	12.1	12.6
Secured term loan	65.0	60.1	55.3	48.8	40.6	27.6	n.a.	n.a.	n.a.
10.5 percent senior notes due in 2003	100.0	100.0	100.0	100.0	n.a.	n.a.	n.a.	n.a.	n.a.
New notes	n.a.	n.a.	n.a.	n.a.	100.0	100.0	100.0	100.0	100.0
Total liabilities	194.4	191.0	185.2	177.5	168.8	156.5	130.1	131.3	132.5
Shareholders' equity									
Paid-in capital	1.0	1.0	1.0	1.0	1.0	1.0	1.0	1.0	1.0
Retained earnings	32.4	48.0	57.6	60.0	60.7	64.8	71.5	79.8	91.2
Total shareholders' equity	33.4	49.0	58.6	61.0	61.7	65.8	72.5	80.8	92.2
Total liabilities and shareholders' equity	227.8	240.1	243.9	238.5	230.5	222.3	202.6	212.1	224.78

n.a. Not applicable.

Table A.4: Actual versus Estimated Balance Sheet as of December 31, 2003
(millions of dollars)

Item	Actual	Estimated
Assets		
Cash and equivalents	9.1	3.8
Other current assets	48.8	48.8
Net property, plant, and equipment	177.9	177.9
Total assets	235.8	230.5
Liabilities		
Accrued interest	5.3	0.0
Accounts payable	17.3	17.3
Accrued expenses	11.0	11.0
Secured term loan	40.6	40.6
10.5 percent senior notes due in 2003	100.0	0.0
New notes	0.0	100.0
Total liabilities	174.1	168.8
Shareholders' equity		
Paid-in capital	1.0	1.0
Retained earnings	60.7	60.7
Total shareholders' equity	61.7	61.7
Total liabilities and shareholders' equity	235.8	230.5

A

due on December 31, 2003. OpCo could not repay its maturing bond debt because the underlying capital markets did not cooperate. Capital markets are fickle, and as the old market adage goes, "Liquidity is a funny thing: it is never there when you really need it." It may be that credit markets are especially tight (like in early 1990 and, more recently, in late 2001 through 2002). Or it may be that credit markets are open, but just not to more highly leveraged companies. For whatever reason, the financing market is closed to OpCo, and the situation requires a balance sheet restructuring (versus a refinancing).

After terminating the investment banker who promised the refinancing, OpCo hires a restructuring banker, who walks in and, after a thorough analysis, declares, "OpCo is a good company with a problem balance sheet."

Situational Assessment

Once engaged, the restructuring banker takes stock of the situation. Assuming that all debts other than the financial debt are being paid on a timely basis (that is, assuming the first focus of the restructuring is not on obtaining the liquidity necessary to fund the immediate operations), the restructuring banker attempts to determine the value of the company's operations and the priority and amount of the various claims against this value. While it is clear from the hypothetical that OpCo cannot pay its bills as they become due, it is not clear that the value of its liabilities exceeds the value of its assets. OpCo may be liquidity constrained, but it is not clear that it is balance sheet insolvent.

In this hypothetical case, I assume that the restructuring banker completes a preliminary valuation analysis of OpCo using four techniques: a market-multiples approach, a transaction-multiples approach, a discounted cash flow approach, and a liquidation approach (see table A.5). Based on these analyses,[3] the professional determines that, as a going concern, OpCo is likely worth between $160 million and $195 million.

Given that OpCo has about $136.8 million of outstanding funded debt obligations, net of any cash it holds, the restructuring banker concludes that OpCo is likely to be balance sheet solvent. Enough value exists to satisfy the debt obligations in full and leave value for equity. A cursory review of OpCo's liabilities reveals the claims shown in table A.6.

As indicated, OpCo has about $145.9 million of funded debt obligations and another $28.2 million of working capital liabilities. OpCo is not underinvested in working capital. In the event OpCo restructures and continues as a going concern, all of the existing working capital liabilities will be settled and renewed in the ordinary course of business. Consequently, a

Table A.5: Valuation Analysis, OpCo
(millions of dollars)

Valuation technique	Total enterprise value
Market-multiples approach	165.0–209.0
Transaction-multiples approach	160.0–195.0
Discounted cash flow analysis	180.0–220.0
Implied total enterprise value[a]	160.0–195.0

a. On a controlling-interest basis.

Table A.6: Analysis of Liabilities, OpCo, as of December 31, 2003
(millions of dollars)

Liability	Amount
Funded debt obligations	
Secured term loan	40.6
10.5 percent senior notes due in 2003	100.0
Accrued interest on 10.5 percent senior notes due in 2003	5.3
Total funded debt obligations	145.9
Working capital liabilities	
Accounts payable	17.3
Accrued expenses	11.0
Total working capital liabilities	28.2
Total liabilities	174.1

A

going-concern restructuring plan only needs to consider the funded debt claims and equity interests.[4]

After determining the overall value of the enterprise and the amount and priority of the claims against it, the restructuring banker is left to determine how best to satisfy the claims. Other than cash, which is not available in this situation (other than surplus cash on the balance sheet), a company has two types of considerations to offer: debt and equity. The restructuring banker performs several analyses designed to determine the debt capacity of the company—that is, the amount of par-value debt the enterprise can reasonably support. This analysis includes, among other things, a review of the appropriate cost of par-value debt securities (as reflected in the prices and indicated yields of the publicly traded debt securities of comparable companies) and a survey to determine the average capital structure in the subject industry (that is, the average mix of debt and equity capital employed by industry participants). Generally, the point of the debt capacity analysis is to determine both the optimal and the maximum amount of par-value debt that an enterprise can support. The debt capacity analysis informs the restructuring banker of the quantity of debt and therefore the quantity of equity potentially available to satisfy the firm's obligations. As an aside, many of the market-based components of the debt capacity analysis are a subset of the research that informs the analysis of the subject firm's weighted average cost of capital, a critical input into the discounted cash flow valuation technique (table A.7).

This analysis estimates debt capacity based on three important operating statistics—EBITDA (earnings before interest taxes and depreciation allowance), the maintenance level of capital expenditures, and the maintenance level of investment in working capital—plus a market analysis of the industry average pretax cost of debt capital. To estimate debt capacity, the analysis sets a target ratio of (EBITDA minus maintenance capital expenditures minus maintenance levels of investment in working capital) divided by interest expense and estimates debt capacity based on assumptions for operating performance and the average pretax cost of debt capital. Once the target ratio is set, the analysis is sensitized across a range of the pretax cost of debt capital and is further sensitized to incorporate a somber view of operating performance (estimating EBITDA at the bottom of the range and maintenance expenditure levels at the high end of the range) and more optimistic views. The analysis also investigates the results of selecting different target ratios. Based on the analysis, the restructuring banker determines that OpCo can support between $100 million and $140 million of par-value debt.

The analysis is but one way to estimate the debt capacity of a firm. However, most of these methods are similar in that they estimate debt capacity based on a firm's ability to generate cash flow (the numerator of the target ratio) to cover the current cost of its debt (namely, the estimated interest expense, the denominator of the ratio). Moreover, the analysis is highly subjective. To begin with, the analyst must determine the appropriate

Table A.7: Analysis of Debt Capacity, OpCo
(millions of dollars)

Operating performance (percent)	Average pretax cost of debt capital given a debt capacity target ratio of 1.5[a]				Average pretax cost of debt capital given a debt capacity target ratio of 1.7[a]			
	15.0	20.0	25.0	30.0	15.0	20.0	25.0	30.0
10.0	100.0	133.3	166.7	200.0	88.2	117.6	147.1	176.5
11.0	90.9	121.2	151.5	181.8	80.2	107.0	133.7	160.4
12.0	83.3	111.1	138.9	166.7	73.5	98.0	122.5	147.1
13.0	76.9	102.6	128.2	153.8	67.9	90.5	113.1	135.7

a. Ration of (EBITDA minus capital expenditures minus maintenance levels of investment in working capital) divided by interest expense.

range of earnings. Next, an assessment must be made of annual maintenance expenditures. While the results of the hypothetical company are reasonably consistent, and thus susceptible to simple techniques such as averaging over a multiple-year period, in the real world, restructuring companies usually exhibit more variability. In practice, estimating the appropriate range of annual maintenance expenditures is rarely a simple exercise. Now the analyst must choose the appropriate range of target ratios. This is informed by, among other things, industry averages. Even the most conservative target ratio in the debt capacity analysis would not generate enough free cash flow from operations after interest (not to mention cash taxes) to fully repay the implied level of debt in any reasonable time frame.[5] In other words, to fully repay the target level of debt when it is likely to become due, the analyst assumes that the firm has access to the capital markets at or before the time when refinancing is required. The point here is that the debt capacity analysis and the valuation analysis are both subjective applications of objective tools; the quality of the analysis is generally a direct function of the quality and experience of the analyst.

At this point in the hypothetical, the restructuring banker has analyzed valuation, existing liabilities, and debt capacity. Armed with this information, he can now assemble an appropriate capital structure and allocate the elements of that capital structure to the various claimants and interest holders. In the case of OpCo, the total allocable value (that is, the total value of OpCo's debt and equity securities) is between $160 million and $195 million, plus any cash on hand. Of this amount, the restructuring banker estimates that he can distribute between $100 million and $140 million in the form of par-value debt securities. The residual amount—between $29.1 million and $104.1 million,[6] depending on the pro forma capital structure and the view of valuation—is the value of OpCo's restructured equity. As indicated in the analysis of existing liabilities, as of the restructuring date, there are three relevant claims against or interests in OpCo: a $40.6 million secured debt claim, a $105.3 million unsecured debt claim (which includes $5.3 million of accrued interest), and 100 percent of the equity interest in OpCo. In the vernacular, three classes of claims need to be satisfied.[7] The restructuring banker now turns to the task of allocating value based on legal entitlements.

The concept of legal entitlement—what a party should be due based on a contract claim and the notion that some claims have priority over other claims by virtue of, among other considerations, a security (or first-priority) interest in a defined collateral pool, contractual subordination, or legal structural priority—is a prerequisite for the development of any sort of capital market. Consider a system where an owner cannot enforce property rights to evict a nonperforming tenant or a lender is prevented from seizing and selling collateral to repay a nonperforming loan. In such a system, possession counts for everything; derivative ownership interests, such as the deed to a house or the mortgage that is secured by the deed, are worthless. For this hypothetical, legal entitlements are assumed to be discernable and enforceable (a subject addressed below). The secured debt has priority over the unsecured debt to the extent of its collateral, and the unsecured debt has priority over the equity.

The Negotiating Dynamics

A restructuring negotiation is best thought of as a multiparty, zero-sum allocation of value. The negotiation is a forced event (the obligor is in default or is very likely to default in the immediate future) and assumes that, if the parties cannot reach a consensual arrangement, a court-officiated process will commence. For this hypothetical, it is assumed that the court process will lead, over time, to a rational result (that is, the accurate enforcement of valid legal entitlements). In this environment, the equity owners have the most to lose and, therefore, the most to gain from a consensual resolution of events. In addition, in the real world, companies in debt restructuring seldom do "better" than they would outside of a restructuring. While certain restructuring regimes give debtors the power to improve performance by, for example, shedding burdensome contracts, over time, the "cloud of distress" has an adverse effect on business performance. Because of the uncertainty caused by a restructuring, customers often choose an alternative supplier, or a firm's most productive employees look elsewhere for more job security. Whatever the manifestation, the uncertainty erodes value over time relative to normal business operations. In a legal environment that recognizes and enforces contractual legal entitlements, this propensity toward erosion of value provides OpCo's owners (that is, the recipients of the residual value) with a strong incentive to work quickly to preserve their remaining value. One of the principal roles of a value-maximizing restructuring banker is to drive parties toward a conclusion and to minimize the destruction of value.

As identified, the equity retains any value left over after the satisfaction of prior claims. Generally, to avoid ownership dilution, equity can do three things to debt: it can repay (or refinance) the debt, it can cure past monetary defaults and reinstate the debt, or it can replace the debt with a new debt instrument (effectively an internal refinancing). With these nondilutive options in mind,[8] the first claim to consider is the $41 million of secured bank debt.

For the purposes here, it is assumed that the value of the underlying collateral exceeds the amount of the outstanding obligation—the claim is fully secured. At this point, it is important to remember that OpCo has been performing on its secured debt obligation; the claim is only in default by virtue of the cross-default tied to the unsecured notes. In theory, if OpCo's equity owners and the unsecured creditors reach a consensual solution to cure the default, then OpCo's equity owners have the option of simply reinstating the secured debt. However, the terms of the existing secured debt indicate significant upcoming amortization payments. OpCo's projections indicate that, even if the unsecured debt is resolved and even if all excess cash flow is reserved for repaying the secured debt, OpCo still will not accumulate enough cash to make the scheduled amortization payments. In other words, reinstating the secured debt (and not seeking an extension of maturity, for example) will cause OpCo, once again, to rely on the external capital markets to avoid default. Clearly, though, the risk of not being able to refinance the top third of the capital structure (with access to all of a firm's collateral and priority over unsecured debts) is much lower than the risk of not being able to refinance the junior-most debt capital.

After careful analysis, the equity owners inform the restructuring banker that reinstating the secured debt is the optimal solution. Given the facts surrounding the case, and based on the assumption that secured debt financing will be available in the future to replace the maturing secured debt, the restructuring banker agrees with the equity owners. The restructuring banker's view is clearly supported by the debt capacity and valuation analyses. And, after all, why engage in a negotiation when one can be avoided or at least delayed? With this plan in mind for the secured creditors, the equity owners and the restructuring banker now turn their attention to the unsecured creditors.

The negotiation with the unsecured creditors is a much more complicated affair. To fully understand the negotiating dynamic, one must investigate the bankruptcy laws of the relevant jurisdiction and assess the judicial process through which the laws are applied. As Stiglitz (2001), among others, has noted, *because bankruptcy law affects the likely outcome if a dispute has*

A

A

to be resolved by the courts, bankruptcy law affects the outcome of the bargaining process designed to avoid the uncertainty and delay of relying on court-mandated solutions. In general, jurisdictions that do not have the infrastructure or the sophisticated and impartial judiciary necessary to administer a complicated set of bankruptcy laws would do well to avoid the situation entirely and enact the simplest set of laws possible (for an example of such a simplified system, see Werbalowsky 1992).

For this hypothetical, OpCo is assumed to be domiciled in a jurisdiction with laws that recognize the rights of unsecured creditors to realize value ahead of equity holders. However, the mechanism for attaining this result— a formal court proceeding—is an uncertain process. Among other things, it is assumed that the equity owners remain in control of business decisions during the court proceeding unless and until the unsecured creditors can demonstrate that their class is impaired on a value basis and that the process for establishing this state of affairs is time-consuming, expensive, and, because valuation is subjective, somewhat uncertain. Also, the filing of a court proceeding is assumed to limit the claim of an unsecured creditor; after a bankruptcy petition is filed, unsecured claims stop accruing interest. Recall also the economic proposition that, while this conflict is playing out in court (and often in public), the overall value of the business is prone to erosion. Based on the uncertain and costly court process and the attendant risks, the two parties attempt to negotiate a consensual solution to the default.

First, I address the likely perspective of the equity owners in this negotiation. In this type of negotiation, where equity is the junior claimant in a zero-sum allocation of value, equity can best be thought of in terms of option theory. The equity owners have an option of uncertain duration on 100 percent of the economic value of the enterprise above a strike price. The strike price is equal to the level of debt; the duration is the time until the date on which the equity owners become disenfranchised (that is, after a lengthy court fight and well after the actual date of payment default). As option theory indicates, equity owners have every incentive to attempt to negotiate a reduction in the strike price and to extend the duration of their option. Volatility, another important component of option value, can also play a critical role in explaining the perspective and behavior of the equity owner. To increase volatility, equity owners should dedicate scarce firm resources to increasingly risky projects; the degree to which equity actually engages in this type of behavior depends on whose value is at risk. For example, if the actual enterprise value of the firm is at or near the value of the debt (that is, the current value of the option is approximately equal to the strike price and there is little intrinsic value to the option), then equity is increasingly investing value that, in bankruptcy and on an absolute-priority basis, belongs to unsecured creditors. There is little incentive to avoid risk; 100 percent of the benefits of a successful bet accrue to equity, and the risk of loss lies largely with unsecured creditors.

But in the current example, OpCo is balance sheet solvent. At the range of current valuation, there is thought to be between $23.2 million and $58.2 million of equity value. In this situation, equity has a lot (of intrinsic value) to lose and conducts itself accordingly. Equity owners judge that they have significant duration to their option and that value-maximizing behavior lies in making investments that enhance intrinsic value without jeopardizing duration (there are far fewer "bet the ranch" types of investments). In fact, because equity has value to lose and because a lengthy and contentious in-court restructuring process tends to erode value, the equity owners in this hypothetical have significant and quantifiable value to gain (or, really, avoid losing) by completing a successful out-of-court negotiation with the unsecured creditors.

From the perspective of OpCo's unsecured creditors, the world is largely unjust. They have a legitimate legal call on value, but forcing the issue through a bankruptcy is likely to cost them present value. If they negotiate today and receive full or near-full value in new, performing securities, they avoid a protracted fight that, at best, yields them a full recovery of their current claim sometime in the future. Because they do not accrue interest in this hypothetical bankruptcy regime, the unsecured creditors also have positive incentives to avoid a failed negotiation. As a further incentive, the unsecured creditors are aware that the cushion they enjoy today (the current difference between OpCo's total enterprise value and the level of debt) will erode in a contentious proceeding and, at some point in time, the erosion will jeopardize the full recovery of their claim.

To initiate the negotiation, the equity owners ask the restructuring banker to design a "fair" restructuring proposal. After meeting with all parties, the restructuring banker designs an offer that meets the principal goal of equity (avoiding or minimizing ownership dilution) and the principal goal of debt (recovering full value, preferably in debt securities). Based on the prior debt capacity analysis, the restructuring banker determines that the preference of the debt holders for a full recovery in debt securities can be achieved without overleveraging the enterprise.

A

A

After careful consideration, the restructuring banker suggests an offer to exchange each $1,000 of notes due in 2003 for $1,030 of new 11.5 percent notes due in 2010; accrued interest would be paid in new notes. In the view of the restructuring banker and based on market comparables, the higher interest rate should create a security with a market value at or near par value. The slight (3.0 percent) premium to par is justified to the equity owners as the "cost of the internal refinancing" and likely less than the value that would be lost to a nonconsensual process. Also, the longer duration of the proposed debt security should give the equity owners plenty of time to refinance this obligation. After internal debate, the restructuring plan is approved by OpCo's equity owners, and the restructuring banker is tasked with "selling" equity's preferred restructuring plan to the holders of OpCo's notes due in 2003.

To begin with, the restructuring banker must organize and coordinate discussions with the holders of the notes due in 2003. This organizational effort often can be quite difficult. Because of the sophistication and liquidity of today's capital markets, unsecured debt is no longer concentrated in the hands of a small number of insurance companies, banks, and other financial institutions. Rather, these institutions continue to own unsecured debt, but holder diversity has expanded to include structured vehicles (for example, collateralized debt obligations and collateralized bond obligations), mutual funds, unregulated hedge funds dedicated to distressed investing, and the "mom and pop" retail holders who invested in "safe bonds" to fund their retirements. The problem of holder dispersion and diversity is significant; when holders of similarly situated claims have different goals, reaching consensus can be very challenging. There are also two interrelated questions: What exactly constitutes a consensus? And, assuming consensus is reached, how does one treat a nonconsenting holder?

For the first hypothetical, I set aside the complexities of intercreditor dynamics and assume that the entire $100 million issue of notes due in 2003 was placed with a single institution. With this simplified dynamic, the restructuring banker meets directly with the institutional investor and presents him with a term sheet that describes the exchange offer. The restructuring banker also reviews the prospects for the company, the value of the proposed new debt security, and the risks of a nonconsensual process. The institutional investor considers the offer and the various options for a counterproposal.

Among other economic benefits, the institutional investor considers asking for (1) a percentage of the equity of OpCo, (2) more new notes for each old note, (3) modifications to the proposed new note, including a higher interest rate, a shorter duration, a second security interest in the available collateral pool, and a package of operating covenants, and (4) accrued interest paid in cash versus new notes. The investor also understands that the owners have acute sensitivity toward equity dilution and that the local bankruptcy regime treats secured creditors very differently than unsecured creditors, particularly with regard to the accrual of interest during a court proceeding. The investor is keen to avoid the situation "the next time around, if there is a next time around." With this in mind, the institutional investor makes a counterproposal to exchange each $1,000 of notes due in 2003 for $1,070 of escalating-rate secured notes due in 2008; the interest rate on the new notes begins at 11.5 percent and increases 50 basis points every six months. The new notes are secured by all of OpCo's assets. To refinance the bank debt and provide liquidity, the investor proposes a carve-out for a $55 million first-priority interest in the collateral pool. The investor indicates that, even after paying accrued interest in cash, this amount provides OpCo with an additional $15 million of available liquidity.

After much back and forth, the parties compromise on the following terms of an exchange: for each $1,000 of notes due in 2003, the holder receives $1,050 of escalating-rate secured notes due in 2008; outstanding accrued but unpaid interest is paid in cash. The new notes have a security interest in all of OpCo's assets; the security interest includes a carve-out for a $65 million, first-priority security interest in the collateral pool to facilitate refinancing the bank debt and to provide OpCo with approximately $25 million of visible liquidity. The parties agree on an initial interest rate of 11.5 percent, an initial interest rate period of 18 months, and a rate increase of 50 basis points every six months thereafter. Table A.8 summarizes the negotiation between OpCo's owners and the institutional investor.

With an agreement in place, the parties move to document and implement the restructuring transaction. In this particular circumstance, the old notes are exchanged for new notes—this simple debt-for-debt exchange achieves the primary goals of the equity holders (minimize the dilution of ownership, improve the maturity profile) and the primary goals of the debt (recover full value, improve the positioning for any future default). Because only one party holds old notes, the exchange transaction is greatly simplified. Table A.9 indicates OpCo's balance sheet before restructuring, the

A

Table A.8: Key Terms of the Negotiated Restructuring Proposal, OpCo

Term	Equity holders' proposal	Negotiated terms	Note holders' proposal
Security	11.5 percent unsecured notes due in 2010	Escalating-rate secured notes due in 2008	Escalating-rate secured notes due in 2008
Amount	$1,030 for each $1,000 principal amount of 10.5 percent senior notes due in 2003	$1,050 for each $1,000 principal amount of 10.5 percent senior notes due in 2003	$1,070 for each $1,000 principal amount of 10.5 percent senior notes due in 2003
Accrued interest	Paid-in 11.5 percent unsecured notes	Paid-in cash	Paid-in cash
Term	Seven years	Five years	Five years
Collateral	None	Second security interest in all of OpCo's assets; carve-out for a $65.0 million first-priority collateral interest	Second security interest in all of OpCo's assets; carve-out for a $55.0 million first-priority collateral interest
Interest	11.5 percent, fixed and payable in cash	11.5 percent through June 30, 2005, payable in cash; interest rate increases 50 basis points every six months thereafter	11.5 percent through June 30, 2004, payable in cash; interest rate increases 50 basis points every six months thereafter
Amortization	Bullet at maturity	Bullet at maturity	Bullet at maturity

accounting adjustments made for the exchange transaction, and OpCo's balance sheet pro forma for the exchange.

Debt-for-Equity Exchange

To illustrate a debt-for-equity exchange, this section stays with OpCo but modifies certain assumptions. The story behind this hypothetical begins at the end of 1999, when OpCo completed a leveraged recapitalization of its balance sheet.

In 1999, the equity public markets valued companies similar to OpCo at between 7.0 and 8.0 times EBITDA for the latest 12 months. With approximately $49 million of EBITDA for this period, OpCo was thought to be worth between $343 million and $392 million. At the time, and based on these valuations, the debt capital markets were offering to lend up to 4.5 times trailing EBITDA to borrowers like OpCo. Unable to resist the opportunity, OpCo's owners completed a leveraged recapitalization transaction. OpCo borrowed a combination of $210 million of bank and high-yield debt,

Table A.9: Balance Sheet Before and After Restructuring and Accounting Adjustments Made for the Exchange, OpCo
(millions of dollars)

Item	Before restructuring	Adjustments	After restructuring
Assets			
Cash and equivalents	9.1	(5.3)	3.8
Other current assets	48.8	0.0	48.8
Net property, plant, and equipment-	177.9	0.0	177.9
Total assets	235.8	(5.3)	230.5
Liabilities			
Accrued interest	5.3	(5.3)	n.a.
Accounts payable	17.3	0.0	17.3
Accrued expenses	11.0	0.0	11.0
Secured term loan	40.6	n.a.	40.6
10.5 percent senior notes due in 2003	100.0	(100.0)	0.0
New notes	0.0	105.0	105.0
Total liabilities	174.1	(0.3)	173.8
Shareholders' equity			
Paid-in capital	1.0	0.0	1.0
Retained earnings	60.7	(5.0)	55.7
Total shareholders' equity	61.7	(5.0)	56.7
Total liabilities and shareholders' equity	235.8	(5.3)	230.5

n.a. Not applicable.

and funds were used to refinance any existing debt, pay a dividend to the owners, and provide working capital. From the debt market's perspective, this debt load was sustainable for the following reasons: at the prevailing interest rates, OpCo's ratio of EBITDA to pro forma cash interest coverage was about 2.5 times; at 4.3 times leverage, OpCo was perceived to have an ample equity cushion (with loan-to-value ratios of between 54 and 61 percent); and, at the end of the transaction, OpCo still had $5 million of available cash to address any unforeseen operating issues. Table A.10 details the sources and uses of funds for the recapitalization.

Subsequent to the transaction, OpCo performed as described in the first hypothetical. Business conditions caused revenue and margins to erode, although cash flow before debt service remained reasonably strong. Despite the interest burden, OpCo continued to invest in its fixed asset base. And even today, OpCo is current with its suppliers. However, as indicated in tables A.11 through A.13, OpCo's balance sheet has finally caught up to it.

On December 31, 2003, the company lacked the cash to make the $7.9 million semiannual interest payment on the outstanding 10.5 percent notes due in 2006. OpCo's counsel reviews the indenture for the notes and determines that the contract provides for a 30-day grace period for payment defaults. Because the payment default on the notes triggers a cross-default on the bank credit agreement, counsel also reviews this document and discovers a similar 30-day grace period. OpCo's owners decide *not* to make the interest

Table A.10: Sources and Uses of Funds for the Leveraged Recapitalization, OpCo
(millions of dollars)

Item	Before restructuring	Adjustments	After restructuring
Assets			
Cash and equivalents	5.0	n.a.	5.0
Other current assets	50.9	n.a.	50.9
Net property, plant, and equipment	175.0	n.a.	175.0
Total assets	230.9	n.a.	230.9
Liabilities			
Accounts payable	18.0	n.a.	18.0
Accrued expenses	11.4	n.a.	11.4
Old secured bank debt	105.0	(105.0)	n.a.
Secured term loan	n.a.	60.0	60.0
10.5 percent senior notes due in 2006	n.a.	150.0	150.0
Total liabilities	134.4	105.0	239.4
Shareholders' equity			
Paid-in capital	1.0	n.a.	1.0
Retained earnings[a]	95.4	(105.0)	(9.6)
Total shareholders' equity	96.4	(105.0)	(8.6)
Total liabilities and shareholders' equity	230.9	n.a.	230.9

n.a. Not applicable.

a. Approximately $5.0 million of fees and expenses charged to retained earnings.

payment (and retain cash and operating flexibility) and to use the 30-day grace period to evaluate their alternatives. The balance sheet in table A.14 reflects OpCo's actual cash position as of December 31, 2003.

As a first step, OpCo's owners hire a restructuring banker to evaluate and recommend alternatives and to manage any negotiations with the lending groups. To gain a rapid understanding of the situation, the restructuring banker reviews OpCo's financial results and projections and schedules interviews with OpCo's managers. During the interviews, he focuses on the assumptions that support the financial projections and whether or not they are achievable. After speaking to the managers responsible for sales and customer service, he discovers that important customers have read the press reports about OpCo's default and are beginning to call and inquire about OpCo's ability to perform in light of its highly leveraged balance sheet. OpCo's payables manager also reports similar inquiries from important suppliers. In fact, suppliers are talking about shortening the number of days of credit they extend to OpCo. Generally, OpCo's managers (who may or may not be significant equity owners) are nervous about the situation. At this point in time, employees are surprised by events, but confident in management's ability to resolve the situation.

After this and other due diligence, the restructuring banker (with the help of his expert staff) produces a preliminary valuation analysis and a preliminary debt capacity analysis. As in the first hypothetical, the restructuring banker concludes that OpCo is currently worth between $160 million and $195 million (before surplus cash) and that OpCo can support between $100 million and $140 million of par-value debt securities. In the presentation to OpCo's board of directors,[9] the restructuring banker makes several important points.

First and foremost, the company is in a precarious state. Because of the uncertainty surrounding OpCo and its financial situation, the company is in jeopardy of spiraling into a cycle of distress. If the situation is not resolved soon, customers may cancel orders and put the projections (and the valuation) at risk; the company is potentially facing a working capital squeeze.[10] Moreover, the current financial debt of the company (about $190.9 million, including accrued interest and net of cash on hand) is just less than the restructuring banker's most optimistic assessment of value; in his view, OpCo is very likely to be balance sheet insolvent (that is, the financial liabilities exceed the mark-to-market value of OpCo's tangible and intangible assets).[11] The restructuring banker also notes several areas that, in his

353

A

Table A.11: Historic and Projected Income Statement Following Leveraged Recapitalization, OpCo, Fiscal Year Ended December 31, 2000–07

(millions of dollars unless otherwise noted)

Item	Actual			Estimated		Projected		
	2000	2001	2002	2003	2004	2005	2006	2007
Revenue								
Amount	300.0	291.0	279.4	273.9	280.7	291.9	303.6	315.8
Percent growth	5.0	-3.0	-4.0	-2.0	2.5	4.0	4.0	4.0
Cost of sales	190.5	189.2	187.2	186.2	186.7	192.7	198.9	205.2
Gross profit								
Amount	109.5	101.9	92.2	87.6	94.0	99.3	104.7	110.5
Percent margin	36.5	35.0	33.0	32.0	33.5	34.0	34.5	35.0
Selling, general, and administrative costs	69.0	71.8	74.6	73.1	73.1	74.6	76.1	77.6
Operating income	40.5	30.1	17.6	14.5	20.9	24.7	28.7	32.9
Interest expense								
Secured term loan	(3.8)	(3.6)	(3.2)	(2.8)	(2.2)	(0.9)	n.a.	n.a.
10.5 percent senior notes due in 2006	(15.8)	(15.8)	(15.8)	(15.8)	(15.8)	(15.8)	(15.8)	n.a.
New notes	n.a.	n.a.	n.a.	n.a.	n.a.	n.a.	n.a.	(18.0)
Interest income	0.1	0.2	0.2	0.1	(0.1)	(1.2)	(3.7)	(3.2)
Pretax income	21.0	11.0	(1.2)	(4.0)	2.8	6.8	9.2	11.7
Less taxes (40 percent)	(8.4)	(4.4)	0.5	1.6	(1.1)	(2.7)	(3.7)	(4.7)
Net income	12.6	6.6	(0.7)	(2.4)	1.7	4.1	5.5	7.0

n.a. Not applicable.

Table A.12: Historic and Projected Cash Flow Statement Following Leveraged Recapitalization, OpCo, Fiscal Year Ended December 31, 2000–07
(millions of dollars unless otherwise noted)

Item	Actual			Estimated		Projected		
	2000	2001	2002	2003	2004	2005	2006	2007
Cash from operations								
Net income	12.6	6.6	(0.7)	(2.4)	1.7	4.1	5.5	7.0
Adjustments								
Depreciation and amortization	14.6	14.7	14.8	14.9	14.8	14.8	14.7	14.7
Net working capital	(1.1)	0.7	0.9	0.4	(0.5)	(0.8)	(0.9)	(0.9)
Net cash from operations	26.1	21.9	14.9	12.9	16.0	18.0	19.4	20.8
Cash from investing activities								
Net property, plant, and equipment	15.8	15.9	16.0	14.3	14.2	14.2	14.1	14.1
Net cash from investing activities	15.8	15.9	16.0	14.3	14.2	14.2	14.1	14.1
After-tax cash from operations	10.4	6.1	(1.0)	(1.4)	1.8	3.8	5.2	6.7
Cash from financing activities								
Repayment of secured term loan	(3.0)	(4.5)	(6.0)	(6.5)	(12.0)	(28.0)	n.a.	n.a.
Repayment of 10.5 percent senior notes due in 2006	n.a.	n.a.	n.a.	n.a.	n.a.	n.a.	(150.0)	n.a.
Proceeds from new notes	n.a.	n.a.	n.a.	n.a.	n.a.	n.a.	150.0	n.a.
Repayment of new notes	n.a.	n.a.	n.a.	n.a.	n.a.	n.a.	n.a.	n.a.
Net cash from financing activities	(3.0)	(4.5)	(6.0)	(6.5)	(12.0)	(28.0)	n.a.	n.a.
Cash								
Increase in cash	7.4	1.6	(7.0)	(7.9)	(10.2)	(24.2)	5.2	6.7
Cash at beginning of period	5.0	12.4	14.0	6.9	(0.9)	(11.2)	(35.3)	(30.1)
Cash at end of period	12.4	14.0	6.9	(0.9)	(11.2)	(35.3)	(30.1)	(23.4)

n.a. Not applicable.

A

Table A.13: Historic and Projected Balance Sheet Following Leveraged Recapitalization, OpCo, Year Ended December 31, 1999–2007

(millions of dollars unless otherwise noted)

Item	Actual				Estimated	Projected			
	1999	2000	2001	2002	2003	2004	2005	2006	2007
Assets									
Cash and equivalents	5.0	12.4	14.0	6.9	(0.9)	(11.2)	(35.3)	(30.1)	(23.4)
Other current assets	50.9	53.4	51.8	49.7	48.8	50.0	52.0	54.1	56.2
Net property, plant, and equipment	175.0	176.2	177.3	178.5	177.9	177.3	176.7	176.2	175.6
Total assets	230.9	242.0	243.1	235.2	225.8	216.2	193.4	200.1	208.4
Liabilities									
Accounts payable	18.0	18.9	18.3	17.6	17.3	17.7	18.4	19.1	19.9
Accrued expenses	11.4	12.0	11.6	11.2	11.0	11.2	11.7	12.1	12.6
Secured term loan	60.0	57.0	52.5	46.5	40.0	28.0	n.a.	n.a.	n.a.
10.5 percent senior notes due in 2006	150.0	150.0	150.0	150.0	150.0	150.0	150.0	n.a.	n.a.
New notes	n.a.	n.a.	n.a.	n.a.	n.a.	n.a.	n.a.	150.0	150.0
Total liabilities	239.4	237.9	232.5	225.3	218.2	206.9	180.1	181.3	182.5
Shareholders' equity									
Paid-in capital	1.0	1.0	1.0	1.0	1.0	1.0	1.0	1.0	1.0
Retained earnings	(9.6)	3.1	9.6	8.9	6.5	8.2	12.3	17.9	24.9
Total shareholders' equity	(8.6)	4.1	10.6	9.9	7.5	9.2	13.3	18.9	25.9
Total liabilities and shareholders' equity	230.89	242.0	243.1	235.2	225.8	216.2	193.4	200.1	208.4

n.a. Not applicable.

Table A.14: Actual versus Estimated Balance Sheet Following Leveraged Recapitalization, OpCo (millions of dollars)

Item	Actual	Estimated
Assets		
Cash and equivalents	6.9	(0.9)
Other current assets	48.8	48.8
Net property, plant, and equipment	177.9	177.9
Total assets	233.6	225.8
Liabilities		
Accrued interest	7.9	0.0
Accounts payable	17.3	17.3
Accrued expenses	11.0	11.0
Secured term loan	40.0	40.0
10.5 percent senior notes due in 2006	150.0	150.0
Total liabilities	226.1	218.2
Shareholders' equity		
Paid-in capital	1.0	1.0
Retained earnings	6.5	6.5
Total shareholders' equity	7.5	7.5
Total liabilities and shareholders' equity	233.6	225.8

A

view, are ripe for cost cutting and recommends that the board bring in an operations consultant to review the cost side of the projections.

Because of the upcoming expiration of the grace period and the looming liquidity crisis, the restructuring banker reviews three possible courses of action with the board. The first option is to maintain the status quo. OpCo needs to "find" about $1 million of liquidity to fund the debt service payments; the company could start to "slow pay" suppliers and possibly generate the liquidity from working capital. The company also has one or two regularly scheduled plant maintenance projects that it can defer, but not cancel. But even deferral puts operations at some risk and would certainly raise the suspicions of employees. All in all, the restructuring banker describes an unappealing scenario where long-term value could be enhanced by cost cutting, but where the company lives hand to mouth in the interim. Further, during the time frame in which the company is working to cut costs and build value, the company is just as likely to experience significant erosion of value as customers look for products from a more financially sound partner. And as if that were not bad enough, "finding" the first $1 million by drawing it out of working capital is very likely to cause a working capital squeeze and trigger an even bigger demand for liquidity.

This course of action may appeal to equity holders. By making the debt service payments, equity holders would, in effect, hope to extend the duration of their option by at least six months (the date of the next coupon payment) and possibly longer, especially if the restructuring banker is correct about the possibility for cost savings and the prospects for enhanced cash flow from operations. As discussed earlier in this appendix, equity is evaluated as an option (on 100 percent of the residual value)—the value of the option is increased by raising the current value, lowering the strike price, increasing the volatility, or extending the duration. The status quo strategy would be to maximize the value of equity by extending the duration of the option and to increase the value of the firm by investing scarce resources in cost savings. The downside to this strategy is that it risks doing serious damage to OpCo's business, reducing its future earnings prospects and long-term value. The high likelihood of a subsequent working capital squeeze undermines the "duration-extension" value of the status quo strategy. And if the squeeze does occur, the potential loss of value from an eroding base of customers and employees would dominate any accretion of value from cost savings.

Equity bears very little of the risk of this loss. OpCo is or is very nearly insolvent. If the current value were monetized (through a sale process, discussed as the second option) and distributed, the residual equity claim would likely receive little or nothing after repaying debt (that is, after an absolute-priority distribution of proceeds). Now consider the expected value of equity's recovery in the status quo scenario. If the company can manage the current liquidity crisis, restore customer confidence, avoid a working capital squeeze, and cut costs, equity will likely enjoy 100 percent of the increase in value. For example, if the aforementioned events occur (assume a 20 percent probability) and firm value increases 20 percent, equity value would increase by about $35 million. However, if the situation devolves, equity would recover nothing. The expected value of "investing" in the status quo scenario is $7.0 million; it is the probability-weighted return of $7.0 million [($35 million x 20 percent) + ($0 million x 80 percent)] less the cost of the investment to equity, which is close to zero.

The cost of failure is borne by two parties: the holders of unsecured claims against the company (principally note holders and vendors) and the stakeholders in the company (individuals and businesses invested in the company because they depend, in some measure, on it for their economic livelihood). Stakeholders include employees, suppliers and their employees, and communities with a high concentration of stakeholders. The creditors suffer because, by the time they disenfranchise equity through a court proceeding and recover 100 percent of the available value, the failed status quo strategy and the subsequent court fight will have depleted the value of the firm. To summarize, the status quo scenario has a low probability of success, and failure would significantly lower the value of the business. Equity would accrue all or nearly all of the benefits of success, while the cost to equity of failure is close to zero. Basically, the status quo scenario gives equity a short-term opportunity to gamble with value that more correctly belongs to creditors and, possibly, stakeholders. This presents what the literature usually refers to as a moral dilemma and causes the restructuring banker to call on the restructuring attorney to explain the concept of fiduciary duties and to determine to whom a fiduciary owes a duty of care.

A fiduciary relationship is one in which a designee, the fiduciary, acts as a trustee for another party. In layman's terms, the designated party, or fiduciary, is entrusted to act in a manner that is in the best interests of the designating party. The concept is relevant because, under the laws of OpCo's jurisdiction of incorporation, the members of the board are fiduciaries. They have been designated by the owners of a business enterprise to act in the economic best interests of the owners. And now it gets complicated. The laws are such that the term owner is interpreted to mean the residual beneficiary. In other words, the fiduciaries (or, in this case, directors) are generally charged with maximizing the value of the firm, because maximizing the value of the firm accrues to the benefit of the owner; the owner is the party to whom the next dollar of benefit accrues. If a company is insolvent, its liabilities exceed the value of its assets. Any increase (or decrease) in value would most directly affect the holder of a claim, not the holder of a share of stock. Thus, under the laws of the jurisdiction, the owners of an insolvent company hold claims against the company, not the equity holders. If OpCo is, in fact, insolvent, the directors owe their allegiance to the company's creditors and not the equity owners.

With that background, the restructuring banker discusses OpCo's other alternatives. The next option to consider is an immediate sale of the firm.

Table A.15: Comparison of a Consensual Sale Versus a Contested Deal, OpCo
(millions of dollars)

Item	Consensual sale	Contested deal
Proceeds from sale	195.0	160.0
Less fees and expenses[a]	(5.9)	(9.6)
Plus cash balance[b]	6.9	6.9
Net distributable proceeds	196.1	157.3
Distribution of secured term loan	40.0	40.0
Amount of proceeds available for distribution to note holders and equity holders	156.1	117.3
Percent of proceeds distributed to note holders	95.0	100.0
Distribution to note holders		
Future value		
Amount of recovery	148.3	117.3
Percent of recovery[c]	93.9	74.3
Present value[d]	143.2	102.3
Amount of recovery		
Percent of recovery	90.7	64.8
Distribution to equity holders		
Future value	7.8	n.a.
Present value[d]	7.5	n.a.

n.a. Not applicable.

a. Assumes fees and expenses of 3 and 6 percent in a consensual sale and a contested deal, respectively.

b. Assumes OpCo is cash neutral until the closing date of either transaction.

c. Assumes note claims equal to $150.0 million of principal plus $7.9 million of accrued interest.

d. Assumes a discount rate of 15 and 20 percent for a consensual sale and a contested deal, respectively, equal to the interest rate on notes plus a premium for uncertainty. A contested deal is more uncertain and warrants a higher risk premium. Assumes a consensual sale closes in three months and a contested deal closes in nine months.

At this juncture, a sale of the company as a going concern is a viable alternative. Current market conditions are unlikely to yield value in excess of the debt but, in exchange for agreeing to initiate and execute the sale, current equity could negotiate with its creditors for some modest split of proceeds. Current equity could get as much as 5 percent of the proceeds of the sale, after repaying the secured debt. When asked why the unsecured creditors would agree to pay anything to equity if creditors were not paid in full, the restructuring banker replies that unsecured creditors would view such a payment as an insurance policy against future erosion of value. From the perspective of an unsecured creditor, there is a time lag between knowing a company is insolvent and being able to assert control over the situation. In the interim, the only source for their recovery, the company, is very likely to decrease in value. Table A.15 demonstrates why this strategy maximizes value for an unsecured creditor.

The restructuring banker also points out that, under the immediate-sale scenario, the expected value to the equity is more than $7 million (equity's expected recovery in the status quo scenario). Although equity is indifferent (on an expected-value basis) between an immediate sale and the status quo, the other affected parties (unsecured creditors and stakeholders) are substantially better off in the immediate-sale scenario. The creditors are better off in simple economic terms; the stakeholders are better off because risk-averse constituents are sheltered from delay and the attendant uncertainty.

And now the restructuring banker turns his attention to the third scenario: a conversion of debt to equity. At present, OpCo's problems are related to the balance sheet; the basic operations of the business are sound. But to protect against the defection of customers and vendors and the erosion of business, the company has to deleverage its balance sheet. The company also could cut its selling, general, and administrative costs in the next year and further improve cash flows and firm valuation. If the company could achieve recurring cost reductions of between $7 million and $8 million (or 6 and 8 percent, respectively, of total selling, general, and administrative costs, after adjusting for inflation), and assuming the prevailing market multiples of 5.5 times to 6.5 times EBITDA, the company could build between $40 million and $50 million of value over the next 12 to 18 months. With a sound balance sheet, OpCo is likely to achieve the reforecast results (see tables A.16–A.18). For the purposes of the forecast, OpCo is assumed to have $40 million of bank debt with a revised amortization schedule (basically a refinancing of the existing bank debt) and no other debt. In other words, the reforecast assumes that all of the existing unsecured notes are exchanged for equity.

The recast projections include real cuts of selling, general, and administrative costs of about 10 percent by year two (2005), tempered by the effects of inflation. The increased capital budget in year one (2004) reflects investments that support the increased cash flow (for example, investment in improved billing systems with added functionality that, over time, will improve collection rates and reduce headcount). If the company achieves the recast projections, it would likely be worth between $200 million and $245 million. The increase in value reflects the capitalization of the incremental cash flow generated by the assumed cost savings. But the assumed cost savings cannot be achieved with a leveraged balance sheet. Based on conversations with OpCo's major customers, the restructuring banker believes that customer defections are likely to occur in the absence of a substantial, and perhaps complete, deleveraging of the balance sheet.

Based on the potentially higher value of OpCo, the restructuring banker presents the absolute-priority distribution analysis as shown in table A.19. The analysis reflects the new valuation range and adjusts for the cash on the balance sheet.

As indicated, if 100 percent of the outstanding unsecured debt is converted into equity, the existing equity would be entitled to between 5.4 and 25.5 percent of the pro forma equity. If 50 percent of the unsecured claim is converted into equity and the balance is left in place, the existing equity would be entitled to between 9.9 and 39.5 percent of the pro forma equity. If half of the unsecured claim is converted into equity, it would take an enterprise valuation of about $274 million before old equity would be entitled to as much as half of the pro forma equity. A negotiated settlement with the unsecured creditors that converts half of their claim into equity would likely leave old equity with between 10 and 30 percent of the pro forma equity; if 100 percent of unsecured claims are converted into equity, old equity could expect to retain between 5 and 20 percent of the pro forma equity. The expected value of each of these scenarios is depicted in table A.20.

The expected value of either the status quo scenario or the immediate-sale scenario is less than $8 million, while the expected value of the debt-for-equity conversion scenario is between $8 million and $40 million. For existing equity owners, the upside to the debt-for-equity scenario is the potential to share in the increased valuation. The downside to the scenario is that the ownership percentage of old equity would be substantially diluted; the unsecured creditors would end up as the new majority owners. From the perspective of a fiduciary, a consensual debt-for-equity exchange scenario maximizes the expected value of the firm and has a much lower expected value of any negative externalities (caused by the failure of a status quo scenario and the protracted in-court negotiation over any remaining value that would follow).

Table A.16: Projected Income Statement in Debt-for-Equity Exchange, OpCo, Fiscal Year Ended December 31, 2000–07
(millions of dollars unless otherwise noted)

Item	Actual			Estimated		Projected		
	2000	2001	2002	2003	2004	2005	2006	2007
Revenue								
Amount	300.0	291.0	279.4	273.9	280.7	291.9	303.6	315.8
Percent growth	5.0	-3.0	-4.0	-2.0	2.5	4.0	4.0	4.0
Cost of sales	190.5	189.2	187.2	186.2	186.7	192.7	198.9	205.2
Gross profit								
Amount	109.5	101.9	92.2	87.6	94.0	99.3	104.7	110.5
Percent margin	36.5	35.0	33.0	32.0	33.5	34.0	34.5	35.0
Selling, general, and administrative costs	69.0	71.8	74.6	73.1	68.7	67.4	68.7	70.1
Operating income	40.5	30.1	17.6	14.5	25.3	31.9	36.0	40.4
Interest expense								
Secured term loan	(3.8)	(3.6)	(3.2)	(2.8)	(2.3)	(1.8)	(1.3)	(0.8)
10.5 percent senior notes due in 2006	(15.8)	(15.8)	(15.8)	(15.8)	n.a.	n.a.	n.a.	n.a.
New notes	n.a.	n.a.	n.a.	n.a.	n.a.	n.a.	n.a.	n.a.
Interest income	0.1	0.2	0.2	0.1	(0.1)	0.0	0.2	0.4
Pretax income	21.0	11.0	(1.2)	(4.0)	22.8	30.1	34.9	40.0
Less taxes (40 percent)	(8.4)	(4.4)	0.5	1.6	(9.1)	(12.0)	(14.0)	(16.0)
Net income	12.6	6.6	(0.7)	(2.4)	13.7	18.0	20.9	24.0

n.a. Not applicable.

A

Table A.17: Projected Cash Flow Statement Following Debt-for Equity Exchange, OpCo, Fiscal Year Ended December 31, 2000–07

(millions of dollars unless otherwise noted)

Item	Actual			Estimated	Projected			
	2000	2001	2002	2003	2004	2005	2006	2007
Cash from operations								
Net income	12.6	6.6	(0.7)	(2.4)	13.7	18.0	20.9	24.0
Adjustments								
Depreciation and amortization	14.6	14.7	14.8	14.9	14.8	15.1	15.0	15.0
Net working capital	(1.1)	0.7	0.9	0.4	(0.5)	(0.8)	(0.9)	(0.9)
Net cash from operations	26.1	21.9	14.9	12.9	28.0	32.3	35.1	38.1
Cash from investing activities								
Capital expenditures	15.8	15.9	16.0	14.3	17.8	14.5	14.4	14.4
Net cash from investing activities	15.8	15.9	16.0	14.3	17.8	14.5	14.4	14.4
After-tax cash from operations	10.4	6.1	(1.0)	(1.4)	10.2	17.8	20.7	23.7
Cash from financing activities								
Repayment of secured term loan	(3.0)	(4.5)	(6.0)	(6.5)	(8.0)	(8.0)	(8.0)	(8.0)
Repayment of 10.5 percent senior notes due in 2006	n.a.	n.a.	n.a.	(150.0)	n.a.	n.a.	n.a.	n.a.
Proceeds from new notes	n.a.	n.a.	n.a.	n.a.	n.a.	n.a.	n.a.	n.a.
Repayment of new notes	n.a.	n.a.	n.a.	n.a.	n.a.	n.a.	n.a.	n.a.
Conversion of debt to equity	n.a.	n.a.	n.a.	150.0	n.a.	n.a.	n.a.	n.a.
Cash flows from financing activities	(3.0)	(4.5)	(6.0)	(6.5)	(8.0)	(8.0)	(8.0)	(8.0)
Cash								
Increase in cash	7.4	1.6	(7.0)	(7.9)	2.2	9.8	12.7	15.7
Cash at beginning of period	5.0	12.4	14.0	6.9	(0.9)	1.3	11.1	23.8
Cash at end of period	12.4	14.0	6.9	(0.9)	1.3	11.1	23.8	39.4

n.a. Not applicable.

A

Table A.18: Projected Balance Sheet Following Debt-for Equity Exchange, OpCo, Fiscal Year Ended December 31, 1999–2007
(millions of dollars unless otherwise noted)

Item	Actual				Estimated		Projected		
	1999	2000	2001	2002	2003	2004	2005	2006	2007
Assets									
Cash and equivalents	5.0	12.4	14.0	6.9	(0.9)	1.3	11.1	23.8	39.4
Other current assets	50.9	53.4	51.8	49.7	48.8	50.0	52.0	54.1	56.2
Net property, plant, and equipment	175.0	176.2	177.3	178.5	177.9	180.9	180.3	179.7	179.1
Total assets	230.9	242.0	243.1	235.2	225.8	232.2	243.4	257.5	274.8
Liabilities									
Accounts payable	18.0	18.9	18.3	17.6	17.3	17.7	18.4	19.1	19.9
Accrued expenses	11.4	12.0	11.6	11.2	11.0	11.2	11.7	12.1	12.6
Secured term loan	60.0	57.0	52.5	46.5	40.0	32.0	24.0	16.0	8.0
10.5 percent senior notes due in 2006	150.0	150.0	150.0	150.0	n.a.	n.a.	n.a.	n.a.	n.a.
New notes	n.a.	n.a.	n.a.	n.a.	n.a.	n.a.	n.a.	n.a.	n.a.
Total liabilities	239.4	237.9	232.5	225.3	68.2	60.9	54.1	47.3	40.5
Shareholders' equity									
Paid-in capital	1.0	1.0	1.0	1.0	1.0	1.0	1.0	1.0	1.0
Retained earnings	(9.6)	3.1	9.6	8.9	156.5	170.3	188.3	209.2	233.2
Total shareholders' equity	(8.6)	4.1	10.6	9.9	157.5	171.3	189.3	210.2	234.2
Total liabilities and shareholders' equity	230.9	242.0	243.1	235.2	225.8	232.2	243.4	257.5	274.8

n.a. Not applicable.

A

365

Table A.19: Absolute-Priority Distribution Analysis Following Debt-for-Equity Exchange
(millions of dollars)

Item	Note holders convert 100 percent of claim to equity		Note holders convert 50 percent of claim to equity	
	Low valuation	High valuation	Low valuation	High valuation
Enterprise value	200.0	245.0	200.0	245.0
Plus cash balance	6.9	6.9	6.9	6.9
Distributable value	206.9	251.9	206.9	251.9
Secured term loan	40.0	40.0	40.0	40.0
10.5 percent senior notes due in 2006	0.0	0.0	75.0	75.0
Implied equity value	166.9	211.9	91.9	136.9
Distribution of outstanding secured debt to note holders				
Amount	157.9	157.9	82.9	82.9
Percent of implied equity	94.6	74.5	90.1	60.5
Distribution of outstanding secured debt to existing equity	9.1	54.1	9.1	54.1
Amount				
Percent of implied equity	5.4	25.5	9.9	39.5

a. Includes $7.9 million of accrued interest.

Before breaking for deliberations, the board asks to be informed of any risks and potential liabilities that either they or the old equity holders face on account of a nonconsensual insolvency proceeding. At this point, the restructuring attorney reenters to discuss the concept of avoidable transfers and the risk to the recipient of such a transfer in the event of a formal insolvency proceeding. In particular, the attorney discusses the concept of a fraudulent conveyance—a transfer of value by a party to a third party in a transaction whereby the transferring party receives less than reasonably equivalent value. If the transferring party is insolvent at the time of the transfer or is rendered insolvent on account of the transfer, the transfer is avoidable.

For example, if a company sells a piece of real estate at less than fair market value and is insolvent at the time of the sale and, subsequently, the company files for protection from creditors, the creditors of the company could seek to avoid the transaction. If successful, they could seek a variety of remedies, ranging from a rescission of the transaction to a payment from the purchaser equal to the difference (at the time of the transaction) between the sale price and the market value. In OpCo's jurisdiction of incorporation, insolvent companies can pursue these avoidance actions for up to one year after the transfer if the transferee is a true third party and for up to five years if the transferee is an insider. Doing the math, the board realizes that if OpCo files for insolvency, the original recapitalization transaction that occurred four years ago (in which a substantial dividend was paid to equity for no consideration) is open to attack. Basically, old equity must consider this additional element of risk.

From the perspective of a fiduciary, most of the discrete risk is mitigated by (1) pursuing legitimate business strategies that maximize the risk-adjusted expected value of the firm and (2) avoiding the potential defrauding of future unsecured creditors by recognizing the moment at which OpCo becomes insolvent (that is, the moment at which OpCo incurs a debt that it knows it cannot repay in full) and, at that moment, by ceasing "trading" or pursuing a court-supervised reorganization. Because it is difficult to know the precise moment at which a firm's assets exceed its liabilities, the board should consider itself at risk of running afoul of the second point if the firm is "in the zone of insolvency." For all practical purposes, unless a firm has at

Table A.20: Results for Old Equity of a Negotiated Settlement That Converts Unsecured Credit into Equity

(millions of dollars)

Percent of pro forma equity going to old equity	Note holders convert 100 per-cent of claim to equity		Note holders convert 50 per-cent of claim to equity	
	Low valuation	High valuation	Low valuation	High valuation
5	8.3	10.6		
10	16.7	21.2	9.2	13.7
15	25.0	31.8	13.8	20.5
20	33.4	42.4	18.4	27.4
25	25.0	25.0	23.0	34.2
30			27.6	41.1

Note: Based on absolute-priority distribution analysis in table A.21.

least a 5 percent cushion between overall value and the value of its liabilities, it should consider itself at risk of being in the zone of insolvency. The attorney concludes by stating that, if a firm is insolvent or in the zone of insolvency, then the residual claimant is the class of unsecured creditors and not equity. And given the legal definition of owner (the residual claimant) and the legal conclusion that a fiduciary owes an obligation to the owner, if OpCo is insolvent or in the zone of insolvency, the board can avoid risk by demonstrating a fiduciary obligation to unsecured creditors and not old equity holders.

In effect, two elements of risk are added to the equation. First, if the company is insolvent, then old equity is at risk from an attack by creditors against the original recapitalization transaction. Next, if a company is either insolvent or in the zone of insolvency, then its fiduciaries are at risk of, in effect, committing fraud.

With this additional information, the board deliberates about the alternatives. As value-maximizing and risk-averse individuals, they determine that OpCo is best served by pursuing a debt-for-equity exchange transaction. Because no reasonable valuation scenario or pro forma balance sheet would leave the old equity with a majority of the pro forma equity, the board determines that a complete conversion of the outstanding notes is the preferred (though not necessarily the most tax-efficient) solution. Among other things, the board recognizes that the new owners (by proxy, through a reconstituted board elected by the pro forma equity owners) can choose to releverage the balance sheet after converting all of the unsecured debt to equity. After deciding on the best course of action (a consensually negotiated debt-for-equity conversion), the board calls on the restructuring banker to organize and negotiate with the relevant creditor groups. The board expects to retain between 10 and 20 percent of the fully deleveraged company.

The Negotiating Dynamics

In the first hypothetical, the negotiating dynamic (and the implementation process) is greatly simplified by assuming that a single institution holds all of OpCo's outstanding unsecured notes. For this example, this assumption is relaxed; in this case, OpCo's outstanding unsecured notes are assumed to be held in unequal amounts by at least 30 institutions, with the five largest holders each owning between 10 and 15 percent of the outstanding notes.

The first goal of the restructuring banker is to put the restructuring proposal in writing and present the written proposal to a group that represents, or speaks for, a consensus amount of each affected class of claims (or interests). In this case, drafting the restructuring proposal is easy; identifying and coordinating the creditor groups are difficult.

With regard to the bank group, it is assumed that a single lending institution holds OpCo's outstanding bank debt. The restructuring banker identifies the appropriate individual (or group of individuals) at the bank, introduces himself, sends the restructuring proposal, and schedules a meeting to follow up. In this hypothetical, the bank debt is either being cured and reinstated (on top of a largely deleveraged capital structure) or being refinanced and repaid. In reality, the restructuring banker is only asking the bank for enough time to negotiate with the note holders and to implement a board-approved restructuring. In the event of a successful debt-for-equity exchange, OpCo would be an attractive borrower for any bank. Despite the current default, OpCo's existing bank lender understands the value of keeping a performing (and fee-paying) loan in its portfolio, agrees that a successful restructuring would create an attractive borrower, and understands the costs to a nonconsensual process.[12] Near the end of the meeting, the bank principal expresses his relief that OpCo's management is addressing the balance sheet in a professional way and wants to help by waiving the current default for 60 days and "giving the company the time it needs to negotiate with note holders." In return for the 60-day waiver, the principal banker indicates that the bank will charge a fee equal to 0.50 percent of the outstanding balance and requests the right to match any proposal the company receives regarding a refinancing of the bank debt.

Given the fact that the bank debt is over-collateralized, in a formal restructuring the bank debt would expect to recover its claim, including accrued interest through the effective date of a restructuring. By asking for a waiver fee, the bank is seeking to increase its claim and hence its overall recovery. From the company's perspective, the value of the 60-day waiver is illusive; absent an agreement with note holders (or at least a standstill during negotiations), the company is still in a default position. Although the bank cannot call a default until the waiver expires, nothing prevents the note holders from doing so. However, in the event the company develops a coherent negotiation with note holders, a bank standstill will have value insofar as it provides a negotiating environment that is within the control of the negotiating parties; it takes the bank out of the immediate negotiation.

A

The restructuring banker takes the matter under advisement and indicates that he will go back to the board with the bank's request and the follow-up with the bank.

After explaining to the board the potential benefits of a standstill, the restructuring banker advises the board that the approximately $200,000 waiver fee is worthwhile in the event it promotes a successful negotiating environment. However, the right of first refusal on a refinancing is over-bearing and would inhibit OpCo's ability to create a competitive process for a bank refinancing. While the waiver is a one-time, relatively modest expense, a chilled refinancing process risks costing the company at least 50 basis points in recurring interest charges. In an effort to realize the value of the standstill, the restructuring banker reports that he has identified and initiated contact with the five largest note holders. Collectively, these institutions owned 65 percent of OpCo's outstanding unsecured notes and wanted to organize themselves into a negotiating committee and hire professional legal and financial advisers.

Based on the foregoing, the restructuring banker advises that the board propose a 90-day standstill that commences on the day the 30-day grace period expires in return for a 50 basis point fee (that is added to the loan balance) and, if absolutely necessary, a right to participate in some material minority amount (for example, 30–40 percent) of any bank refinancing that is agreed to during the restructuring process.

With regard to the note holders, the restructuring banker recommends that the board approve the retention of professionals on behalf of the committee, subject to certain restrictions. To begin with, the role these professionals play is similar to the role the restructuring banker and the restructuring attorney play for the board—they provide analysis and advice (to the committee) regarding restructuring options. If properly informed, the theory goes, the committee is more likely to engage in a rational (that is, value-maximizing) negotiation. In addition, the restructuring banker recommends structuring the retention contracts to incorporate a financial incentive (a transaction fee) that rewards a timely and consensual result.[13] While the transaction fee should not motivate these professionals to achieve any particular result, and thus not create any credibility-sapping conflict of interest, a properly structured transaction fee will motivate the professionals to be proactive and work to catalyze a consensus within the group they are advising. As a precondition to hiring the outside professionals on acceptable terms, the restructuring banker recommends that the board require the five large note holders to agree to "get restricted"[14] and actively participate in a negotiating committee. After active deliberations, the board agrees to support the recommendations and directs the restructuring banker to (1) negotiate acceptable terms for a 90-day standstill with the bank, (2) organize the note holders into a committee, and (3) initiate a negotiation with the committee. The last task includes negotiating acceptable (that is, transaction-motivating) terms for the retention of committee professionals.

After another meeting between the bank principal and the restructuring banker, the two sides agree on a waiver of defaults and a 90-day standstill commencing on expiration of the grace period in exchange for a 50 basis point fee, to be added to the loan balance and payable at maturity. Ultimately, the bank does not insist on participating in any future lending agreement, but the restructuring banker does commit the company to review and respond within one week to any refinancing proposal the bank has to offer. With this agreement in place, the restructuring banker turns his attention to the matter of organizing a formal committee.

It is assumed that the notes are held by a large number of institutions but that 65 percent of the notes are concentrated with five large holders. To understand the significance of the ownership figures, two interrelated questions posed (but assumed away) in the first hypothetical must be addressed. First, according to the bankruptcy laws of the jurisdiction, what constitutes "consensus" for any particular class? And next, according to the bankruptcy laws of the jurisdiction, what treatment is afforded to nonconsenting members of a consenting class? These questions are important because they affect the methodology by which a company can hope to implement any negotiated exchange–based solution.

In the first hypothetical, there is a single holder of the unsecured notes. Any negotiated solution can be implemented by way of a bilateral exchange agreement. Because the company is only dealing with a single counterparty, the company knows it would achieve participation by 100 percent of the outstanding notes. If more than one party holds notes, the company has no guarantee of full participation. Any settlement negotiated between the company and the bankruptcy-consensus majority is exposed to holdout risk, or the risk that some holders of a minority amount of notes may elect not to participate in the negotiated exchange offer. When debt issues are widely held, holdout risk always exists. However, holdout risk is particularly acute when debt holders are being impaired on a value basis and when debt

A

securities, like the notes, are being exchanged for more junior securities (for example, an equity interest in a company).

In a situation where debt securities are being impaired on a value basis, holdout risk is driven by economic considerations. For example, recall that in the second hypothetical, OpCo has $40 million of bank debt and $150 million of notes and the preliminary valuation range, before credit for likely cost savings, is between $160 million and $195 million. Assuming that an average note holder uses the low end of the range for the exchange decision (not an unlikely assumption), the note holder might produce the analysis presented in table A.21.

As indicated, if 100 percent of the notes participate in an exchange offer that converts all participating notes into a ratable share of 100 percent of the subject company's post-exchange equity, each note would recover 80.4 percent of its claim value. In the event that less than 100 percent of the outstanding notes participate, the holdout notes (enjoying priority in a newly equitized capital structure) would retain their claim. If the holdout percentage is low enough (in this case, 34 percent), then unexchanged claims are valued at par (as in the above analysis) and the post-exchange equity value is reduced dollar-for-dollar to account for the holdout claims. The participating notes still get 100 percent of the pro forma equity, and the equity is spread over a smaller pool of claims (that is, each participating claim receives a higher percentage of the pro forma equity), but the equity is now worth less than before and, as indicated, the expected recovery for participating notes is reduced to 70.3 percent of the claim value. The disparity in recovery—100 percent for a holdout versus 70.3 percent for an exchanging holder—is the principal driver of holdout risk in a value-impairment situation.

Table A.21: Holdout Analysis Using Low End of the Valuation Range, OpCo
(millions of dollars unless otherwise noted)

Type of note holder	Claim	Distribution	Percent recovery
Holdout (34 percent of total)	53.7	53.7	100.0
Participating (66 percent of total)	104.2	73.3	70.3
Aggregate	157.9	126.9	80.4

Note: The distributable value to note holders is determined as follows. The enterprise value is $160 million plus 6.9 million in cash equals a distributable value of $166.9 million minus $40 million for payment of the secured term loan, yielding a distributable value of $126.9 million.

Even at the high end of the valuation, where note holders are arguably unimpaired on a value basis, holdout risk is high. For one thing, being unimpaired is not the same as being "arguably unimpaired." Unless note holders are clearly receiving full value, economic holdout risk is relevant. Next, institutions and individual holders that invest in bonds are investing in fixed-income securities, either by choice or by charter. They either do not want to own a different asset class or may be prohibited (or significantly disincentivized) from owning other asset classes. For example, consider the case of a high-end valuation in which the note holder is a regulated financial institution that must meet risk-based capital adequacy ratios. These types of calculations cause the regulated entity to follow prescribed rules for valuing its investment portfolio and, because the value of an equity instrument is less certain and more volatile than the value of a debt instrument of the same issuer, regulatory agencies often structure rules to encourage the regulated institution to hold securities of more determinate and stable value. So, even if the regulated financial institution is convinced of the high-end valuation and thus is economically indifferent between participation and holdout, it will likely not participate in a voluntary exchange if participation causes the institution to have to increase its risk-based capital (relative to the value of the institution's investment portfolio).

Other types of investors that tend to hold out when fixed-income securities are exchanged for equity include closed-end bond funds. Closed-end bond funds (for example, collateralized debt obligations and collateralized loan obligations) are a prominent form of leveraged investment vehicle that raises a fixed amount of debt and equity capital and invests it in fixed-income securities. By their charter or indentures, they are unable to hold equities and, hence, a holdout risk. For this category of investor, only cash (to reinvest) or new fixed-income securities will suffice. To address this problem, many debt-for-equity exchanges require the company to take all reasonable steps to create a public market for the new equity and, hence, a way for these (and other) investors to monetize consideration.

The cost of holdouts to participating note holders can be substantial. To eliminate this free-rider problem, one generally has to look at the bankruptcy laws of the relevant jurisdiction. In most jurisdictions, in the event a consensus majority of a class of creditors approves a particular class treatment (and assuming certain other conditions are met), the bankruptcy laws allow equal treatment to be imposed on nonconsenting creditors of the consenting class. In other words, most bankruptcy laws allow a consensus

A

majority of claimants of a particular class to bind the minority, nonconsenting claimants of that class to the treatment agreed to by the consensus majority. Because of the ability to bind holdouts, a bankruptcy code can be a powerful tool to drive negotiations to a consensual resolution (by freeing the negotiation from the "tyranny of the minority") and to implement transactions in a manner that eliminates free-rider inefficiencies without unfairly discriminating against the member of any particular class. The hypothetical adopts the U.S. standard for bankruptcy consensus—namely, that a class of claims accepts a plan treatment if it is accepted by creditors holding at least two-thirds in amount and more than half in number of the allowed claims of the class voting to accept or reject the plan treatment.[15]

With this in mind, the restructuring banker reviews his list of note holders. In this case, nearly two-thirds of the claims are held by a limited number of institutions. Clearly reaching an agreement with this group would go a long way toward achieving a supermajority consensus. To organize a dialogue with this group, the restructuring banker speaks to several of the large note holders and invites them to form an ad hoc negotiating group that includes the five large note holders. He indicates that the company has agreed to pay for legal and financial advisers for the group, subject to reviewing and approving the engagement contracts.

Once professionals are retained for the committee, they execute confidentiality agreements with the company and begin to review and analyze material and nonpublic information about OpCo, its operations, and contractual commitments. These professionals are also likely to spend time communicating with members of the committee to establish a schedule for a negotiating process and to begin assessing the views and goals of the individual holders regarding an optimal restructuring outcome. At this point in time, committee professionals are researching and attempting to draw conclusions about the same issues that concerned the company's professionals. What is the company worth? How much debt can it support? What are the amount and priority of the various classes of claims? And what are the time, cost, and expected value of achieving a court-supervised, absolute-priority distribution of value?

With less than a week to go in the 30-day grace period, the restructuring banker calls the committee banker and invites him and his clients to present the background and support for the board's preferred restructuring solution. At the meeting, the restructuring banker and management present OpCo's revised operating plan and discuss the risks to the plan. In particular, the presentation outlines risks that could immediately reduce the going-concern value of OpCo, such as the potential for customer defections due to OpCo's highly leveraged balance sheet.

The restructuring banker indicates that, to reduce the risk to the business, the board has made the courageous decision to cede control of the company to note holders in connection with a full conversion of the outstanding notes into equity. Specifically, the restructuring banker presents the analysis in table A.22 to the note holder group and its advisers.

At this juncture, the restructuring banker makes the specific offer to convert all of the outstanding notes into 80 percent of the post-restructuring equity and conveys the company's willingness to reconstitute OpCo's board of directors to reflect the new ownership percentages. The restructuring banker explains that the board considered several other alternatives, including a sale of the company, which was rejected because it did not take advantage in the expected, "highly likely" improved performance and valuation, and an alternative-exchange consideration, including a combination of debt and equity, but, for a variety of reasons, preferred a full equitization. First and foremost, a deleveraged balance sheet would help the company to repair its reputation with customers and suppliers and would increase the probability of achieving forecasted results. And next, if note holders insist on retaining a substantial debt claim, then the tradeoff is control of the

Table A.22: Proposed Full Conversion of Debt to Equity, OpCo
(millions of dollars)

Item	Accrued interest on paid-in equity	Paid-in equity	Accrued interest on paid-on cash	Paid-in cash
Enterprise value	200.0	245.0	200.0	245.0
Plus cash	6.9	6.9	6.9	6.9
Distributable value	206.9	251.9	206.9	251.9
Secured term loan	40.0	40.0	40.0	40.0
Distributable value after secured term loan	166.9	211.9	166.9	211.9
Less cash paid for accrued interest	0.0	0.0	7.9	7.9
Implied equity value	166.9	211.9	159.1	204.1
10.5 percent senior notes due in 2006 claim	157.9	157.9	150.0	150.0
Percent of implied equity	94.6	74.5	94.3	73.5

equity. Because the directors believe that a deleveraged balance sheet gives OpCo its highest expected value, they are willing to concede control of the firm to achieve this result.

With that, the restructuring banker and the company end their presentation, and the committee and its professionals retire to consider their alternatives and response.

To begin with, the financial and legal professionals make sure the committee is clear on the laws and process that would govern a nonconsensual process. The committee's banker also notes that a prolonged, nonconsensual process would pose a very real risk to enterprise value. Because the duration of a nonconsensual process rests on valuation, the committee's banker expresses his opinion that the company's valuations may be aggressive, especially in the "assumed cost savings" case, but, on balance, are defensible. And the attorney reminds creditors that, if OpCo has to file for bankruptcy protection, they will not accrue interest on their claim during the proceedings. In other words, a nonconsensual process is uncertain and, most likely, would cost creditors absolute economic value and time value. The committee's restructuring professionals also note that, in this particular circumstance, OpCo's owners seem particularly enlightened; in an effort to maximize value for all parties, they are willing to cede control of the equity (and hence, the company). The more traditional response would be to offer enough new debt so that old equity can retain control and claim that the still leveraged balance sheet would not affect customer and vendor confidence. Both professionals also note that the 30-day grace period on the interest payment default expires in less than a week and, after expiring, the company is at risk of being forced involuntarily into a bankruptcy proceeding. In summary, time is of the essence, and the committee should take the opportunity to negotiate aggressively to a consensual resolution.

After considering the advice of their professional advisers and seizing on the good judgment of the board, the five note holders agree to support a full equitization but agree that taking less than 90 percent of the equity is "a mistake." The committee's professionals work to get the five holders to agree to a counterproposal that converts 100 percent of the outstanding notes into 91 percent of the pro forma equity and pays the outstanding accrued interest in cash. With that, the committee ends the deliberations, and the committee professionals convey the counterproposal to the restructuring banker.

Over the next two days, the parties engage in spirited negotiations that result in an agreement to convert 100 percent of the outstanding notes into

86 percent of the pro forma equity, with accrued interest (through the closing of any transaction) paid in cash, on the closing date. The agreement is contingent on the company obtaining a new bank facility that provides enough liquidity to pay the accrued interest and leaves the company with a minimum of $10 million of available liquidity. After all, if the note holders are about to become equity holders, they want to create as much "duration" as possible. The parties agree to attempt to complete the transaction through an exchange offer, but closing the exchange offer is conditioned on achieving a 95 percent acceptance rate. In other words, participating note holders are willing to tolerate a limited free-rider tax from holdouts. But what happens if less than 95 percent of the outstanding notes agree to exchange?

In sophisticated jurisdictions, there is a useful trend toward using the bankruptcy laws to implement negotiated settlements between a company (really, the equity owners) and a consensus group of creditors. The principal reason for relying on bankruptcy laws is the embedded ability to bind holdouts to a transaction and eliminate free-rider taxes. In such jurisdictions, a company would seek to gain an agreement with the required bankruptcy consensus and then either work to complete an out-of-court exchange with a very high minimum acceptance rate or simply file for bankruptcy, with either a prenegotiated or presolicited plan of reorganization. In the case of a presolicited deal (in the United States, known as a prepackaged plan), the company solicits acceptances to an exchange and acceptances to a plan of reorganization with the same ballot. If the company reaches the minimum tender condition, it closes on the exchange offer; if the exchange offer fails the minimum tender condition but achieves a bankruptcy consensus, the company seeks bankruptcy court approval to implement its presolicited plan. In permitting jurisdictions, the bankruptcy court assumes that the out-of-court solicitation process (which is supervised by the relevant securities regulatory authorities) is valid and waives the need for any in-court solicitation of a plan of reorganization. While a presolicited transaction can save substantial time in court (where costs grow and enterprise values shrink), it assumes that the company can generate a solicitation document that is acceptable to the relevant securities regulatory authorities. In the United States, it is often faster (and sometimes easier) to seek and gain the approval of the bankruptcy court on the sufficiency of a solicitation document rather than look to the Securities and Exchange Commission. In this circumstance, a company would prenegotiate a transaction with a consensus or near-consensus group of creditors, prepare all relevant documentation,

A

then file for bankruptcy. While in bankruptcy, the court would review and comment on the solicitation document and then, if certain defined criteria are met, approve the document and the solicitation process. After solicitation (very similar, whether in-court or out-of-court) and achievement of a consensus vote, the bankruptcy court would approve the plan of reorganization. This process is known as a prearranged or prenegotiated bankruptcy. In practice, the decision between a prearranged versus a prepackaged process rests on the whether one expects an easier and faster approval process for the solicitation document with the relevant securities commission or the bankruptcy court.

In our hypothetical, OpCo is assumed to execute voting agreements with the five largest holders. The voting agreements contractually obligate the committed bondholder to vote for the negotiated transaction. They also allow the signing holder to sell the committed bonds to another investor, as long as the purchaser also agrees to support the transaction. This sort of arrangement gives the company certainty regarding achievement of a consensus and gives the holder more options for liquidity. With 65 percent of the notes committed to support a transaction, the company only needs to gain the support of one more significant holder to achieve a "value" consensus. Until the solicitation takes place, the company can never really be certain about achieving a "numerosity" consensus.

At this juncture, the company decides whether a prepackaged plan or a prearranged plan is more expeditious and publicly announces the terms of the exchange transaction, the percentage of note holders supporting the transaction, and any other material facts, including that the company will likely seek to implement the transaction through a formal court proceeding. In practice, if a company garners the support of an ad hoc committee that represents a significant amount of bonds and includes sophisticated institutions, it is very likely to be able to "up sell" the transaction to a larger group of note holders. Usually, enough other holders (in this case, the other 25 holders that own 35 percent of the notes) will respect an arm's-length transaction negotiated by adversarial parties as fair and either support the settlement or abstain from voting. This market dynamic often gives a company confidence in its ability to achieve a consensus despite negotiating with a committee that owns less than a threshold amount of claims.

With 65 percent support in hand and a draft solicitation document at the ready, OpCo elects to file for a prearranged bankruptcy. After receiving approval for the solicitation document from the court (a 60- to 90-day process in the United States) and conducting a solicitation (a 30-day process) where the company garners the support of more than two-thirds of the amount and at least 50 percent of the holders of the notes that actually voted to accept or reject the plan, OpCo seeks to have its plan confirmed by the court. With no significant objections, OpCo's plan of reorganization is approved. After a 10-day appeal period, OpCo's plan "goes effective." The old notes are canceled, and shares are issued to holders of old notes. After emerging from bankruptcy (about 120 to 150 days after filing a bankruptcy petition), OpCo is newly recapitalized and has a new ownership structure.

References

Stiglitz, Joseph E. 2001. "Bankruptcy Laws: Basic Economic Principles." In Claessens, S., S. Djankov, and A. Mody (eds.), *Resolution of Financial Distress: An International Perspective on the Design of Bankruptcy Laws*. World Bank: Washington, D.C.

Werbalowsky, Jeffrey I. 1992. "Reforming Chapter 11: Building and International Restructuring Model." *Journal of Bankruptcy Law and Practice* 8 (6).

Notes

1. This analytical perspective uses a measure of cash flow from operations to assess the sustainability of balance sheet leverage. In reality, a company also has some level of access to capital markets that has to be considered. A more accurate assessment of balance sheet sustainability would compare free cash flow from operations to interest expense and would look at the separate issue of debt maturities in the context of the prevailing conditions of the relevant capital markets.

2. This is an oversimplification. In fact, almost every business begins in a cash flow negative proposition. In successful ventures, capital is raised and invested in an aggregation of resources that produces profits (a return on the invested capital). If a company is in this start-up phase, it falls into sector C. After all, it is free cash flow negative. But the start-up phase is usually the province of equity investors. Of course, in the late

1990s, the telecommunications sector provided several notable exceptions to this "rule" of investing.

3. See the appendix to the conference version of this paper for an explanation of the valuation analysis.

4. A valuation of OpCo (or any company) is based largely on observed public market trading and transaction multiples for companies deemed comparable to the subject company. Generally, these comparable companies are healthy public companies with adequate investment in working capital. The other prominent valuation technique, a discounted cash flow analysis, also assumes adequate investment in working capital. The assessment of OpCo's liabilities assumes that, like the comparable public companies, OpCo has adequate working capital. If, for some reason, OpCo is underinvested in working capital (if, for example, OpCo has stretched its payables to vendors), then OpCo's funded liabilities have to be expanded to account for any investment necessary to normalize its working capital position. In a restructuring, if certain suppliers are critical to ongoing operations, debt owed to them is often afforded priority beyond its legal entitlement.

5. Assuming zero cash taxes and the application to debt repayment of 100 percent of free cash flow from operations after interest expense to debt repayment, the formula for years to debt repayment—that is, debt divided by free cash flow from operations after interest—can be expressed in terms of two variables: r, the target ratio, and i, the estimated average pretax cost of debt capital. Once simplified, years to debt repayment equals $[(1\,/\,r)\,/\,i]\,/\,[1 - (1\,/\,r)]$. According to this formula, assuming a target ratio of 2.0 times EBITDA and an average pretax cost of debt capital of 10.0 percent, it would take a company 10 years to repay the maximum amount of par-value debt it could support.

6. Includes $9.1 million of cash on hand.

7. Each of the three classes of claims discussed—secured debt claims, unsecured debt claims, and equity interests—has a call on value; the secured and unsecured claimants have a call on a fixed amount of value, and the equity holders have a call on all of the residual value. However, only the secured and unsecured debt claims are fixed, liquidated claims. Because of its uncertain value, the equity "claim" is usually referred to as an "interest."

8. In the case of OpCo, the total allocable value—$160 million to $195 million of enterprise value plus cash of approximately $9.1 million—

exceeds the total secured and unsecured debt claims of $145.9 million. As a result, the holders of both secured and unsecured debt expect to be paid in full or left unimpaired. Further, because the company has enough debt capacity to satisfy existing claims in full with new claims, equity holders also expect to be left unimpaired (that is, equity holders do not expect to have their ownership interest diluted).

9. In most jurisdictions, both privately and publicly held companies manage corporate governance through some form of proxy methodology. In other words, the equity owners nominate and elect individuals to serve on a council to represent their interests in matters of corporate strategy and governance. In this case, the governing council is called a board of directors.

10. As news of their distress spreads to customers and suppliers, companies like OpCo often face a working capital squeeze. In this situation, customers elect either to hold or to delay payments until long after goods are received or even until the next order is shipped or received. The first action increases receivables; the second does the same and causes overinvestment in inventory. Further, as suppliers learn of the situation, they are likely to reduce their credit exposure to OpCo by reducing the number of days they give OpCo to pay for goods or services. The net result of these actions or combination of actions is to increase the amount of working capital OpCo requires to run its operations and to increase OpCo's near-term need for cash.

11. If a company is (arguably) insolvent, a question of appropriate corporate governance arises. The goal of good corporate governance (and the duty of a board member) should be to maximize the risk-adjusted, or expected, value of the firm. If a company is solvent, maximizing the expected value of the equity and maximizing the expected value of the firm are congruent. If equity is out-of-the-money, it may be rational to pursue higher-risk, higher-reward investments because (a high probability) failure costs equity nothing, while success brings a massive return on equity's "investment" (near-infinite returns because the amount of equity's investment, defined as how much they have at risk in the event of failure, is zero or near zero). Because corporate governors are elected by equity at a time when the company is solvent, they may be tempted to show a filial loyalty to their electors versus a fiduciary duty to the company. Such behavior must be considered contrary to any acceptable concept of good corporate governance.

A

12. Among other costs, a bank needs to consider the impact of having one of its loans fall into the nonperforming category and the attendant impact on its risk-adjusted capital adequacy ratios. As an individual bank approaches the point of having inadequate risk-adjusted capital (and absent negative ramifications that result from "ignoring the problem"), the owners of the bank have less of an incentive to identify and categorize a loan as nonperforming.

13. While the professionals work on behalf of the committee, the engagement contract is an obligation of the company.

14. In restructurings, it is common for some (or most) of the outstanding claims to be structured as publicly traded securities. Depending on the jurisdiction, there are usually restrictions on buying and selling securities when in possession of material, nonpublic information. By participating in a restructuring negotiation, the security holder becomes privy to some level of material, nonpublic information (even if the only additional information is the bid and the ask) and thus is prevented from trading in the securities of the company. In the context of a rapidly evolving and potentially unstable restructuring environment, this restriction is often an important concession for a security holder to make and reflects a sincere desire to negotiate to a conclusion.

15. See 11 U.S.C. §1126 (6).